Contemporary African Linguistics

Editors: Akinbiyi Akinlabi, Laura J. Downing

In this series:

1. Payne, Doris L., Sara Pacchiarotti & Mokaya Bosire (eds.). Diversity in African languages: Selected papers from the 46th Annual Conference on African Linguistics.

2. Persohn, Bastian. The verb in Nyakyusa: A focus on tense, aspect and modality.

ISSN: 2511-7726

The verb in Nyakyusa

A focus on tense, aspect and modality

Bastian Persohn

language
science
press

Bastian Persohn. 2017. *The verb in Nyakyusa: A focus on tense, aspect and modality* (Contemporary African Linguistics 2). Berlin: Language Science Press.

This title can be downloaded at:
http://langsci-press.org/catalog/book/141
© 2017, Bastian Persohn

ISBN: 978-3-96110-014-9 (Digital)
    978-3-96110-015-6 (Hardcover)
ISSN: 2511-7726
DOI:10.5281/zenodo.926408
Source code available from www.github.com/langsci/141
Collaborative reading: paperhive.org/documents/remote?type=langsci&id=141

Cover and concept of design: Ulrike Harbort
Typesetting: Sebastian Nordhoff, Bastian Persohn
Proofreading: Andreas Hölzl, Bev Erasmus, Caroline Rossi, Christian Döhler, Elizabeth Bogal-Allbritten, Grace Temsen, Jan Wohlgemuth, Jean Nitzke, Jeroen van de Weijer, Lea Schäfer, Matthew Czuba, Mike Aubrey, Mykel Brinkerhoff, Prisca Jerono, Rosetta Berger, Sandra Auderset
Fonts: Linux Libertine, Arimo, DejaVu Sans Mono
Typesetting software: XƎLᴬTEX

Language Science Press
Unter den Linden 6
10099 Berlin, Germany
langsci-press.org

Storage and cataloguing done by FU Berlin

Freie Universität Berlin

Contents

Contents

Acknowledgments

An academic monograph, such as this one, may have a single author, but is really a project dependent on the support of many more people.

First of all, I wish to thank my three PhD supervisors:[1] Gerrit Dimmendaal for all the time he has dedicated to mentoring my work, for the cordial reception at the Institute for African Studies and Egyptology and for believing in my abilities from the very first moment on; Martin Becker for hours of discussion and answering tons of e-mails on the mind-twisting issues of tense, aspect and modality; and Silvia Kutscher for motivating me to pursue a doctorate and for channelling my work.

I am further indebted to Dan King and Helen Eaton of SIL International for access to their data and for lengthy discussions of Nyakyusa, to Dörte Borchers for encouraging me to continue working on this language and to Robert Botne, Thera Crane, Tiffany Kershner, Axel Fleisch and Frank Seidel for debating all things tense and aspect.

My trips to Lwangwa would not have been possible without the accommodation offered by Kai and Susanne Hoffmann. Further thanks go to Marcelo and Melanie Reimer and to Heinke Schimanowski for their help in times of need.

Nancy Winters and Martin Werner helped me a great deal with my first steps in the village and have provided great companionship far from home. My first contacts in the Nyakyusa community were established with the help of Astol Benson and Anthon Mwangake. Martin Mwakaje has been a great help in finding further speakers for text collecting.

Descriptive linguistic research greatly relies on the cooperation of native speakers. I am thankful to all my language assistants, especially Elisha Mwakyoma, who has been so patient from my first steps in empirical linguistics on, and Herbert Zabron "The Professor" Mwaikema, who has been a dedicated language teacher.

The Institute for African Studies and Egyptology with all of its members has been a welcoming and supportive environment. Further thanks go to Monica Feinen, who has provided the map used in this study.

---

[1] The work presented in this book is based on my doctoral dissertation, which was accepted by the University of Cologne's Faculty of Arts and Humanities in 2016.

Acknowledgments

I also wish to express my gratitude towards a.r.t.e.s. Graduate School for the Humanities Cologne for the great working conditions and for awarding me a generous scholarship that made this research possible.

Further thanks go to Lee Bickmore and Sebastian Nordhoff for providing helpful feedback and for guiding me through the publication process. This book has also benefited greatly from the comments of the two anonymous reviewers. I wish to thank Mary Chambers and the Language Science Press community proofreaders for improving my non-native English.

Last but not least, I wish to thank all my friends, who lifted my spirits when writing or fieldwork strained my nerves, especially Alexandra, Anne, Benjamin, Eka, Hares, Jens and Willi.

Abbreviations and symbols

Morphemes throughout this study are glossed using the Leipzig Glossing Rules, with some minor additions to fit the needs of Nyakyusa morphology.

-	segmentable morpheme boundary
=	clitic boundary
<>	infix boundary; graphemic representation
.	syllable boundary
*	ungrammatical form; reconstructed form
#	contextually inadequate
?	questionable or only marginally acceptable
<	source language
//	phonological representation
[]	phonetic form
~	reduplication; variation between forms
´	marked rise in pitch
ˌ	syllabicity of nasal segment

1...18	noun classes	CAUS	causative
1PL	first person plural	COM	comitative ('with'/'and')
1SG	first person singular	COMP	complementizer
2PL	second person plural	CMPR	comparative
2SG	second person singular	COND	conditional
ADJ	deverbal adjective	COP	copula
AGNR	agent nominalizer	DE	German
APPL	applicative	DEM	demonstrative
ASSOC	associative	DESDTV	desiderative
AUG	augment	DIST	distal demonstrative
AUX	auxiliary verb	EN	English
C	consonant segment;	[ET]	example from elicitation
	coda phase	FUT	future

FV	final vowel	PROX	proximal demonstrative
G	glide segment	Q	question marker
HORT	hortative particle	RECP	reciprocal
IMP	imperative	REDUPL	reduplication
INDEF.FUT	indefinite future	REF	referential demonstrative
INF	infinitive	S	time of speech
INTENS	intensifier	SG	singular
INTS	intensive	SM	subject marker
intr.	intransitive	SUBJ	subjunctive
INTERJ	interjection	SUBSEC	subsecutive
IPFV	imperfective	SWA	Swahili
ITV	itive	TMA	tense, mood, aspect
LOC	locative	tr.	transitive
MOD.FUT	modal future	V	vowel segment
N	nasal segment;	VB	verb base
	nucleus phase	WH	wh-question word
n/a	not applicable		
NARR	narrative tense		
NCL	noun class		
NEG	negation		
NEUT	neuter (derivation)		
NPX	nominal prefix		
O	onset phase		
OM	object marker		
PART	partitive		
PASS	passive		
PST	past		
PB	Proto-Bantu		
p.c.	personal communication		
PCU	perception, cognition, utterance		
PERS	persistive		
PFV	perfective		
PL	plural		
POSS	possessive		
PRS	present		
PROG	progressive aspect		
PROH	prohibitive		
PPX	pronominal prefix		

1 Introduction and Background

1.1 Introductory remarks

This monograph deals with the verb in Nyakyusa, a Bantu language of south-western Tanzania. As Nurse (2008: 21) puts it, "Bantu languages are 'verby', that is, they are morphologically agglutinating languages, expressing by verbal inflection what other languages may express lexically or syntactically." Grammatical categories marked on the verb include subject, object, negation, a number of derivational categories and tense, mood and aspect (TMA).

Perhaps one of the most striking features of verbs in Bantu are the highly nuanced systems of marking tense and aspect distinctions. Dahl (1985: 185) even speaks of "the most complex TMA systems in general". While most descriptive accounts of individual languages deal with formal aspects of these systems, their meaning and usage are commonly disregarded. Typically, the authors confine themselves to giving a label for each construction and presenting a few examples with approximate translations. Recent and noteworthy exceptions include Fleisch (2000), Kershner (2002), Botne et al. (2006), Botne (2008), and Crane (2011). Given this lacuna, the following description puts a special focus on TMA constructions, encompassing both their sentence-level meaning as well as their patterns of employment in discourse. The description is synchronically orientated and aims at scholars of comparative Bantu studies as well as the general linguistic audience.

In the following sections, the language and its speakers are presented (§1.2), followed by an exposition of the methods of data collection used (§1.3). Lastly, the theoretical framework is described (§1.4).

1.2 The Nyakyusa language and its speakers

1.2.1 Geography and demography

Nyakyusa is a Bantu language spoken in the Mbeya region of south-western Tanzania, in the coastal plains of lake Nyassa (Lake Malawi) and the hills extending to the north of it (e.g. M. Wilson 1963: 1), with the biggest urban centres being Tukuyu and Kyela. Its homeland forms part of the so-called Nyasa-Tanganyika Corridor (henceforth: the Corridor; see §1.2.4) and is characterized by heavy rainfalls and fertile ground. In the updated version of Guthrie's referential system Nyakyusa has the code M31 (Maho 2009).[1]

The Ethnologue estimates 1,080,000 speakers in Tanzania (Simons & Fenning 2017), while Muzale & Rugemalira (2008) give a number of 732,990. Nyakyusa is vigorously used by all generations and also learned by local non-native speakers (Lewis 2009). Most speakers are bilingual in Swahili. Nyakyusa is surrounded by other Bantu languages, among them Kinga (G65) to the east, Kisi (G67) to the southeast, and Safwa (M25) and Wanji (G66) in the north. Its closest relatives are Ngonde (M31d), spoken further south in Malawi and Ndali (M301). Nyakyusa and Ngonde are typically treated as one language. However, the limited data available on Malawian Ngonde points towards major structural divergences, as will be pointed out at various points throughout this study.

The linguistic and cultural closeness of Nyakyusa and Ndali (also see §1.2.4) is reflected in a shared myth of origin. According to this myth, Nyakyusa and Ndali were part of one ethnic group originating in Mahenge, half way between their current homelands and the coast. The Ndali people took the longer path, thus the name Ndali 'long (class 9)' (Konter-Katani 1989: 39). A different myth, however, sees a common origin with the Kinga, a group with whom an important cult is shared (Weber 1998: ch. 7).

1.2.2 On the name Nyakyusa

Over the course of time, the names used to refer to the Nyakyusa people and their language have changed and caused some confusion in the literature. Therefore, a short excursion into the history of research on them, with a focus on glossonyms, seems to be appropriate before turning to the linguistic research itself.

The first Europeans to at the area around the north shore of Lake Nyasa on the Zambezi-Shire-Nyasa water way in the 1870s, landed in the Ngonde kingdom of present-day Malawi. Hence they called the local groups, among them those that later came to be known as Nyakyusa, by the name Konde (Prein 1995: 36–40; M. Wilson 1963: 1–5). This is reflected in the first descriptions of and notes on the Nyakyusa language (Meinhof 1966; Schumann 1899; Cleve 1904). A wordlist

---

[1]The referential system devised by Malcolm Guthrie, which refers to Bantu languages by a combination of a letter (zone) and digits (group and language) is to be understood as purely geographical, with no direct reference to phylogenetic or areal relationships; see Maho (2003).

by Merensky (1894), however, features "Iki Nyakyusa" in its subtitle, which is presumably the first scholarly mention of the language by that name.

A turning point in the linguistic treatment of Nyakyusa is Endemann's (1914) grammatical sketch "Erste Übungen im Nyakyusa". The anglophone tradition, however, takes a different path: until the 1930s reference is made to the local varieties dealt with (Bain 1891; Hodson 1934), with Johnston (1977: 208 et passim) somewhere in-between, using "Ikinyi-kiusa (Nkonde)" and listing a number of dialects. Berger (1933; 1938), and Stolz's (1934) posthumously published wordlist edited by Berger, however, still speak of "Konde", as does Busse in 1942, although he later on (1949; 1957; n.d.) adopts the denomination *Nyakyusa*. This term had in the meantime been established in the ethnological literature by Geoffrey and Monica Wilson (1936; 1937 amongst others), mainly to differentiate between the divergent political systems on either side of the Songwe river, i.e. scattered chiefdoms to the north vs. the Ngonde kingdom to the south. Originally, *Nyakyusa* designated a local chiefdom, and was extended to name all of the peoples living north of the Konde and their closely related mutually intelligible language varieties. The name Nyakyusa relates to a legendary chief Mwakyusa, whose name again is a matronym 'son of Kyusa' (Labroussi 1998: 42f; Weber 1998: 91–95). The prefix *nya-* designates group, clan or family membership and is a widespread Bantu element (Meeussen 1967). From that period onwards all linguistic publications dealing with Tanzanian varieties speak of Nyakyusa (see e.g. Guthrie 1967; Mwangoka & Voorhoeve 1960c; von Essen & Kähler-Meyer 1969).[2]

1.2.3 Previous linguistic research

In comparison to other, mostly un(der)described, Corridor languages, there has been a relatively high number of publications on Nyakyusa. Description nevertheless remains very sketchy.

The only more or less comprehensive grammatical sketches, with around 90 pages each, are Schumann (1899) and, partly based on that work, Endemann (1900), the former being the oldest monograph on any of the Corridor languages.[3] In the mid-20th century another short grammatical sketch was produced at the University of Leiden (Mwangoka & Voorhoeve 1960c), accompanied by a prac-

---

[2]For a valuable discussion of linguistic work in the colonial period, although somewhat coloured by the Moravian perspective, see Kröger (2011).

[3]Another shorter, typewritten and unpublished grammatical sketch of unknown authorship was found in possession of Reverend Mwasamwaja of Lwangwa. This work, which has gone unnoticed so far, is said to be the product of Scandinavian missionaries and seems to be heavily based on Schumann's and Endemann's grammars.

tical language guide by the same authors (Mwangoka & Voorhoeve 1960a). An even shorter grammatical sketch of just eight pages is Nurse (1979). The domain of tense, mood and aspect in particular is only rudimentarily dealt with in all of these; they limit themselves mainly to labelling certain constructions and providing a few translations of sample sentences into German or English.

A number of publications deal with more specific aspects of Nyakyusa grammatical structure.[4] Meinhof (1966) is the first approximation to an account of Nyakyusa phonology, Meyer (1919) an unpublished proposal for developing an official orthography. Endemann (1900) is an attempt at explaining the morphophonology of applicativized causatives (see §4.3.3). Labroussi (1998; 1999), apart from genetic classification, discusses some aspects of phonology and morphology, and von Essen & Kähler-Meyer (1969) deal with the prosody of nouns (including verbal nouns) in isolation. Method's (2008) master's thesis presents a generative approach to aspects of phonology in a dialect of Nyakyusa. Konter-Katani (1989) discusses the reflexes of Proto-Bantu plosives in Nyakyusa and Ndali, a topic seemingly also dealt with by Mulinda (1997). Some aspects of reduplication are analyzed in Lusekelo (2009a). Berger (1938) is a first attempt to describe regularities in the formation of perfective stems (§6.4.2).

Concerning morphosyntax we find a manuscript by Duranti (1977) and a description of the linear structure of the noun phrase by Lusekelo (2009b). Lusekelo also published several papers dealing with aspects of motion verbs (Lusekelo 2008b) and adverbials (Lusekelo 2010). Object marking and some aspects of verbal derivation are dealt with in his PhD dissertation (Lusekelo 2012), parts of which were published as a paper beforehand (Lusekelo 2008a). A master's thesis by Hawkinson (1976) deals, according to its title, with aspects of cross-reference marking. Persohn (2017b) discusses postfinal clitics (§3.3.8). Lusekelo's (2007) master's thesis, which has been published in a slightly modified version (Lusekelo 2013), deals with tense and aspect categories. See i.a. p. 115 for a critical discussion. Lusekelo (2016) discusses some aspects of conditional sentences in Nyakyusa. Persohn (2016) discusses the semantic shifts that have lead to the present-day narrative tense (§7.3) and modal future (§9.5) constructions. Persohn & Bernander (2016) give an overview of present tense markers in the Corridor and several languages of Guthrie's zones G and N and discuss their grammaticalization.

Concerning lexicography, the first known wordlist is Bain (1891), further lists of varying lengths and reliability are found in Johnston (1897; 1977), Nurse (1979),

---

[4]The following studies were inaccessible to the author: Anonymous (1939), Busse (n.d.), Duranti (1977), Hawkinson (1976), Konter-Katani (1988), Lusekelo (2010), Meyer (1919) and Mulinda (1997).

Schumann (1899), Merensky (1894) and Mwangoka & Voorhoeve (1960b). Stolz (1934) deals with botanical vocabulary, while Greenway (1947) lists veterinary lexemes in several languages, one of which is Nyakyusa. There are further unpublished word lists and dictionaries (Anonymous 1939; Busse n.d. Konter-Katani 1988). Some scattered words can be found in Werner (1919) and M. Wilson (1958). The only published and extensive lexicographic work is Felberg (1996). The latter has been of immense help for the creation of the present monograph, although it has deficits and inconsistencies in the transcription of vowel length as well as of the vowel quality of the two pairs of high vowels.[5]

Social aspects of language use are specifically dealt with by Hodson (1934) on name giving, Walsh (1982) on greetings and Kolbusa (2000) on the avoidance register *ingamwana*. The latter also contains an extensive discussion of previous notes on onomastics. A short note by Cleve (1904) is the first known mention of *ingamwana*. Mwakasaka (1975; 1978) deals with oral literature, although without presenting any original texts. Some narratives, written down by native speakers and without translation, can be found at Felberg's web page (Felberg 2010) and Mwangoka & Voorhoeve (1960d). There is also a number of edited narratives with German translations: Berger (1933), Busse (1942; 1949) and also in the appendix of Schumann (1899). Busse (1957) is a collection of riddles including translation into German. An overview of educational and religious materials can be found in Kröger (2011) and Felberg (2010).

Unfortunately, some of the more recent publications on Nyakyusa either transcribe Nyakyusa with orthography of Swahili, which has only 5 vowels and no vowel length distinctions, or, when attempting to transcribe the 7x2 vowel system, are very inconsistent, even to the point of self-contradiction. This impedes any meaningful analysis not only of TMA constructions, but also of morphological processes applying within the verb stem (e.g. §4.2.1.1–4.2.1.2, 6.4.2).

Several further papers include some discussion of Nyakyusa data, among them Hyman (1999) on vowel harmony, Hyman (2003) on the emergence of morphophonological patterns, Bostoen (2008) on spirantization, Eaton (2013) on narrative markers in the Corridor and Persohn & Bernander (2016) on the grammaticalization of present tenses in southern Tanzanian Bantu languages. Furthermore, SIL International is working on a standardized orthography and a re-translation of the Bible, but not planning any linguistic publications (Helen Eaton, p.c.; Daniel King,, p.c.). For an overview of ethnological work on the Nyakyusa and Ngonde people as well as religious material see Mwalilino (1995).

---

[5]Knut Felberg (p.c.) himself recognizes these shortcomings.

1.2.4 Nyakyusa within Bantu

Attempts at an internal classification of the Bantu languages have, apart from smaller subgroups such as Guthrie's zone S, so far not yielded any comprehensive or broadly accepted results. This can be attributed to the high number of languages, the very limited documentation of most of these and the difficult task of disentangling inherited innovations from geographical diffusion of structural and lexical traits. For an overview of different attempts of classification as well as a discussion of some methodological problems, the reader is referred to Möhlig (1981: 102–114) and Nurse & Philippson (2003c).

The Nyakyusa language area forms part of the Nyasa-Tanganyika Corridor, a geographical stretch that was named by social anthropologist Monica M. Wilson (1958) after the two lakes defining it to the south and north. The area's cultural and linguistic coherence has been noted from early on (see e.g. Fülleborn 1906; Johnston 1977). Even on this smaller scale, linguistic classification proves a difficult task, with the specific problems of most languages being underdescribed and the data available, until recently, being heavily biased towards Tanzania (Nurse 1988).

Concerning Nyakyusa, there is broad agreement that its closest relative, apart from Ngonde, is Ndali.[6] This has led some scholars to consider at least the aforementioned two tongues, or even all three of them, as dialects of one and the same language (see M. Wilson 1958: 9). Especially on the lexical level this group is very unlike its neighbours. Says Nurse (1988: 72f), "moving from the three eastern groups to Nyakyusa-Ndali one has the impression of entering a different lexical world". Some of these uncommon lexemes are suggested by Nurse (1988) and Ehret (1973) to be of South Cushitic and Central Sudanic origin. On the structural level however, Nyakyusa proves to be quite divergent from Ndali and Ngonde as described by Botne (2008), Labroussi (1998) and Kishindo (1999) (see also Nurse 1988: 55).

In the following paragraphs the various proposed classifications of Nyakyusa and the neighbouring tongues are briefly summarized and discussed. The names of different varieties are adapted to NUGL (Maho 2009) and may not conform to the original sources. As the reader will notice, the various attempts at classification differ not only with regards to their results, but also to the languages examined, rendering the results only partially comparable.

Bernd Heine, in his often-cited (1972) work, presents a lexicostatistic classification of Bantu that is supposed to reflect diachronic reality. In his study of

---

[6]The Sukwa language of Malawi (see Kershner 2002) is usually subsumed under Ndali.

137 languages, he considers Nyakyusa together with Fipa and Nyika to be part of a Fipa-Konde branch of Eastern Highland (*Osthochland*), which again represents a sub-branch of his Congo branch (*Kongozweig*), the most numerous of 11 postulated primary Bantu branches.

Derek Nurse, together with his colleagues Gérard Phillipson and George Park, has presented various classifications of the Corridor languages over the years. In an early lexicostatistically-based classification (Nurse 1979) he proposes that Nyakyusa should be grouped with Ndali and Lambya, without proposing a higher level grouping. A decade later this idea changed: in Nurse (1988), on the basis of lexicostatistics and phonological innovations, a Corridor group consisting of three subgroups, one of them Nyakyusa/Ndali, is proposed, although in Nurse & Park (1988) this subgroup is separated from the other Corridor languages, a position maintained in Nurse (1999). Nurse & Philippson (2003c) keep the basic grouping of the Corridor languages (Figure 1.1), expressing doubts as to whether Nyakyusa/Ndali should be included.

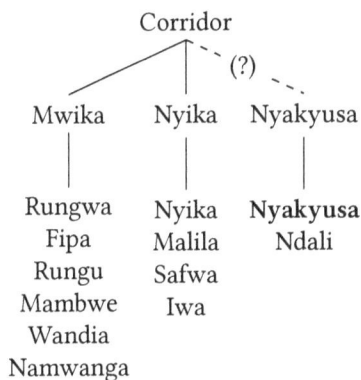

Corridor

(?)

Mwika	Nyika	Nyakyusa
Rungwa	Nyika	**Nyakyusa**
Fipa	Malila	Ndali
Rungu	Safwa	
Mambwe	Iwa	
Wandia		
Namwanga		

Figure 1.1: Nurse & Phillipson's (2003c) classification of the Corridor languages

Catherine Labroussi's (1998, 1999) work is a valuable contribution to our understanding of the Corridor languages: apart from phonological traits and lexico-statistic calculations, it examines patterns of diffusion and also discusses social factors, mostly retrieved by archaeology and oral history. As for the classification of the Corridor languages, it fundamentally reflects Nurse's position concerning Nyakyusa.

Historian Christopher Ehret (1973) proposed a Corridor-group ("Mambwe-Fipa-Nyiha") which excludes Nyakyusa. What distinguishes his proposal is that he postulates that Corridor and Nyakyusa may belong to different branches of eastern Bantu. This position is revised in Ehret (2001: 36f, 55), where the Corridor languages are split into two major groups, Rungwe (Nyakyusa, Ndali, Safwa, Nyika, Wandia) and Mwika (Pimbwe, Fipa, Mambwe, Namwanga). Ehret qualifies this insofar as he admits that this synchronic grouping need not reflect linguistic genealogy.

Ehret's student Catherine Fourshey, however, has returned to Ehret's earlier views (Fourshey 2002). In an attempt to reconstruct the pre-colonial history of the Corridor based mainly on linguistic data, she proposes a genetic unit comprising the Corridor languages, the internal structure of the unit in essence reflecting Nurse's classification. Fourshey arrives at this assumption primarily on the basis of lexicostatistics supplemented and refined by an examination of the distribution of certain cultural lexemes. Unfortunately Fourshey did not have access to the linguistically more fine-grained analysis of Labroussi (1998).

To conclude, it seems safe to assert at this point – as stated more or less explicitly in Nurse (1988), Labroussi (1998), Nurse & Philippson (2003c) – that the languages of the Corridor might best be understood not as a genetically uniform unit, but as forming an area of long-term linguistic convergence. In this context, Nyakyusa can be understood as the special case, being more strongly isolated from its geolinguistic environment. Although it shares a number of lexical and structural features with its neighbouring languages, especially Ngonde and Ndali/Sukwa, it seems to have been rather resistant to external influences, and in the development and spreading of innovations it seems to have played the role of donor rather than that of recipient.

1.2.5 Dialects and variety described

The dialectal geography of the Corridor as a whole, as well as for the specific case of Nyakyusa, remains relatively unknown (Walsh & Swilla 2002: 4, 25). However, a number of topolectal divisions can be stated. Some first observations concerning subgroups and varieties of Nyakyusa were made by Johnston (1977: 61), with subsequent refinements by M. Wilson (1963: 2). The following notes are based on the latter, as well as on Walsh & Swilla's (2002) comments upon it. These sources have been supplemented by consultation with a number of native speaker informants as well as by an unpublished survey by SIL International.[7] The following

---

[7]Kindly made available to the author by Helen Eaton.

list gives the identifiable subgroups within Nyakyusa, together with their respective Guthrie codes according to Maho (2009):[8]

- Nyakyusa of the lake-shore plains. This variety is often referred to as *MuNgonde* by speakers of northern varieties, although speakers from the area do not use this name themselves. It is considered clearly distinct from Malawian Ngonde (*IkyaNgonde*).
- Central Nyakyusa, around Masoko. The Nyakyusa variety of this area, seat of chief Mwaipopo, is considered the variety with the highest prestige. In Maho (2009) this variety is grouped with that of the lake-shore plains as *Nyakyusa proper* (M31A).
- Northern Nyakyusa (M31B), also called *Kukwe* or *Ngumba* ('innermost plateau').
- Nyakyusa of the mountains (M31C), also referred to as *Mwamba* ('Mountains'), *Lugulu* (name of an aboriginal group) or *Sokelo* ('East'), in the area around Mwakaleli.
- Selya (M31E), at the foot of the Livingstone Mountains. Wilson distinguishes this from another eastern subgroup named Saku.

The denominations for the various groups and varieties within Nyakyusa are used differently by speakers from different areas. As Monica Wilson states:

> AbaMwamba means by derivation 'the hill people', but is generally used for 'the people of the north'. The Ngonde of Karonga call those on the plain around Mwaya BaMwamba, the men of Mwaya apply the name not to themselves, but to the people of Selya, while the people of Selya apply it to those in the hills to the north of them. (M. Wilson 1963: 2 FN2)

Two further varieties of unclear status might be added to the list above. M. Wilson (1958: 9) observed that the group of Penja M302, as well speakers of the eastern variety of Nyika M23, were being absorbed by the Nyakyusa. While the case of Penja remains unsolved (Walsh & Swilla 2002: 26), a recent sociolinguistic survey provides further indications of a language shift of the Eastern Nyika people, suggesting an additional Nyakyusa topolect (Lindfors et al. 2009).

Although diatopic variation within Nyakyusa exists and speakers readily identify the speech varieties of different regions, intercomprehension is not affected. Given the high number of speakers, Nyakyusa can be considered relatively uniform in comparison to many of the other, smaller Corridor languages (see La-

---

[8]It has to be kept in mind that ethnic or group identity and linguistic varieties need not overlap.

broussi 1998: 204). Most speakers consulted stress that the main dividing line lies between the variety of the lake-shore plains (Kyela district) on the one side and the varieties of the more mountainous terrains on the other.

The focus of this study lies on the Selya and Mwamba/Lugulu varieties. The Germany-based language assistants are originaly from Ikama (Mwamba/Lugulu) and Itete (Selya). In Mbeya city, preliminary work was performed with speakers from Itete. The main part of the fieldwork (§1.3) took place in the village of Lwangwa, which is said to be at the transition between the Mwamba/Lugulu and Selya varieties. The map in Figure 1.2 shows the position of the three villages.

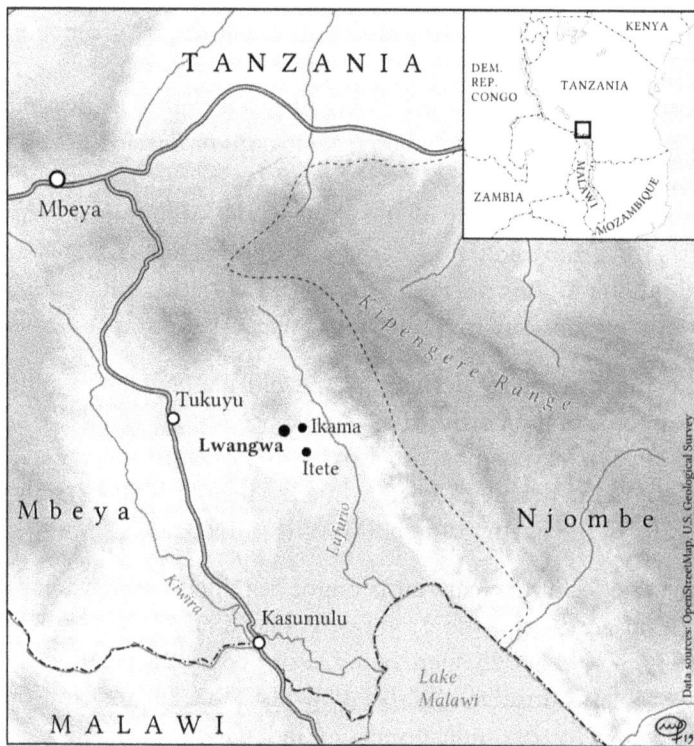

Figure 1.2: Field base and origin of language assistants. Map courtesy of Monika Feinen

1.3 Data collection

The main data for this study was collected during three research trips to Tanzania. The first trip took place in November and December 2013, during which time research was carried out with speakers living in the city of Mbeya. On the second trip, in November and December of 2014, as well as on the third trip, from late September to early December of 2015, Lwangwa village in Busekelo district was chosen as the field base. Further intensive work, mainly guided elicitation, was carried out with two language assistants living in Germany between 2012 and 2016.

All language assistants that participated in this study are native speakers of Nyakyusa, fluent in Swahili and between 25 years and 78 years of age during the period of research. The expatriate speakers have been living in Germany since 2009 and 2005 respectively. Since that time they have returned periodically to the language area and continue to converse with family members on a regular basis in their native language. The contact language used in research has mainly been English, plus some Swahili (in Tanzania) and German (in Germany).

The main practices of data collection were one-on-one elicitation and text collection, predominantly of folk narratives. Elicitation is here to be understood not as a mere production task, but in a broad and interactive sense, in line with Mous (2007: 2), who states that "elicitation is guided conversation about language data". See Cover (2015: 245–256) for a recent discussion of elicitation with a focus on semantic fieldwork.

The collection of lexical items, apart from basic approaches such as the elicitation of semantic fields and sound-substitution (Crowley 2007: 104–111), was greatly aided by previous work on Nyakyusa, especially Felberg's (1996) dictionary. Although a great number of entries had to be checked for accuracy, it served as a valuable starting point for enlarging the lexical corpus. All lexical items were entered into a database using Fieldworks Language Explorer (FLEx) software. In the course of research this was supplemented and double-checked with usage in texts and spontaneous speech. FLEx software was also used for morphological segmentation and creating lexical cross-references. Given the problematic representation of Nyakyusa in several recent publications (see §1.2.3), a great amount of time and scrutiny was dedicated to checking and re-checking all transcriptions.

With regard to the semantics of TMA, elicitation encompassed a variety of tasks. One of them was translation from the contact language, mostly together with a discourse context. Here Dahl's (1985; 2000a) tense and aspect questionnaires served as valuable points of departure. In other cases, the compatibility of a given construction with specific adverbials or lexical items was checked through grammaticality judgements, or possible contexts of use for constructed sentences were narrowed down through dialogue with the language assistants. The more research advanced, the more elicitation on TMA became intertwined with the analysis of texts and naturally observed data. Specific utterances were checked for their applicability and/or meaning in other contexts, and examples were manipulated in a targeted way, again checking for acceptability, changes in meaning, and possible contexts of use.

The texts used in this study came from two main sources. First, oral monologues, mostly folk narratives plus a few eexpository texts, were recorded with single speakers and later transcribed by the researcher. The transcription was then checked and the texts were translated into English with the help of a language assistant. Apart from minor exceptions, these were not the recorded speakers themselves. Additionally, two retellings of the Pear Story (Chafe 1980) were recorded and one oral rendering of a traditional narrative was made available by Knut Felberg. Furthermore, a number of written texts were made available by SIL International's Mbeya office. These stem from literacy workshops and are mostly fictitious narratives but also include a few expository and procedural and one behavioural text. Five of these came edited and with translations into English, the others were translated with the language assistants. One additional written expository text was provided by one of the main language assistants. All written texts were double-checked for pronunciation. The composition of the text corpus is given in Table 1.1. A few additional examples were taken from a current draft of a Bible translation by SIL International (kindly made available by Helen Eaton),[9] HIV prevention materials produced by the same organization and older text collections (Berger 1933; Busse 1942; 1949).

The focus on discourse is due to a number of reasons. The first reason is the availability of texts and the comparatively easy segmentation of narrative texts, given the time limits imposed upon this study. The second reason is the need for an adequate description of the dedicated narrative markers (§7). Third, though monological in their form, narratives often contain language of other communicative situations, for instance episodes in dialogue form or embedded expository or behavioural discourse. The use of certain grammatical devices, especially TMA, in everyday discourse constitutes an area that is open for further research.

---

[9]Scripture quotations from The Authorized (King James) Version. Rights in the Authorized Version in the United Kingdom are vested in the Crown. Reproduced by permission of the Crown's patentee, Cambridge University Press.

Table 1.1: Composition of the text corpus

Genre	Medium	Source	N° of texts	Avg. N° of words
Narrative	Oral	Own fieldwork	15	324
Narrative	Oral	Knut Felberg	1	856
Narrative	Written	SIL	16	285
Retelling	Oral	Own fieldwork	2	430
Exposition	Oral	Own fieldwork	3	351
Exposition	Written	Own fieldwork	1	95
Exposition	Written	SIL	2	247
Behavioural	Written	SIL	1	129
Procedural	Written	SIL	1	205

Apart from elicitation and text collection, a great deal of everyday life in the field was carried out using Nyakyusa. This allowed for the observation of language use in a more natural environment and proved a fruitful source for contextualized examples, which served as jumping-off points for further elicitation. Lastly, Proto-Bantu reconstructions stem from the Bantu lexical reconstructions 3 database (Bastin et al. 2002).

Throughout this study, examples from elicitation sessions are marked with the abbreviation "[ET]". Textual data is marked with a short version of the text's name, often the title of the narrative, such as "[Crocodile and Monkey]". Examples from participant observation or conversation are marked as "[overheard]".

1.4 Theoretical framework

1.4.1 Overview

For most parts of this grammar, no particular framework has been adopted. Instead, the description is based on well-known descriptive and typological concepts. In those parts dealing with phonological, morphological and syntactic aspects, the description is guided by structural considerations, whereas in the discussion of the meaning and use of TMA categories, functional considerations are in the foreground.

However, to gain a more profound understanding of the organization of tense and aspect, the cognitive framework developed by Botne & Kershner (2008) has been adopted, although an attempt was made to give a broad and dense description so as to facilitate translation into other frameworks. Botne & Kershner's framework will be outlined in §1.4.2–1.4.3.

Further, to approach the uses of TMA categories in Nyakyusa narrative texts, the analytic tools developed by Labov & Waletzky (1967 and subsequent works) were applied and augmented by a number of concepts stemming from the works of Fleischman (esp. 1990) and Longacre (esp. 1990), as well as some insights into activation status by Prince (1981; 1992). These are described in §1.4.4.2. Lastly, while the approaches mentioned so far are synchronically oriented, in various cases it was found that applying a diachronic perspective helped the understanding of the present-day situation. Therefore, findings from grammaticalization theory (e.g. Heine et al. 1991; Bybee et al. 1994) were included, particularly with regard to identifying the sources of a given construction, delimiting newer and older readings and disentangling the interplay between the various constructions available within an area of grammar.

1.4.2 Tense and grammatical aspect

1.4.2.1 Tense

Tense is a deictic category that localizes a described state-of-affairs in time (see Comrie 1985 among others). According to the most commonly expressed view, the linguistic construal of time is best described in terms of an abstract time line. Thus Comrie (1985: 2), in his reference work on tense, declares that "such a diagrammatic representation of time is adequate for an account of tense in human language." Figure 1.3 illustrates this conception. Throughout this study, in the illustration of temporal relations, S stands for 'time of speech'.

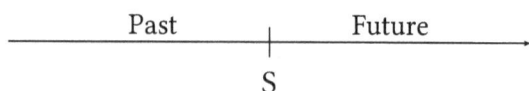

Figure 1.3: Linear conception of time

Bantu languages are well known for their complex TMA systems which include various degrees of remoteness in time, especially in the past (Dahl 1985: 185; Nurse 2008: 21f). Following the common conception of tense, these are usually described in terms of distance on a mono-dimensional timeline, as illustrated in Figure 1.4. The subscript digits indicate the degree of remoteness.

$$P_4 \quad P_3 \quad P_2 \quad P_1 \qquad F_1 \quad F_2 \quad F_3 \quad F_4$$

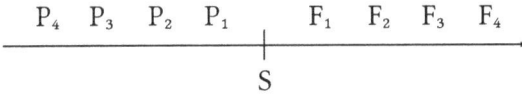

Figure 1.4: Remoteness distinctions in a linear conception of time

Such a representation, however, fails in many cases to explain patterns of morphological marking, as well as the systematic employment of these constructions. For example, the Malawian Bantu language Sukwa M301, as discussed by Kershner (2002: 93f), possesses four non-imperfective paradigms with past time reference. At first glance, their meanings seem to represent a progression from immediate past to to remote past. Figure 1.5 illustrates these paradigms together with their morphological composition on the traditional timeline.

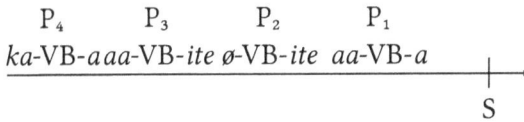

$$P_4 \qquad P_3 \qquad P_2 \qquad P_1$$
$$ka\text{-VB-}a \quad aa\text{-VB-}ite \quad \textit{ø-}\text{VB-}ite \quad aa\text{-VB-}a$$

Figure 1.5: Sukwa paradigms with past reference. Adapted from Kershner (2002: 94)

The linear approach to tense fails to give a motivated explanation for the morphological composition of these constructions, e.g., why there is a zero-prefix in past$_2$, whereas past$_1$ and past$_3$ have *aa-*, or why past$_3$ combines the prefix of past$_1$ with the suffix of past$_2$. Further, it does not allow us to adequately describe their patterns of employment, which are described at length by Kershner (2002).

To address such cases, Botne & Kershner (2008) develop a cognitive model of tense and aspect, which is based on the tenet that there are two basic conceptualizations of time. One conceptualization has Ego, the conceptualizer, moving along a stationary timeline (TIME IS A PATH); see Evans & Green (2006: 84f) on the concept of Ego. In the other, time itself is construed as moving (TIME IS A STREAM), which allows for two perspectives. Either the metaphorical stream of time moves Ego along, passing eventualities as they take place, or time floats eventualities past a stationary Ego. Figure 1.6 depicts the two basic construals.

These two distinct conceptualizations of time are not mutually exclusive. A language may rather encode different aspects of both in different verbal paradigms. Botne & Kershner go on to decompose Reichenbach's (1947) concept of reference time into two separate concepts: reference frame ("temporal domain" in Botne

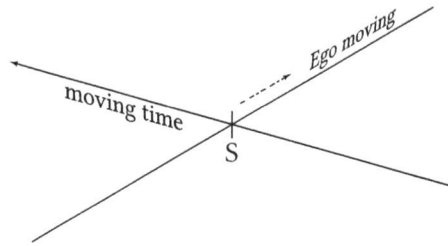

Figure 1.6: Two perspectives on time

& Kershner's terms) and reference anchor. The first is said to be "comparable, but not identical" (Botne & Kershner 2008: 152) to Klein's (1994) concept of topic time. Tense is then understood as the relationship between time of speech as the deictic locus and a reference frame. When the time span of the reference frame includes the deictic locus, this "denot[es] a primary, prevailing experiential past and future perspective" (Botne & Kershner 2008: 153). In cases where the deictic locus is not included in the time span of the reference frame (domain), they speak of a dissociated past or future. Exclusion corresponds to the conceptualization of TIME is a PATH.

The split between reference frame and reference anchor allows Botne & Kershner to further account for temporal relations within a reference frame, which correspond to the conceptualizatioan of TIME is a STREAM.

Figure 1.7 illustrates these two types of temporal relationships, with the reference frames (domains) as rectangular plains. Figure 1.8a depicts a past tense, such as the English simple past. With the reference frame excluding the time of speech, the conceptualizer is instructed to move to a different cognitive domain, where the eventuality takes place. Figure 1.8b illustrates an associated past ("tenor" in Botne & Kershner's terminology), which situates an eventuality prior to the time of speech but within the same reference frame.

In the case of Sukwa addressed above, constructions with past time reference can now be described on a compositional basis (Kershner 2002). The suffix -*ite* denotes *completive aspect*.[10] The prefix *aa-* situates the described state-of-affairs in a preceding time unit within the same reference frame. In out-of-the-blue utterances this is understood as being shortly before the time of speech, but depending on the discursive environment, it can also refer to units such as the preceding day, month, season, etc. The sense of heightened remoteness of the configuration *aa*-VB-*ite* then derives from viewing an event as already completed within a pre-

---

[10]See §1.4.2.2, 6.5.3.2 on grammatical aspect and the notion of completion respectively.

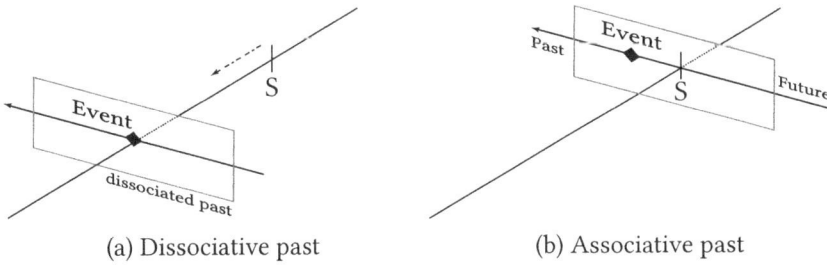

(a) Dissociative past   (b) Associative past

Figure 1.7: Dissociative and associative pasts

ceding time unit. Lastly, *ka-* is a true tense in that it situates the state-of-affairs in a past reference frame. Figure 1.9 illustrates the pasts of Sukwa. See Botne & Kershner (2008) for a discussion of a number of such cases across Bantu.

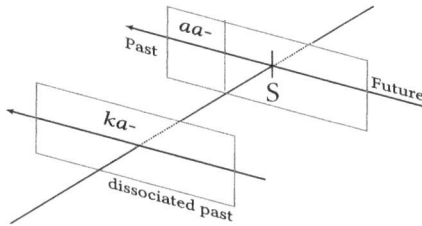

Figure 1.9: Organization of the past in Sukwa. Adapted from Kershner (2002: 113).

Apart from Botne & Kershner's own work (among others Botne 2003b; 2006; 2008; Botne & Kershner 2000; 2008; Kershner 2002) their framework has proven fruitful in Seidel's (2008) grammar of Yeyi R41, Crane's (2011) treatise of tense and aspect in Totela K41 as well as Dom & Bostoen's (2015) work on the Kikongo cluster of Bantu languages. As will be seen in Chapters 6–8, the core assumption of two linguistic perspectives on time will also guide our understanding of the organization of the Nyakyusa tense and aspect system.

1.4.2.2 Grammatical aspect

While tense, as defined in §1.4.2.1, is a deictic category, aspect is not. According to the most common and widely agreed-upon definition, "aspects are different ways of viewing the internal temporal constituency of a situation" (Comrie 1976: 3).

As has been pointed out variously in the theoretical literature on aspectuality, it is essential to distinguish aspect as a grammatical device from the aspectual potential encoded in the lexical verb or verb phrase. Sasse (2002) speaks of "bidimensional approaches" to aspectuality. Within these bidimensional approaches, a prominent position is taken by those approaches which Sasse (2002), adopting a term first introduced by Bickel (1997), calls "radical selection theories". In these theories, aspect as a morphosyntactic device and the lexical dimension of aspect are understood as standing in a strict correspondence relationship: grammatical aspect serves as a phase-selector that selects matching temporal phases from the lexical dimension (the concept of phase will be developed in §1.4.3). As Sasse points out, other prominent bi-dimensional approaches to aspectuality, such as the one put forward by Smith (1997) are conceptually closely related to radical selection theories or might even constitute only a notional variant of them.

The need to distinguish two dimensions of aspectuality also holds for an adequate description of Nyakyusa. As will become clear in Chapters 5–8, grammatical aspect in Nyakyusa is sensitive to the aspectual potential in the lexical (and verb phrase) dimension and hence the choice of an inflectional paradigm greatly depends upon the latter. A central distinction here is that which falls between inchoative and non-inchoative verbs; see §1.4.3.1. In compliance with the tenets of radical selection theories, Botne & Kershner define grammatical aspect as follows:

> [Grammatical, BP] [a]spect denotes the particular temporal view of time in the narrated event. More precisely, a specific aspect denotes a particular temporal phase of the narrated event as the focal frame for viewing the event. This focal frame depicts the status of the event in relation to the vantage point determined by Ego, by default typically the moment of speaking. (Botne & Kershner 2008: 171)

It is not entirely clear how far the idea of a temporal phase as the "focal frame" serves our understanding of grammatical aspect in Nyakyusa. Rather, it seems, especially in the case of perfective aspect (§6.5.3.2), that Ego's vantage point may be construed in relation to a particular phase without necessarily being contained in the eventuality itself. Throughout this study, grammatical aspect will therefore be understood in a slightly simplified version of Botne & Kershner's definition as denoting a particular temporal view of an eventuality by relating Ego's vantage point to a particular temporal phase of it.

As can be gathered from the preceding discussion, Botne & Kershner's approach to tense and grammatical aspect is a compositional one. Concerning

Nyakyusa, this has proven especially fruitful for the analysis of the past tense paradigms (see Chapter 6), the function of the future enclitic *aa=* (§8.2) and the analysis of the present perfective (§6.5.3) vis-à-vis the past perfective (§6.5.5). In a few other cases, such as the narrative tense (§7.3) and the modal future (§9.5), the meanings and uses of the paradigms in question can, however, only be taken as a function of the entire construction. This situation can, in turn, be explained by taking into account the diachronic axis.

1.4.3 Inherent temporal structure of the verb

Grammatical aspect, as defined in the previous subsection, relates Ego's vantage point to a particular temporal phase of an eventuality. The key to the interpretation of any particular verbal expression in Nyakyusa is thus the interaction between grammatical aspect and the temporal structure inherently encoded in the verb. In spite of its central role, this facet of grammar hardly receives any attention in descriptive work on Bantu languages. It is common in Bantu studies, however, to recognize that a number of verbs tend to show a particular behaviour, appearing mainly in certain inflectional paradigms and encoding a state. This class of verbs is commonly labeled "inchoative verbs" (e.g. Cole 1955: 55–60); this class of verbs will be dealt with in more detail below. A brief theoretical digression will lay out the concepts and analytical tools central to understanding the interaction between the lexical and the inflectional dimension in Nyakyusa.

1.4.3.1 Aristotelian aspect ('lexical aspect')

Aristotelian aspect, also named 'lexical aspect' or 'verb aspect' by some scholars, refers to the obligatory classification of the aspectual potential encoded in the lexical (and phrasal) dimension in terms of abstract temporal phases. Sasse (2002) speaks of 'aspect$_2$'. The present study follows Binnick's terminology, as Aristotle is generally credited with discovering these distinctions (Binnick 1991: 171f).

The most familiar categorization of verbal expressions in the linguistic literature are the categories postulated by the philosopher Vendler (1957) and developed to explain the behaviour of different verbal expressions in English. Vendler distinguishes four types of expressions based on temporal criteria and their behaviour or compatibility in particular syntactic frames: states, activities, achievements and accomplishments. A major split between these categories is along the lines of telicity (delimitedness): achievements and accomplishments are understood as telic, whereas states and activities are understood as atelic. The latter two again differ in dynamicity, while accomplishments and achievements differ in regards to their duration (see below). Vendler's categories have been accepted by a great number of scholars as being valid for all natural languages, as they are supposed to be based on universals of logic and are therefore understood not to be subject to cross-linguistic variation (see e.g. Tatevosov 2002: 322); for critical evaluations of this assumption see Filip (2011) and Bar-el (2015). The broad acceptance of Vendler's categorization is not challenged by certain tweaks proposed by different scholars: for instance Verkuyl (1972) and Kenny (1969) conflate achievements and accomplishments, while Smith (1997) adds semelfactives as a further category. A number of tests to determine the category of different expressions have been developed in the literature, the most cited test being one for telicity, by checking for compatibility with adverbials of the type "in X time" and "for X time". For an overview of tests put forward by a number of scholars, see Binnick (1991: 173–197).

For the study of Bantu languages Vendler's categories are hardly applicable. As Crane puts it:

> Rather than having a basic telic-atelic distinction, Bantu languages in general appear to divide verbs differently. This is due to a distinction between non-inchoative verbs (roughly corresponding to Vendler's states, activities, and accomplishments) and inchoative verbs, which encompass many of Vendler's achievements and other verbs. (Crane 2011: 34)

Crane hints at two closely related points of central importance. First, one essentially problematic category in Vendler's classification is that of achievement verbs. In a Vendlerian understanding, as echoed by Binnick (1991: 195), "an achievement is all culmination; although the achievement is possibly preceded by some activity [...] the verb refers only to the achievement phase, not to the preceding activity". Persohn (2017a), by drawing on the Nyakyusa data presented in Chapter 5 and incorporating data from Sukwa (Kershner 2002) and Ndali (Botne 2008), shows that the morphosemantic behaviour of numerous verbal lexemes and verb phrases in these languages can only be explained by assuming the lexicalization of transitional patterns that consist of a state or process of origin, a change-of-state and a resultant state; similar assumptions have so far been mostly implicit in recent studies of aspectuality in Bantu languages. This leads to the second point: Crane picks up the notion of *inchoative verbs*, which has come to be used as an umbrella term for those classes of verbal lexemes that encode a resultant state as part of their aspectual potential. As will become more explicit in Chapters 5–6, this notion of inchoativity plays a central role in the choice of grammatical aspect in Nyakyusa.

Within radical selection theories of aspectuality (§1.4.2.2), certain modifica-
tions of the Vendlerian categories have been stipulated. To give an example,
Breu and Sasse (e.g. Breu 1984; Sasse 1991) understand grammatical aspect as
making reference to boundaries of situations, the basic assumption being that
the lexical or verb phrase dimension can potentially encode one situation, a left
boundary that represents the ingression into the situation and a right boundary,
that is, the egression out of the situation. This yields five potential types of verbs.
Other radical selection theories, such as Bickel (1997) or Johanson (1996; 2000)
offer comparable classifications; see Croft (2012: 48–52) for an overview. What
these approaches share is the basic assumption that the lexical or verb phrase dimension may encode only one situation (or 'middle phase'), which by definition
excludes any lexicalizations of a transition from a state or process of origin into
a resultant state; see Persohn (2017a) for more extensive discussion.

For the description of aspectuality in Nyakyusa the present study thus draws
on a framework developed by Botne and Kershner (see Botne 1983; Kershner
2002; Botne & Kershner 2008 among others; see also §1.4.2), which has its origin
in Botne's study of aspectuality in Ruanda JD61 and has been extended by Kershner's study of Sukwa M301. Botne and Kershner's categorization of verbs is based
on Freed (1979), a study of English phasal verbs ('aspectualizers') and their interaction with verbal semantics and the syntax of the verbal complement, in which
Freed provides a formalization of Vendler's categories. In analogy with syllable
phonology Freed proposes that the underlying temporal structure of verbs can
be understood as a combination of three phases ("segments" in her terminology).
The Onset constitutes a preliminary or preparatory phase, while the Nucleus
corresponds to the characteristic act encoded in the verb. The Coda constitutes a
culminative phase following the characteristic act. In doing so, Freed subscribes
to Vendler's understanding of achievements as pure transitions. Botne and Kershner, in their works, adopt Freed's understanding of phases; their central mod-
ification is to allow for more combinations of phases. Thus achievement verbs,
apart from a punctual Nucleus, may further encode an extended Onset (state of
origin) and/or an extended Coda (resultant state), yielding four types of achievements. Likewise, accomplishments may either contain a punctual or extended
Coda phase. In both cases, the presence or absence of an extended Coda phase is
equivalent to the distinction between inchoative and non-inchoative verbs. Activities, in Botne & Kershner's understanding, comprise an extended Nucleus,
whereas a state does not possess any internal structure. Throughout this study,
in illustration of aspectual classes the three possible constituent phases will be
abbreviated as O, N and C respectively. Note that the choice of Botne & Kersh-

ner's model is to be understood as a useful descriptive tool; see Persohn (2017a) for a critical evaluation.

What must be emphasized in this context is the essential need to distinguish between the ontology of a real world state-of-affairs on the one hand and the linguistic construction (lexicalization) on the other which need not be congruent (Botne 1981: 77–100; Bickel 1997). Stated differently, cross-linguistic differences can arise when different phases of a situation are included in the lexical semantics of a verb. This is illustrated by Botne (2003b), a case study on 'to die' verbs, traditionally understood as a primary example of an achievement in Vendler's sense. Furthermore, the alleged polysemy of many inchoative verbs in Bantu ('to become X'; 'to be X') can thus be understood as a result of an inadequate meta-language translation, rather than an as inherent ambiguity (cf. Seidel 2008: 269, FN 249).

1.4.3.2 Aktionsart

Having broached the issues of grammatical aspect and Aristotelian (lexical) aspect, a further analytical distinction is to be made between Aristotelian aspect and Aktionsart. While Aristotelian aspect classifies the phasal structure of the verb in a wider sense, Aktionsart is "rather a classification of (expressions for) phases of situations and subsituations" (Binnick 1991: 170), which is optional and best described in more specific terms such as inceptive or resumptive (Binnick 1991: ibid). Formally, Aktionsart in Nyakyusa is expressed by verbal derivation (Chapter 4) and phasal verbs (Chapter 5).

To give an example, in the single-event reading of (1) the phasal verb *leka* 'cease, stop' refers to a cessation of the Nucleus phase of the lexical verb *moga* 'dance':

(1) a-lek-ile   ʊ-kʊ-mog-a
     1-cease-PFV AUG-15(INF)-dance-FV
     'S/he has stopped dancing.'

1.4.4 Tense and grammatical aspect in discourse

1.4.4.1 Remarks on textual analysis and grammaticography

In the following description of tense and aspect categories, apart from their use in a sentence-level frame, an attempt is made to further include their use in discourse. A number of factors speak in favour of this approach. The 'traditional' perspective on tense and aspect is most clearly expressed by Comrie:

> [T]he investigation of the use of a grammatical category in discourse should not be confused with the meaning of that category; instead, the discourse function should ultimately be accounted for in terms of the interaction of meaning and context. (Comrie 1985: 29)

Among the well-known feature of Bantu languages, however, are constructions whose main function lies in the structuring of narrative discourse (Nurse 2008: 24), typically labelled *narrative tense* and/or *consecutive tense*; see Chapter 7 for such constructions in Nyakyusa. Thus Comrie's perspective seems problematic with regard to descriptive adequacy. A similar argument is put forward by Güldemann (1996) in his discussion of Doke's grammar of Lamba M54 (translated from the original German, BP):

> In the otherwise extensive and precise grammatical analysis by Doke one hardly encounters useful indications concerning the construction's functional classification [...] The author only describes the verbal paradigm within the limits of sentence semantics [...] Within such an approach the result of the analysis can only produce a relatively vague term such as tempus historicum, which semantically speaking seems the more vacuous as the paradigms characterized by it are not the only ones that can denote historical events. (Güldemann 1996: 208)

Furthermore, as Levinson (1983: 77ff) notes, in most languages there is no one-to-one correspondence between temporal reference, in the physical sense, and linguistic categories. It is a common feature of natural languages to employ the latter for a broader variety of meanings. Assuming these notions surface especially in discourse contexts, an analysis limiting itself to the sentence-level misses many defining characteristics.

The opposite pole to a position such as Comrie's is prominently represented by Weinreich (1964) and Hopper (1982), who consider temporal and aspectual categories to be of discourse origin and sentence-level meanings to be but mere correlates of discourse functions. Hopper says:

> [M]orphological and local-syntactic accounts of aspect are either incomplete, or, to the extent that they are valid, essentially show the sentence-level correlates of discourse structures [...][O]ur understanding of aspect should be rooted in the last resort in discourse. (Hopper 1982: 16)

An intermediate position is taken by Suzanne Fleischman, who considers discursive uses of tense and grammatical aspect as "motivated extensions that [...] may ultimately contribute to a reshaping of the basic meanings" (Fleischman 1990: 23). In other words, she sees a certain dialectic relationship between meaning and use, although with a primacy of meaning.

Further intermediary positions can be found in the field of cognitive linguistics, with approaches considered to be holistic. Mental space theory (Fauconnier 1994) deals with the construction of discursive worlds through the use of TMA markers among other features. To a certain extent Botne & Kershner's principle of inclusion and exclusion (§1.4.2.1) can also be understood as holistic, although no direct reference to discourse is made. What both approaches and further cognitive frameworks have in common is that, in their understanding, temporal and aspectual interpretations of these inflectional categories represent just the special case of a more general notion of cognitive distance and accessibility.

Independently of which one of these intermediary positions is taken, this short excursion has shown that it is necessary to include sentence-level as well as discursive data, whether they permit us to draw conclusions as to the "basic" meanings of the categories in question, which might be in the process of being reshaped by discursive use, which again is culture- and language-specific, or because sentence-level semantics and discourse uses are understood as two sides of one abstract conceptualization.

1.4.4.2 Tools and concepts of narrative analysis

The key concepts used in this study to approach the use of tense and grammatical aspect in discourse stem from Labov & Waletzky (1967 and subsequent works). These authors propose a classification of independent clauses within narratives, based on whether and to what degree they can be displaced without changing the temporal and sequential interpretation:

- *Narrative clauses* cannot be displaced without changing the inferred sequence of eventualities.
- *Restricted clauses* can be displaced throughout a determined part of a narrative.
- *Co-ordinate clauses* can be interchanged only with each other.
- *Free clauses* can range throughout the whole narrative.

By moving each clause to the beginning of its respective displacement set and coalescing coordinate clauses into a single unit, the "primary sequence" of events is obtained. Labov & Waletzky further put forward a structural outline of a typical narrative text (Table 1.2).

A minimal narrative, according to Labov & Waletzky (1967), consists of a sequence of clauses of which at least two are temporarily ordered. Thus a minimal
narrative may consist of only the complicating action, although Labov & Waletzky emphasize that such a narrative would be pointless. As Fleischman (1990:
136) observes, there is a close relationship between narrative structure and TMA
categories. The abstract and coda relate to the now of the speaker, thus one can
expect the corresponding verbal categories to be used, whereas the orientation
section, the complicating action and the resolution relate to the story-now and
thus demand the use of different categories.

Table 1.2: Narrative structure according to Labov & Waletzky (1967)

Abstract	A short summary that primarily serves to license the speaker to take the conversational turn.
Orientation	Formally defined as those free clauses preceding the first narrative clause. Its function is to "orient the listener in respect to person, place, time and behavioural situation" (Labov & Waletzky 1967: 32).
Complicating action	The core of the text.
Evaluation	The point of the narrative, defined semantically through evaluation of eventualities, allocation of blame, etc. The evaluation can coincide with other structural parts of the narrative.
Resolution	Formally defined as the part of the narrative following or coinciding with the evaluation. In Labov (1997: 414) the definition is refined to "the set of complicating actions that follow the most reportable event."
Coda	"[A] functional device for returning the verbal perspective to the present" (Labov & Waletzky 1967: 39). The coda pro-vides definite closure.

Labov & Waletzky's analytic tools were originally designed for analysing "oral
versions of personal experience" (Labov & Waletzky 1967: 12), which, according
to the authors, exhibit the most simple and fundamental narrative structures.
They were later successfully applied to more complex narrative texts, perhaps
most prominently in the works of Suzanne Fleischman. Thus Fleischman (1990)
is an extensive treatment of tense and grammatical aspect in narrative discourse.
Her analyses over a variety of languages, historical stages and genres is guided

by the distinction of four separate but interdependent functional components on which tense and grammatical aspect operate:

- The so-called *referential component* encompasses truth-conditional relations and what Fleischman takes to be the basic functions of TMA categories. As the term *referential* is often associated with so-called referential theories of meaning (e.g. Ogden & Richards 1923), this component will be referred to as *semantics* in the narrow sense throughout this study.
- The *textual component* deals with grounding (the construction of relative salience within the text), with marking textual boundaries and with controlling the flow of information.
- The *expressive component* provides social and attitudinal meanings, including evaluations and points of view.
- The *metalinguistic component* characterizes the discourse as such, by signalling specific styles, genres, registers and types of discourse.

The assumption of a textual component of meaning will prove fruitful in the analysis of the employment of the past tense categories in narrative discourse (§6.5.5.3), while the expressive component plays a role for the narrative present (§6.7.1) and the employment of tense in relative clauses (§6.7.2.3). Lastly, a metalinguistic component must be assumed, at least for the dedicated narrative markers (Chapter 7).

From Longacre (1996) the concept of narrative peak has been adopted. Longacre puts forth a structural outline of narratives comparable to the one proposed by Labov & Waletzky. Unlike the latter authors, however, he distinguishes between two tiers: a notional structure and a surface structure. Peak is then understood as the surface realization of the notional elements of climax ("everything comes to a head [...] contradictions, [...] all sorts of tangles until confrontation is inevitable"; Longacre 1996: 35) and/or denouement ("a crucial event happens which makes resolution possible"; Longacre 1996: 35). Considering the grammatical and pragmatic devices used, peak is characterized as "a zone of turbulence in regard to the flow of the discourse in its preceding and following parts" (Longacre 1996: 38). Common strategies of peak-marking include a shift in tense and grammatical aspect, rhetorical underlining such as repetitions and paraphrases, the concentration of participants as if on a crowded stage, over-specification of referents, or a shift in vantage point, to name just a few.

Lastly, in the analysis of tense usage in relative clauses (§6.7.2.3), Prince's (1992) classification of information status has proven helpful. Prince introduces two binary distinctions, depending on whether information is new or old to the hearer (hearer-new/hearer-old) and new or old to the discourse (discourse-new/discourse-old). In an older taxonomy (Prince 1981), discourse-new/hearer-new information is labelled "brand new information". As information that is new to the hearer is likewise new to the discourse, these distinctions yield three logical combinations: discourse-new/hearer-new, discourse-new/hearer-old, and discourse-old/hearer-old. As a separate category, Prince proposes inferable information: a discourse may contain information that is technically discourse-new/hearer-new but can be inferred from schemata, general beliefs or context. For Prince, information means referents in discourse. In the analysis of tense-use in relative clauses this study follows Levinsohn (2007) in applying the classification of activation status not only to referents, but to whole propositions, too. This combined approach to relative clauses has been adapted from Karels (2014).

2 Grammatical sketch

2.1 Typological overview

Nyakyusa classifies as a typical Narrow Bantu language, while also showing some unique characteristics. This section will provide a summary of these characteristics, giving examples of a number of commonly mentioned defining features (Möhlig 1981; Nurse & Philippson 2003a). It will then provide a short grammatical sketch that will serve as a point of departure for a more detailed description of the verb.

The phonology of Nyakyusa proves to be typical for Narrow Bantu in terms of its symmetrical inventory of seven vowel qualities and its phonotactics, although it can be considered innovative with regard to the loss of tone (§2.2.3) and also shows a rather particular variation from typical Narrow Bantu vowel harmony and related processes (§4.2.1).

Concerning morphology, Nyakyusa is a highly agglutinative language, with a productive system of verbal derivation. As will be described in §6.3, it features various verbal negations, the functional distribution of which is uncommon from a pan-Bantu perspective. Nyakyusa further has an elaborate system of tense, aspect and mood categories. An outstanding feature of Nyakyusa in this regard are the great number of futurate constructions (Chapter 8) in comparison to past tense forms, and the existence of two different narrative markers (Chapter 7). Bantu morphology, especially derivational morphology, has been described as showing a strong tendency towards templatic structures (Hyman 2002). Nyakyusa shows some intriguing cases of templatic requirements in the phonological realisation of certain affixes and affix combinations (see §4.3.3, 6.4.2) that are noteworthy even within the broader Bantu context.

When it comes to syntax, the Nyakyusa "basic" word order is SVO. The language has compound verbs, that is auxiliaries taking an inflected verb as a complement (see §6.6.2, 6.6.3). The language further has a well developed system of noun classes and both subject- and object-marking on the verb.

2.2 Basic phonology

2.2.1 Vowels and syllables

2.2.1.1 Syllable structure

Syllables in Nyakyusa can have any of the following structures:

(1) V   ɪ.kɪ.ko.ta   'chair'
     VV   ii.si.kʊ   'day'
     CV   ʊ.n.jwe.**go**   'noise'
     CVV   a.**kaa**.ja   'homestead'
     CGV   ɪ.**kya**.lo   'field'
     N   ʊ.**m**.pʊ.nga   'rice'
     NCV   ʊ.mu.**ndʊ**   'person'
     NCVV   ʊ.lʊ.te.**ngaa**.no 'peace'
     NCGV   ɪ.**ngwe**.go   'spear'

The possible syllable structures are subject to several distributional constraints: Syllables featuring an initial NC-cluster are not permitted following a syllabic nasal and syllabic nasals do not occur in word-final position. V and VV only occur in the initial position of a word or clitic group. Word-final vowels as a general rule are short, although there are several exceptions: the negated copula (optional, see §10.2.1), some cases of the associative marker -*a*, some interjections such as *ee* 'yes' and a number of ideophones.

2.2.1.2 Vowel inventory

Nyakyusa has a system of seven phonemic vowel qualities, as has also been reconstructed for Proto-Bantu (Schadeberg 2003b: 147). Phonetically, the mid-vowels are realized as open-mid vowels [ɛ, ɔ]. All seven vowel qualities occur as short and long. Following Bantuist conventions, long vowels are represented by a sequence of two identical vowels.[1] Figure 2.1 illustrates the vowel inventory.

2.2.1.3 Vowel length

Nyakyusa has both short and long vowels. They can be lexically specified or can arise through morphophonemic processes such as contact between heteromorphemic vowels (§2.2.1.4) or as a compensation for the deletion of word-internal

---

[1]This stands in contrast to Ndali, which has a reduced inventory of five phonemic vowel qualities, maintaining the inherited length opposition (Labroussi 1998; Botne 2008), and Ngonde, which has further lost the opposition in quantity (Labroussi 1998; Kishindo 1999).

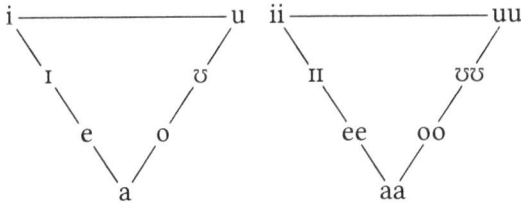

Figure 2.1: Nyakyusa vowel system

non-syllabic nasals (see p. 61 in §3.3.4.1). It is these contexts in which vowel length is distinctive. The minimal pairs in (2) exemplify the distinctive lexical function of vowel length, while those in (3) show that vowel length is grammatically distinctive.

(2) ʊkʊtima   'to rain'   vs. ʊkʊtiima   'to herd'
    ʊkʊlɪla   'to cry'   vs. ʊkʊlɪɪla   'to eat with/for/at'
    ʊkʊmeta   'cut (esp. hair)'   vs. ʊkʊmeeta   'bleat, cry like a goat'
    ʊkʊsala   'choose; pick'   vs. ʊkʊsaala   'be(come) happy'
    ʊkʊbola   'rot, go bad'   vs. ʊkʊboola   'cut; slaughter'
    ʊkʊtʊla   'err, make a mistake'   vs. ʊkʊtʊʊla   'take from the head'
    ʊkʊfula   'castrate'   vs. ʊkʊfuula   'undress; open knots'

(3) ajengile   's/he has built'   vs. aajengile   's/he built'
    ʊkʊmanya   'to know'   vs. ʊkʊʊmanya   'to know me'
    ʊkʊsala   'to choose; pick'   vs. ʊkʊʊsala   'to choose me'

A number of Bantu languages, including some of the neighbouring Corridor languages, restrict the occurrence of long vowels. For instance in Malila M24, a long vowel cannot surpass the fourth mora reckoned from the word end (Kutsch Lojenga 2007). Nyakyusa, however, does not know such a constraint as the following examples illustrate.

(4) jaakatala   '(then) it (class 9) got angry'
    aalaalʊʊsiisye   's/he asked'
    baalʊʊki   'oranges'

Long vowels can further be the result of compensatory lengthening before prenasalized plosives (see §2.2.2.3). Vowels following glides (§2.2.2.2) are also realized with a slightly increased duration. As vowel length in these two environments is predictable, it is not given in the orthographic representation. Generally speaking, vowels in a syllable bearing primary stress tend to be realized with a longer phonetic duration, especially in the penultimate syllable of a phrase. Nevertheless, the phonemic length distinction is still discernible in stressed syllables.[2] The only exception to the regular lengthening before prenasalized plosives is in imperatives (§9.2).

The opposite of compensatory lengthening is triggered by syllabic nasals (see §2.2.2.4).[3] Any vowel preceding a syllabic nasal surfaces as short. The examples in (5) illustrate the opposition between prenasalized plosives and syllabic nasals. In the practical orthography employed throughout this work, syllabic nasals are marked <ņ, m̦> preceding <b, d, g>, thus differentiating them from the voiced prenasalized plosives. As a nasal preceding a voiceless plosive or another nasal is always syllabic in Nyakyusa – see §2.2.2.4, 2.2.2.3 – syllabicity is not overtly indicated in these cases. Examples in (6) show that a short vowel is pronounced where the outcome of morphophonology would otherwise be a long or lengthened vowel.

(5)   [a.ŋ.ga.ˈni.ɾɛ] 's/he loves him/her   vs.   [aː.ⁿga.ˈni.ɾɛ] 's/he loves me'

(6)   a. Long vowel (triggered by 1SG prefix) shortened:
         [na.ŋ.kʰɔ.ˈma.ɥa] (°n-a-mu-kom-aga) 'I was beating him/her'

      b. Long vowel (outcome of vowel coalescence) shortened:
         [βa.ŋ.kʰɔ.ˈma.ɥa] (°ba-a-mu-kom-aga) 'they were beating him/her'

      c. Vowel shortening overrides compensatory lengthening:
         [tʷa.ŋ.kʰɔ.ˈma.ɥa] (°tʊ-a-mu-kom-aga) 'we were beating him/her'

2.2.1.4 Vowel coalescence and glide formation

When heteromorphemic vowels within a word are juxtaposed, vowel coalescence and glide formation take place. The regularities differ slightly to the left and to the right of the root. (7–11) illustrate the outcome to the left of the stem, using the combination of subject prefix and verb stem. In the case of /u/-initial stems, the examples are nouns.[4] Note that the outcome of vowel contact is independent of syllable count.

---

[2] The accoustic study by von Essen & Kähler-Meyer (1969) notes the same for nouns produced in citation form, hence a phonological phrase. Such cases of phonetic penultimate lengthening have been reported for a number of Bantu languages; see Hyman (2013: 313) and references therein.

[3] The same effect is triggered by the object marker of noun class 1; see p. 63 in §3.3.4.2.

[4] No verb stems beginning with /u/ are attested and no prefix contains the mid-vowels /e, o/; see §3.2.

(7) i + i → ii   *siisile*   (°si-is-ile)   'they (class 10) have come'
     i + ɪ → yɪ   *syɪmile*   (°si-ɪm-ile)   'they (class 10) have stopped'
     i + e → ye   *syegile*   (°si-eg-ile)   'they (class 10) have taken'
     i + a → ya   *syagile*   (°si-ag-ile)   'they (class 10) have found'
     i + o → yo   *syogile*   (°si-og-ile)   'they (class 10) have bathed'
     i + ʊ → yʊ   *syʊmile*   (°si-ʊm-ile)   'they (class 10) have dried'
     i + u → yu   *ɪfyuga*   (°ɪ-fi-uga)   'hoofs'

(8) ɪ + i → ii   *liisile*   (°lɪ-is-ile)   'it (class 5) has come'
     ɪ + ɪ → yɪ   *lyɪmile*   (°lɪ-ɪm-ile)   'it (class 5) has stopped'
     ɪ + e → ye   *lyegile*   (°lɪ-eg-ile)   'it (class 5) has taken'
     ɪ + a → ya   *lyagile*   (°lɪ-ag-ile)   'it (class 5) has found'
     ɪ + o → yo   *lyogile*   (°lɪ-og-ile)   'it (class 5) has bathed'
     ɪ + ʊ → yʊ   *lyʊmile*   (°lɪ-ʊm-ile)   'it (class 5) has dried'
     ɪ + u → yu   *ɪkyuga*   (°ɪ-ki-uga)   'hoof'

(9) a + i → ii   *biisile*   (°ba-is-ile)   'they have come'
     a + ɪ → ɪɪ   *bɪɪmile*   (°ba-ɪm-ile)   'they have stopped'
     a + e → ee   *beegile*   (°ba-eg-ile)   'they have taken'
     a + a → aa   *baagile*   (°ba-ag-ile)   'they have found'
     a + o → oo   *boogile*   (°ba-og-ile)   'they have bathed'
     a + ʊ → ʊʊ   *bʊʊmile*   (°ba-ʊm-ile)   'they have dried'
     a + u → uu   *amungu*   (°a-ma-ungu)   'mushrooms'

(10) ʊ + i → wi   *twisile*   (°tʊ-is-ile)   'we have come'
     ʊ + ɪ → wɪ   *twɪmile*   (°tʊ-ɪm-ile)   'we have stopped'
     ʊ + e → we   *twegile*   (°tʊ-eg-ile)   'we have taken'
     ʊ + a → wa   *twagile*   (°tʊ-ag-ile)   'we have found'
     ʊ + o → oo   *toogile*   (°tʊ-og-ile)   'we have bathed'
     ʊ + ʊ → ʊʊ   *tʊʊmile*   (°tʊ-ʊm-ile)   'we have dried'
     ʊ + u → uu   *ʊtungu*   (°ʊ-tʊ-ungu)   'little mushrooms'

(11) u + i → wi   *mwisile*   (°mu-is-ile)   'you (pl.) have come'
     u + ɪ → wɪ   *mwɪmile*   (°mu-ɪm-ile)   'you (pl.) have stopped'
     u + ɪ → we   *mwegile*   (°mu-eg-ile)   'you (pl.) have taken'
     u + a → wa   *mwagile*   (°mu-ag-ile)   'you (pl.) have found'
     u + o → oo   *moogile*   (°mu-og-ile)   'you (pl.) have bathed'
     u + ʊ → ʊʊ   *mʊʊmile*   (°mu-ʊm-ile)   'you (pl.) have dried'
     u + u → uu   *ʊmuunyu*   (°ʊ-mu-unyu)   'salt'

The table in (12) summarizes the outcome of left-of-the-stem (prefixing) vowel contact.

(12) Adjacent vowels (left of the stem):

V1＼V2	i	ɪ	e	a	o	ʊ	u
i	ii	yɪ	ye	ya	yo	yʊ	yu
ɪ	ii	yɪ	ye	ya	yo	yʊ	yu
a	ii	ɪɪ	ee	aa	oo	ʊʊ	uu
ʊ	wi	wɪ	we	wa	oo	ʊʊ	uu
u	wi	wɪ	we	wa	oo	uu	uu

Noun class 9 prefix *jɪ-* is exceptional. Its vowel assimilates to any following vowel (one may alternatively analyse this as vowel deletion with subsequent compensatory lengthening). (13) illustrates this for the subject prefix.

(13) *jiisile*   (°jɪ-is-ile)   'it (class 9) has come'
  jɪɪmile   (°jɪ-ɪm-ile)   'it (class 9) has stopped'
  jeegile   (°jɪ-eg-ile)   'it (class 9) has taken'
  jaagile   (°jɪ-ag-ile)   'it (class 9) has found'
  joogile   (°jɪ-og-ile)   'it (class 9) has bathed'
  jʊʊmile   (°jɪ-ʊm-ile)   'it (class 9) has dried'

Juxtaposition of heteromorphemic vowels to the right of the root (suffixation and infixation) occurs productively only in a limited number of cases, one of which is derivational suffixes attached to monosyllabic verbs. This yields slightly ideosyncratic results; see §4.2.1.1. The other two are the suffixing of inflectional affixes to monosyllabic verbs and a process of infixing referred to as *imbrication* (§6.4.2). Unlike with prefixes, the low vowel /a/ followed by a front vowel yields /ee/.

(14) i + i → ii   *inamiike*   (°inami<i>k-e)   'bend (tr).PFV'
  ɪ + i → ii   *pɪliike*   (°pɪlɪ<i>k-e)   'hear; feel.PFV'
  e + i → ii   *kemiile*   (°keme<i>l-e)   'bark at.PFV'

(15) a + i → ee   *peegwa*   (°pa-igw-a)   'be given'
        egeeme   (°ega<i>m-e)   'lean.PFV'
  a + ɪ → ee   *peela*   (°pa-ɪl-a)   'give away'

(16) o + e → we   *bwene*   (°bo<e>n-e)   'see.PFV'
  o + i → wi   *kosomwile*   (°kosomo<i>l-e)   'cough.PFV'
  ʊ + i → wi   *alwike*   (°alʊ<i>k-e)   'stand up.PFV'
  u + i → wi   *afwile*   (°afu<i>l-e)   'crawl.PFV'

2.2.2 Consonants

2.2.2.1 Consonant inventory

Table 2.1 shows the 16 phonemic consonants of Nyakyusa as they are spelt in this study. Where the phonetic value differs from the graphic representation it is given in square brackets.

Table 2.1: Nyakyusa consonant inventory

	Bilabial	Lab. dent	Alveolar	Palatal	Velar	Glottal
Plosive	p		t	ɟ <j>	k	
Nasal	m		n	ɲ <ny>	ŋ <ng'>	
Fricative		f	s			h
Approx.	β <b>				ɰ <g>	
Lat. Appr.			l			
Glide				(j) <y>	(w)	

The glottal fricative is very rare. In most cases it can be regularly traced back to loans from Kinga and Kisi (Labroussi 1998: 218). Nurse (1979) even considers it to be so marginal as to make its phonemic status dubious. The velar nasal is frequent phonetically, but rare in its occurrence underlyingly. The approximants are realized as plosives when following a nasal and as approximants elsewhere. Lateral /l/ is optionally realized as [ɾ~ɹ] after a front vowel in unstressed sylla-bles, unless it is followed by a glide. The palatal plosive is typically realized as an affricate [dʒ] when following a nasal. Voiceless plosives tend to be aspirated. The fricative /f/ in native material can regularly be traced back to a diachronic or synchronic process of spirantization; see Bostoen (2008) on Bantu spirantization. Morphophonemic processes can, however, obscure this relationship, detaching the fricative from the triggering vowel (see §4.3.1, 4.3.3).[5] Nasals preceding an-other consonant are generally homorganic and will be written as <m> before a labial and as <n> elsewhere. Consonants in loans from Swahili that are not adapted to the phoneme inventory of Nyakyusa will be written with their re-spective phonetic symbols.

---

[5]Note also the verb stem *fifa* 'hide (intr.)' (variant *fisa*) < PB *píc, a clear case of historical assimilation.

2.2.2.2 Glides

Glides can be synchronically or diachronically traced back to the desyllabifica-
tion of a vowel, although the quality of the underlying vowel is not synchronically discernible in all cases. The palatalized alveolar nasal is clearly distinct from
the palatal nasal. In monitored speech it is realized as [nʲ]. The palatalized alveolar nasal will be written as <ni> throughout this study in order to distinguish
it from the palatal nasal /ɲ/, represented by the digraph <ny>. Glides normally
do not appear before rounded back vowels, although some lexicalized exceptions
occur. Vowels following glides are slightly lengthened (§2.2.1.3).

2.2.2.3 Prenasalized plosives

Prenasalization in Nyakyusa is limited to plosives (see Table 2.2).

Table 2.2: Prenasalized consonants

Bilabial	Alveolar	Palatal	Velar
ᵐb <mb>	ⁿd <nd>	ⁿdʒ <nj>	ᵑg <ng>

Prenasalized plosives are always voiced and homorganic.[6] Voiceless plosives
turn into their voiced counterparts when preceded by a non-syllabic nasal, and
the approximants /β, l, ɥ/ into their plosive counterparts. (17) shows that preceding vowels the prefix of noun class 9/10 surfaces as *ny-* (note that any vowel
preceding or following this prefix surfaces as long; see §2.3.2) and (18) illustrates
how this prefix induces prenasalization. (19) illustrates prenasalization with the
subject prefix of the first person singular.[7]

(17) ɪɪmyiifi   (°ɪ-ny-ifi)   'chameleons'
      ɪɪnyɪmbo (°ɪ-ny-ɪmbo) 'songs'
      ɪɪmyendo (°ɪ-ny-endo) 'journeys'
      ɪɪmyaala   (°ɪ-ny-ala)   'grindstones'
      ɪɪmyoobe (°ɪ-ny-obe)   'fingers'
      ɪɪmyʊʊbo (°ɪ-ny-ʊbo)   'big knives'

---

[6]This voicing rule distinguishes Nyakyusa from the Ngonde variety described by Labroussi
(1998: 278), although it does apply in the variety described by Kishindo (1999).
[7]Before certain object prefixes, the 1SG subject prefix turns into a syllabic nasal; see §3.3.2.1.

(18)   *ɪmbepo*   (°ɪ-ny-pepo)   'cold; air(s); spirit(s)'
       ɪndʊmi   (°ɪ-ny-tʊmi)   'message(s), news'
       ɪnjʊni   (°ɪ-ny-jʊni)   'bird(s)'
       ɪnguuto   (°ɪ-ny-kuuto)   'cry / cries'
       ɪmbatɪko   (°ɪ-ny-batɪko)   'procedure(s)'
       ɪndagɪlo   (°ɪ-ny-lagɪlo)   'law(s); commission(s)'
       ɪngolo   (°ɪ-ny-golo)   'louse(s)'

(19)   *mbinyile*   (°n-piny-ile)   'I have bound'
       ndaagile   (°n-taag-ile)   'I have thrown'
       njaatile   (°n-jaat-ile)   'I have taken a walk'
       ngeetile   (°n-keet-ile)   'I have watched'
       mbalile   (°n-bal-ile)   'I have counted'
       ndɪlile   (°n-lɪl-ile)   'I have cried'
       ngelile   (°n-gel-ile)   'I have tested'

Prenasalized consonants are not considered phonemic for a number of reasons. First, when they occur across morpheme boundaries, as in the above examples, they can clearly be analysed as the result of a nasal segment followed by a plosive or approximant. Second, the nasals involved are also found as single phonemes and the voiced plosives are regular allophones of /β, l, ɥ/ in a post-nasal context, as can also be seen with the syllabic nasals (§2.2.2.4). Further, their stem-internal distribution is very limited, the majority of cases being the second consonant of the stem. Last, they are rarely found in affixes. All of this speaks in favour of assuming syllable structures of the type /NC.../ rather than an additional set of phonemes. Note that prenasalization triggers lengthening of a preceding vowel, as discussed in §2.2.1.3.

2.2.2.4 Syllabic nasals

Syllabic nasals in the great majority of cases are the result of a series of morphophonemic processes affecting noun class affixes. The most frequently applying of these processes is deletion of the underlying high back vowel of the prefixes of noun classes 1, 3, and 18 in most pre-consonantal environments and subsequent syllabification of the nasal segment. Other sources include the first person singular subject prefix in determined phonemic and morphological contexts (see §3.3.2.1).

Syllabic nasals hardly ever appear morpheme-internally. Exceptions include *mma* ['m̩.ma] 'no' and related forms such as *somma* [sɔ.'m̩.ma] 'don't!', as well as *nnoono* [n̩.'nɔː.nɔ] 'so much' and *nsyɪsyɪ* [n̩.'sʸɪ.sʸɪ] 'skunk' (pl. *bansyɪsyɪ*). In contrast to prenasalized plosives, syllabic nasals do not trigger voicing. Thus, in the graphic representation, the syllabicity of nasals is ambiguous only in sequences involving a voiced plosive, and will be marked <m̩, n̩> in this context. Further, syllabic nasals induce shortening of preceding long or lengthened vowels (see §2.2.1.3). Phonetically they are realized with a longer duration than non-syllabic nasals. As with prenasalized plosives, syllabic nasals as a general rule are homorganic to the following segment, and approximant phonemes are hardened to plosives. A syllabic nasal preceding /h/ is realized as velar.

(20) ʊm̩belo   (°ʊ-mu-belo)   'wind'
      ʊn̩dʊme   (°ʊ-mu-lʊme)   'husband'
      ʊŋgʊnda   (°ʊ-mu-gʊnda)   'field, farm'
      ʊnhɪɪji   (°ʊ-mu-hɪɪj-i)   'thief'

2.2.3 Suprasegmentals

Nyakyusa is not a tonal language, unlike the majority of Bantu languages (Kisseberth & Odden 2003 amongst others). The loss of inherited tone in Nyakyusa has been noted even in early studies (e.g. Nurse 1979; Guthrie 1967; von Essen & Kähler-Meyer 1969). Instead, Nyakyusa features a regular penultimate accent. The lack of phonemic tone makes Nyakyusa quite different from its close relative Ndali (see e.g. Nurse 1988; Botne 2008), although this characteristic is apparently shared with Ngonde (Kishindo 1999; Labroussi 1999). Every word in Nyakyusa is assigned stress on the penultimate syllable. However, words are often grouped together as a prosodic unit, in which case the penultimate syllable of the rightmost word receives a more pronounced stress.[8] Typical cases are nouns followed by a determiner:

(21) ʊˌmwan(a) ˈʊjʊ
      ʊ-mu-ana   ʊ-jʊ
      AUG-1-child AUG-PROX.1
      'this child'

(22) iiˌgalɪ ˈlyangʊ
      ii-galɪ lɪ-angʊ
      5-car   5-POSS.1SG
      'my car'

---

[8]See Bickmore & Clemens (2016) on Tooro JE12 for a similar case.

In the same fashion, a determiner introducing a relative clause (see §2.4) forms a prosodic unit with the following verb:

(23) ʊŋˈdʊngʊ   ˌʊgʊ   gʊˈkwisa   aˈtwale   ɪɪˌheela
      ʊ-mu-lʊngʊ ʊ-gʊ   gʊ-kʊ-is-a   a-twal-e   ɪɪ-heela
      AUG-3-week AUG-PROX.3 3-PRS-come-FV 1-carry-SUBJ AUG-money(9)

      ˈjangʊ
      jɪ-angʊ
      9-POSS.1SG

      'Next week [lit. the week that comes] he must bring my money.' [Monkey and Tortoise]

2.3 Nouns and noun phrase

2.3.1 Noun classes

Bantu languages are well-known for their noun class systems; for an introduction see Maho (1999: ch. 3) and Katamba (2003). Nyakyusa has a typical system of 18 noun classes, of which some are further differentiated into subclasses. Each noun class is characterized by a series of agreement prefixes. Agreement in the noun phrase occurs between the head and its modifiers, as (24) illustrates. See Lusekelo (2009b) on the linear structure of the Nyakyusa noun phrase.

(24) a-**ba**-ana   a-**ba**-lʊmyana a-**ba**-tupe **b**-angʊ   ba-bɪlɪ ba-la
      AUG-2-child AUG-2-boy   AUG-2-fat 2-POSS.1SG 2-two 2-DIST

      'these two fat sons of mine' [ET]

As to agreement marking, two sets of prefixes can be distinguished within the noun phrase:
- The *nominal prefix* (NPX) is used with nouns and adjectives and the numerals 2–5, as well as with the bound roots *nandɪ* 'little, few', *ingi* 'many, much' and *lɪnga* 'how much, how many'.
- The *pronominal prefix* (PPX) is used to form demonstratives (see §2.3.3), and also occurs with the associative and possessives as well as the bound roots *mo* 'one, some', *ngɪ* 'other', *ki* 'what kind of, which', *ope* 'also', *ene* 'self; owner' (except for class 1), *osa* 'all', and is also used as a secondary prefix (see §2.3.2).

As the list indicates, there are a number of additional complexities concerning the choice and shape of these agreement prefixes, of which only the most frequent can be discussed here. In noun class 1, the pronominal prefix is *gʊ-* with possessives, the associative and *osa* 'all' (yielding irregular *gwesa*), and *jʊ-* elsewhere. Further, the bound root *ene* 'self; owner' takes the nominal prefix in noun class 1, but the pronominal prefix in all other classes. Numerals in class 10 are marked by a prefix *i-*.

Subclasses (1a, 2a, 9a, 10a) differ from their main class in the marking of the head noun – in the first three cases they lack an overt nominal prefix. Dependent constituents, however, take the agreement forms of the respective main classes. Throughout this study, subclasses will not be explicitly marked in glossing. The agreement prefixes are further subject to a number of morphophonological alternations, some of which will be discussed in §2.3.2.

Nouns, adjectives and a number of other bound roots can also carry the augment, which is commonly referred to as the pre-prefix or initial vowel. This morpheme has the shape of a single vocalic segment /ɪ, a, ʊ/, whose place of articulation harmonizes with that of the respective noun class's underlying prefix vowel. See §2.3.2 for a short discussion of the distribution of the augment.

The semantics of the Nyakyusa noun classes are only semi-transparent and can best be described in terms of some common core meanings.

Table 2.3 gives an overview of the various noun classes in Nyakyusa, their nominal agreement prefixes and frequent semantic elements of each class; cross-reference markers on the verb will be discussed in §3.3.2, 3.3.4, 3.3.8.1. The noun classes are numbered according to the common Bleek-Meinhof system. The ascribed meanings are based on a synthesis of previous grammatical sketches[9] and have been refined by the author through the inclusion of subclasses.

As can be gathered from Table 2.3, Nyakyusa noun classes form a number of regular singular-plural pairings. Figure 2.2 illustrates these pairings, which for the main classes represent one of the most frequent patterns across Bantu (Katamba 2003: 109). Examples for each of these pairings are given in (25). See (27) below for examples of the locative noun classes and Chapter 11 on the infinitive noun class 15. Note that when it comes to nominal agreement, the discourse participants (first and second person) fall within noun classes 1 (singular) and 2 (plural).

---

[9]Schumann (1899), Meinhof (1966), Endemann (1914), Nurse (1979), Lusekelo (2007) and Felberg (1996)

Table 2.3: Nyakyusa noun classes

Class	AUG	NPx	PPx	Semantics
1	ʊ-	mu-	jʊ- (gʊ-)	human beings
1a	(ʊ-)	ø-		kinship terms; proper names
				some living beings; some loans
2	a-	ba-	ba-	regular plural of class 1
2a	(a)-	baa-		regular plural of class 1a
3	ʊ-	mu-	gʊ-	plants, other non-animates
				natural phenomena
4	ɪ-	mi-	gɪ-	regular plural of classes 3 and 14
				regular plural of class 5 augmentatives
5	ɪ-	li- (ii-)	lɪ-	fruits, produce; body parts; miscellanea
				augmentatives
6	a-	ma-	ga-	regular plural of class 5
				mass terms and liquids; paired objects
7	ɪ-	kɪ-	kɪ-	characteristics, mannerisms, languages
				instruments, utensils, tools
				derogatives
8	ɪ-	fi-	fi-	regular plural of class 7
9	ɪ-	ny-	jɪ-	animals; frequently used objects
				some abstracts
9a	ɪɪ-	ø-		primarily loans
10	ɪ-	ny-	si- (i-)	regular plural to class 9
				plural to concrete nouns of class 11
10a	ɪɪ-	ø-		regular plural to class 9a
11	ʊ-	lʊ-	lʊ-	long, thin entities; some abstracts
				single instances of collectives
				particular instances of class 9 stems
12	a-	ka-	ka-	large quantities; some miscellanea
				diminutives
13	ʊ-	tʊ-	tʊ-	regular plural of class 12
14	ʊ-	bʊ-	bʊ-	qualities, characteristics, materials
				abstracts; localities, countries
				some concretes
15	ʊ-	kʊ-	kʊ-	infinitives
16	/	pa-	pa-	locative: 'at', 'proximity'
17	/	kʊ-	kʊ-	locative: 'general area', 'far away'
18	/	mu-	mu-	locative: 'in'

Sg.   Pl.

```
1 ─────────────────────► 2
1a ────────────────────► 2a
3 ──────────────────────► 4
5 ──────────────────────► 6
7 ──────────────────────► 8
9 ──────────────────────► 10
9a ────────────────────► 10a
11
12 ─────────────────────► 13
14
```

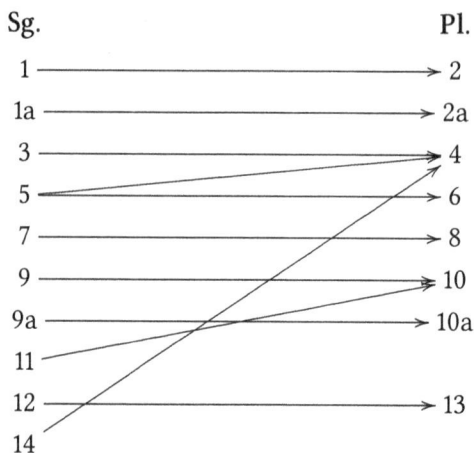

Figure 2.2: Attested noun class pairings

(25)   a.   Classes 1/2:

        ʊmwana   (°ʊ-mu-ana)   'child'
        abaana   (°a-ba-ana)   'children'

    b.   Classes 1a/2a:

        taata   (°ø-ø-taata)   'my father'
        baataata   (°ø-baa-taata) 'my fathers'

    c.   Classes 3/4:

        ʊmpiki   (°ʊ-mu-piki)   'tree'
        ɪmipiki   (°ɪ-mi-piki)   'trees'

    d.   Classes 5/6:

        iitooki   (°ii-tooki)   'type of banana'
        amatooki (°a-ma-tooki) 'bananas'

    e.   Classes 5/4 (augmentatives):

        iibwa   (°ii-bwa)   'big/bad dog'
        ɪmibwa   (°ɪ-mi-bwa)   'big/bad dogs'

    f.   Classes 7/8:

        ɪkɪkombe (°ɪ-kɪ-kombe) 'cup'
        ɪfikombe   (°ɪ-fi-kombe)   'cups'

g. Classes 9/10:

ɪmbwa	(°ɪ-ny-bwa)	'dog'
ɪmbwa	(°ɪ-ny-bwa)	'dogs'

h. Classes 9a/10a:

ɪɪpʊsi	(°ɪɪ-ø-pʊsi)	'cat' (<EN)
ɪɪpʊsi	(°ɪɪ-ø-pʊsi)	'cats'

i. Classes 11/10:

ʊlʊnywili	(°ʊ-lʊ-nywili)	'hair (sg.)'
ɪɪnywili	(°ɪ-ny-nywili)	'hair (pl.)'

j. Classes 12/13:

akapango	(°a-ka-pango)	'story'
ʊtʊpango	(°ʊ-tʊ-pango)	'stories'

k. Classes 12/13 (diminutives):

akabwa	(°a-ka-bwa)	'little dog'
ʊtʊbwa	(°ʊ-tʊ-bwa)	'little dogs'

l. Classes 14/4:

ʊbooga	(°ʊ-bʊ-oga)	'mushroom'
ɪmyoga	(°ɪ-mi-oga)	'mushrooms'

2.3.2 Nominal morphology

The linear structure of a canonical nominal in Nyakyusa can be schematized as in Figure 2.3.

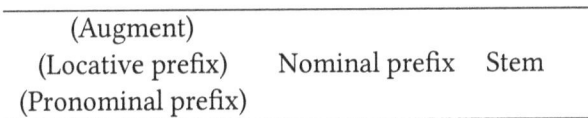

(Augment)		
(Locative prefix)	Nominal prefix	Stem
(Pronominal prefix)		

Figure 2.3: Structure of Nyakyusa nominals

The grammatical functions of the augment in Bantu are complex and need further research; see Hyman & Katamba (1991; 1993) and also van der Wal & Namyalo (2016) for an insightful discussion of a number of pragmatic and syntactic functions of the augment in Ganda JE15. In Nyakyusa use of the augment is optional, although it is excluded in a number of contexts: following the associative -*a*, in predicative and vocative use, following *ngatɪ* 'as, like', *kʊkʊtɪ* 'every' and *(ɪ)kɪsita/(ʊ)kʊsita* 'without', and when the head noun is modified by *ki* 'which, what kind of'. Nouns carrying a pronominal prefix instead of an augment, express an emphatic notion translatable along the lines of 'just X; the very X':

(26) *lʊ-lw-ala*   'the very grindstone (class 11)'
      gʊ-n-tʊ   'the very head (class 3)'

Inherently locative nouns are rare. Locatives are commonly formed by additive marking, that is by prefixing a locative noun class prefix to a noun already marked for a noun class of its own:

(27) *pa-lw-ɪsi*   'at (class 16) a/the river'
      kʊ-lw-ɪsi   'at (class 17) a/the river'
      mu-lw-ɪsi   'in (class 18) a/the river'

In a manner analogous to the prefixing of pronominal prefixes discussed above, locative nouns may carry more than one prefix of the same locative class in addition to the noun's basic noun class prefix. This twofold or even threefold locative marking seems to give emphasis to the specific locative semantics.

(28) *pa-pa-kɪ-lo*   'on that very (class 16) night'
      mu-n-k-iina   'in (class 18) the pit'
      mu-mu-n'-dw-ɪsi   'in (class 18) the river'

The nominal prefixes (§2.3.1) are subject to a number of morphophonological alternations, of which only the most general ones can be discussed here. The nominal prefix *mu-* of noun classes 1, 3 and 18 is commonly realized as a syllabic nasal when preceding consonants other than the prenasalized plosives; see §2.2.2.4 for some examples. The nominal prefix *ny-* of classes 9/10 does not surface when preceding a stem-initial nasal or voiceless fricative, unless the resultant word would be monosyllabic, in which case it surfaces as a syllabic nasal (29). Any prefix preceding an underlying *ny-* (the augment, a locative prefix or a prepositional prefix) is realized with a long vowel. The same holds for any following stem-initial vowel (30). Similarly, augments and other prefixes on subclass 9a/10a nouns always feature a long vowel (31).

(29) *ɪɪnongwa*   (°ɪ-ny-nongwa)   'affair(s); case(s)'
      ɪɪswi   (°ɪ-ny-swi)   'fish(es)'
      nswi   (°ny-swi)   'it is (a/the) fish(es)'

(30) *ɪɪnyuma*   (°ɪ-ny-nyuma)   'back'
      jɪɪnyuma   (°jɪ-ny-nyuma)   'the very back'
      kʊʊnyuma   (°kʊ-ny-nyuma)   'behind, after'
      ɪɪnyaala   (°ɪ-ny-ala)   'grindstones'

(31)   ɪɪlefani   (°ɪ-lefani)   'spoon'
       ɪɪpʊsi   (°ɪ-pʊsi)   'cat'

Further, there are a few class 9/10 stems where the prefix and the stem-initial consonant fuse due to a fossilized morphophonemic process known as Meinhof's law (32). In noun class 5, with consonant-initial stems, most commonly a prefix *ii-* is used, with no distinction concerning the presence or absence of an augment (33).

(32)   ɪɪng'ombe (°ɪ-ny-gombe) 'cow'   cf. *akagombe* 'little cow (class 12)'
       ɪɪnyumba (°ɪ-ny-jumba) 'house'   cf. *akajumba* 'little house (class 12)'

(33)   *ii-bole*   'leopard'
       ii-lʊʊka   'shop'
       ii-syʊ   'word'

2.3.3 Demonstratives and pronominals

Three basic demonstratives can be distinguished. First, a proximal of the shape AUG-PPX.[10] This demonstrative is always used with the augment. Second, a demonstrative with a referential function (AUG-PPX-*o*). Used without the augment, this further serves as an emphatic copulative. Following common Bantuist terminology, throughout this study these demonstratives will also be called substitutives. Third, there is a distal demonstrative (PPX-*la*). Table 2.4 illustrate these forms.

Numerous emphatic forms can be constructed through various patterns of reduplication, for instance *kɪkɪɪkɪ* 'this very one (class 7)', *kɪɪkyo* 'the very one (class 7) (e.g. already mentioned)' or *kɪlakɪla* 'that very one (class 7)'. Locative classes 17 and 18 (but not 16) differ in that their proximal demonstrative has the shape PPX-*no*. Parallel forms also exist for class 14 (*bʊno* 'this way, thus, so') and class 5 (*lɪno, lɪlɪno* 'now; today').

A number of demonstratives have acquired special meanings and functions. The class 14 substitutive *bo* serves a number of circumstancial functions, such as introducing adverbials of comparison. It also has an aspectual function of establishing or reintroducing a temporal anchor (34) and introducing temporal adverbial clauses (35).

---

[10] Sometimes (but not consistently) a Swahili-influenced variant /hVCV/ is heard: e.g. *hɪkɪ* 'this (7)'.

Table 2.4: Noun class demonstratives

Class	Proximal	Referential	Distal	Class	Proximal	Referential	Distal
1	ʊjʊ	ʊ-jo	jʊla	11	ʊlʊ	ʊ-lo	lʊla
2	aba	a-bo	bala	12	aka	a-ko	kala
3	ʊgʊ	ʊ-go	gʊla	13	ʊtʊ	ʊ-to	tʊla
4	ɪgɪ	ɪ-gyo	gɪla	14	ʊbʊ	ʊ-bo	bʊla
5	ɪlɪ	ɪ-lyo	lɪla	15	ʊkʊ	ʊ-ko	kʊla
6	aga	a-go	gala	16	apa	a-po	pala
7	ɪkɪ	ɪ-kyo	kɪla	17	kʊno	ʊ-ko	kʊla
8	ɪfi	ɪ-fyo	fila	18	muno	ʊ-mo	mula
9	ɪjɪ	ɪ-jo	jɪla				
10	ɪsi	ɪ-syo	sila				

(34) bo   a-a-bomb-ag-a   fi-ki?
     14.REF 1-PST-do-IPFV-FV 8-what

     'What was he doing then?' [ET]

(35) bo   fi-kw-and-a   ʊ-kʊ-bɪfw-a,   ɪ-n-gambɪlɪ
     14.REF 8-PRS-begin-FV AUG-15-ripen-FV, AUG-10-monkey
     si-lɪnkw-and-a   ʊ-kʊ-ly-a   ɪ-fi-lombe   m-mi-gunda gy-a
     10-NARR-begin-FV AUG-15-eat-FV AUG-8-maize 18-4-farm   4-ASSOC
     ba-ndʊ   ba-la
     2-person 2-DIST

     'When it began to ripen, monkeys started to eat the maize in those
     people's field.' [Thieving monkeys]

Similarly, the locative determiners are used as temporals. Further cases of specialized meanings include class 11 proximal ʊlʊ 'in this way; now' and class 18
reduplicated substitutives *muumo, momuumo* 'right, all right; accordingly; com-
plete'.

The pronouns for the discourse participants (substitutives) are given in Table 2.5. In contrast to the substitutives of the noun classes, they have the shape
AUG-C(G)-*e*. Note the change of the consonant in the first person plural when
preceded by a vowel.

Table 2.5: Participant pronouns

Participant	Pronoun
1SG	ʋ-ne
2SG	ʋ-gwe
1PL	twe, ʋ-swe
2PL	ʋ-mwe

Emphatic personal pronouns are formed with a reduplicated class 1 pronominal prefix. This holds for the singular as well as for the plural: *jʋ~jʋʋ-ne* 'just me', *jʋjʋʋgwe* 'just you', *jʋjʋʋswe* 'just us', *jʋjʋʋmwe* 'just you (pl.)'.

2.4 Basic syntax

The basic word order in Nyakyusa is Subject–(Auxiliary)–Verb–1^{ary} Object–2^{ary} Object (–Adjuncts).

(36) a-lɪ pa-kʋ-ba-p-a a-ba-ana ɪ-fi-ndʋ pa-ka-aja
1-COP 16-15-2-give-FV AUG-2-child AUG-8-food 16-12-homestead

'She is giving the children food at home.' [ET]

However, as Bearth (2003) observes, word order in Bantu is typically not as much a question of syntactic restrictions as it is governed by the needs of discourse. Modifiers most commonly follow their head:

(37) ɪɪ-heela ny-ingi
AUG-money(10) 10-many

'much money'

(38) ʋ-tʋ-ndʋ tw-ɪtʋ
AUG-13-thing 13-POSS.1PL

'our things'

A key element in Nyakyusa syntax are the noun classes (§2.3.1) and their respective agreement or cross-reference. Agreement in Nyakyusa occurs between a head and its modifiers in the noun phrase, as well as between the predicate and its subject and possibly an object. There is also endophoric agreement with demonstratives and relative clauses. The reader is referred to Katamba (2003) and Bearth (2003) for an introduction.

Unlike many other Bantu languages (see Güldemann 1996: ch. 3.3), Nyakyusa does not have dedicated morphological paradigms for relative clauses. Instead these are introduced by demonstratives that agree with the head of the phrase. Typically the proximal or distal demonstratives are used, although emphatic reduplicated pronouns (see §2.3.3) are also found. (39, 40) illustrate subject and object relatives respectively. (41) exemplifies a relative clause modifying a locative adjunct.

(39) ba-mo **a-ba**   **ba-tol-iigwe**   ʊ-kʊ-ly-ag-a
      2-one AUG-2.PROX 2-win-PASS.PFV AUG-15-5-find-FV
      ɪ-ly-ʊndʊ,   ba-a-gelek-el-aga   ɪ-mi-pʊpa
      AUG-5-thatching_grass 2-PST-thatch-APPL-IPFV AUG-4-banana_leaf

      'Some who were unable to get the type of grass would roof with banana leaves.' [Nyakyusa houses of long ago]

(40) leelo   ʊ-lw-ifi   bo lʊ-pɪliike **a-ma-syʊ** g-a   kalʊlʊ
      now/but AUG-11-chameleon as 11-hear.PFV AUG-6-word 6-ASSOC hare(1)
      a-ga   a-a-job-aga,   lʊ-lɪnkw-amul-a   lʊ-lɪnkʊ-tɪ
      AUG-PROX.6 1-PST-speak-IPFV 11-NARR-answer-FV 11-NARR-say

      'When Chameleon heard the words that Hare had been speaking, he answered:' [Hare and Chameleon]

(41) a-lɪnkʊ-ga-ag-a a-m-ɪɪsi   ma-nandɪ **ŋ-dʊ-kʊbo**   **mu-no**
      1-NARR-6-find-FV AUG-6-water 6-little   18-11-pasture 18-PROX
      a-a-tiim-aga   ɪɪ-ng'ombe
      1-PST-herd-IPFV AUG-cow(10)

      'He found a little water in the pasture where he was herding cows.' [Water and toads]

Relative clauses referring to discourse participants are introduced by their respective substitutives without the augment. (42, 43) illustrate this for the first and second person singular.

(42) n-dɪ   na=a-ma-hala   jʊʊ~jʊ-ne   **ne n-ga-job-a**
      1SG-COP COM=AUG-6-intelligence REDUPL~1-1SG 1SG 1SG-NEG-speak-FV
      na=si-mo
      COM=10-one

      'I'm the only smart one, I who haven't said anything.' [Invaders]

(13) ʊ-ne   n-gʊ́-fi-tol-a   n=ɪ-fi-nyamaana   fi-f-ingi,
AUG-1SG 1SG-PRS-8-beat-FV COM=AUG-8-animal 8-8-many

aa=kʊ-j-a   jo   ʊ-gwe   **gwe ʊ-bagiile**
FUT=PRS-be(come)-FV REF.1 AUG-2SG 2SG   2SG-be_able.PFV

ʊ-kʊ-tolan-a   na=niine?
AUG-15-compete-FV COM=COM.1SG

'I beat [i.e. have beaten] many animals, will you be the one who is able to compete with me?' [Hare and Chameleon]

Lastly, a relative clause need not have a lexical head. Endophoric reference and the inherent semantics of noun classes may substitute for this. (44) illustrates a headless relative clause.

(44) pa-lʊ-komaano lʊ-la, j-aa-sal-iigwe   ɪɪ-fubu
16-11-meeting   11-DIST 9-PST-choose-PASS.PFV AUG-hippo(9)

ʊ-kʊ-j-a   mw-ɪmɪlɪli gw-a   **ba-la bi-kʊ-j-a**
AUG-15-be(come)-FV 1-supervisor 1-ASSOC 2-DIST 2-PRS-be(come)-FV

pa-kʊ-tolan-a
16-15-compete-FV

'At that meeting, Hippo was chosen as the referee of those that were going to race.' [Hare and Chameleon]

3 Structure of the verb

3.1 Introduction

The purpose of this chapter is to give an introduction to the phonological and morphological structure of the verbal word in Nyakyusa, as well as to give a description of several morphemes that do not fit in the following chapters.

First, the phonological structure of verbal morphemes will be laid out (§3.2), followed by a description of the linear morphological structure of the finite verb (§3.3). The latter includes a description of each of the slots that make up the finite verbs and the morphemes that may fill these slots. Specific focus is laid on subject and object prefixes as well as on post-final enclitics. Last, the hierarchical structure of the verbal root, base and stem will be discussed (§3.4).

3.2 Phonological structure of verbal morphemes

The basic segmental shape of the verbal root is CVC, where C_1 can be followed by a glide and C_2 can be a prenasalized plosive; C_1 is never prenasalized. One of the consonantal segments can be zero and V might be short or long. For vowel-initial roots, all vowels in the inventory but /u/ are attested, which is most likely an accidental gap, as nominal stems with initial /u/ are attested, e.g. ʊ-mu-unyu 'salt', ɪ-ly-ungu 'pumpkin'.

Although disyllabic roots can be considered the most basic structure, more complex forms outnumber these in the present-day language. Most verbs with a more complex shape can be analysed as the outcome of derivational processes, although in many cases such an analysis can only be arrived at through a comparative Bantu perspective. Only 17 monosyllabic verbs exist in Nyakyusa. These, however, include some very basic concepts. (1) lists their isistem forms; see §3.4 on roots and stems. Note that <ni> in nia stands for a sequence of coronal nasal plus palatal glide.

(1)   a. shape Cɪ (defective verbs)

       lɪ   'be'

       tɪ   'say; think; do like'

   b. shape C(V)-a

       pa (p(a)-a) 'give'[1]

       ja (j-a)   'be, become'

   c. shape Cy-a

       kya 'cease raining; dawn'

       lya 'eat'

       nia 'defecate'

       pya 'be burnt'

       sya 'grind'

   d. shape Cw-a

       fwa 'die'

       gwa 'fall'

       kwa 'pay dowry'

       lwa 'fight'

       mwa 'shave'

       nwa 'drink'

       swa 'spit; forgive'

       twa 'be plenty (esp. of fish)'

The typical verbal prefix has the shape CV-, with a very limited number of exceptions having VCV-, V- or N-. Prefixes do not contain the mid vowels /e/ and /o/. Suffixes typically have the mirrored form -VC, with a few cases of -V. Of the few suffixes having -VCV, some might be understood as bipartite -VC-V. The final vowel segment of the verbal word is always short. This also holds when post-final clitics (§3.3.8) are attached.

3.3 Linear morphological structure of the finite verb

The highly agglutinative structure of the finite verb in Nyakyusa can be understood as consisting of a number of slots for derivational and inflectional affixes that frame the basic unit, the verbal root.

The linear arrangement of the verbal morphemes and the functions associated with each slot can be represented as in Figure 3.1, adopting the segmentation and terminology proposed by Güldemann (1999: 546). Slots with a subscript N may be filled with various affixes, as will be described in the corresponding sections.

---

[1]The verb *pa* 'give' behaves ambiguously with regard to its segmentation. Both vowel quality and length in the perfective stem *peele* (§6.4.2), the applicative *peela* (§4.2.1) and the passive *peegwa* (§4.2.7) indicate a root *pa*. With the imperfective suffix however, the stem takes the shape *paga* (*pege* in the imperfective subjunctive), not **paaga, peege*. With post-final clitics it also surfaces as *pa* (*pe* in the subjunctive). Thus it is treated as *p* in these cases.

slot	pre-initial	initial	post-initial~N~	pre-radical	radical
function	tense/ emphasis	subject	TMA/ polarity	object	verbal root

slot	pre-final~N~	final	post-final
function	derivation/ voice	TMA	locative/WH/ adverbial

Figure 3.1: Linear structure of the finite verb

Examples (2) and (3) illustrate the imperative as the morphologically minimal possible structure and the use of all verbal slots respectively.[2]

(2) job-a
    speak-FV
    'Speak!'

(3) aa=tʊ-ti-kʊ-ba-jaat-ɪl-a=ko
    FUT=1PL-NEG-PRS-2-walk-APPL-FV=17(LOC)
    'We will not visit them there'

In the following subsections, each of the individual slots, together with the morphemes that may fill them, will be described.

3.3.1 The pre-initial slot

The pre-initial slot of the verbal word may only contain a single morpheme. As Güldemann (2003: 186) notes, morphemes in this slot are typically the result of the truncation of a formerly bi-predicate structure. This is most likely the case for the de-itive future proclitic *aa=* (§8.2) and its de-ventive counterpart (*i*)*sa=* (§8.3). Other morphemes that may occupy this slot are a proclitic form of comitative *na=* as well as a proclitic *a=*, both of which add specific interlocutory and modal nuances to certain uses of the subjunctive paradigm (§9.3.1.1). Last, in some southern varieties of Nyakyusa, a proclitic *naa* with a future-oriented meaning is found (§8.4), which might be a portmanteau of comitative *na* and the future proclitic *aa=*.

---

[2] The gloss PRS 'present' is here to be understood as shorthand for a non-past imperfective; see §6.5.1.

3.3.2 The initial slot

In the initial slot of the verbal word, the subject is marked. Any finite Nyakyusa verb, with the exception of imperatives (§9.2) and subjunctives in their directive use (§9.3.1.1), carries a subject prefix.

In the Bantuist and general linguistic tradition, the subject prefixes, as well as the object prefixes (§3.3.4), are most often referred to as *agreement* markers. Given the origin of the term agreement in the treatment of person-marking in European languages and the typological problems associated with it (see e.g. Haspelmath 2013), the more neutral and also widespread term *cross-reference* is used throughout this study. This nomenclature has the further advantage of capturing not only subject- and object-markers but also the locative morphemes described in §3.3.8.1.

Concerning the subject markers, two paradigmatic sets of prefixes will be assumed in this study. The choice between the sets depends on the following formant: when the subject prefix directly precedes the simple present prefix *kʊ-*, set 2 is used. Otherwise set 1 is used.

These two distinct sets are postulated for two reasons. First, the subject prefix for the second person singular is zero before simple present *kʊ-* and has the shape *(g)ʊ-* elsewhere. Second, the shape of the other subject prefixes preceding *kʊ-* is not completely predictable in the varieties that are in the focus of this study. While /a/ regularly changes to /i/ in this environment and the front vowel of some subject prefixes is raised to /i/, this is not a regularly predictable process (see Tables 3.1 and 3.2). In other topolects, such as the one described by Berger (1938) and the lake-shore-plains variety, which is the subject of ongoing research by SIL International, there is greater regularity. In those varieties all unrounded vowels preceding simple present *kʊ-* are raised to /i/ and all rounded back vowels change to /u/. The findings of the present study, however, basically agree with those of Mwangoka & Voorhoeve (1960c) and Labroussi (1998). While the former work gives no information as to the variety studied, Labroussi's main assistant is a speaker of the Kukwe/Ngumba topolect.

Similar alternations, in which a vowel segment /i/ surfaces in at least one allomorph of the simple present (and constructions based on this paradigm), are found in numerous languages in a coherent area encompassing Nyakyusa as well as most of Guthrie's zones G60 and N10.[3] Persohn & Bernander (2016) trace this back to a grammaticalization process the source structure of which consists of a

---

[3]The variety of Ngonde described by Kishindo (1999) does not have this alternation in subject prefixes. This seemingly also holds for the Ngonde described by Labroussi (1998).

reflex of Proto-Bantu * jikad* 'dwell, be, sit' plus infinitive and the cradle of which is found in zone G60.

In the following subsections, first the subject prefixes for the discourse participants (first and second person) will be described (§3.3.2.1), followed by the prefixes for the noun classes (third persons) (§3.3.2.2).

3.3.2.1 Participant subject prefixes

The subject prefixes for the discourse participants are listed in Table 3.1.[4]

Table 3.1: Participant subject prefixes

Participant	Set 1	Set 2
1SG	*n-*	*n (ni-)*
2SG	*ʊ-*	*ø-*
1PL	*tʊ-*	*tʊ-*
2PL	*mu-*	*mu-*

The prefixes of the first and second person singular display some morphophonemic peculiarities. In the first person singular, set 2 contains an alternative form *ni-*. This was found in older descriptions and text collections (e.g. Schumann 1899; Endemann 1914; Berger 1933). The younger speakers consulted were unaware of this alternation and it was considered antiquated by the older generation.

Preceding those noun class object prefixes featuring a voiceless plosive (noun classes 7, 12, 13, 15, 16 and 17), the first person singular subject prefix is realized as a syllabic nasal. This is illustrated in (6). Before any other prefix with an initial voiceless plosive, it regularly triggers prenasalisation; see (4) for the object prefixes of the second person singular and first person plural, and (5) for TMA prefixes. For stem-initial plosives see (19) in §2.2.2.3. This allopmorphy can hence not be accounted for on a purely phonological base.

(4) *ngʊmeenye* (°n-kʊ-many-ile) 'I know you'
     ndʊmeenye (°n-tʊ-many-ile) 'I know us'

---

[4] The second person plural is also used as an honorific. This usage seems to be limited to the exchange of greetings; also see Walsh (1982: 32).

(5)   *ngamanya*   (°n-ka-many-a)   'I do not know'
      ngamanye   (°n-ka-many-e)   'I should go get to know'
      ndikʊjoba   (°n-ti-kʊ-job-a)   'I do not speak'

(6)   *nkameenye*   (°n-ka-many-ile)   'I know it (class 12)'
      ntʊmeenye   (°n-tʊ-many-ile)   'I know them (class 13)'
      nkʊmeenye   (°n-kʊ-many-ile)   'I know it (class 15)'
      mpameenye   (°n-pa-many-ile)   'I know the place (class 16)'
      nkʊmeenye   (°n-kʊ-many-ile)   'I know the place (class 17)'

The first person singular subject prefix also surfaces as a syllabic nasal before a fricative or another nasal:

(7)   *mmalile*   (°n-mal-ile)   'I have finished'
      mmumeenye (°n-mu-many-ile) 'I know it inside (class 18)'
      nnusiisye   (°n-nus-ile)   'I have smelled'
      nng'walile   (°n-ng'wal-ile)   'I have scratched'
      nnyeelile   (°n-nyeel-ile)   'I have jumped'
      nhobwike   (°n-hobok-ile)   'I have rejoiced'
      mfibwene   (°n-fi-bon-ile)   'I have seen them (class 8)'
      mfumile   (°m-fum-ile)   'I have come (from)'
      nsibwene   (°n-si-bon-ile)   'I have seen them (class 10)'
      nswile   (°n-sw-ile)   'I have spilled'

The first person singular subject prefix is further realized as a syllabic nasal before monosyllabic stems with an initial plosive or approximant in the subjunctive mood, that is, in those cases in which prenasalization would result in a monosyllabic word (8). In the imperfective subjunctive and when post-final clitics are attached, the resultant word is no longer monosyllabic and the prefix surfaces as prenasalization (9). Likewise, when the subjunctive of *tɪ* 'say; think; do like' merges with the following interrogative *bʊle* (see §10.3), the first person singular subject prefix surfaces as prenasalization (10). A similar avoidance of monosyllabic words is found with the corresponding object prefix in the imperative; see §3.3.4.1.

(8)   *ɲje*   (°n-j-e)   'I should be(come)'
      ndye   (°n-ly-e)   'I should eat'
      ndɪ   (°n-tɪ)   'I should say'[5]
      ŋgwe   (°n-gw-e)   'I should fall'

(9)   *ndyege*   (°n-ly-ege)   'I should be eating'
      ndyepo   (°n-ly-e=po)   'I should eat a bit'

    ndyemo (°n-ly-e=mo) 'I should eat some'

    ndɪgɪ   (°n-t-ɪgɪ)   'I should be saying'

(10)   *ndʊbʊle* (°n-tɪ bʊle)   'What should I say/do'

When the object prefix of noun class 1 follows the subject prefix of 1SG, an epenthetic vowel /u/ is inserted.

(11)   *nummʊʊliile* (°n-mu-ʊl-ɪl-ile) 'I have bought for him/her'

    nummwagile (°n-mu-ag-ile)   'I have found him/her'

    nunkomile   (°n-mu-kom-ile) 'I have hit him/her'

A vowel following the first person singular subject prefix is regularly long (12), with the exception of the indefinite future prefix *isakʊ-* (§8.6).

(12)   *niisile*   (°n-is-ile)   'I have come'

    nɪɪmile   (°n-ɪm-ile)   'I have stopped'

    neegile   (°n-eg-ile)   'I have taken'

    naagile   (°n-ag-ile)   'I have found'

    naataagile (°n-a-taag-ile) 'I threw'

    noogile   (°n-og-ile)   'I have bathed'

    nʊʊlile   (°n-ʊl-ile)   'I have bought'

The subject prefix of the second person singular is realized as *gʊ-* preceding a vowel (13). The usual rules for vowel juxtaposition apply (see §2.2.1.4).

(13)   *gwisile*   (°ʊ-is-ile)   'you have come'

    gwɪmile   (°ʊ-ɪm-ile)   'you have stopped'

    gwegile   (°ʊ-eg-ile)   'you have taken'

    gwagile   (°ʊ-ag-ile)   'you have found'

    gwataagile (°ʊ-a-taag-ile) 'you threw'

    googile   (°ʊ-og-ile)   'you have bathed'

    gʊʊlile   (°ʊ-ʊl-ile)   'you have bought'

When the subject prefix of the second person singular is adjacent to the object prefix of the first person singular or noun class 1, there is free variation between *gʊ-* and *ʊ-*. The only paradigms in which these two sets of morphemes can be adjacent are the subjunctive (§9.3) and the present perfective (§6.5.3):

---

[5]For the subjunctive of defective *tɪ*, see §10.3.

(14) Subject prefix 2SG and object prefix 1SG:

(g)ʋʋnyʋʋliile (°ʋ-ny-ʋl-ɪl-ile) 'you have bought for me'
(g)ʋndaagile (°ʋ-ny-taag-ile) 'you have thrown me'
(g)ʋʋsalile (°ʋ-ny-sal-ile) 'you have chosen me'
(g)ʋʋnyʋʋlɪle (°ʋ-ny-ʋl-ɪl-e) 'you should buy for me'
(g)ʋndaage (°ʋ-ny-taag-e) 'you should throw me'
(g)ʋʋsale (°ʋ-ny-sal-e) 'you should choose me'

(15) Subject prefix 2SG and object prefix class 1:

(g)ʋmmʋʋliile (°ʋ-mu-ʋl-ɪl-ile) 'you have bought for him/her'
(g)ʋmmwagile (°ʋ-mu-ag-ile) 'you have found him/her'
(g)ʋnsalile (°ʋ-mu-sal-ile) 'you have chosen him/her'
(g)ʋmmʋʋlɪle (°ʋ-mu-ʋl-ɪl-e) 'you should buy for him/her'
(g)ʋmmwage (°ʋ-mu-ag-e) 'you should find him/her'
(g)ʋnsale (°ʋ-mu-sal-e) 'you should choose him/her'

Given this free variation as well as the fact that the second person singular subject before consonants in other contexts surfaces as *ʋ-*, the monosegmental form can be assumed to be the underlying representation.

3.3.2.2 Noun class subject prefixes

Table 3.2: Noun class subject prefixes

Noun class	Series 1	Series 2	Noun class	Series 1	Series 2
1	*a-*	*i- (ʋ-)*	10	*si-*	*si-*
2	*ba-*	*bi-*	11	*lʋ-*	*lʋ-*
3	*gʋ-*	*gʋ-*	12	*ka-*	*ki-*
4	*gɪ-*	*gɪ-*	13	*tʋ-*	*tʋ-*
5	*lɪ-*	*li-*	14	*bʋ-*	*bʋ-*
6	*ga-*	*gi-*	15	*kʋ-*	*kʋ-*
7	*kɪ-*	*ki-*	16	*pa-*	*pi-*
8	*fi-*	*fi-*	17	*kʋ-*	*kʋ-*
9	*jɪ-*	*jɪ-*	18	*mu-*	*mu-*

The subject prefixes for the noun classes are given in Table 3.2. Except for noun class 1, the first series is identical to the pronominal prefixes (§2.3.1). In the second series, *i-* is the most common and most widely accepted subject prefix of noun class 1. A variant form *ʊ-* is attested for speakers of the northernmost varieties. The speakers consulted on this subject considered this a feature common for the northernmost topolects, but of low prestige. Given that all the other subject prefixes recorded for that variety have the predictable alternation between /a/ in series 1 and /i/ in series 2, this is most likely an innovative case of assimilation.[6]

3.3.3 The post-initial slot

In the post-initial slot, polarity, tense, aspect and mood/modality are marked. The following prefixes may fill this slot: *ti-* 'negation', *ka-* 'negation', *nga-* 'negative subjunctive' (see §6.3 on negation in Nyakyusa), *kʊ-* 'simple present (also: modal future)', *a(lɪ)-* 'past', *a-* 'subsecutive', *lɪnkʊ-* 'narrative tense', *isakʊ-* 'indefinite future', *ka-* 'itive/distal', and *lɪ-* 'desiderative'.

Concerning the order of prefixes in this slot, negative markers are followed by the respective tense-aspect prefixes. The exception is desiderative *lɪ-*, which stands before the negative subjunctive prefix. Table 3.3 lists the possible co-occurrences of prefixes in the post-initial slot. Note that some of the mentioned paradigms require the addition of specific suffixes other than the default final vowel *-a* (§3.3.7). For a detailed description of the individual tense, aspect and mood/modal construction as well as their negative counterparts see §6–9.

Table 3.3: Co-occurrences of prefixes in the post-initial slot

Prefixes			See
	ka- 'NEG'	a(lɪ)- 'PST'	§6.5.6, 6.5.8
	ti- 'NEG'	kʊ- 'PRS'	§6.5.1, 9.5
	ti- 'NEG'	isakʊ- 'INDEF.FUT'	§8.6
lɪ- 'DESDTV'	nga- 'NEG.SUBJ'		§9.3.4
lɪ- 'DESDTV'	ka- 'ITV'		§9.4

---

[6]In the (north-)eastern neighbour languages Kinga and Wanji the combination of noun class 1 subject prefix and simple present prefix yields *i/ikʊ*, while Safwa, bordering to the north, has *ahu-/a-*. The choice of allomorphs depend on the type and shape of the following morpheme (Wolff 1905; Voorhoeve n.d. Helen Eaton, p.c.). Influence from the neighbouring languages can thus be excluded.

3.3.4 The pre-radical slot

The pre-radical slot is the locus of object-marking. In the following subsections the object prefixes will be described, beginning with those of the discourse participants (§3.3.4.1), followed by the object prefixes of the noun classes (third persons) (§3.3.4.1) and the reflexive object prefix (§3.3.4.3). The focus lies mainly on the shape of the prefixes and a number of morphophonological particularities.

Concerning the syntactic and discourse-pragmatic factors licensing the object prefixes, some first observations are found in Lusekelo (2012). As observed therein and as previously noted by Schumann (1899: 20f) and Endemann (1914: 17–20), Nyakyusa allows for only a single object to be marked in pre-radical position. In the typology of Bantu languages put forward by Bearth (2003), Nyakyusa thus classifies as an OM-1 language. This characteristic is shared by the surrounding languages Nyika Nyika M23, Malila M24, Safwa M25 (Helen Eaton, p.c.), Kinga G65 (Wolff 1905), Wanji G66 (Helen Eaton, p.c.), and Kisi G67 (Gray n.d.).

3.3.4.1 Participant object prefixes

Table 3.4 lists the object prefixes for the discourse participants.

Table 3.4: Participant object prefixes

Participant	Object prefix
1SG	*ny-*
2SG	*kʊ-*
1PL	*tʊ-*
2PL	*ba-*

The object prefix of the first person singular displays some morphophonemic peculiarities. Before a vowel it surfaces as *ny-*. In this case, both the vowel of the preceding prefix and the following stem-initial vowel are long (16).

(16)   *ikʊʊnyiitɪka*   (°i-kʊ-ny-itɪk-a)   's/he believes me'
       muunyootile   (°mu-ny-ot-ile)   'you (pl.) have invited me'
       baanyaagile   (°ba-ny-ag-ile)   'they have found me'
       syalɪɪnyaagile   (°si-alɪ-ny-ag-ile)   'they (class 10) found me'
       ʊkaanyʊʊlɪle   (°ʊ-ka-ny-ʊl-ɪl-e)   'go buy for me'

Preceding a plosive or an approximant, the first person singular object prefix follows the general phonological rules and triggers prenasalization. Note that prenasalization induces lengthening of the preceding vowel (see §2.2.2.3), which, as it is predictable, is not indicated in the practical orthography.

(17) *bambinyile* (°ba-ny-piny-ile) 'they have bound me'
   bambʊʊlile (°ba-ny-bʊʊl-ile) 'they have told me'
   bandaagile (°ba-ny-taag-ile) 'they have thrown me'
   bandobile (°ba-ny-log-ile) 'they have bewitched me'
   banjobile (°ba-ny-job-ile) 'they have spoken to me'
   bangeetile (°ba-ny-keet-ile) 'they have watched me'
   bangogile (°ba-ny-gog-ile) 'they have killed me'

There is one exception: in the imperative (§9.2), when a monosyllabic root contains an initial plosive or an approximant and prenasalization would thus result in a monosyllabic word, the first person singular object prefix surfaces as a syllabic nasal (18). Accordingly, in the imperfective imperative and with post-final clitics (§3.3.8), the first person singular object prefix surfaces as prenasalization (19). This behaviour is shared with the first person singular subject prefix in the subjunctive mood; see §3.3.2.1.

(18) *ṇdya* (°ny-ly-a) 'Eat me!'
   ŋgwa (°ny-kw-a) 'Pay me dowry!'
   ṃba (°ny-p-a) 'Give me!'

(19) *ndyaga* (°ny-ly-aga) 'Be eating me!'
   ngwaga (°ny-kw-aga) 'Be paying me dowry!'
   mbaga (°ny-p-aga) 'Be giving me!'
   mbako (°ny-p-a=ko) 'Give to me!'

When the object prefix of the first person singular stands between a prefix and a stem-initial nasal or fricative, it has no segmental realization. However, it is discernible through the length of the preceding vowel (20). To summarize, any word-internal vowel preceding or following the first person singular object prefix is phonetically realized as long.[7]

---

[7]Interestingly, the same holds for the noun class 9/10 noun prefix, which also has the underlying shape *ny-*.

(20) a. Deletion of object prefix 1SG in simple present:

ikʊʊmeta	(°i-kʊ-ny-met-a)	's/he shaves me'
ikʊʊnangɪsya	(°i-kʊ-ny-nangɪsi-a)	's/he shows me'
ikʊʊnyomosya	(°i-kʊ-ny-nyomosi-a)	's/he frightens me'
ikʊʊng'amula	(°i-kʊ-ny-ng'amul-a)	's/he recognizes me'
ikʊʊfwɪma	(°i-kʊ-ny-fwɪm-a)	's/he hunts me'
ikʊʊhobosya	(°i-kʊ-ny-hobosi-a)	's/he makes me happy'
ikʊʊsala	(°i-kʊ-ny-sal-a)	's/he chooses me'

   b. Deletion of object prefix 1SG in other paradigms:

aafwɪmile	(°a-ny-fwɪm-ile)	's/he has hunted me'
aalɪɪfwɪmile	(°a-alɪ-ny-fwɪm-ile)	's/he hunted me'
aametile	(°a-ny-met-ile)	's/he has shaved me'
aalɪɪmetile	(°a-alɪ-ny-met-ile)	's/he shaved me'
(g)ʊʊsalile	(°ʊ-ny-sal-ile)	'you have chosen me'
ʊngaasyobaga	(°ʊ-nga-ny-syob-aga)	'don't cheat on me'

3.3.4.2 Noun class object prefixes

Table 3.5 lists the object prefixes for the noun classes. These are identical to the pronominal prefixes, except for class 1, the object prefix of which is identical to the nominal prefix (§2.3.1).

Table 3.5: Noun class object prefixes

Noun class	Object prefix	Noun class	Object prefix
1	*mu-*	10	*si-*
2	*ba-*	11	*lʊ-*
3	*gʊ-*	12	*ka-*
4	*gɪ-*	13	*tʊ-*
5	*lɪ-*	14	*bʊ-*
6	*ga-*	15	*kʊ-*
7	*kɪ-*	16	*pa-*
8	*fi-*	17	*kʊ-*
9	*jɪ-*	18	*mu-*

The object prefix of noun class 1 becomes a syllabic nasal before a consonant (21) and thus triggers shortening of a preceding vowel (22).[8]

(21) *bikʊmpinya*   (°bi-kʊ-mu-piny-a)   'they bind him/her'
   bikʊmbʊʊla   (°bi-kʊ-mu-bʊʊl-a)   'they tell him/her'
   bikʊɲjoba   (°bi-kʊ-mu-job-a)   'they speak to him/her'
   bikʊnsala   (°bi-kʊ-mu-sal-a)   'they choose him/her'
   bikʊmmeta   (°bi-kʊ-mu-met-a)   'they shave him/her'

(22) *bampinyaga*   (°ba-a-mu-piny-aga) 'they were binding him/her'
   bambʊʊlaga   (°ba-a-mu-bʊʊl-aga) 'they were telling him/her'
   baɲjobaga   (°ba-a-mu-job-aga) 'they were speaking to him/her'
   bansalaga   (°ba-a-mu-sal-aga) 'they were choosing him/her'
   bammetaga   (°ba-a-mu-met-aga) 'they were shaving him/her'

When a following vowel induces glide formation or vowel coalescence (see §2.2.1.4), the nasal segment of the noun class 1 object prefix is realized with a longer phonetic duration and also triggers vowel shortening (23), which is orthographically indicated by <mm> in these cases. The nasal in these cases, however, does not constitute a syllable of its own. In summary, any vowel preceding the noun class 1 object prefix surfaces as short.

(23) *bammwega*   [βa.ˈmːʷɛˑ.ɰa]   'they (then) took him/her'
   bammʊʊlɪlaga [βa.mːʊː.lɪ.ˈla.ɰa] 'they were buying for him/her'
   bammootaga   [βa.mːoː.ˈtʰa.ɰa] 'they were inviting him/her'

Unlike its class 1 counterpart, the noun class 18 object prefix *mu-* does not become a syllabic nasal before a consonant. The nasal segment is neither realized with a longer duration, nor does it trigger vowel shortening:

(24) *amumeenye*   (°a-mu-many-ile)   's/he knows it inside'
   aamumeenye   (°a-a-mu-many-ile)   's/he knew it inside'
   ikʊmwinogona (°i-kʊ-mu-inogon-a) 's/he considers the inside'

Note that locative object prefixes are extremely rare in the text corpus, whereas enclitic forms of locative substitutives (§3.3.8.1) occur frequently. A similar distribution is also attested in languages such as Kiluba L33, Ruund L53, and Luvale K14; see Persohn & Devos (2017) for an overview.

---

[8]The vowel of the noun class 1 prefix is given as /u/, as the process of reduction and syllabification is shared with the nominal concords of classes 1, 3 and 18, which have the shape *mu-*. Due to the rules of hiatus resolution for verbal prefixes (§2.2.1.4) and the fact that the prefix surfaces as a mere consonantal segment preceding another consonant, the quality of the vowel cannot be directly observed.

3.3.4.3 Reflexive object prefix

The reflexive object prefix has the shape *i-* before consonants (25) and *ij-* preceding vowels. Stem-initial vowels following the reflexive are always long (26).

(25) *koma*   'hit'   > *ikoma*   'hit oneself'
      nyomosya 'frighten' > *inyomosya* 'frighten o.s.'
      joba   'speak'   > *ijoba*   'speak about o.s.'
      baaja   'kick'   > *ibaaja*   'kick o.s.'
      fisa   'hide'   > *ifisa*   'hide o.s.'

(26) *ima*   'not give; deprive'   > *ij-iima*   'abstain from'
      ɪmika   'erect; respect'   > *ij-ɪɪmika*   'stand o.s. up; praise o.s.'
      elʊsya   'clean; rinse'   > *ij-eelʊsya* 'cleanse o.s.'
      abʊla   'help; open, release'   > *ij-aabʊla* 'make o.s. free'
      onanga 'destroy'   > *ij-oonanga* 'destroy, spoil o.s.'
      ʊbatɪla 'embrace'   > *ij-ʊʊbatɪla* 'embrace o.s.'

With some verbs the reflexive gives an idiosyncratic meaning:

(27) *i-kanyanga* 'talk nonsense'   < *kanyanga* 'trample'
      i-bona   'consider o.s. different' < *bona*   'see'
      i-bɪɪka   'pretend'   < *bɪɪka*   'put, store'
      i-gana   'like, prefer'   < *gana*   'like, love'
      i-pɪlɪka   'act arrogantly'   < *pɪlɪka*   'hear'
      i-pʊʊla   'actively seek'   < *pʊʊla*   'thresh'
      i-puuta   'pray, worship'   < *puuta*   'blow out (in prayer)'
      i-kasya   'bear; try one's best'   < *kasya*   'encourage; fasten'
      i-kinya   'knock, bump (LOC)'   < *kinya*   'hit'

Given an adequate context, at least some of the verbs with idiosyncratic meaning with the reflexive allow for a second object prefix, including a second instance of the reflexive (28). The examples in (29, 30) show that two object prefixes in the same verb are otherwise not licensed. See Marlo (2014) for a discussion of object marking exceptionalities involving the reflexive in several Bantu languages.

(28) *k-ii-gana*   'like it (class 7)' (not all speakers)
      ij-ii-gana   'like oneself; be vain'
      ny-ii-puut-ɪl-a   'pray for/with (APPL) me'
      mmw-i-puut-ɪl-a 'pray for/with (APPL) him/her'
      ij-ii-puut-ɪl-a   'pray for/with (APPL) oneself'

(29) a. * bi-kʊ-si-m-p-a   ʊ-ɲ-dʊmyana ıı-heela
         2-PRS-10-1-give-FV AUG-1-boy   AUG-money(10)

      b. * bi-kʊ-n-si-p-a   ʊ-ɲ-dʊmyana ıı-heela
         2-PRS-1-10-give-FV AUG-1-boy   AUG-money(10)

      (intended: They give the boy money.')

(30) a. * ʊ-ɲ-dʊmyana i-kʊ-si-i-p-a   ıı-heela
         AUG-1-boy   1-PRS-10-REFL-give-FV AUG-money(10)

      b. * ʊ-ɲ-dʊmyana i-kw-i-si-p-a   ıı-heela
         AUG-1-boy   1-PRS-REFL-10-give-FV AUG-money(10)

      (intended: 'The boy gives himself money.')

At least with the following two verbs, the reflexive has an intransitivizing or middle function:

(31) *i-kola*   'be(come) caught, stuck' < *kola*   'grasp, hold'
      i-kyela 'consent; be pleased'   < *kyela* 'please'

Lastly, at least the following verbs exist only as reflexives:

(32) *i-fun-a*   'boast'   no *funa* attested
      ij-eekel-a 'be in privacy' no *ekela* attested

3.3.5 The radical slot

As discussed in §3.3, the radical slot contains the verbal root and can thus be considered the centre of the verbal word. For the phonological structure of verbal roots see §3.2.

3.3.6 The pre-final slot

The pre-final slot is the locus of verb-to-verb derivation by means of suffixes (verbal extensions). This will be described in detail in §4. For a discussion of co-occurrences of verbal derivation suffixes see §4.3.

3.3.7 The final slot

In the final slot of the verb, tense, aspect and isimood/modality are marked. By default this slot is filled with the final vowel -*a*; see §3.4. Other suffixes that may occur in this slot are imperfective -*a(n)ga*, subjunctive -*e*, imperfective subjunctive -*e(n)ge* – see §6.4.1 on the morphophonology of the imperfective suffix – as well as perfective *-ile*. The latter is subject to complex alternations, which may obscure the boundary between the radical, pre-final and final slot; see §6.4.2 for a detailed discussion.

3.3.8 The post-final slot

The post-final slot of the verb may be filled with one of a set of morphemes of the shape CV.[9] Although there is no clear boundary between clitics and affixes, these morphemes will be referred to as enclitics in this study. The reasons for this analysis are mainly syntactical and morphological. First, in case of the WH enclitics, these stand in alternation with their free forms. Second, post-final enclitics are often optional and – in the cases of non-locative =*po* and =*mo* – show a lower selectivity than affixes. Further, they lie outside the scope of stem reduplication. In terms of their (morpho-)phonology, however, the post-finals show a tight integration into the verbal word. First, when they are attached, stress shifts to the new penultimate syllable. More importantly, all enclitics except =*ki* 'what' trigger certain morphophonological changes in the verb stem, namely prenasalization of the imperfective suffix (§6.4.1) and raising of the vowel in the copula (see §10.2.3).

   In the following subsections, first enclitic forms of locative substitutives will be discussed, which serve as locative cross-reference markers, (§3.3.8.1), followed by a description of several adverbial enclitics that can mostly be traced back to extended functions of the locative enclitics (§3.3.8.2–3.3.8.4) and frequent or lexicalized collocations between verbs and these enclitics (§3.3.8.5). Last, two enclitic forms of question words ('WH enclitics') will be described (§3.3.8.6).

3.3.8.1 Enclitic locative substitutives

Locations can be marked on the verb with enclitic forms of the substitutives of locative noun classes 16–18. Note that the locative enclitic is licensed even when the overt locative noun phrase directly follows the verb, as in (34), unlike what has been reported for interlacustrine Bantu languages (e.g. Diercks 2011; Gray 2013).

---

[9]The analysis and some of the data presented in this section are also found in Persohn (2017b). The limitation to a single enclitic stands in contrast to (the Malawian variety of) Ndali, where enclitics can be stacked (Botne 2008: 92).

(33) bo i-kʊ-gon-a   mu-n-k-iina mula~mu-la   ɪ-n-jala
     as 1-PRS-live-FV 18-18-7-pit   REDUPL~18-DIST AUG-9-hunger
     j-a-ṇ-dʊm-aga   fiijo,   a-lɪnkʊ-tendeel-a pa-mwanya ʊkʊtɪ
     9-PST-1-bite-IPFV INTENS 1-NARR-peep-FV 16-up   COMP
     a-sook-e   a-bʊʊk-e n-kʊ-ly-a. a-lɪnkw-ag-a   ɪ-n-giisi
     1-leave-SUBJ 1-go-SUBJ 18-15-eat-FV 1-NARR-find-FV AUG-9-darkness
     jɪ-li=po   ngatɪ mu-ndʊ ɪɪm-ile=**po**,   ngɪmba ii-syanjʊ
     9-COP=16 like   1-person 1.stand/stop-PFV=16 behold 5-leave
     lɪ-ṇ-gw-ɪl-iile=**po**
     5-1-fall-APPL-PFV=16

     'While he [Hare] was staying there in the pit, he was plagued by hunger.
     He had a look upwards to leave and go to eat. He found there was
     darkness, as if a person was standing **there**, in fact a leaf had fallen
     (**there**) on him.' [Saliki and Hare]

(34) p-ii-sɪɪlya   a-aly-and-ile ʊ-kʊ-bop-a   kɪsita   kʊ-keet-a-**ko**
     16-5-other_side 1-PST-start-PFV AUG-15-run-FV without 15-watch-FV-17
     kʊʊ-nyuma
     17-back(9)

     'On the other side, he started to run without looking **back**.' [Saliki and
     Hare]

Locative enclitics were also found with reference not to a formal locative, but to a noun phrase that simply denotes a location. Thus in (35) the class 17 clitic =*ko* refers to *ʊngʊnda* 'field', while in (35) the class 18 clitic =*mo* can be understood to refer to the inside of *ɪndeko* 'earthen pot'. This kind of use often has an infinitive as the dependent element of the associative construction (37).

(35) n-kamu   gw-angʊ Pakɪɪndɪ, ɪɪ-ng'ombe si-k-oonang-a   fiijo
     1-relative 1-POSS.1SG P.   AUG-10.cow 10-PRS-destroy-FV INTENS
     a-ma-jabʊ   ga-ako   a-ka-balɪlo a-ka-a   pa-muu-si,
     AUG-6-cassava 6-POSS.2SG AUG-12-time AUG-12-ASSOC 16-3-daytime
     n-gʊ-kʊ-sʊʊm-a   ʊkʊtɪ ʊ-bʊʊk-e   ʊ-ka-sigɪl-e=**ko**   paapo
     1SG-PRS-2SG-beg-FV COMP 2SG-go-SUBJ 2SG-ITV-check-SUBJ=17 because
     a-ma-jabʊ   g-oonang-iike   fiijo
     AUG-6-cassava 6-destroy-NEUT.PFV INTENS

     'My friend Pakyindi, the cows are destroying your cassava during the day,
     I beg you go and have a look **there**, because the cassava is very spoiled.'
     [Sokoni and Pakyindi]

(36) bo a-fik-ile   a-a-jɪ-bwene   ɪ-n-deko   jɪ-lɪ pa-m-ooto.
     as 1-arrive-PFV 1-PST-9-see.PFV AUG-9-earthen_pot 9-COP 16-3-fire
     a-a-kuputwile,   a-aly-eg-ile=**mo**   ɪ-fi-balali
     1-PST-uncover.PFV 1-PST-take-PFV=18 AUG-8-piece

     'When she arrived, she saw that the pot was on the fire. She uncovered it, she took **out** pieces [of the food].' [Thieving woman]

(37) gw-ijʊʊl-e   ʊ-kʊ-lond-a   ʊ-bʊ-jo   ʊ-bʊ-nunu
     2SG-work_hard-SUBJ AUG-15-search-FV AUG-14-place AUG-14-good
     ʊ-bw-a   kʊ-jeng-a=**po**
     AUG-14-ASSOC 15-build-FV=16

     'You should try to look for a good place to build **on**.' [How to build modern houses]

Note that there are homophonous enclitics =*po* and =*mo* which serve non-locative functions. These are discussed in the following subsections.

3.3.8.2 Partitive =*po*

An enclitic =*po*, derived from the locative class 16 substitutive serves as a partitive. For an overview over such de-locative partitives across Bantu, see Persohn & Devos (2017). Concerning the core function of verbal partitive markers, Persohn & Devos adopt the follwing definition by Budd: "[A verbal partitive marker denotes] an indefinite partial degree, to which an action is carried out or to which a situation pertains" (Budd 2014: 524).

    The use of partitive =*po* in Nyakyusa is frequently, but not exclusively, combined with the adverbial *panandɪ* 'a little'. Formally speaking, *panandɪ* can be segmented into *pa-nandɪ* '16-little'. This collocation thus seems like a reasonable candidate for the development of the non-locative function of the enclitic. This fits the fact that Nyakyusa =*po* often retains a minimizing meaning of low intensity, short duration or limited affectedness of the object, whereas a more general indefinite meaning is expressed by enclitic =*mo* (see §3.3.8.4). The scope of partitive =*po* may be over the object (in transative clauses), as in (38), or over the entire predicate, in which case it quantifies the degree of the state-of-affairs, as in (39). Note that in (40) the partitive seems to also function on the intersubjective level, qualifying the imperative's imposition on the hearer rather than only the propositional content.

(38) kangɪ na=nungwe kʊ-m-bon-a   lɪnga   a-ka-ndʊ   ka-mo
     again COM=COM.2SG 2SG.PRS-1SG-see-FV if/when AUG-12-thing 12-one

ka-m-balamaasiisye=**po** ʊ-m̩-bɪlɪ   gw-angʊ, n-gw-andʊl-a
12-1SG-touch.PFV=PART AUG-3-body 3-POSS.SG 1SG-PRS-change-FV
ɪ-my-enda ɪ-gɪ   m-fwele,   nakalɪnga
AUG-4-cloth AUG-PROX.4 1SG-dress/wear.PFV immediately
n-gʊ-fwal-a   ɪ-gɪ-ngɪ   ɪ-mi-nunu ɪ-gy-a   lʊ-ko
1SG-PRS-dress/wear-FV AUG-4-other AUG-4-good AUG-4-ASSOC 12-type
ʊ-lʊ-ngɪ
AUG-11-other

'You too see me [habitually], when something touches my body **a bit**, I change the clothes I wear and immediately put on other beautiful ones of a different type.' [Hare and Chameleon]

(39) lʊmo bo a-bomb-ile=**po** **panandɪ** kw-ag-aga
maybe as 1-work-PFV=PART a_little 2SG.MOD.FUT-find-MOD.FUT
a-b-eene   na=fyo   b-iis-ile   kʊ-kw-eg-a
AUG-2-owner COM=REF.8 2-come-PFV 17-15-take-FV

'Or when he has worked **for a little while**, you will find they [owner of the tools] have come to take them back.' [Types of tools in the home]

(40) tw-ɪmb-ɪl-e=**po**   kangɪ mwa=li-ndʊ,   kʊb-a kangɪ!
1PL-sing-APPL-IMP=PART again matronym=5-monster beat-FV again

'Sing **a little** for us again, Mr. Monster, play again!' (Monster with Guitar)

On negated verbs, the partitive =*po* strengthens the negation, having the meaning 'not a bit' or 'not at all'.

(41) a-a-bop-ile   mw-ene, a-a-bop-ile   mw-ene kalʊlʊ.
1-PST-run-PFV 1-only   1-PST-run-PFV 1-only   hare(1)
mwa=n-dugutu   **a-ka-a-bop-ile=po**
matronym=9-type_of_bird 1-NEG-PST-run-PFV=PART

'He [Hare] had run alone, Hare had run alone. Mr. Tugutu did not run at all.' [Hare and Tugutu]

(42) ʊ-gwe kʊ-job-a   ɪ-s-ingi   itolo ɪ-si
AUG-2SG 2SG.PRS-speak-FV AUG-10-many just AUG-PROX.10
a-ka-kʊ-lagɪl-a=po,   fiki ʊ-ti-kʊ-pɪlɪkɪsy-a   kanunu?
1-NEG-2SG-order-FV=PART why 2SG-NEG-PRS-listen-FV well

'You say many things that he hasn't told you at all, why don't you listen properly?' [Saliki and Hare]

As with the semantically locative enclitics, minimizing =*po* triggers prenasalization of the imperfective suffix (§6.4.1):

(43) a. nw-anga=po!
     drink-IPFV=PART
     'Drink a little!'

 b. ʊ-tʊʊsy-enge=po
    2SG-rest-IPFV.SUBJ=PART
    'You should rest a little.'

Partitive =*po* is also used with predicative adjectives (44) and is also attested with adverbials (45). This has been observed before by Schumann (1899: 63) and Endemann (1914: 80).

(44) a-ka-aja   a-ko   ka-lɪ   pa-tali=po
     AUG-12-village AUG-REF.12 12-COP 16-long=PART
     'That village is a bit far.' [ET]

(45) bo end-ile=po   n-ky-eni=po   panandɪ,
     as 1.walk/travel-PFV=PART 18-7-forehead=PART a_little
     a-lɪnkʊ-ba-bon-a Jaakobo na   Johani, a-ba-nya-Sebetai
     1-NARR-2-see-FV J.   COM J.   AUG-2-kinship-S.
     'When he had gone a little farther, he saw James son of Zebedee and his brother John.' (Mark 1:19)[10]

3.3.8.3 Comparative =*po*

Another enclitic, =*po*, likewise derived from the locative class 16 substitutive, is used in comparisons of inequality. Nyakyusa's primary means of encoding comparisons of inequality features the verb *kɪnda* 'pass, surpass', which takes the standard of comparison as its object. Stassen (2013) terms this pattern, which is the most common means of forming comparisons in languages south of the Sahara, "exceed comparatives".

(46) ɪɪ-nyumba   ɪ-jɪ   nywamu ʊ-kʊ-kɪnd-a   jɪ-la
     AUG-house(9) AUG-PROX.9 big(9)   AUG-15-pass-FV 9-DIST
     'This house is bigger than that one' [ET]

---

[10] *nkyeni* (lit. 'in the forehead') has grammaticalized to an adverbial 'in front, ahead'.

The verb *kında* often features the comparative enclitic =*po*. According to the speakers consulted, this emphasizes the comparison.

(47) ʊ-mw-ana ʊ-jʊ   a-lɪ   na=a-ma-hala
     AUG-1-child AUG-PROX.1 1-COP COM=AUG-6-intelligence

     ʊ-kʊ-kɪnd-a=**po**   ʊ-jʊ-ngɪ   ʊ-jʊ
     AUG-15-pass-FV=CMPR AUG-1-other AUG-PROX.1

     'This child is cleverer than this other one.' [ET]

Note that *kında* even in non-comparative contexts often features an enclitic =*po*:

(48) bo ka-kɪnd-ile=po   a-ka-balɪlo   ka-nandɪ, Pakyindi a-lɪnkʊ-bʊʊk-a
     as 12-pass-PFV=CMPR AUG-12-time 12-little, P.   1-NARR-go-FV

     kʊ-ṇ-gʊnda
     17-3-field

     'When a short time had passed, Pakyindi went to the field.' [Paykindi and Sokoni]

The host of the comparative enclitic may also be an inflected verb (49) or a predicative adjective (50) functioning as the object of comparison.

(49) ʊ-ṇ-dʊmyana ʊ-jʊ   **i-kʊ-bomb-a=po**   kanunu
     AUG-1-boy   AUG-PROX.1 1-PRS-work-FV=CMPR well

     ʊ-kʊ-n-kɪnd-a   ʊ-jʊ
     AUG-15-1-pass-FV AUG-PROX.1

     'This boy works better than this one.' [ET]

(50) **kʊ-pepe=po** ɪ-n-gamila   ʊ-kw-end-a   pa-bw-asi
     15-easy=CMPR AUG-9-camel(<SWA) AUG-15-walk/travel-FV 14-gap

     bw-a   sindaano ʊ-kʊ-kɪnd-a   ʊ-n-kabi ʊ-kw-ingɪl-a
     14-ASSOC needle(9) AUG-15-pass-FV AUG-1-rich AUG-15-enter-FV

     ṃ-bʊ-nyafyale bw-a   Kyala
     18-14-chiefdom 14-ASSOC God

     'It is easier for a camel to go through the eye of a needle than for someone who is rich to enter the kingdom of God.' (Mark 10:25)

The comparative clitic is also found on predicative adjectives without any form of *kında* in the clause (51). Lastly, note that a sequence /po/ is also found in the invariant stem *paakipo* 'preferable' and in *kyajɪ* ~ *kyajɪpo* 'better'.

(51) ɪ-m-bwa   ɪ-jɪ   n-galɪ, jɪ-la   **n-galɪ=po**
      AUG-9-dog AUG-PROX.9 9-fierce 9-DIST 9-fierce=CMPR
      'This dog is fierce, that one is fiercer.' [ET]

The use of an originally locative enclitic to express comparison is not limited to Nyakyusa: Persohn & Devos (2017) observe comparative uses in Kanyoka L32, Kaonde L41, Tumbuka N21 and Umbundu R11. As has been noted above, in Nyakyusa there is a strong attraction between the exceed-verb *kɪnda* and the enclitic *=po*. It is conceivable that the enclitic originally indexed the (implied) landmark, beyond which motion continues. Through metaphorical transfer this may be a temporal landmark, as in (48) or the standard of comparison NP. A likely source construction is found in the following example:

(52) n-ambɪliile   fy-osa ɪ-fi   mu-m-b-eele,   kangɪ
      1SG-receive.PFV 8-all   AUG-PROX.8 2PL-1SG-give-PFV again
      n=ʊ-kʊ-kɪnd-a=po   palɪ ɪ-fi   n-aa-lond-aga
      COM=AUG-15-pass-FV=16 16   AUG-PROX.8 1SG-PST-want-IPFV
      'But I have all, and abound. [lit. I have received everything that you have given me and even more than what I needed]' (Philippians 4:18)'

In this scenario, *=po* turns into a comparative marker of its own when it attaches to the inflected verb, predicative nominal or predicative invariant stem that expresses the object of comparison.

3.3.8.4 Some(time) *=mo*

The enclitic *=mo* can have a range of non-locative readings. The collocation with perfective *-ile* (see §6.5.3,6.5.5) typically denotes a state-of-affairs that has occurred at some previous time, a reading similar to what has been labelled the "experiential perfect" (Comrie 1976) or "existential perfect" (McCawley 1971).

(53) ʊ-ka-bagɪl-a   ʊ-kʊ-n-dol-a   ʊ-ne,   paapo ɪ-fi-nyamaana
      2SG-NEG-be_able-FV AUG-15-1SG-beat-FV AUG-1SG because AUG-8-animal
      bo ɪ-m-babala,   ɪɪ-senjebele n=ɪ-fi-nyamaana   ɪ-fi-ngɪ,
      like AUG-9-gazelle AUG-zebra(9) COM=AUG-8-animal AUG-8-other
      ɪ-fi   ʊ-fi-meenye   ʊkʊtɪ fi-kʊ-bop-a fiijo   ʊ-lʊ-bɪlo,
      AUG-PROX.8 2SG-8-know.PFV COMP 8-PRS-run-FV INTENS AUG-11-running
      fy-ope fi-gel-**ile=mo**   ʊ-kʊ-tolana   na=niine,   fy-osa
      8-also 8-try-PFV=some AUG-15-compete COM=COM.1SG 8-all

n-aa-fi-tol-ile
1SG-PST-8-beat-PFV

'You can't beat me, because animals like Gazelle, Zebra and many animals that you know to race fast have [at some point] tried to compete with me, I beat them all.' [Hare and Chameleon]

(54) Context: When you came to this place, did you know my brother?
tw-ag-an-**iilee**=mo
1PL-find-RECP-APPL.PFV=some

'We met [at least once before].' [ET]

In questions, =*mo* can be combined with *sikʋ* 'ever':[11]

(55) ʋ-l-iile=mo sikʋ ɪ-kɪ-nanaasi?
2SG-eat-PFV ever AUG-7-pineapple(<SWA)

'Have you ever eaten pineapple?' [ET]

With negated verbs, =*mo* adds the notion of 'not once, never'.

(56) a-ka-balɪlo ka-mo a-alɪ-m̩-bwene n=ʋ-n-nyambala ʋ-jʋ-ngɪ
AUG-12-time 12-one 1-PST-1-see.PFV COM=AUG-1-man AUG-1-other

mu-ɳ-gʋnda ʋ-gw-a   ma-jabʋ ʋ-gw-a   ɳ-dʋme   bo
18-3-field   AUG-3-ASSOC 6-cassava AUG-3-ASSOC 1-husband as

i-kʋ-logw-a.   leelo   Sokoni a-ka-alɪ-m̩-bʋʋl-ile=**mo**
1-PRS-copulate-FV now/but S.   1-NEG-PST-1-tell-PFV=some

ʋ-ɳ-dʋme
AUG-1-husband

'One time he [Sokoni] saw her with another man in her husband's cassava field while was having sex. But Sokoni did not ever tell the husband.' [Sokoni and Pakyindi]

(57) po na=jʋ-mo a-ti-kw-i-tuufy-a=**mo**   kʋʋ-nongwa j-aa
then COM=1-one 1-NEG-PRS-REFL-praise-FV=some 17-issue(9)   9-ASSOC

m-bombo ɪ-si   i-kʋ-bomb-a
10-work   AUG-PROX.10 1-PRS-work-FV

'So no one ever praises oneself for the work s/he does.' [Division of labour]

Negation involving =*mo* is frequently strengthened through the use of the postverbal *sikʋ*, yielding a sense of 'never ever' (58). The enclitic is also used on infinitives negated by *(ʋ)kʋsita, (ɪ)kɪsita* 'without' (59).

---

[11]The adverbial *sikʋ* 'ever' seems to be derived from the root *sikʋ* 'day'.

(58) n-ga-fwal-a=**mo**   **sikʊ** a-ma-koti   ma-nywamu
      1SG-NEG-dress/wear-FV-some ever AUG-6-coat(<SWA) 6-big
      'I have never ever put on a thick jacket.' [ET]

(59) ba-lɪnkʊ-j-a   ba-ndʊ b-a   lʊ-sulumanio fiijo
      2-NARR-be(come)-FV 2-person 2-ASSOC 11-grief   INTENS
      ʊ-kʊ-kong-an-a   n=ʊkʊsita   kʊ-kab-a=**mo** ʊ-mw-ana
      AUG-15-follow-RECP-FV COM=without 15-get-FV=some AUG-1-child
      na=jʊ-mo n-katɪ   m̩-bʊ-ʊmi bw-abo
      COM=1-one 18-middle 18-14-life   14-POSS.PL

      'They became very sad because they did not [ever in all that time] get
      even a single child in their life.' [Pregnant women]

As with the semantically locative enclitics, =*mo* in its indefinite function triggers prenasalization of the imperfective suffix (§6.4.1):

(60) ba-ka-a-bomb-anga=mo   sikʊ
      2-NEG-PST-work-IPFV=some ever

      'They were never ever working.' [ET]

Note that an enclitic =*mo* is also found with predicative nominals. This gives a
qualifying or mitigating reading. Thus (61) was given as a response to the author
asking for the relationship between the addressee and another person who had
just left. The mini-dialogue in (62) was suggested when discussing possible uses
of =*mo* on nouns and adjectives.[12]

(61) m-manyaani=mo gw-angʊ
      1-friend=some   1-POSS.1SG

      'He is somewhat of a friend of mine.' [overheard]

(62) bʊle, pa-Lwangwa pa-piipi? – mma, pa-tali=mo
      Q   16-L.   16-close   no   16-far=some

      'Is it close to Lwangwa?' – 'No, it is somewhat far.' [ET]

3.3.8.5 Frequent or lexicalized collocations

Some verbal roots frequently occur in combination with a post-final clitic. To
begin with, with the movement verb *sooka*, whose core meaning can be para-

---

[12]Enclitic =*mo* is not only homophonous to the class 18 substitutive but also to the bound root
mo 'one; some'. One is lead to wonder if this might have motivated the extra-locative uses.

phrased as 'leave, set off',[13] the locative enclitics in most cases do not refer to an overt location, but specify the spatial relation to the source (63). An example within its discoursive co-text is given in (64). Note that there is no antecedent for the locative.

(63)   *sooka=po*   'go away; go off; pull out (train, bus)'
        sooka=ko   'go away'
        sooka=mo   'get out'

(64) i-kw-eg-a   ɪ-n-jɪnga,   a-ka-bagɪl-a   pa-kʋ-pot-a,   paapo
    1-PRS-take-FV AUG-9-bicycle 1-NEG-be_able-FV 16-15-steer-FV because
    a-fuleele   ɪ-kɪ-lʋndɪ. **i-kʋ-sook-a=po.**
    1-be(come)_hurt.PFV AUG-7-leg 1-PRS-leave-FV=16

    'He takes the bike, he cannot ride it, because he has injured his leg. He
    sets off.' [Elisha pear story]

The same use of enclitics is found with the causative *soosya*:

(65)   *soosya*   'remove, get rid of; discharge; donate; yield'
        soosya=po   'omit; remove; expel; dismiss; displace; send away'
        soosya=ko   'deduct, subtract; remove'
        soosya=mo 'exclude; bring out from within'

Locative enclitics are also frequently used with *pa* 'give', in which case the reference is to the recipient/goal:

(66) popaa~po   ʋ-mu-ndʋ   jʋ-la a-lɪnkʋ-bʋʋk-a pa-kɪ-syanjʋ
    REDUPL~then AUG-1-person 1-DIST 1-NARR-go-FV 16-7-thicket
    pa-kʋ-tʋʋsy-a, a-lɪnkʋ-j-aag-a   ɪɪ-nyama.   a-lɪnkʋ-jɪ-koolel-a
    16-15-rest-FV   1-NARR-9-find-FV AUG-meat(9) 1-NARR-9-call-FV
    ɪ-m-bwa j-aake,   a-lɪnkʋ-p-a=po   ʋkʋtɪ jɪ-ly-ege
    AUG-9-dog 9-POSS.SG 1-NARR-give-FV=16 COMP 9-eat-IPFV.SUBJ

    'That man went into the thicket to rest, he found the meat. He called his
    dog, he gave [the meat] **to him** to eat.' [Dogs laughed at each other]

A few collocations of verbal root plus enclitic have acquired a specialized meaning, which must be considered lexicalized or on the path to becoming so. First, the verb *lya* 'eat', when used with a human subject, is more frequently than

---

[13]Botne (2005: 66) states about the seemingly functionally equivalent verb in Ndali: "*ny'amuka* denotes separation of the figure from the source, with latent motion away from that source." The encoding of motion in Nyakyusa is the subject of ongoing research.

not used with an enclitic =*mo*, whose semantic contribution is not entirely clear (67). The only counterexamples in the corpus feature anthropomorphized animals as the protagonists of fables, as in (68). This association with humans also became clear in elicitation, where constructed examples with animals as subjects of *lya=mo* were either only accepted with a locative reading or considered as humanizing the animal.

(67) ba-lɪnkʊ-m'-bʊʊl-a ʊkʊtɪ iik-e   paa-si   **a-ly-e=mo**
      2-NARR-1-tell-FV   COMP 1.descend-SUBJ 16-below 1-eat-SUBJ=some(?)
      ɪ-fi-ndʊ   ɪ-fi   ba-alɪ-n-twal-iile
      AUG-8-food AUG-PROX.8 2-PST-1-carry-APPL.PFV

      'They told her to come down and eat the food they brought for her.' [Myfage turns into a lion]

(68) bo **ba-l-iile=mo**   kalʊlʊ n=ʊ-lʊ-bʊbi,   ba-lɪnkʊ-buj-a
      as 2-eat-PFV=some(?) hare(1) COM=AUG-11-spider 2-NARR-return-FV
      kʊ-my-abo
      17-4-POSS.PL

      'When Hare and Spider had eaten they went home.' [Hare and Spider]

Lastly, at least the verbs in (69) have related, but idiosyncratic meanings when combined with an enclitic:

(69) *tala*   'do first; be first to do'   > *tala=po*   'go ahead'
      gela   'try; examine'   > *gela=po*   'dare to'
      ingɪla 'enter'   > *ingɪla=po* 'succeed, inherit from'
      ikinya 'knock at, bump into (LOC)' > *ikinya=mo* 'take offence'

In the cases of *tala=po* and *gela=po*, the partitive *po* suggests itself as the source of the divergent meaning. Concerning *ingɪla=po* and *ikinya=mo*, the ideosyncratic readings most likely originate in collocations with locative possessives, which are still sometimes found in the present-day language: *ingɪla=po pamyake* 'enter his/her place' > 'succeed' and *ikinya=mo mmyake* lit. 'bump into his/hers' > 'take offence'.

3.3.8.6 WH-enclitics

Two question morphemes can attach to the verb: *ki* 'what' and *kʊ* 'where'. The bound root *ki* has a meaning along the lines of 'what kind of; which'. Its employment as an enclitic is derived from its use in noun class 8 (70).[14]

(70) kʊ-lond-a=ki?   ~ kʊ-lond-a   fi-ki?
      2SG.PRS-want-FV=what   2SG.PRS-want-FV 8-what
      'What do you want?' [overheard]

    Enclitic *ki* cannot be employed together with its full form:

(71)   * *kʊlondaki fiki?*

    The clitic *kʊ* is a shortened form of *kʊʊgʊ*, the question word for locative noun class 17.

(72) ba-fum-ile   kʊʊgʊ? ~ ba-fum-ile=kʊ?
      2-come_from-PFV where   2-come_from-PFV=where
      'Where have they come from?' [ET]

    The enclitic *kʊ* also forms part of the fixed expression *kʊtwakʊ* 'Where are you going?'. As is the case with =*ki*, =*kʊ* is incompatible with the full form:

(73)   * *bafumilekʊ kʊʊgʊ?*

3.4 Root, base and stem

The verbal root being its basic unit, the Nyakyusa verb can be described in terms of a hierarchy. According to this view, the hierarchically lowest element is the root, which is not further analysable in its morphology. The root together with the derivational elements in the pre-final slot form the base, which is the domain of the morphophonological process of imbrication (§6.4.2). The base together with the final affix form the stem, which is the domain of clitizication (§3.3.8). Figure 3.2 illustrates this structure.

    In another common terminology, what is labelled *root* and *base* here corresponds to *simple base* and *extended base* (Schadeberg 2003a). Downing (2001) uses *derivational stem* and *inflectional stem* instead of *base* and *stem*.

---

[14] *fiki* is also used as an interrogative of reason 'why?'. Some speakers stated that the enclitic =*ki* is emblematic of the Mwamba/Lugulu and/or Kukwe/Ngumba dialect.

stem

base　　　final

root　(derivational
suffixes)

Figure 3.2: Hierarchical structure of the verb

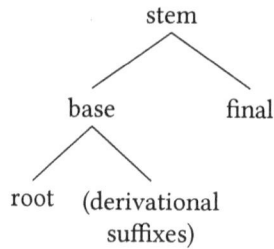

A number of verbs with initial /i/ are formally reflexive verbs, that is, they are preceded by the reflexive object marker *i-* (§3.3.4.3). However, with some of these the reflexive semantics has become obscured and there may not exist a corresponding stem without the reflexive marker. There are at least two diagnostic criteria regarding the status of initial /i/. First, object prefixes do not count as stem syllables. Trisyllabic formal reflexives are thus treated as disyllabic in the formation of the perfective stem (see §6.4.2).

(74)　*itoga*　　'mount (horse, donkey)'　> *itogile*　(not *itwige)
　　　ikifya　　'do your best'　　> *ikifiifye* (not *ikiifye)

Second, any object prefix other than first person singular triggers a final vowel *-e* in the imperative (§9.2) (75). Verbs in which initial /i/ is part of the stem have *-a* (76),

(75)　*i-jʊʊl-e!*　'work hard!'　　　　(not *ijʊʊla)
　　　i-nogon-e! 'think!'　　　　　(not *inogona)

(76)　*inamika!*　'turn (sthg) upside down!'
　　　igʊla!　　'open!'

The final slot of the stem is obligatory and by default is occupied by the final vowel (FV) *-a*, except for certain TMA paradigms and the defective verbs *lɪ* and *tɪ* (§10). Following Bantuist tradition, throughout the rest of this study verbs are listed as stems, except when explicitly making reference to hierarchically lower structures. Note that the verb stem is generally not a possible morphological word in Nyakyusa.[15]

---

[15]The exception is the imperative (§9.2), for those verbs that can figure in this paradigm and are not monosyllabic.

4 Verbal Derivation

4.1 Introduction

Verbal derivation in Nyakyusa is accomplished by means of several devices. The most frequent is the use of derivational suffixes. These are also known as verbal extensions in Bantu studies (Schadeberg 2003a) and are common in the postulated Niger-Congo phylum (Hyman 2007). The canonical verbal extension has the shape VC, with the exception of the passive and causative extensions (V and VCV). While some verbal extensions, e.g. the applicative, are highly productive, others like the tentive can be segmented on the basis of their shape and meaning, but are not used productively to derive new verbs. Between these two extremes lie other extensions whose productivity is harder to determine as there seems to be a close interaction with verbal semantics (see Fleisch 2000). In these cases productivity is described on a tentative basis.

Verbal derivation by means of derivational suffixes is cyclic: once a derived verbal base has acquired a special or idiosyncratic meaning, this functions as the point of departure for subsequent derivations.

(1) *fuma*
    'come from'
    > *fumuka*
       'be(come) known, famous' (separative)
       > *fumusya*
          'announce' (separative + causative)
          > *fumusigwa*
             'be announced' (separative + causative + passive)

Verbal derivations cover a set of functions that can be subsumed under valency changing operations, semantic alternations, aktionsart (see §1.4.3.2) and alternations in Aristotelian aspect (see §1.4.3.1). Some devices express a combination of these functions.

This chapter begins with an account of morphophonological processes affecting verbal extensions (§4.2.1), followed by a section on the form and function of

each verbal extension (§4.2.2–4.2.15). The treatment of the less productive extensions includes observations on lexical co-occurrences that are derived forms from
the same root (commutations). Thereafter the combinations of verbal extensions
are dealt with in more detail, including their respective order and some cases
of specialized combinations (§4.3). Following the verbal extensions, denominal
verb bases are dealt with (§4.4). Lastly, there is a note on partially reduplicated
verbs (§4.5).

4.2 Verbal extensions

4.2.1 Morphophonology of verbal extensions

Verbal extensions in Nyakyusa are subject to two progressively operating processes affecting the degree of vowel opening: vowel height harmony and high
vowel raising.

4.2.1.1 Vowel height harmony

The verbal extensions with an underlying front vowel /ɪ/ surface with mid vowel
/e/ following a syllable containing mid vowels /e, o/. The examples in (2) illustrate this for the applicative extension (only one possible reading given for each
example).

(2)   *fikɪla*   'arrive at'   < *fika*   'arrive'
       pɪmɪla   'measure with'   < *pɪma*   'weigh, measure'
       temela   'cut with'   < *tema*   'cut'
       jabɪla   'give off to'   < *jaba*   'divide; distribute'
       bopela   'run to'   < *bopa*   'run'
       bʊʊkɪla 'go to'   < *bʊʊka* 'go (to)'
       guulɪla 'wait for'   < *guula* 'wait'

A similar rule applies to extensions beginning with the back vowel /ʊ/. The
separative extensions *-ʊl* and *-ʊk* occur as *-ol* and *-ok* following a syllable with
/o/ (but not /e/). They surface as *-ul/-uk* following a syllable with the high back
vowel /u/. That is, front and back vowels are treated asymmetrically. Previous
discussions of vowel harmony in Nyakyusa (e.g. Mwangoka & Voorhoeve 1960c;
Labroussi 1998; Hyman 1999) did not notice the raising of /ʊ/ to /u/. This rule
of high vowel rising seems to be the expression of a more general constraint
against stem-internal /*uCʊ/. These rules are illustrated in (3) for the separative
transitive extension.

(3) *kingʋla*   'uncover'   < *kinga*   'cover'
     pɪndʋla   'convert'   < *pɪnda*   'bend; wrap'
     niembʋla 'disentangle' < *niemba* 'wrap up'
     matʋla   'demolish'   < *mata*   'plug, stop up'
     bonola   'pay off'   < *bona*   'see'
     tʋngʋla 'pick'   < *tʋnga*   'hang; string together'
     fumbula 'solve'   < *fumba*   'enclose in mouth or hands'

In principle, the rules of vowel harmony apply to all verbal extensions in question. (4) gives a formalized account. Extensions containing /i/ or /a/ such as the passive or the reciprocal do not change their vowel quality.

(4) $\text{ɪ} \rightarrow \text{e} / \begin{cases} \text{e C} \_ \\ \text{o C} \_ \end{cases}$
    $\text{ʋ} \rightarrow \text{o} / \text{o C}\_$
    $\text{ʋ} \rightarrow \text{u} / \text{u C}\_$

The shape of the verbal extensions subject to vowel height harmony on monosyllabic roots is not predictable in a straightforward fashion, at least in synchronic terms. (5) lists the applicative forms of monosyllabic verbs together with their Proto-Bantu forms.[1]

(5) a. *pa*   (**pá*)   'give'   > *peela*
       ja   (**gì*)   'be(come)'   > *jɪɪla*
    b. *fwa* (**kú*)   'die'   > *fwɪla*
       gwa (**gò*)   'fall'   > *gwɪla*
       kwa (**kó*)   'pay dowry'   > *kwela*
       lwa (**dò*)   'fight'   > *lwɪla*
       mwa (**mò*)   'shave'   > *mwela*
       nwa (**ɲó*)   'drink'   > *nwela*
       swa (**tu?*) 'spit; forgive'   > *swela*
       twa (**tó?*) 'be plenty (esp. fish)'   > *twɪla*
    c. *kya* (**ké*)   'dawn; cease to rain'   > *kyela*
       lya (**lí*)   'eat'   > *lɪɪla*
       nia (**nè*)   'defecate'   > *niela*
       pya (**pí*)   'be(come) burnt'   > *pɪɪla*
       sya (**cè*)   'grind'   > *syela*

---

[1]Defective *lɪ* and *tɪ* do not take derivational suffixes.

As can be gathered, *pa* is treated as underlying *pa-a* for derivational purposes. With all other monosyllabic roots, the surface glide is retained, unless the sequence is /*ɪ-ɪ/. The vowel quality of the derivational suffix as such is conditioned by the historic root vowel and shows the same alternations as with longer verbs. The only exceptions are *twa* 'be plenty (esp. of fish)', whose origin in **tó* 'bite' is merely tentative, and *swa* 'spit; forgive' < **tú* 'spit', where **fwa* would be expected according to the rules of diachronic phonology.

4.2.1.2 High vowel raising

Two further and related processes affect the quality of vowels in verbal extensions. What both have in common is the raising of the second degree vowels /ɪ, ʊ/ to the first degree /i, u/. First, the underlying vowels of verbal extensions are raised to first degree vowels when following the palatal nasal,[2] as illustrated in (6) with the applicative (*-ɪl*), neuter (*-ɪk*), causative₂ (*-ɪsi*) and the separative (*-ʊl/-ʊk*) extensions.

(6) *manyila* (°many-ɪl-a) 'learn'   < *manya* 'know'
     manyika (°many-ɪk-a) 'be known'
     manyisya (°many-ɪsi-a) 'teach'
     kanyisya (°kany-ɪsi-a) 'fill up, stuff' < *kanya* 'tread on'
     tuunyila (°tuuny-ɪl-a) 'throw at'   < *tuunya* 'throw'
     tuunyuka (°tuuny-ʊk-a) 'fall (from)'
     kinyula (°kiny-ʊl-a) 'disencourage' < *kinya* 'hit'

This rule does not apply when the vowel in question is affected by vowel height harmony (7). Also, only the directly adjacent vowel is subject to high vowel raising (8).

(7) *toonyesya* 'cause to fall or drip'   < *toonya* 'drip, ooze'
     keenyesya 'insult, shout at'   < *keenya* 'insult'
     konyola   'break, wreck; harvest corn' < **kóny* 'fold, bend, twist'
     konyoka   'break (intr.)'

(8) *manyilɪla* 'know (much)'   < *manya* 'know'
     pinyilɪla 'tie up, bind repeatedly'   < *pinya* 'bind; detain; fix'
     kenyulɪla 'add too much; oversalt'

---

[2] This seems to be the expression of a more general constraint against stem-internal /*nyɪ, nyʊ/, cf. also nominal stems like *unyu* 'salt' < PB **jínyʊ̀*.

The underlying second degree vowels /ɪ, ʊ/ of verbal extensions are also realized as first degree /i, u/ when they follow a sequence of low vowel /a/ plus the coronal or bilabial nasal /n/ or /m/. Examples are given in (9) for the extensions in question when following the reciprocal and positional extensions, while (10) illustrates this for root-final sequences.[3]

(9) *komanila* (°kom-an-ɪl-a) 'fight for' < *koma* 'hit'
     swiganika (°swig-an-ɪk-a) 'wonder (much)' < *swiga* 'wonder'
     sulamika (°sulam-ɪk-a) 'turn upside down' < *sulama* 'bend, droop'
     batamisya (°batam-ɪsi-a) 'silence, caress' < *batama* 'be silent'

(10) *ganila*   (°gan-ɪl-a)   'love + APPL'   < *gana*   'love'
     ganisya   (°gan-ɪsi-a) 'cause to love'
     kaanika   (°kaan-ɪk-a) 'dispute'   < *kaana* 'refuse'
     kaanila   (°kaan-ɪl-a) 'refuse'
     kaanisya (°kaan-ɪsi-a) 'forbid'
     kamila   (°kam-ɪl-a)   'milk + APPL'   < *kama*   'milk, squeeze'
     kamula   (°kam-ʊl-a)   'squeeze out'
     lamula   (°lam-ʊl-a)   'stop fight; judge' *dàm-ʊd* 'settle dispute'
     saamila   (°saam-ɪl-a) 'move + APPL'   < *saama* 'move, migrate'
     saamisya (°saam-ɪsi-a) 'transfer; displace'

Again, only the directly adjacent vowel undergoes raising:

(11) *fwanikɪsya* (°fwan-ɪkɪsi-a) 'compare'   < *fwana* 'resemble'
     kaanilɪla (°kaan-ɪlɪl-a) 'refuse +INTNS' < *kaana* 'refuse'
     saamikɪsya (°saam-ɪkɪsi-a) 'transfer; exile to' < *saama* 'move, migrate'
     saamilɪla (°saam-ɪlɪl-a) 'migrate + INTNS'
     sanukɪla   (°sanuk-ɪl-a)   'turn to'   < *sanuka* 'alter'
     amulɪsya   (°amul-ɪsi-a)   'make answer'   < *amula* 'answer'

The examples in (12) show that other /aC/ sequences do not induce raising of the second degree vowels.[4] The examples in (13) show that other /VN/ sequences likewise do not induce high vowel raising (but see above on the effects of the palatal nasal, and below on the sequence /mu/).

---

[3] Again, this seems to be the expression of a more general phonotactic constraint: Regardless of syntactic class, no stem containing /an, am/ followed by a second degree vowel is attested in the data.

[4] A few combinations are not attested in the data: /aɲɪ, afɪ, afu/. The lack of the first is due to the scarcity of the velar nasal, while the lack of the other two stems from the fact that the bilabial fricative /f/ has its main diachronic source in sequences of Proto-Bantu plosives followed by a first degree vowel.

(12) /ap, at, ak/   /amb, and, aɲɟ, aŋg/

paapɪla	'give birth + APPL'	*bambɪka*	'arrange in line'
tapʊka	'separate'	*sambʊka*	'rebel'
ʊbatɪla	'embrace'	*andɪsya*	'establish; repeat'
latʊla	'rip'	*andʊla*	'change; convert'
pakɪla	'load + APPL'	*nangɪsya*	'show'
sakʊka	'reappear'	*pangʊla*	'dismantle'

/aβ, al, aɟ, aɰ/   /as, ah/

laabɪla	'get up early; be early'	*lasɪla*	'stab + APPL'
abʊla	'release; open'	*pasʊka*	'burst'
malɪka	'(be) finish(ed) (intr.)'	*hahɪla*	'propose + APPL'
saalʊka	'be(come) unravelled'		/aɲ/
baajɪka	'kick + APPL'	*kang'ʊla*	'remove stopper'
tajʊka	'break up (intr.)'		
bagɪla	'be able; suit'		
pagʊka	'fall apart'		

(13) /V≠a{n, m}/

pɪmɪla	'measure + APPL'
inɪsya	'dirty (tr.)'
inʊla	'lift'
timɪla	'rain + APPL'
ʊmɪla	'dry + APPL'

A formalized account of the rules of high vowel raising is given in (14, 15).

(14) $\left\{ \begin{matrix} \text{ɪ} \\ \text{ʊ} \end{matrix} \right\} \rightarrow \left\{ \begin{matrix} \text{i} \\ \text{u} \end{matrix} \right\}$ / ny__

(15) $\left\{ \begin{matrix} \text{ɪ} \\ \text{ʊ} \end{matrix} \right\} \rightarrow \left\{ \begin{matrix} \text{i} \\ \text{u} \end{matrix} \right\}$ / a{n, m}__

Lastly, in a few stems the sequence /mu/ is found in contexts where it cannot be accounted for by the above rules (16). This seems to be the expression of a general phonotactic constraint against /mʊ/.[5] While the latter sequence may be the outcome of vowel coalescence between the vowel of a prefix and a vowel-initial stem (§2.2.1.4), no stem or affix containing it is attested.[6]

---

[5] This kind of constraint against certain CV sequences may be more widespread in Bantu. Bennet & Lee (2015) describe in detail how the sequence /li/ is strongly dispreferred in Tsonga S53.

[6] Note that this constraint alone cannot explain the raising of the front vowel /ɪ/ after /a{m, n}/, nor can it explain the raising of /ʊ/ after /an/, as /mɪ, nɪ, nʊ/ are licensed stem-internal syllables.

(16)   *lendemuka*   'crack'
      nyenyemusya 'excite'
      telemuka   'slip'   < *tèdɪmʊk
      syelemuka   'slip'   < *tìedɪmʊk
      tyemula   'sneeze'   < *tíemʊd
      tyesemula   'sneeze'

4.2.2 Causative 1

The verbal suffix -*i* serves to derive causative verbs. Before turning to a closer examination of its function, some formal aspects require discussion.

Synchronically speaking, the vowel of this extension is not directly observable; instead it surfaces as the glide /y/. It is interpreted as -*i* because of the morpho-phonological changes it induces, which in diachronical terms go back to a first degree front vowel. Lingual plosives and approximants preceding this causative suffix are spirantized to /s/, while their labial counterparts change to /f/. This rule, which constitutes a typical case of Bantu spirantization (see Bostoen 2008), is given (17) and illustrated in (18).

(17)   Spirantization triggered by causative -*i*
     a. { t, l, j, k, g } → s / _i
     b. { p, b } → f / _i

(18)   *bosya*   'cause to rot'   < *bola*   'rot'
     sesya   'make laugh'   < *seka*   'laugh'
     osya   'bathe (tr.); baptize'   < *oga*   'bathe (intr.)'
     pyʊfya 'warm, heat up'   < *pyʊpa* 'get warm'
     sofya   'loose; mislead'   < *soba*   'be lost; be wrong'

When prenasalized plosives are spirantized, the preceding vowel becomes long (19).[7] The causative -*i* followed by passive -*igw* surfaces with a short vowel; see p. 94 in §4.2.7.

(19)   *kɪɪsya* 'make pass, pass through; allow' < *kɪnda* 'pass'
     joosya 'elope with girl; lose'   < *jonga* 'run away'

When serving as a typical causative, this extension increases the valency of the verb by one. It introduces an agent that causes the act of the underlying verb

---

[7] This can be analyzed either as retention of the compensatory lengthening triggered by the NC cluster or as subsequent deletion of the word-internal non-syllabic nasal plus compensatory lengthening, cf. the first person singular object prefix (§3.3.2.1).

and demotes the original subject to an object. The following examples illustrate this.

(20) | | | | | |
|---|---|---|---|---|
| elʊsya | 'clean, rinse' | < elʊka | 'become white, clean' |
| fulasya | 'hurt (tr.)' | < fulala | '(be)come hurt' |
| isʊsya | 'fill' | < isʊla | '(be)come full' |
| sumusya | 'make stand up, get up' | < sumuka | 'get up, depart' |
| kusya | 'blow away' | < kula | 'blow (intr.), drift' |

Causative -*i* has developed idiosyncratic readings with a number of verbs, but it is no longer productive in the present-day language. These issues are dealt with in more detail in §4.2.4.

4.2.3 Causative 2

The extension -*ɪsi* (allomorphs -*esi*, -*isi*, see §4.2.1,) serves to derive causative verbs. -*ɪsi* is the only causative extension used with monosyllabic verbs and verbs ending in the palatal nasal (21a). It is also the only productive causative in Nyakyusa; see §4.2.4 for discussion.

(21) a. Causatives of monosyllabic verbs:

gwa	'fall'	> gwɪsya	'overturn, throw down'
lwa	'fight'	> lwɪsya	'cause to fight'
nwa	'drink'	> nwesya	'make drink, water'
lya	'eat'	> lɪɪsya	'feed'
sya	'grind'	> syesya	'make grind'

  b. Causatives of bases ending in -*ny*:

manya	'know'	> manyisya	'teach'
pinya	'bind; detain; fix'	> pinyisya	'make bind'
kuunya	'push, bump'	> kuunyisya	'make push, bump'

The suffix -*ɪsi* may be analysed as consisting of two morphemes -*ɪs-i*. In combination with the reciprocal/associative it often surfaces as -*ɪs-an-i*; see also §4.3.1. Also note that any causative followed by the passive -*igw* surfaces with a short vowel; see p. 94 in §4.2.7.

(22) | | | | |
|---|---|---|---|
| lwɪsania | 'make fight each other' | < lwa | 'fight' |
| sobesania | 'loose each other' | < soba | 'be lost' |

Causative₂ -*ɪsi* increases the valency of the verb by one, introducing an agent-causer and demoting the original subject to an object. See (25–27) in §4.2.4 for numerous examples. Causative₂ can further be used to add an intensive, evaluative meaning without changing the verb's argument structure (23, 24). Such an intensifying use of the causative has also been reported for neighbouring Ndali (Botne 2003a: 73f) and other Bantu languages such as Chewa N20 (Anonymous 1969: 78f), Bemba M42 (van Sambeek 1955: 83–92) and Kalanga S16 (Mathangwane 2001: 397). For a typological perspective see Kittilä (2009).

(23) i-kʊ-mmw-amul-ɪsy-a
      1-PRS-1-answer-CAUS-FV

      '1. S/he makes him/her answer.'
      '2. S/he answered him/her snottily.' [ET]

(24) i-kʊ-ba-hah-ɪsy-a   a-ba-kiikʊlʊ
      1-PRS-2-persuade-CAUS-FV AUG-2-woman

      'He goes around proposing to women.' [ET]

4.2.4 The relationship between the two causatives

As was seen in the preceding sections, Nyakyusa has two causative morphemes: -i and -ɪsi. Their distribution is partly conditioned by phonology. Only -ɪsi applies with mono-syllabic verbs and following /ny/. These phonological contexts aside, in the variety described by Schumann (1899) and Endemann (1914), causative₁ -i figures as the more productive morpheme of the two. For the present-day language, however, Labroussi (1999) observes that causative₂ -ɪsi has widely replaced causative₁ -i. Labroussi's observations are corroborated in the data. First, in a number of cases, causative₁ -i is lexicalized with idiosyncratic meanings, whereas causative₂ -ɪsi yields a more transparent meaning and syntax. (25) illustrates a few of these.

(25) *kʊba* 'beat; ring; play' > *kʊfya*   'cause trouble' not: 'make beat'
                               > *kʊbɪsya* 'make beat, ring, play'
      oga   'bathe (intr.)' > *osya*   'bathe (tr.); baptize'
                               > *ogesya*   'bathe (tr.)' not: 'baptize'
      pona 'recover; escape' > *ponia*   'greet, visit' not: 'cure'
                               > *ponesya* 'cure, rescue'
      syala 'remain'   > *syasya*   'leave over' not: 'make remain'
                               > *syalɪsya* 'make remain'
      taama 'moo'   > *taamya*   'trouble; persecute'
                                           not: 'make moo'
                               > *taamisya* 'make moo'

In other cases, both causatives are attested without any apparent difference in meaning. With most of these, there is a preference for the long causative₂. However, with a few verbs, the short causative₁ is strongly preferred or is the only acceptable form (26). The data at hand suggest that this kind of lexicalization is particularly the case with verbs featuring the separative intransitive (§4.2.11) and the extensive (§4.2.15).

(26) *fulala* 'be(come) hurt' > *fulasya* 'hurt (tr.)'
  hoboka 'be(come) happy' > *hobosya* 'amuse
          **hobokesya*
  kalala 'be(come) angry' > *kalasya* 'enrage'
          **kalalısya*
  lıla i.a. 'cry' > *lısya* 'make cry' (preferred)
      > *lılısya* 'make cry'
  pyʊpa i.a. 'get warm' > *pyʊfya* 'heat, warm up'
          **pyʊpısya*

Furthermore, causative₂ -*ısi* is the only one which is applied productively (27). Causative₁ -*i* was rejected with most roots, including a number of those listed by Meinhof (1966)[1910], Schumann (1899), and Endemann (1914).[8]

(27) *baaja* 'kick' > *baajısya* 'make kick' not: **baasya*
  bona 'see' > *bonesya* 'show' not **bonia*
  funja 'harvest' > *funjısya* 'make harvest' not: **fuusya*
  ikʊta 'be(come) satisfied' > *ikʊtısya* 'satisfy' not: **ikʊsya*
  jaata 'walk' > *jaatısya* 'make walk' not: **jaasya*
  jenga 'build' > *jengesya* 'make build' not: **jeesya*
  keeta 'look, watch' > *keetesya* 'make look' not: **keesya*
  lıma 'cultivate' > *lımıya* 'make cultivate' not: **lımya*
  pıija 'cook' > *pıijısya* 'make cook' not: **pıisya*

Lastly, causative₂ -*ısi* is found with the same function as causative₁ -*i* in the derivation of pluractionals (see §4.3.2). It is also subject to the same templatic requirements as -*i* in the formation of applicativized causatives (§4.3.3) and stems

---

[8] *hobokesya* is acceptable nevertheless as the applicativized causative. Felberg (1996) lists *kalalısya* for the variety of the lake-shore plains, so topological differences might also come into play. Some of these forms exist as causatives of other verbs: *baasya* < *baala* 'increase, thrive', *pıisya* < *pya* 'be(come) burnt'. Mwangoka & Voorhoeve (1960b) list *keesya* < *keeta*, which was rejected by the speakers consulted for this study.

(§6.4.2), both of which can be diachronically traced back to spirantization triggered by causative₁ -i.

Labroussi (1999) regards the loss of productivity of causative₁ -i as an epiphe-
nomenon of the more general decline of spirantization in Nyakyusa, which is
also observed in the agent noun suffix -i. The latter is lexicalized with spirantizing forms, but does not productively cause consonant mutation. What Labroussi
does not consider is the fossilization of passive *-ʊ (§4.2.8), which has been replaced by the reflex of PB *-ibʊ (§4.2.7). The alternation between these two was
historically also triggered by phonological context (Schadeberg 2003a: 78). Thus,
apart from a general decline of spirantization,spirantization present-day Nyakyusa also shows a general preference for suffixes of the shape -VCV over -V.

4.2.5 Reciprocal/Associative

The reciprocal/associative extension has the shape -an. With some roots, this extension surfaces with a long vowel, which is maintained in complex derivations
(§4.3). The long allomorph is induced predominantly, but not exhaustively, by
roots of the shape (C)VNC.

(28)   Long reciprocals -aan:

    a. Following (C)VNC:

bʊngaana	'gather, be assembled'	< *bǒnga*	'gather up'
jʊgaania	'shake, aggitate'		
lɪngaania	'explain; narrate'	< *lɪnga*	'peep through'
lʊngaana	'join together (intr.)'	< *lʊnga*	'join; add spice'
ongaana	'be together, be mixed'	< *onga*	'suck'
sangaana	'kill each other with blade'	< *sanga*	'slaughter'
tengaana	'settle; live in peace'	< *tenga*	'make bed'

    b. Following (C)VC:

jʊʊgaania	'shake, aggitate'		
jʊʊgaanika	'tremble'		
kolaana	'grasp, hold e.o.; accuse e.o.'	< *kola*	'grasp, hold'
kolaania	'multitask'		
lekaana	'leave e.o.; release e.o.'	< *leka*	'release; let'
manyaana	'be(come) acquainted'	< *manya*	'know'

However, not all (C)VNC roots have the long allomorph (29). Further, one
minimal pair -an vs. -aan is attested (30).

(29) Short reciprocal -*an* following (C)VNC:

andana   'be early'   < anda   'start'
kongana 'follow e.o.; depend upon e.o.' < konga 'follow'
ningana 'give e.o.; be opposite e.o.'   < ninga 'give'
pɪngana 'debate, disagree'   < pɪnga 'obstruct'

(30) komana   'fight'   < koma   'hit'
komaana 'hold a meeting'

Having broached the formal issues of the reciprocal/associative, its function can now be examined. The reciprocal/associativ is commonly used with transitive verbs and yields a reciprocal action. The verb's valency in this case decreases by one.

(31) sekana   'make fun of each other'   < seka 'laugh (at)'
tʊʊlana 'help each other'   < tʊʊla 'help'
titana   'pinch each other'   < tita   'pinch'

Another reading of the reciprocal/associative is that of a joint action. Accordingly, valency remains unchanged:

(32) jabana   'divide amongst each other' < jaba 'divide; distribute'
gonana 'sleep together, copulate'   < gona 'rest, sleep'

A closer look at examples (28, 29) above shows that the reciprocal/associative often expresses a further range of related meanings in the area of middle voice (Kemmer 1993). A preliminary classification, including some of the above examples, is given in the following:

(33) a. Verbs of being (dis-)connected:
pangʊkana 'break apart'   < pangʊka 'collapse'
ongaana   'be together, be mixed' < onga   'suck'
b. Collective eventualities:
bʊngaana 'gather, be assembled' <* bʊ́nga 'gather up'
palamana 'be close to each other'
papatana 'be squeezed together' < *pát   'hold'
c. Chaining relation:
kongana 'follow each other'   < konga 'follow'

d. Intransitive, resultative:[9]

andana	'be early'		< *anda*	'start'
bulungana	'be(come) round'		< *bulunga*	'roll up; knead'
tengaana	'be(come) quiet; settle'		< *tenga*	'make bed'

The majority of these readings include a plurality of participants. Thus the grammatical subject is often expressed as plural (34). Depending on the specific verb and on context, other strategies are also encountered. Two conjoined noun phrases may form a plural subject (35). Lastly, conjoined subjects may be expressed discontinuously. In this case, the corresponding plural may be cross-referenced on the verb (36). Alternatively, the first noun phrase or a participant in the context (37) may be cross-referenced. This latter strategy is attested muss less frequently in the data.

(34) ɪ-fi-nyamaana ɪ-fi   **fy-a-many-eene**   fiijo
      AUG-8-animal AUG-PROX.8 8-PST-know-RECP.PFV INTENS
      n=ɪ-m-bombo   sy-abo   sy-osa **fy-a-tʊʊl-an-aga**
      COM=AUG-10-work 10-POSS.PL 10-all 8-PST-help-RECP-IPFV
      'These animals were close friends and helped each other with everything.'
      [Hare and Chameleon]

(35) kalʊlʊ **n=ʊ-lʊ-bʊbi**   **ba-lɪnkʊ-job-an-a**   kʊ-kʊ-mwanya
      hare(1) COM=AUG-11-spider 2-NARR-speak-RECP-FV 17-17-high
      kʊ-m-piki
      17-3-tree
      'Hare and Spider talked high in the tree.' [Hare and Spider]

(36) paapo **ba-al-iitɪk-eene**   na kalʊlʊ ʊ-kʊ-bop-a
      because 2-PST-agree-RECP.PFV COM hare(1) AUG-15-run-FV
      a-ma-eli   ma-haano
      AUG-6-mile(<EN) 6-five
      'Because they (Tugutu and Hare) had agreed to run five miles.' [Hare and Tugutu]

(37) jʊ-la **i-kw-itɪk-an-a**   na=nuuswe
      1-DIST 1-PRS-agree-RECP-FV COM=COM.1PL
      'That one agrees with us.' [ET]

---

[9]Botne (2008), observing that a number of verbs with -(*a*)*an* in Ndali are aspectually inchoative and have a resultative meaning, stipulates a homophonous "resultative" extension.

4.2.6 Applicative

The applicative extension, also called *dative* (Schadeberg 2003a), has the under-lying shape *-ɪl*. Allomorphs are *-el*, *-il*; see §4.2.1. In its most productive use, the applicative increases the valency of the verb by one. The semantic roles of the additional argument can be grossly classified as being beneficiary (38), location or direction/goal (39), instrument (40), manner (41) or reason (42).

(38) Beneficiary:
bo g-ʊʊl-ile   ʊ-lond-e   ʊ-mu-ndʊ   ʊ-gw-a
as 2SG-buy-PFV 2SG-search-SUBJ AUG-1-person AUG-1-ASSOC
kʊ-kʊ-jeng-el-a
15-2SG-build-APPL-FV

'When you have bought one [place to build], you should look for a person to build for you.' [How to build modern houses]

(39) Direction:
ba-lɪnkw-igʊl-a ʊ-tʊ-supa   tʊ-la   **n=ʊ-kʊ-si-sop-el-a**
2-NARR-open-FV AUG-13-bottle 13-DIST COM=AUG-15-10-throw-APPL-FV
ɪ-n-gambɪlɪ
AUG-10-monkey

'They opened those little bottles and threw them at the monkeys.' [Thieving monkeys]

(40) Instrument:
ʊ-n-nyambala i-kʊ-lond-igw-a   ʊ-kʊ-j-a   n=ii-kʊmbʊlʊ
AUG-1-man   1-PRS-want-PASS-FV AUG-15-be(come)-FV COM=5-hoe
ly-ake   ɪ-ly-a   **kʊ-lɪm-ɪl-a.**   ɪ-n-gwego ɪ-j-aa
5-POSS.SG AUG-5-ASSOC 15-farm-APPL-FV AUG-9-spear AUG-9-ASSOC
kʊ-las-ɪl-a.   ɪɪ-sengo   ɪ-j-aa   **kʊ-seng-el-a**   ...
15-stab-APPL-FV AUG-sickle(9) AUG-9-ASSOC 15-chop-APPL-FV

'A man is required to have his hoe for farming with. A spear for stabbing. A sickle for clearing with ...' [Types of tools in the home]

(41) Manner:[10]
ʊ-swe   tʊ-ka-pɪliike   a-ka-jʊni   a-ka   mu-no
AUG-1PL 1PL-12-hear.PFV AUG-12-bird AUG-PROX.12 18-DEM

ki-kw-ɩmb-ɩl-a
12-PRS-sing-APPL-FV

'We have heard how the little bird is singing.' [Man and his in-law]

(42) Reason:
Pakyɩndɪ a-alɪ-n-kalal-**iile**   fiijo   ʊ-n-kasi
P.   1-PST-1-be(come)_angry-APPL.PFV INTENS AUG-1-wife
kʊ-m-bombo ɪ-si   a-a-si-bomb-ile ɪ-li-sikʊ   lɪ-la
17-10-work   AUG-PROX.10 1-PST-10-do-PFV AUG-5-day 5-DIST

'Pakyindi got very angry with his wife for what she had done that day.'
[Sokoni and Pakyindi]

An applicative is sometimes found with an indefinite locative or directional
meaning 'somewhere; someplace', as in (43–45).

(43) kʊ-m-malɪɪkɪsyo ɪɪ-sofu   jɪ-lɪnkw-igal-a   ʊ-lʊ-komaano. po
      17-3-end   AUG-elephant(9) 9-NARR-close-FV AUG-11-meeting then
      ɪ-fi-nyamaana fy-osa **fi-lɪnkʊ-bal-an-ɪl-a**
      AUG-8-animal 8-all   8-NARR-shine-RECP-APPL-FV

'Finally Elephant closed the meeting. All the animals dispersed.' [Hare
and Chameleon]

(44) **jɪ-lɪnkw-ag-an-ɪl-a**   n=ɪ-m-bwa   ɪ-jɪ   jɪ-l-iile
      9-NARR-find-RECP-APPL-FV COM=AUG-9-dog AUG-PROX.9 9-eat-PFV
      ɪɪ-nyama
      AUG-meat(9)

'He [somewhere on his way] met the dog that had eaten the meat.' [Dogs
laughed at each other]

(45) kɪ-laabo   ɪ-kɪ-ngɪ   Sokoni a-lɪnkʊ-bʊʊk-a kangɪ **kʊ-kʊ-kʊng-ɪl-a**
      7-tomorrow AUG-7-other S.   1-NARR-go-FV   again 17-15-tie-APPL-FV
      ɪɪ-ng'ombe
      AUG-cow(10)

'The next day Sokoni went again to tie the cows [someplace].' [Sokoni
and Pakyindi]

In many verbs the applicative has become lexicalized with a divergent meaning, with or without an increase in valency:

---

[10]The expression of manner is a common extension of locative class 18.

(46)   *angalıla*   'tease, mock'   < *angala*   i.a. 'be well, converse'
       ımıla   'preside'   < *ıma*   'stand, stop'
       lagıla   'enforce; dictate; rule'   < *laga*   'bid farewell'
       manyila   'learn'   < *manya*   'know'
       sookela   'appear at; happen'   < *sooka*   'leave'

4.2.7 Productive Passive

The productive passive extension has the shape -*igw*. While the category of passive rather belongs to the inflectional than the derivational domain, it is discussed at this place because it fills the pre-final slot of the verb template, just as other verbal extensions.

(47)   *bomba*   'do; work'   > *bombigwa*   'be done; be worked'
       ega   'take; marry'   > *egigwa*   'be taken; be married'
       senga   'chop'   > *sengigwa*   'be chopped'

When the passive follows one of the causative extensions, the resultant vowel remains short:

(48)   *fumusigwa*   (°fum-ʊk-i-igw-a)   'be announced'
       sofigwa   (°sob-i-igw-a)   'be mislead'
       taamigwa   (°taam-i-igw-a)   'be troubled'
       manyisigwa   (°many-ısi-igw-a)   'be taught sthg.'

The passive of monosyllabic verbs is formed by inserting -*ıl*/-*el* between the root and the passive extension. See §4.2.1 on vowel alternations.

(49)   *pa*   'give'   > *peeligwa*
       mwa   'shave'   > *mweligwa*
       nwa   'drink'   > *nweligwa*
       lya   'eat'   > *lıılıgwa*
       sya   'grind'   > *syeligwa*

For *pa* 'give', a variant *peegwa* exists, while for *lya* 'eat' there is a variant form *lııgwa* (see §6.4.2.2 for the perfective stems of these verbs).[11] The speakers consulted preferred the regular forms *peeligwa* and *lıılıgwa*, which are also the only ones found in the textual data.

---

[11] According to Berger (1938: 212f), *lııgwa* is semantically restricted to human beings being eaten by beasts of prey. This could not be confirmed by the present data and is contradicted by Berger's (1933) own text collection, where on page 122 it is found in reference to beans being eaten by birds.

The original or underlying subject of the passive can be introduced by a pro-clitic form of the comitative *na*:[12]

(50) jo   a-a-pon-ile   kʊsita   kʊ-seng-**igw**-a   **n=ʊ-mw-ene**
      REF.1 1-PST-save-PFV without 15-chop-PASS-FV COM=AUG-1-owner
      ka-aja   ʊ-jʊ   a-a-kol-ile   ıı-sengo
      12-homestead AUG-PROX.1 1-PST-hold-PFV AUG-sickle(9)

      'He was saved without being cut by the owner of the house, who held a sickle.' [Wage of the thieves]

(51) ı-kı-siba   ı-kyo   kı-sisya   kangı kı-syʊngʊʊtıl-**iigwe**
      AUG-7-pond AUG-REF-8 8-frightening again 8-surround-PASS.PFV
      n=ı-fy-amba   na a-m-ıısi   ga-ake   ma-sisya
      COM=AUG-8-mountain COM AUG-6-water 6-POSS.SG 6-frightening

      'That pond is frightening. It is surrounded by mountains and its water is frightening.' [Selfishness kills]

With locative subjects, passives of intransitive verbs can be formed. This yields an impersonal meaning:

(52) paa-sokoni   pi-kʊ-jweg-igw-a
      16-market(9)(<SWA) 16-PRS-shout-PASS-FV

      'At the market, there is shouting.' [ET]

(53) kʊ-ka-aja   kʊ-my-ınʊ kʊ-kʊ-hobok-igw-a   fiijo
      17-12-homestead 17-4-POSS.1PL 17-PRS-be(come)_happy-PASS-FV INTENS

      'At our home, they rejoice much.' [ET]

(54) n-nyumba mu-la mu-kʊ-mog-igw-a
      18-house(9) 18-DIST 18-PRS-dance-PASS-FV

      'In that house, there is dancing.' [ET]

For a discussion of the syntax of the passive see Lusekelo (2012). Nyakyusa has symmetric passives (see e.g. Bresnan & Moshi 1990): Both objects of three-argument-verb can be promoted to subject in passivization. The following examples illustrate this with objects occupying various semantic roles.

---

[12]In the variety described by Schumann (1899: 35) and Endemann (1914: 88), the agent/force of the passive is introduced by the locative class 17 *kʊ-*. In elicitation this was rejected as agent marking and only accepted with a locational reading.

(55) a. Active voice:

i-kʊ-ba-pɪɪj-ɪl-a   ɪ-fi-ndʊ   a-ba-heesya

1-PRS-2-cook-APPL-FV AUG-8-food AUG-2-foreigner

'S/he cooks food for the guests.'

b. Passive voice, theme as subject:

ɪ-fi-ndʊ   fi-kʊ-pɪɪj-ɪl-igw-a   a-ba-heesya

AUG-8-food 8-PRS-cook-APPL-PASS-FV AUG-2-foreigner

'The food is cooked for the guests.'

c. Passive voice, beneficiary as subject:

a-ba-heesya   bi-kʊ-pɪɪj-ɪl-igw-a   ɪ-fi-ndʊ

AUG-2-foreigner 2-PRS-cook-APPL-PASS-FV AUG-8-food

'(The) food is cooked for the guests.'[13]

(56) a. Active voice:

i-kʊ-kolog-el-a   ʊ-n-tingo   ɪ-fi-ndʊ

1-PRS-stir-APPL-FV AUG-3-wooden_spoon AUG-8-food

'S/he stirs (the) food with a/the spoon.'

b. Passive voice, theme as subject:

ɪ-fi-ndʊ   fi-kʊ-kolog-el-igw-a   ʊ-n-tingo

AUG-8-food 8-PRS-stir-APPL-PASS-FV AUG-3-wooden_spoon

'(The) food is stirred with a/the spoon.'

c. Passive voice, instrument as subject:

ʊ-n-tingo   gʊ-kʊ-kolog-el-igw-a ɪ-fi-ndʊ

AUG-3-wooden_spoon 3-PRS-stir-APPL-PASS-FV AUG-8-food

'A/the spoon is used to stir (the) food.'

(57) a. Active voice:

ʊ-mw-ana i-kʊ-sop-el-a   ɪ-m-bwa a-ma-bwe

AUG-1-child 1-PRS-throw-APPL-FV AUG-9-dog AUG-6-stone

'A/the child throws stones at a/the dog.'

b. Passive voice, theme as subject:

a-ma-bwe gi-kʊ-sop-el-igw-a   ɪ-m-bwa

AUG-6-stone 6-PRS-throw-APPL-PASS-FV AUG-9-dog

'Stones are thrown at a/the dog.'

c. Passive voice, goal as subject:

ɪ-m-bwa   jɪ-kʊ-sop-el-igw-a   a-ma-bwe
AUG-9-dog 9-PRS-throw-APPL-PASS-FV AUG-6-stone

'A/the dog is thrown stones at.' [all examples elicited]

4.2.8 Fossilized Passive

For Proto-Bantu, the passive extension has been reconstructed with two allo-morphs *-ʊ/-*ibʊ, the latter of which came to be used only with vowel-final bases (Schadeberg 2003a: 78). While the reflex of the longer passive extension is pro-ductive in Nyakyusa (§4.2.7), the short allomorph is only found in a relatively small number of lexicalized cases.[14] These have in most cases undergone a se-mantic shift, as shown in the following examples.

(58) *gogwa*   'dream; have vision' < *goga* 'kill; destroy'
 komwa 'sob'   < *koma* 'hit'
 logwa 'copulate'   < *loga* 'bewitch'
 milwa 'drown'   < *mila* 'swallow; devour'
 pondwa 'fail to; miss'   < *ponda* 'forge'
 tolwa   'be burdened, weak' < *tola* 'defeat'

Some of these fossilized passives are transitive:

(59) *ibwa*   'forget (tr.)'   < *iba*   'steal'
 syʊkwa 'miss sadly (tr.)' < *syʊka* 'be resurrected'

For some of these short passives, no underived base is available, but commu-tations can be found in most cases (60). With other verbs that appear from their shape to be fossilized passives, neither is attested and it may be questionable whether diachronically these verbs constitute passives at all (61). However, all of these verbs except *ilaamwa* pattern together with fossilized passives in the formation of their passive stems; see §6.4.2.2.

---

[13]This example created some amusement, as it also allows for a reading of the subject being the instrument, hence cannibalism.

[14]Schumann (1899: 36) observes for a number of stems that "[s]ome verbs are only formally passives, but also concerning formation of the perfect deviate from the regular passive form (deponentia)" (translated from the original German, BP). See Good (2007) for a discussion of deponency in Bantu.

(60) *fukwa*   'be full beyond capacity' cf. *fukula* 'dig up'
     sulwa   'dare to, presume'   cf. *sulula* 'pour'
     keelwa   'be plentiful'   no **keela* or commutations
     kunwa   'be in great need'   no **kuna* or commutations

(61) *ilaamwa* 'disregard, doubt'   no **(i)laama* attested
     nyonywa 'long for, desire'   no **nyonya* attested
     miimwa   'crave, envy'   < **miim* 'sprinkle'?

The fossilized passive extension often co-occurs with the applicative (62). It is further apparent in a number of deverbal nouns (63).

(62) *agɪlwa*   'diminish (by); lack'   < *aga*   'diminish (tr.)'
     kʊbɪlwa   'suffer'   < *kʊba*   'beat; ring'
     lakɪlwa   'choke (on)'   cf. *ʊlʊlaka* 'great thirst'
     tumukɪlwa   'be(come) short on; late for'   cf. *tumula* 'cut; come to decision'
     ʊmɪlwa   'be thirsty (for)'   < *ʊma*   'dry; wither'

(63) *ʊmfwalwa*   'clothing, dress'   < *fwala*   'dress, wear'
     iikolwa   'shell'   < *kola*   'grasp, hold'
     ɪkɪsʊʊjwa   'porridge from maize milk'   < *sʊʊja*   'filter, strain'
     ʊntʊmwa   'slave, servant'   < *tʊma*   'send'

When asked in elicitation to form true passives of fossilized passives, the language assistants replaced the fossilized extension (or what is treated as such) with the productive long passive extension:

(64) *ibwa*   'forget'   > *ibigwa*   'be forgotten'
     milwa   'drown'   > *miligwa*   'be drowned at' (LOC subject)
     miimwa   'crave, envy'   > *miimigwa*   'be craved for'
     ilaamwa   'disregard, doubt' > *ilaamigwa*   'be disregarded, doubted'

However, this was felt to be an artificial device, and with some roots it creates ambiguity (65). Topicalization of the patient/theme through fronting (66) was suggested as more natural for such verb constructions.

(65) a. *ɪngamu jangʊ jɪ-kw-ib-igw-a nagwe*
       1. 'My name is being forgotten by him/her.'
       2. 'My name is being stolen by him/her.' [ET]
    b. *ɪnjosi jɪ-kʊ-gog-igw-a nagwe*
       1. 'A dream is dreamt by him/her.'
       2. 'A dream is killed by him/her.' [ET]

(66) a. ɪ-n-gamu   j-angʋ   i-kʋ-j-iibw-a
AUG-9-name 9-POSS.1SG 1-PRS-9-forget-FV

'(As for) my name, s/he forgets it.' [ET]

  b. ɪ-n-josi   i-kʋ-jɪ-gogw-a
AUG-9-dream 1-PRS-9-dream-FV

'(As for) the dream, s/he dreams it.' [ET]

4.2.9 Neuter

The neuter (also commonly called *stative*) extension has the underlying shape -ɪk (allomorphs -ek, -ik; see §4.2.1). The neuter promotes the object of a transitive verb to the subject of a now intransitive verb, which is construed as potentially or factually experiencing a certain state. (67) gives some examples. Further research is needed to determine the productivity and the semantic and syntactic constraints on the use of the neuter.

(67) *malɪka*   'finish (intr.), be finished'   < *mala*   'finish (tr.)'
  manyika   'be known; be famous'   < *manya*   'know'
  nweka   'be drinkable'   < *nwa*   'drink'
  oneka   'gush; be spilled, scattered'   < *ona*   'spill'
  onangɪka   'be(come) spoiled; perish'   < *onanga* 'destroy'
  ongeleka   'increase (intr.)'   < *ongela* 'increase (tr.)'
  swɪlɪka   'be(come) tame'   < *swɪla*   'feed; rear; tame'

At least the following two verbs derived with the neuter extension have idiosyncratic meanings:

(68) *boneka* 'happen; also: appear, be seen' < *bona* 'see'
  silɪka   'faint'   < *sila* 'protest by refusal (tr.)'

Unlike with the passive, the original agent or force of a neuter verb cannot be expressed:

(69) * ʋ-n-nyambala i-kʋ-bon-ek-a   (na=)a-ba-ndʋ
AUG-1-man   1-PRS-see-NEUT-FV (COM=)AUG-2-person

(intended: 'The man is seen by people.')

(70) * ɪ-n-jʋni   si-la   si-kʋ-peeny-ek-a
AUG-10-bird 10-DIST 10-PRS-remove_feathers-NEUT-FV

> (na=)a-ba-kiikʊlʊ
> (COM=)AUG-2-woman
>
> (intended: 'Those birds have their feathers plucked by women.')

(71)   * ɪɪ-nyumba   ɪ-jɪ   jɪ-kʊ-jeng-ek-a
      AUG-house(9) AUG-PROX.9 9-PRS-build-NEUT-FV
      (na=)a-ba-fundi
      (COM=)AUG-2-worker(<SWA)

      (intended: 'This house is being built by workers.')

    With one verb the combination of neuter and passive is attested: *malɪkigwa* 'run out' < *mala* 'finish (tr.)'.

4.2.10 Intensive

The intensive extension has the underlying shape *-ɪlɪl* (and allomorphs, see §4.2.1). It denotes repetition, greater intensity and/or continuity. As the meaning of this extension is very much dependent on the semantics of the underlying verb as well as on the context, it is best illustrated with some examples from texts.

(72)   a-lɪnkw-and-a ʊ-kʊ-pɪɪj-a,   kangɪ a-a-lʊng-ɪliile   kanunu
      1-NARR-start-FV AUG-15-cook-FV again 1-PST-add_spice-INTS.PFV well
      fiijo
      INTENS

      'She started to cook [it] and spiced [it] very well.' [Thieving woman]

(73)   ba-kʊ-tuufiifye fiijo   ʊ-gwe ʊkʊtɪ ʊ-lɪ   n-nunu, looli fi-fy-ɪma
      2-2SG-praise.PFV INTENS AUG-2SG COMP 2SG-COP 1-good but 8-8-thigh
      fy-ako   fi-kɪnd-ɪliile   ʊ-bʊ-nywamu
      8-POSS.2SG 8-pass-INTS.PFV AUG-14-big

      'They have praised you a lot, that you are a good person, but your thighs are too big [lit. have intensively surpassed size].' [Hare and Hippo]

(74)   bo muu~mo   iisib-ɪliile   ʊ-n-kasi   gw-a
      as REDUPL~REF.18 1.be(come)_accustomed-INTS.PFV AUG-1-wife 1-ASSOC
      Pakyɪndɪ, a-lɪnkʊ-bʊʊk-a kʊ-kw-aganil-a n=ʊ-n-nyambala ʊ-jʊ-ngɪ
      P.   1-NARR-go-FV   17-15-meet-FV   COM=AUG-1-man AUG-1-other
      kʊ-ṇ-gʊnda gw-a   ma-jabʊ g-a   ṇ-dʊme   Pakyɪndɪ
      17-3-field   3-ASSOC 6-cassava 6-ASSOC 1-husband P.

      'Just as she was very accustomed to do, Pakyindi's wife went to meet with another man in Pakyindi's cassava field.' [Sokoni and Pakyindi]

(75) ʊ-ne   kʊ-my-angʊ kʊ-no   n-gʊ-fuma,   n-dɪ   malafyale.
      AUG-1SG 17-4-POSS.1SG 17-PROX 1SG-PRS-come_from-FV 1SG-COP chief(1)

      mu-n-geet-**elel**-e=po   panandɪ!
      2PL-1SG-look-INTS-SUBJ=PART a_little

      'At my home where I come from I am a king. You should look at me a
      little!' [Hare and Hippo]

With a number of verbs, the intensive gives an idiosyncratic reading:

(76) *ambɪlɪla*   'receive; entertain guests'   < *amba*   'hold out to receive'
      bombelela   'weed'   < *bomba* 'work; do'
      endelela   'continue'   < *enda*   'walk, travel'
      keetelela   'take care of; watch'   < *keeta* 'watch'
      kʊbɪlɪla   'flap, fan'   < *kʊba*   'beat; ring'
      paatɪlɪla   'prune'   < *paata* 'way of harvesting'
      tabɪlɪla   'stammer'   < *taba*   'extend; crawl'

A handful of verbs feature *-ɪɪl/-eel* (77). Where the underived root is available,
a comparison of meaning suggests that these verbs feature lexicalized intensives
where the first /l/ has dropped out.

(77) *bʊʊkɪɪlwa* 'drown and be carried by water' < *bʊʊka* 'go'
      boteela   'be calm; be settled'   < *bota* 'be calm'
      eleela   'float'
      embeela   'wander; prostitute'
      obeela   'rumble, scorn'
      ogeela   'swim'   < *oga*   'bathe (intr.)'
      tendeela   'peep'

4.2.11 Separative

There are two separative extensions in Nyakyusa, one yielding transitive verbs
(*-ʊl*) and one yielding intransitive ones (*-ʊk*). See §4.2.1 for morphophonological
processes affecting the vowel quality of these extensions. Schadeberg (2003a: 78)
characterizes the abstract semantic core of the separative as "movement out of
some original position". Other common labels in Bantu studies include *reversive*
and *inversive*. Although the separative extensions are essentially unproductive,
derived verbs are frequent in the lexicon. The following list gives some examples:

(78) baalʊla 'widen (tr.)' – baalʊka 'bloss, expand' < baala 'thrive'
baalʊla 'widen (tr.)' – baalʊka 'bloss, expand' < baala 'thrive'
bulutula 'shell corn' – bulutuka 'collapse'
fyogola 'sprain' – fyogoka 'be(come) sprained'
hobola 'free, relax' – hoboka 'be(come) happy'
kingʊla 'uncover' – kingʊka 'be(come) uncovered' < kinga 'cover'
lumbula 'expand' – lumbuka 'stretch, expand'
pagʊla 'force open' – pagʊka 'be(come) dislocated'
pɪndʊla 'convert' – pɪndʊka 'repent' < pɪnda 'bend'
konyola 'break; harvest' – konyoka 'be(come) broken'
tonola 'dab' – tonoka 'bounce'
kuupula 'uproot' – kuupuka 'be uprooted'

As can be observed in (78), there is frequent commutation between the two separative extensions. This is a strong tendency rather than an absolute rule. Other
attested commutations are with the impositive (§4.2.14) and positional (§4.2.13)
extensions. The separative extensions are also found in denominal derivations. If
the underlying stem ends in a first degree vowel, this is elided and the separative
extension surfaces with /u/ (i.e., the height feature is maintained).

(79) biibuka 'be(come) bad, ugly' < biibi 'bad, ugly'
gangʊla 'treat medically, heal' < ʊŋganga 'doctor; healer'
niinuka 'decrease (intr.)' < niini 'little'
pimbʊka 'be(come) short' < pimba 'short'

In a few verbs, two separative extensions are found. With the exception of
sʊngʊlʊla (80), the separative intransitive follows the separative transitive (81).

(80) sʊngʊlʊla 'dissolve' cf. sʊngʊla 'choose; sift'

(81) bululuka 'scatter (intr.)' cf. bulula 'scatter (tr.)'
bunguluka 'toss and turn' < *búng 'wrap up'
kololoka 'slacken' < kola 'grasp, hold'
kunguluka 'foretell, prophecy' < kunga 'pour out'
sololoka 'descend; appear (spirit)' < solola 'prophecy'
sululuka 'drip' cf. sulula 'pour'

4.2.12 Tentive

The tentive extension has the shape -at. It is not productive and relatively few
verbs are found that contain this suffix. Schadeberg (2003a: 77) notes that the
semantic core for this Bantu extension can be stated as "actively making firm

contact". This characterization holds for Nyakyusa in most cases, see the list in
(82). No noticeable pattern of commutation is attested.

(82) *finyatıla*   'put close to'
      fumbata   'enclose in hands or mouth'
      isunyata   'brood; ponder'
      kambatʋla   'grip'
      lalata   'become paralytic'
      pagata   'put in lap, pull to chest; hold child'

4.2.13 Positional

The non-productive positional extension has the shape *-am*. A common semantic
element of assuming a physical posture or position can be observed (Schadeberg
2003a: 75). All Nyakyusa verbs derived by means of the positional extension
are inchoative. The positional appears not to be productive in Nyakyusa. The
following list gives some representative examples.

(83) *alama*   'settle at bottom; duck'
      asama   'gape'
      batama   'be(come) quiet, silent'
      fugama   'kneel'
      kupama   'lie on stomach'
      egama   'lean'

Some positional verbs have their transitive counterpart formed with the combination of the positional and impositive extensions (84), while others replace
the positional with the impositive (85). In a few cases, both devices are attested
without any apparent difference in meaning (86). Further commutations include
the separative (§4.2.11) (87).

(84) Positional plus impositive:
      bılamika   'bend (tr.)'   < *bılama*   'bend (intr.)'
      gundamika 'bend over/down'   < *gundama* 'stoop, incline'
      telamika   'lower'   < *telama*   'be(come) low'

(85) Commutation between positional and impositive:
      batama   'be(come) quiet, silent' cf. *batıka*   'soothe'
      pıngama   'turn sidewards (intr.)' cf. *pıngıka* 'set across'

(86) Commutation as well as additive derivation:

egama	'lean (intr.)'	cf. *egeka*	'lean (tr.)'
		> *egamika*	'lean (tr.)'
sulama	'bend'	cf. *sulɪka*	'turn upside down'
		> *sulamika*	'turn upside down'

(87) Commutation between positional and separative:

alama	'settle at bottom'	cf. *alʊla*	'remove from top'
sulama	'bend'	cf. *suluka*	'descend'
gasama	'open mouth in surprise'	cf. *gasʊka*	'be astonished'

4.2.14 Impositive

The impositive has the underlying shape *-ɪk*. Allomorphs are *-ek*, *-ik* (see §4.2.1; also note the exceptions below). It is thus homophonous to the neuter extension (§4.2.9). The core meaning of the impositive may be paraphrased as "to put (sth.) into some position" (Schadeberg 2003a: 73). The following list provides some examples.

(88)

bambɪka	'arrange in line'	< *bamba*	'stand in line'
bɪɪka	'put; store; calve'	< *bá*	'dwell; be; become'
jubɪka	'dip, soak'		
jumbɪka	'praise'	< *jumba*	'swell (river)'
olobeka	'soak (tr.)'	< *oloba*	'get wet'
ɸubɪka	'soak (tr.)'		
tegeka	'set a trap for'	< *tega*	'trap; catch'

The impositive extension can be considered the transitive counterpart to the positional extension, with which a number of commutations are attested (see §4.2.13). Other commutations include the separative (89). In one verb, the impositive is found as the transitive counterpart to the extensive; see §4.2.15.

(89)

anika	'set out to dry'	cf. *anula*	'remove from drying'
baatɪka	'arrange; fix'	cf. *baatʊla*	'offload, unload'
bambɪka	'arrange'	cf. *bambʊla*	'peel'
ɸyɪka	'insert'	cf. *ɸyʊla*	'remove'
lɪmbɪka	'accumulate'	cf. *lɪmbʊla*	'serve out; gather honey'
lʊndɪka	'pile up'	cf. *lʊndʊla*	'take cows out; divide'
sulɪka	'turn upside down'	cf. *sulula*	'pour'

In a few cases, what appears to be the impositive extension is found with a first degree vowel /i/ that cannot be accounted for by any regularity:

(90)   ɪmika   'erect; bring to halt; respect'   < ɪma   'stand (up), stop'
                                                     cf. ɪmɪla   'preside'
        ʊmika   'dry (tr.)'   < ʊma   'dry; wither'
        binika   'spoil, ruin, destroy'   < bina   'fall sick'?
                                                     < bini   'malicious'?
                                                     cf. binɪsya   'make sick'

        kitika   'set up; stick into ground'

4.2.15 Extensive

The extensive extension has the shape -*al*. It is unproductive in Nyakyusa. There is no overarching semantic element for verbs derived with this extension. As observed by Schadeberg (2003a: 77), there is a certain tendency for it to occur with verbs denoting two semantic fields: being in a spread-out position (91) and debilitation or illness (92). Some verbs with miscellaneous meanings are given in (93). No reoccurring pattern of commutation is attested in the data.

(91)   *bagala*   'carry load on shoulder'
        tʊʊgala   'get seated, sit; live, inhabit; stay'
        twala   'carry load, bring'

(92)   *fulala*   'be(come) hurt, injured'
        kalala   'be(come) angry annoyed'
        katala   'be(come) tired, exhausted'
        kangala   'be(come) old and worn'
        lemala   'be(come) crippled, disabled'

(93)   *angala*   'be well, feel fine; converse, talk, be in good company'
        langala   'glisten, glitter, shine'
        niongala   'be(come) bent, crooked, twisted'
        syala   'remain'

In two verbs, what seems to be a reduplicated extensive suffix was found. One of these has the combination of extensive plus impositive (§4.2.14) as its transitive counterpart:

(94)   *lambalala* 'lie down, sleep'   cf. *lambalɪka*   'make lie down, put to bed'
        tambalala 'lie flat'

4.3 Combinations of verbal extensions

Often more than one verbal extension appears on a single verb base. In the follow-ing sub-sections, some generalizations over the respective order of morphemes will be given (§4.3.1), followed by a discussion of the derivation of pluractionals by means of combining the reciprocal/associative and the causative (§4.3.2) and a discussion of the shape of applicativized causatives (§4.3.3).

4.3.1 Morpheme order

When several extensions appear in a verbal base, their respective ordering is sub-ject to several restrictions. The group of unproductive extensions appear closest to the root and follow the ordering illustrated in Figure 4.1.

Positional	Impositive
Extensive	Separative
	Tentive

Figure 4.1: Order of unproductive verbal extensions

The following examples illustrate the attested combinations of unproductive extensions:[15]

(95) a. Positional and impositive:
        gundamika 'bend over/down (tr.)'
      b. Extensive and impositive:
        lambalıka 'put to bed'
      c. Extensive and separative:
        nyagalʋka 'get well (health)'

The more productive extensions follow the unproductive ones. The passive (including the fossilized passive) always occupies the last position.

(96) a. Fossilized passive:

kʋbɪlwa	(°kʋb-ɪl-ʋ-a)	'suffer'
ʋmɪlwa	(°ʋm-ɪl-ʋ-a)	'be thirsty (for)'
agɪlwa	(°ag-ɪl-ʋ-a)	'diminish (by); lack'
tumukɪlwa	(°tum-ʋk-ɪl-ʋ-a)	'be(come) short on; late for'

---

[15]The verb *pangalatʋla* 'destroy by taking part after part out' (cf. *pangʋla* 'dismantle') has the sequence *-al-at-ʋl*, which resembles the combination of extensive plus tentive plus separative. It is unclear if this is a chance resemblance or a case of three unproductive extensions.

b. Productive passive:

bɪɪkɪligwa	(°bɪɪk-ɪl-igʊ-a)	'be put for'
meleligwa	(°mel-ɪl-igʊ-a)	'owe'
bombeleligwa	(°bomb-ɪlɪl-igʊ-a)	'be weeded'
manyisigwa	(°many-ɪsi-igʊ-a)	'be taught'
fumusigwa	(°fum-uk-i-igʊ-a)	'be announced'
ɪmikigwa	(°ɪm-ɪk-igʊ-a)	'be respected'
saamikɪsigwa	(°saam-ɪsi-ɪl-igʊ-a)	'be made exile to'

A causative *-i*, either the short causative₁ *-i* or the last segment of a split-up long causative₂ *-ɪs-i*, normally occupies the last position within the base, unless it is followed by the passive.[16]

(97) *fulasania* (°fulal\<an>i-a)   'hurt each other'
      ʊlɪkɪsania (°ʊl-ɪkɪs\<an>i-a) 'sell each other sth.'

Apart from these generalizations, the ordering of the productive extensions in Nyakyusa requires a dedicated study of its own, given the high number of logical possibilities and the question of how morpheme order, meaning and syntax relate to each other. As Hyman (2002) points out, in many Bantu languages the relative order of certain verbal extensions follows a default pattern, which can have both a compositional reading (morpheme order reflecting semantic scope) and a non-compositional one, while the opposite order exclusively receives the compositional reading. Further, Lusekelo (2013) indicates that the relative position of the applicative in Nyakyusa may be linked to the semantic role of the argument it licenses.

Lastly, a few cases of doubled verbal extensions are attested in the data. In most cases it is unclear what the semantic and syntactic functions of these are. Doubling of a verbal extension may serve the purpose of fulfilling the requirement for both a default morpheme order and a compositional order at the same time (Hyman 2002),

(98) a. Two applicatives:

lɪɪlanila	'eat together with sb.'	<	*lya*	'eat'
lwɪlanila	'fight with each other for'	<	*lwa*	'fight'

    b. Two reciprocals/associatives:

sopanilana	'throw to each other'	<	*sopa*	'throw'

---

[16]See §4.2.2 for the process of spirantization induced by the causative₁ *-i*, and §4.3.3 for the formation of applicativized causatives.

c. Two causatives:

tiimɪsyanisya 'make each other herd'[17]   < *tiima* 'herd'

4.3.2 Complex derivations: pluractional

The combination of the reciprocal and causative extensions often gives a pluractional reading. The range of possible meanings includes re-iteration, intensification or the involvement of multiple subjects or objects (also cf. Schumann 1899: 79). This combination is used on transitive bases and verbs of motion (99a, 99b), the only attested exception being the intransitive *sulumania* 'afflict, be sorry'. With verbs denoting 'to return', this combination gives a cyclic reading. When the short causative *-i* is used, sometimes spirantization takes place. This seems not to be predictable and is probably a function of time depth and lexicalization. Concerning the length of the vocalic segment in the reciprocal, see §4.2.5.

Botne (2008: 86) and Gray (n.d.) observe a similar pluractional function of *an-y-* / *an-i-* in neighbouring Ndali and Kisi G67 respectively and Kisseberth (2003: 557) for Makhuwa P30 gives *ú-hókól-an-yáán-ih-a* 'to go and come back the same day'. All these suggest that the combination of the causative and the reciprocal yielding pluractionality might have a wider distribution in Bantu.

The intransitive counterpart to the pluractional has the shape *-anik* and can be analysed as consisting of the reciprocal *-an* and neuter *-ɪk* extensions. It is used on transitive as well as intransitive bases (99c).

(99)   a. Pluractionals derived from transitive verbs:

buuta	'cut; slaughter'	> *buutania*	'cut into pieces'
		> *buutanika*	'break into pieces (intr.)'
joba	'speak to/about'	> *jobesania*	'dispute about'
		> *jobanika*	'speak much'
lɔnga	'add spice;	> *lɔngaania*	'join, connect (tr.)'
	put together'	> *lɔngɪsaania*	'join, connect (tr.)'
		> *lɔngaanika*	'be confused'
menya	'break; chop'	> *menyania*	'chop into pieces'
		> *menyanika*	'be chopped into pieces'
nyamba	'throw'	> *nyambania*	'scatter'
		> *nyambanika*	'disperse, be scattered'
pinya	'bind; detain; fix'	> *pinyania*	'splice; tie together'
		> *pinyanika*	'be spliced; tied manifold'

---

[17]This example was elicited on the basis of Lusekelo (2012).

b. Pluractionals derived from verbs of motion:

buja	'return (to)'	> bujɪsania	'go & return (same day)'
		> busania	'go & return (same day)'
gomoka	'return; reprove'	> gomosania	'go & return (same day)'
kɪnda	'pass'	> kɪɪsania	'pass by'

c. Pluractionals derived from intransitive verbs:

jeeta	'turn pale'	> jeetanika	'faint'
lɪla	'cry; sound; mourn'	> lɪlanika	'complain'
tʊʊja	'pant; breathe out'	> tʊʊjanika	'pant heavily'

4.3.3 Applicativized causatives

Applicativized causatives have a special form -(ɪ)kɪsi / -(ɪ)kɪfi. The alternations in vowel height as described in §4.2.1 apply. When they are derived from a causativized base subject to spirantization (see §4.2.2) -kɪsi / -kɪfi is suffixed to the underlying non-causativized base, with /k/ replacing the base-final consonant. The fricative is /f/ if the replaced consonant is a labial, and is /s/ elsewhere. In other words, it is the fricative that causative spirantization would produce.

(100)
buja	'return'	> busya	'return (tr.)'	> bukɪsya	'return (tr.) + APPL'
fulala	'be hurt'	> fulasya	'hurt'	> fulakɪsya	'hurt + APPL'
oga	'bathe'	> osya	'baptise'	> okesya	'baptise + APPL'
pyʊpa	'get warm'	> pyʊfya	'warm up'	> pyʊkɪfya	'warm up + APPL'

If the causativized base is derived by causative₁ -i following non-spirantizing consonants or if it is derived by causative₂ -isi, a suffix -ɪkɪsi is attached to the non-causativized base:

(101)
saama	'migrate'	> saam-y-a	'transfer'	> saam-ikɪsy-a	'transfer + APPL'
ʊla	'buy'	> ʊl-ɪsi-a	'sell'	> ʊl-ɪkɪsy-a	'sell to/for/at'

This uncommon phonological realization of applicativized causatives has been noticed from the first treatments of Nyakyusa on. Meinhof (1966), as well as Schumann (1899), mentions this and Endemann (1900) presents an attempt at a purely phonological explanation. Unfortunately, Endemann does not discuss cases of the suffixing of -ɪkɪsi after nasals, which cannot be accounted for by his approach. In his later grammar sketch, he further gives a rather curious explanation in which he tries to link this phenomenon to distal/itive ka- (Endemann 1914: 51).

The examples given by Botne (2008: 76) suggest a comparable formation in Ndali. Wolff (1905: 63) describes a similar phenomenon for neighbouring Kinga, where applicativized causativizes take the shape -*ihitsa*, although without replacing the final consonant.

Alhough non-transparent from a synchronic point of view, the morphophonology of applicativized causatives finds a diachronic explanation in a sequence of analogy formations, as Hyman (2003) plausibly illustrates (Berger 1938: 266f develops a parallel interpretation). In this scenario, the point of departure would have been a stage in which infixing of the applicative, together with a cyclic application of spirantization (thus e.g. *sook-a* > *soos-i-a* > *soos-el-i-a* > **soos-es-i-a*), took place, followed by despirantizationspirantization of the root-final consonant (> *sook-es-i-a*). See Nyamwezi F22 (Schadeberg & Maganga 1992: 20ff) for a comparable case. In the next stage, despirantizationspirantization to /k/ was generalized; note that spirantization leads to a merger of the six non-labials affected. In the case of non-labials, one possible interpretation of the sequence /kɪs/ would be that the final consonant spirantized in the first place was being post-posed. This re-analysis was then extended to cases of labials, yielding -*kɪfi*. Once established, this pattern of applicatived causativizes surfacing as /kɪ{s, f}i/ was extended to non-spirantizing consonants (introducing what Hyman labels an "extra k") and thus fully generalized.

The main source for Hyman's interpretation is the chronolect described by Schumann (1899), in which causative$_1$ -*i* is the most productive of the two derivations. The present data show that Nyakyusa has gone one step further, extending this pattern to causative$_2$ -*isi* and thus generalizing the requirement that any applicativized causative must surface with the sequence /kɪ{s, f}/ (and respective vowel alternations).[18]

4.4 Denominal verbs

A number of verbal stems are derived from nominals (including adjectives) by means of suffixation. This seems not to be a particularly productive process. Three monosegmental suffixes are found in denominal verbs: while -*p* yields intransitive verbs (102), -*l* seems to yield only transitives (104). -*k* (103) is not

---

[18]Lusekelo (2012) also discusses the shape of applicativized causatives in Nyakyusa. Though he rejects Hyman's (2003) analysis, at no point throughout his work does he give either an alternative reconstruction for the diachronic origin of these forms, or a motivated explanation for their spread to non-spirantizing bases and forms containing the long causative$_2$ -*isi*.

associated with any specific valency. Further, the separative extensions are employed in noun/adjective to verb derivation; see §4.2.11.

(102) kalɪpa   'be(come) fermented, sour' < kalɪ   'spicy; strict; sour'
       kiikʊlʊpa   'grow up to puberty (girl)' < ʊnkiikʊlʊ   'woman'
       kʊʊlʊpa   'become old and worn'   < kʊʊlʊ   'old'
       tʊngʊlʊpa   'lie'   < ʊbʊtʊngʊlʊ   'lie'
       tungupa   'lie'   < ʊlʊtungu   'testicle'[19]

(103) bulika   'hit with the fist'   < ɪkɪbuli   'fist'
       mulika   'glow'   < ɪɪmuli   'light, brightness'
       tolika   'drip'   < iitoli   'drop'
       pafuka   'be greedy'   < pafu   'greedy'
       tiitʊka   'be(come) dark, black'   < tiitʊ   'black'

(104) heelula   'abuse'   < iiheelu   'abusive language'
       tusula   'shoot'   < ɪndusu   'gun, rifle'

4.5 Partial reduplication

A number of verbs begin with two identical sequences of consonant and vowel. For many of these, the path of derivation is hard to track down. Possible sources are partial reduplication of a verbal base, reduplicated nouns or ideophones. See also Schadeberg (2003a: 79) for a pan-Bantu perspective and Seidel (2008: 262) for a similar observation in Yeyi R41. For some of these verbs, a semantic element of repetition, oscillation or intensification can be observed. Examples are given in (105), ordered by the attested patterns of reduplication.

(105) a. Shape $C(G_1)V_1.C(G_1)V_1C_2$:
           fufula   'endure, tolerate'   < fula 'hurt'?
           lelema   'have shaky voice'
           tetema   'shake, shiver; be afraid; care for'
           bwabwata   'blab, talk nonsense'
           bwabwaja   'blab, talk nonsense'
           mwemweka   'glitter'   cf. mweka 'glow'

---

[19]While 'testicle' > 'lie' might at first seem an implausible metaphor, note that much of Nyakyusa profanity is based on body parts; see Meyer (1989: 146).

b. Shape $C_1V_1.C_1V_1V_1C_2$:

boboota   'grunt'
hohoola   'jeer, laugh at'
ng'ong'oola   'grimace at'
ng'ung'uuta   'whine'
nyinyiila   'squint'
sisiila   'close (eyes)'
sosoola   'point finger at'

The list in (106) illustrates verbs containing reduplication of the initial syllable as well as further suffixes.

(106)   a. Shape $C_1(G_1)V_1.C_1(G_1)V_1C_2$:

kakajʊla   'break by chewing'< kajʊla   'force open'
myamyasya   'smoothen out'   < myasya 'smear, spread'
nyenyemusya   'excite'
i-ng'weng'wesya   'grumble'
papatana   'be squeezed together'< pát   'hold'
popotoka   'bend, twist'   < pota   'steer; twist'
popotola   'strain; strangle'
sasanusya   'overturn; annul' < sanusya 'altern'
sosomela   'protude'

b. Shape $C_1V_1.NC_1V_1C_2$:

jenjelʊka   'dawn'
junjumala   'crouch'

c. Shapes $C_1V_1.C_1V_1V_1C_2 / C_1V_1.C_1V_1NC_2$:

bobonjala   'be(come) flat'
babanjala   'be(come) flat'
luluutila   'ululate'
nyonyoofya   'attract desire'   < nyoofya 'allure'
pʊpʊʊtɪka   'stagger'

5 Verb categorization

This chapter deals with the classification of verbal expressions according to their inherent aspectual potential (Aristotelian aspect). The focus is on lexical verbs, although some observations on the phrasal level are also included. After a short introduction to the distinction between inchoative and non-inchoative verbs (§5.1), the language internal diagnostics for distinguishing verb classes will be presented (§5.2), followed by a discussion of each Nyakyusa verb class (§5.3).

5.1 Introduction

As mentioned in §1.4.3.1, an essential lexical distinction in many, if not all, Bantu languages, is the one between inchoative and non-inchoative verbs, i.e. those verbs that encode a change-of-state as well as a resultant state on the one hand, and those that do not on the other hand. A prototypical case of an inchoative verb in Nyakyusa is *kalala* 'be(come) angry'. With the aspectually imperfective (§6.5.1) this verb denotes an ongoing change-of-state (1) (habitual/generic and futurate readings aside). When used with the present perfective (§6.5.3), *kalala* typically has a stative meaning of being angry (2).

(1) i-kʊ-kalal-a
   1-PRS-be(come)_angry-FV
   'S/he is becoming angry.'

(2) a-kaleele
   1-be(come)_angry.PFV
   (Default reading:) 'S/he is angry.'

At first sight, this might seem like the result of a conversational implicature: stating that one has become angry normally serves to indicate one's state of anger. That this resultant state is in fact part of the verb's lexical meaning becomes clear by contrasting it with a non-inchoative verb like *fika* 'arrive'. Like *kalala*, this verb has a coming-to-be reading in the (3). However, when used in the present perfective it does not denote a state (4).

(3) i-kʊ-fik-a
     1-PRS-arrive-FV
     'S/he is arriving.'

(4) a-fik-ile
     1-arrive-PFV
     'S/he has arrived.'

The distinction between inchoative and non-inchoative verbs is not a mere question of translation, but has morphosyntactic repercussions. An inchoative like *kalala* 'be(come) angry' that is inflected for perfective aspect can stand as the complement of the persistive auxiliary (§6.6.2), where it denotes a continuing state (5). A non-inchoative verb like *fika* 'arrive' is not licensed in this construction (6), as it does not have a resultant state as part of its lexical meaning. Instead, to denote a persistent state, it is necessary to resort to other grammatical devices, in this case the existential construction (ex. 7; see §10.2.3).

(5) a-kaalɪ a-kaleele
     1-PERS 1-be(come)_angry.PFV
     'S/he is still angry.'

(6) * a-kaalɪ a-fik-ile
       1-PERS 1-arrive-PFV
     (intended: 'S/he is still present due to his/her arrival.')

(7) a-kaalɪ a-li=po
     1-PERS 1-COP=16
     'S/he is still present.'

Botne & Kershner (2000: 165), in a discusssion of Zulu S42, summarize inchoative verbs as expressing "a change of condition or location of the experiencer or patient". For a verb denoting a mental state such as anger, this is fairly transparent from the perspective of English as the metalanguage. It is important to notice, however, that inchoative verbs are not limited to typical experiencer verbs.For instance, 'to carry', an activity in English, is expressed by an inchoative verb in Nyakyusa (8). The distinction between inchoative and non-inchoative verbs is thus central to tense and aspect inflection in Nyakyusa.

(8) (a-kaalɪ) a-twele   ɪ-kɪ-kapʊ
     (1-PERS) 1-carry.PFV AUG-7-basket
     'S/he is (still) carrying a/the basket.'

The basic opposition between inchoative and non-inchoative verbs will serve as a guiding line through most parts of the description of tense and grammatical aspect in Nyakyusa. A closer look, however, reveals more fine-grained distinctions and patternings of verbs. This is the topic of the following sections, which are intended as a first systematic approach towards Aristotelian aspect in Nyakyusa, ultimately to be enhanced by further research, and which is among the first such analyses for Bantu languages.[1] The analysis presented here is based on some 50 verbs which have been tested in targeted elicitation with at least two speakers each. Where available, uses in texts were also considered.

5.2 Diagnostic criteria

Based on the tenets of radical selection theories of aspect (§1.4.3.1), a combination of various language-specific semantic and syntactic diagnostic criteria have been applied to determine the lexicalized phasal structure of the verbs in question. Some of the diagnostics are adapted from Botne's (2008) and Kershner's (2002) work on Ndali and Sukwa, others are taken from the typological literature or have emerged during the course of the present study.

As indicated in the previous section, only inchoative verbs, that is those verbs that lexicalize a Coda state, are compatible with the syntactic frame of the persistive aspect auxiliary plus a complement inflected for perfective aspect. Another diagnostic criterion is the possible readings with the imperfective simple present (§6.5.1), or, more precisely, whether a progressive reading is available. As an extension of this, this study tested whether the verbs in question allow for a single event reading in the syntactic frame of the persistive aspect auxiliary plus the simple present, and if so, which phase of the eventuality this denotes: A persistent process is taken as an indication of an extended Nucleus phase, whereas the lack of such a reading, but the possibility to coerce a reading of a persistently sustained result state is taken as secondary evidence for the lexical encoding of the result state. Related to the possible readings in the simple present is the verb's behaviour with the periphrastic progressive (§6.6.1), which shows mostly similar, but slightly different selectional properties.

---

[1]Lusekelo (2013) includes a short discussion of the topic in Nyakyusa, which unfortunately is highly unsystematic and does not include any diagnostic criteria. Concerning other Bantu languages see Mreta (1998) on Chasu G20, who applies a variation of Breu and Sasse's framework (§1.4.3.1), Fleisch (2000) on Luchazi K13, also within the Breu-Sasse framework and Kershner (2002), Botne et al. (2006), Seidel (2008), Botne (2008) on Sukwa M301, Saamia JE34, Yeyi R41, Ndali M301, respectively. The latter authors apply Botne and Kershner's approach to Aristotelian aspect.

A further diagnostic criterion for the classification of a given verb is its compatibility with the time-span phrase 'take X time'. Only telic verbs, that is, verbs that encode an inherent endpoint or change-of-state, are predicted to appear readily in this construction, although repair readings are available for other types of verbs (see e.g. Dowty 1979: 57).

Further indications of the phasal structure of lexical verbs are found in their behaviour with phasal verbs ('Aktionsart verbs' or 'aspectualizers'), which patterns in significant ways with the tense-aspect constructions presented so far. The ingressive auxiliary *anda* 'begin, start' denotes the beginning of the state-of-affairs encoded in the lexical verb. This can be a subphase of a single occurrence as well as the beginning of multiple occurrences. In the latter sense it can also be used to single out the first of various occurrences (9). Similarly, the auxiliaries *mala* 'finish' (10) and *leka* 'cease, stop' (11) can refer to the termination or cessation of either a single or multiple occurrences.

(9) tw-and-ile   ʊ-kʊ-mog-a
     1PL-begin-PFV AUG-15-dance-FV

   1. 'We have (just) started dancing.'
   2. 'We have begun to dance (e.g. repeatedly or as a new habit).'
   3. 'We have begun (were the first) to dance.'

(10) tʊ-mal-ile   ʊ-kʊ-mog-a
     1PL-finish-PFV AUG-15-dance-FV

   1. 'We have (just) finished dancing.'
   2. 'We are done dancing (multiple times).'

(11) tʊ-lek-ile   ʊ-kʊ-mog-a
     1PL-cease-PFV AUG-15-dance-FV

   1. 'We have (just) stopped dancing.'
   2. 'We have given up dancing.'

What is relevant as a diagnostic of the aspectual potential encoded in the lexical verb is the possibility of a single event reading, together with the specific phase of the eventuality that is selected: is there a pre-culmination phase (either Onset or Coda) that can be said to start? If not, is there a resultant state whose early stages *anda* can refer to? Likewise, is there a process (i.e. an extended Nucleus) that can be said to cease (*leka*) or finish (*mala*)? If not, does the behaviour with these phasal verbs give support for the phase structure diagnosed by means of the basic verb inflections? In the following discussion of aspectual classes, it is thus the single event reading that is referred to, without excluding further readings (unless stated otherwise).

Table 5.1 gives an overview of the verb classes identified and their behaviour in the respective constructions. The labels for the individual classes follow Botne (2003a). Values in brackets refer either to criteria that are not directly applicable, but for which the semantic clash can be resolved through repair readings, or to specific readings that are conditioned by semantic factors outside of aspectuality. In both cases, these are discussed in more detail in the sections on the individual verb classes.

Table 5.1: Overview of aspectual classes. Columns with a grey background designate tentative classes; see §5.3.6. The criteria 'PRS as progressive', 'Persistive of PRS' and *anda/ mala/ leka* refer to a possible single event reading only; see p. 117

	Activity	Simple accomplishment	Transitional accomplishment	Transitional achievement	Resultative achievement	Inceptive achievement	Acute achievement
Persistive of PFV	no	no	yes	yes	yes	no	no
PRS as progressive	yes	yes	yes	yes	no	yes	no
Persistive of PRS	ongoing	ongoing	ongoing	(result state)	(result state)	n/a	n/a
Periphrastic PROG	ongoing	ongoing	ongoing	ongoing	result state	ongoing	n/a
'take X time' refers to	(n/a)	culmination	culmination	culmination	culmination	culmination	culmination
anda 'start' refers to	process	process	process	pre-change	result state	pre-change	n/a
mala 'finish' refers to	process	process	process	(result state)	(result state)	n/a	n/a
leka 'cease' refers to	process	process	process	(result state)	(result state)	n/a	n/a

5.3 Verb classes

5.3.1 Activities

Activity verbs encode a durative nuclear phase. Their phasal structure can be schematized as in Figure 5.1 for *moga* 'dance'.

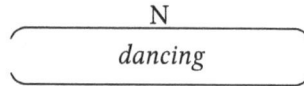

N

dancing

Figure 5.1: Phasal structure of activity

The traditional label *activity* has been adopted for reasons of familiarity. It is important to notice that in Nyakyusa this class of verbs not only encompasses actions performed by a volitional agent, such as *kama* 'milk', *keeta* 'look', *lɪma* 'cultivate' or *lya* 'eat', but also dynamisms such as *bala* 'shine (of sun)', *tima* 'rain' and verbs traditionally subsumed under states, such as *swiga* 'wonder' and *tiila* 'fear, obey, respect'. All of these pattern together in their syntactic and semantic behaviour. Seidel (2008: 271f) makes a similar observation for Yeyi R41. Semelfactives such as *kema* 'bark' or *kosomola* 'cough' may also be subsumed under the category of activities. These verbs normally give a series reading and otherwise pattern with activities in the relevant diagnostic criteria.

In the simple present, activity verbs denote ongoing activity or process (12), although they may also have a habitual/generic or futurate reading. Similarly, the periphrastic progressive gives an ongoing reading (13).

(12) a. i-kʊ-mog-a
         1-PRS-dance-FV
         'S/he is dancing.'

     b. ɪɪ-fula   jɪ-kʊ-tim-a
         AUG-rain(9) 9-PRS-rain-FV
         'It is raining.'

     c. ɪ-m-bwa jɪ-kʊ-kem-a
         AUG-9-dog 9-PRS-bark-FV
         'A/the dog is barking.'

(13) a. a-lɪ   pa-kʊ-mog-a
         1-COP 16-15-dance-FV
         'S/he is dancing.'

    b. ɪɪ-fula   jɪ-lɪ   pa-kʊ-tim-a
          AUG-rain(9) 9-COP 16-15-rain-FV

          'It is raining.'

    c. ɪ-m-bwa   jɪ-lɪ   pa-kʊ-kem-a
          AUG-9-dog 9-COP 16-15-bark-FV

          'A/the dog is barking.'

The simple present as the complement of the persistive aspect auxiliary has a reading of a continuing process and can also have a persistent habitual/generic reading:

(14)   a. a-kaalɪ i-kʊ-mog-a
          1-PERS 1-PRS-dance-FV

          1. 'S/he is still dancing.'
          2. 'S/he still dances.'

    b. ɪɪ-fula   jɪ-kaalɪ jɪ-kʊ-tim-a
          AUG-rain(9) 9-PERS 9-PRS-rain-FV

          1. 'It is still raining.'
          2. 'It still rains.'

    c. ɪ-m-bwa   jɪ-kaalɪ jɪ-kʊ-kem-a
          AUG-9-dog 9-PERS 9-PRS-bark-FV

          1. 'A/the dog is still barking.'
          2. 'A/the dog still barks.'

In the present perfective, activity verbs denote a past eventuality (15). Note that this also holds for state-like verbs such as *tiila* 'fear' (15d). As the class of activities does not encode a resultant state, perfective aspect is not licensed in the complement of the persistive (16).

(15)   a. a-mog-ile
          1-dance-PFV

          'S/he has danced.'

    b. ɪɪ-fula   jɪ-tim-ile
          AUG-rain(9) 9-rain-PFV

          'It has rained.'

    c. ɪ-m-bwa   jɪ-kem-ile
          AUG-9-dog 9-bark-PFV

          'A/the dog has barked.'

    d. a-kʊ-tiil-ile
          1-2SG-fear-PFV

          'S/he has feared you.'

(16) a. * a-kaalı a-mog-ile
         1-PERS 1-dance-PFV

    b. * ıı-fula   jı-kaalı jı-tim-ile
         AUG-rain(9) 9-PERS 9-rain-PFV

    c. * ı-m-bwa   jı-kaalı jı-kem-ile
         AUG-9-dog 9-PERS 9-bark-PFV

    d. * a-kaalı a-kʊ-tiil-ile
         1-PERS 1-2SG-fear-PFV

As activity verbs do not encode an inherent endpoint, they are not directly compatible with the time-span verb phrase 'take X time'. Two repair readings are available, however, and most activity verbs allow for at least one of the two. The first is a conative reading denoting the time that elapses before the beginning of the lexical act (see Dowty 1979: 57 for a similar observation for English). The second repair reading is that of a quasi-accomplishment; see p. 121 below for discussion.

(17) a. eeg-ile   a-ka-balılo a-ka-tali   ʊ-kʊ-mog-a
         1.take-PFV AUG-12-time AUG-12-long AUG-15-dance-FV

        1. 'S/he took a long time to (begin to) dance.'
        2. 'S/he took a long time to finish dancing (i.e. at a social event).'

    b. eeg-ile   a-ka-balılo a-ka-tali   ʊ-kʊ-ly-a
         1.take-PFV AUG-12-time AUG-12-long AUG-15-eat-FV

        1. 'S/he took a long time to begin to eat.'
        2. 'S/he took a long time to eat (i.e. finish the meal).'

    c. eeg-ile   a-ka-balılo a-ka-pimb-a ʊ-kʊ-kosomol-a
         1.take-PFV AUG-12-time AUG-12-short AUG-15-cough-FV

        'S/he took a short time to finish coughing (i.e. overcome illness).'

The auxiliary *anda* 'begin, start' refers to the beginning of the activity (18a, 18b), or in the case of semelfactives the beginning of the series (18c).

(18) a. and-ile   ʊ-kʊ-mog-a
         1.begin-PFV AUG-15-dance-FV

        'S/he has started to dance.'

    b. ıı-fula   j-and-ile   ʊ-kʊ-tim-a
         AUG-rain(9) 9-begin-PFV AUG-15-rain-FV

        'It has started to rain.'

   c. ɪ-m-bwa j-and-ile   ʊ-kʊ-kem-a
      AUG-9-dog 9-begin-PFV AUG-15-bark-FV
      'A/the dog has started to bark.'

The terminative auxiliary *mala* can be used with some but not all activity verbs. This is apparently dependent on two factors. First, a "quasi-accomplishment sense" (Binnick 1991: 176) needs to be available. Binnick, on the basis of Dowty (1979: 61), observes that this is the case when one speaks about an activity that forms part of or constitutes a specific task or habit. The second requirement is not one of phasal structure, but of thematic relations, namely that the subject be an agent or force. The latter is in agreement with the findings on simple and transitional accomplishments (§5.3.2, 5.3.3 respectively); see also Freed (1979: 135) on English *finish*. Thus compare (19a, 19b) to (19c, 19d).

(19) a. a-mal-ile   ʊ-kʊ-mog-a
        1-finish-PFV AUG-15-dance-FV
        'S/he has finished dancing.'

      b. ɪ-m-bwa jɪ-mal-ile   ʊ-kʊ-kem-a
        AUG-9-dog 9-finish-PFV AUG-15-bark-FV
        'The dog has finished barking.'

      c. * ɪɪ-fula   jɪ-mal-ile   ʊ-kʊ-tim-a
        AUG-rain(9) 9-finish-PFV AUG-15-rain-FV
        (intended: 'The rain has finished.')

      d. * a-mal-ile   ʊ-kʊ-n-diil-a
        1-finish-PFV AUG-15-1SG-fear-FV
        (intended: 'S/he is done fearing me.')

Lastly, the egressive auxiliary *leka* denotes a cessation or interruption:

(20) a. a-lek-ile   ʊ-kʊ-mog-a
       1-cease-PFV AUG-15-dance-PFV
       'S/he has stopped dancing.'

      b. ɪɪ-fula   jɪ-lek-ile   ʊ-kʊ-tim-a
       AUG-rain(9) 9-cease-PFV AUG-15-rain-PFV
       'It has stopped raining.'

      c. ɪ-m-bwa jɪ-lek-ile   ʊ-kʊ-kem-a
       AUG-9-dog 9-cease-PFV AUG-15-bark-FV
       'A/the dog has stopped barking.'

5.3.2 Simple accomplishments

Simple accomplishments encode an activity that is delimited by an endpoint. That is, they correspond to Vendler's (1957) *accomplishments*. Following Botne (2008), the qualification *simple* has been adopted to distinguish them from their transitional counterpart (§5.3.3). The phasal structure of simple accomplishments can be schematized as in Figure 5.2 for *pona* 'recover'. Other lexical verbs of this class are *bɪfwa* 'ripen', *lembʊka* 'wake up, get up' and *talalɪla* 'cool (intr.)'. Accomplishments can also be derived from activities, e.g. by means of a quantized primary object, as in *lya ɪngʊkʊ joosa* 'eat a whole chicken' or *kama ɪɪng'ombe syosa* 'milk all cows' (see Verkuyl 1972; Dowty 1979). The derivation of accomplishments through other means, such as measure ('walk a mile') or goal noun phrases ('walk to the park') is open to further research. Note that in Nyakyusa, objects, once they have been introduced into discourse, are often understood from context without repetition or cross-referencing. Lastly, it should be noted that not all simple accomplishments constitute actions performed by a volitional agent. The same is true for activity verbs,

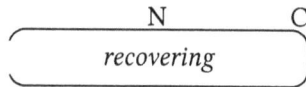

Figure 5.2: Phasal structure of simple accomplishment

Like activity verbs and transitional accomplishments, simple accomplishments denote an ongoing process in the simple present (21), although they may also have a futurate and habitual or generic reading. In the same vein, the periphrastic progressive refers to the process of change (22).

(21)   a.   ʊ-m̩-bine i-kʊ-pon-a
            AUG-1-ill 1-PRS-recover-FV

            'A/the sick person is recovering.'

       b.   i-kʊ-lembʊk-a
            1-PRS-awake-FV

            'S/he is waking up.'

       c.   i-kʊ-ly-a   ɪ-n-gʊkʊ   j-oosa
            1-PRS-eat-FV AUG-9-chicken 9-all

            'S/he is eating a whole chicken.'

(22)   a.   ʊ-m̩-bine a-lɪ   pa-kʊ-pon-a
            AUG-1-ill 1-COP 16-15-recover-FV

            'A/the sick person is recovering.'

       b.   a-lɪ   pa-kʊ-lembʊka-a
            1-COP 16-15-awake-FV

            'S/he is waking up.'

       c.   a-lɪ   pa-kʊ-ly-a   ɪ-n-gʊkʊ   j-oosa
            1-COP 16-15-eat-FV AUG-9-chicken 9-all

            'S/he is eating a whole chicken.'

As expected, the combination of persistive aspect and the simple present denotes the continuation of the process and further allows for a persistent habit-
ual/generic reading:

(23)   a.   ʊ-m̩-bine a-kaalɪ i-kʊ-pon-a
            AUG-1-ill 1-PERS 1-PRS-recover-FV

            1. 'A/the sick person is still recovering.'
            2. 'A/the sick person still recovers (frequently).'

       b.   a-kaalɪ i-kʊ-lembʊk-a
            1-PERS 1-PRS-awake-FV

            1. 'S/he is still waking up.'
            2. 'S/he still wakes up.'

       c.   a-kaalɪ i-kʊ-ly-a   ɪ-n-gʊkʊ   j-oosa
            1-PERS 1-PRS-eat-FV AUG-9-chicken 9-all

            1. 'S/he is still [occupied with] eating a whole chicken.'
            2. 'S/he still eats whole chickens.'

In the present perfective, simple accomplishments denote that the eventuality
has passed (24). As they do not encode a resultant state, perfective aspect is not
licensed in the complement of the persistive aspect auxiliary (25).

(24)   a.   ʊ-m̩-bine a-pon-ile
            AUG-1-ill 1-recover-PFV

            'A/the sick person has recovered.'

       b.   a-lembwike
            1-awake.PFV

            'S/he has woken up.'

c. a-l-iile   ɪ-n-gʊkʊ   j-oosa
   1-eat-PFV AUG-9-chicken 9-all

   'S/he has eaten a whole chicken.'

(25) a. * a-kaalɪ a-pon-ile
        1-PERS 1-recover-PFV

        (intended: -lq S/he is still healed.')

   b. * a-kaalɪ a-lembwike
        1-PERS 1-awake.PFV

        (intended: 'S/he is still awake.')

   c. * a-kaalɪ a-l-iile   ɪ-n-gʊkʊ   j-oosa
        1-PERS 1-eat-PFV AUG-9-chicken 9-all

        (intended: 'S/he is still full from eating a whole chicken.')

With simple accomplishments, the time-span verb phrase 'take X time' unambiguously refers to the time that elapses before the culmination of the process.

(26) a. ʊ-m̩-bine eeg-ile   a-ka-balɪlo a-ka-tali   ʊ-kʊ-pon-a
        AUG-1-ill 1.take-PFV AUG-12-time AUG-12-long AUG-15-recover-FV

        'A/the sick person has taken a long time to recover.'

   b. eeg-ile   ɪɪ-sala   j-oosa ʊ-kʊ-lembʊka-a
      1.take-PFV AUG-hour(9) 9-all   AUG-15-awake-FV

      'S/he has taken a whole hour to wake up.'

   c. eeg-ile   a-ka-balɪlo a-ka-pimba ʊ-kʊ-ly-a   ɪ-n-gʊkʊ
      1.take-PFV AUG-12-time AUG-12-short AUG-15-eat-FV AUG-9-chicken
      j-oosa
      9-all

      'S/he has taken a short time to eat a whole chicken.'

The ingressive auxiliary *anda* 'start, begin' refers to the beginning of the process:

(27) a. ʊ-m̩-bine and-ile   ʊ-kʊ-pon-a
        AUG-1-ill 1.begin-PFV AUG-15-recover-FV

        'A/the sick person has begun to recover.'

   b. and-ile   ʊ-kʊ-lembʊka-a
      1.begin-PFV AUG-15-awake-FV

      'S/he has begun to wake up.'

    c. and-ile   ʊ-kʊ-ly-a   ɪ-n-gʊkʊ   j-oosa
       1.begin-PFV AUG-15-eat-FV AUG-9-chicken 9-all

       'S/he has started to eat a whole chicken.'

The terminative auxiliary *mala* is compatible with some, but not all, accomplishments and denotes that the process has been completed. As with activity verbs in their quasi-accomplishment reading, and as will be seen for transitional accomplishments (§5.3.3), *mala* requires a subject with the semantic role of agent or force:

(28) a. a-mal-ile   ʊ-kʊ-lembʊk-a
         1-finish-PFV AUG-15-awake-FV

         'S/he has finished getting up.'

      b. a-mal-ile   ʊ-kʊ-ly-a   ɪ-n-gʊkʊ   j-oosa
         1-finish-PFV AUG-15-eat-FV AUG-9-chicken 9-all

         'S/he has finished eating a whole chicken.'

      c. * ʊ-m̩-bine a-mal-ile   ʊ-kʊ-pon-a
         AUG-1-ill 1-finish-PFV AUG-15-recover-FV

         (intended: 'A/the sick person has accomplished recovery.')

      d. * a-ma-tooki   ga-mal-ile ʊ-kʊ-bɪfw-a
         AUG-6-banana 6-finish-PFV AUG-15-ripen-FV

         (intended: 'The bananas have become completely ripe.')

   Lastly, *leka* 'cease, stop' denotes a cessation or interruption of the process:

(29) a. ʊ-m̩-bine a-lek-ile   ʊ-kʊ-pon-a
         AUG-1-ill 1-cease-PFV AUG-15-recover-FV

         'A/the sick person has ceased to recover.'

      b. a-lek-ile   ʊ-kʊ-lembʊka-a
         1-cease-PFV AUG-15-awake-FV

         'S/he has ceased to wake up (viz. fallen asleep again).'

      c. a-lek-ile   ʊ-kʊ-ly-a   ɪ-n-gʊkʊ   j-oosa
         1-cease-PFV AUG-15-eat-FV AUG-9-chicken 9-all

         'S/he has ceased eating a whole chicken.'

5.3.3 Transitional accomplishments

Transitional accomplishments encode a process that leads to a new state. They thus share characteristics of activity verbs and simple accomplishments on the one hand and inchoative achievement verbs (§5.3.4, 5.3.5) on the other. Note that a distinction between transitional achievements and transitional accomplishments has so far only been observed for neighbouring Ndali (Botne 2008). Its importance for a theory of Aristotelian aspect is highlighted in Persohn (2017a). More systematic research on Aristotelian aspect in other Bantu languages might bring to light similar distinctions.

The phasal structure of transitional accomplishments can be schematized as in Figure 5.3 for *gaala* 'get drunk, be drunk'. Other verbs of this class include *fwala* 'dress, wear', *isʊla* 'swell, be full', and *onangɪka* 'be(come) spoiled'. As becomes most clear with the last two verbs, and as is the case with activity verbs and simple accomplishments, the lexicalized process need not be dependent on a volitional agent.

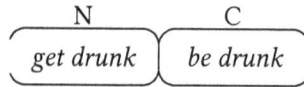

Figure 5.3: Phasal structure of transitional accomplishment

Like activity verbs and simple accomplishments, transitional accomplishments denote an ongoing process in the simple present (30), as well as a possible futurate or habitual/generic reading. In the same vein, the periphrastic progressive refers to the process of change (31).

(30) a. i-kʊ-gaal-a
         1-PRS-be(come)_drunk-FV
         'S/he is getting drunk.'
      b. i-kʊ-fwal-a   (ii-koti)
         1-PRS-dress/wear-FV (5-coat<SWA)
         'S/he is dressing (putting on a/the coat).'

(31) a. a-lɪ   pa-kʊ-gaal-a
         1-COP 16-15-be(come)_drunk-FV
         'S/he is getting drunk.'
      b. a-lɪ   pa-kʊ-fwal-a   (ii-koti)
         1-COP 16-15-dress/wear-FV (5-coat)
         'S/he is dressing (putting on a/the coat).'

Also like activities and simple accomplishments, but unlike transitional achievements, the simple present as the complement of the persistive aspect auxiliary denotes the continuation of the pre-culmination process:

(32)   a.   a-kaalı i-kʊ-gaal-a
           1-PERS 1-PRS-be(come)_drunk-FV

           1. 'S/he still gets drunk (regularly).'
           2. 'S/he is still getting drunk.'

       b.   a-kaalı i-kʊ-fwal-a   (ii-koti)
           1-PERS 1-PRS-dress/wear-FV (5-coat)

           1. 'S/he still dresses (puts on a/the coat).'
           2. 'S/he is still dressing (putting on a/the coat).'

As with all inchoative verbs, but unlike activities and simple accomplishments, the perfective of transitional accomplishments is licensed as the complement of the persistive aspect auxiliary (33), a combination that denotes a persistent resultant state.

(33)   a.   a-kaalı a-gaal-ile
           1-PERS 1-be(come)_drunk-PFV

           'S/he is still drunk.'

       b.   a-kaalı a-fweele   (ii-koti)
           1-PERS 1-dress/wear.PFV (5-coat)

           'S/he is still dressed (with a/the coat).'

The time-span phrase 'take X time', as with simple accomplishments, refers to the time elapsing before the culmination:

(34)   a.   eeg-ile   a-ka-balılo a-ka-tali   ʊ-kʊ-gaal-a
           1.take-PFV AUG-12-time AUG-12-long AUG-15-be(come)_drunk-FV

           'S/he took a long time to get drunk.'

       b.   eeg-ile   a-ka-balılo a-ka-tali   ʊ-kʊ-fwal-a   (ii-koti)
           1.take-PFV AUG-12-time AUG-12-long AUG-15-dress/wear-FV (5-coat)

           'S/he took a long time to dress (put on a/the coat).'

The auxiliary *anda* 'begin, start' in the single event reading denotes the beginning of the process of change:

(35)   a.   and-ile   ʊ-kʊ-gaal-a
           1.begin-PFV AUG-15-be(come)_drunk-FV

           'S/he has begun to get drunk.'

       b.   and-ile   ʊ-kʊ-fwal-a   (ii-koti)
           1.begin-PFV AUG-15-dress/wear-FV (5-coat)

           'S/he has started to dress (to put on a/the coat).'

The auxiliary *mala* 'finish' with transitional accomplishments can have a single event reading, in which case it refers to the culmination of the process. This behaviour is shared with activities and simple accomplishments, but not transitional achievements. To be compatible with *mala* requires the subject to have the semantic role of agent or force, as in (36a, 36b) but not (36c).

(36) a. a-mal-ile   ʊ-kʊ-gaal-a
           1-finish-PFV AUG-15-be(come)_drunk-FV

           'S/he has finished getting drunk (purposefully).'

     b. a-mal-ile   ʊ-kʊ-fwal-a   (ii-koti)
           1-finish-PFV AUG-15-dress/wear-FV (5-coat)

           'S/he has finished dressing (putting on a/the coat).'

     c. * ii-galı lı-mal-ile   ʊ-k-oonangık-a
           5-car 5-finish-PFV AUG-15-be(come)_spoiled-FV

           (intended: 'A/the car has broken down completely.')

Lastly, *leka* 'cease, stop' in a single event reading refers to a cessation or interruption of the process:

(37) a. a-lek-ile   ʊ-kʊ-gaal-a
        1-cease-PFV AUG-15-be(come)_drunk-FV

        'S/he has ceased to get drunk (e.g. stopped drinking).'

     b. a-lek-ile   ʊ-kʊ-fwal-a   (ii-koti)
        1-cease-PFV AUG-15-dress/wear-FV (5-coat)

        'S/he has stopped dressing (putting on a/the coat).'

5.3.4 Transitional achievements

Transitional achievements encode a change-of-state as well a pre-culmination state and a resultant state. Their phasal structure can thus be schematized as in Figure 5.4 for *kalala* 'be(come) angry'. This class of verbs makes up the vast majority of achievements in the sample. Other examples include *fugama* 'kneel', *fwa* 'die', *gwa paasi* 'fall down', *katala* 'be(come) tired', *kola* 'grasp, hold' and *nyala* 'be(come) dirty'.

In the simple present, transitional achievements have a coming-to-be reading (38), as well as a habitual/generic and a futurate one. Likewise, the periphrastic progressive refers to the coming-to-be. Typically this is understood as being close to a change-of-state (39).

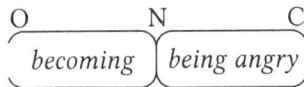

Figure 5.4: Phasal structure of transitional achievement

(38) a. i-kʊ-kalal-a
           1-PRS-be(come)_angry-FV

          'S/he is becoming angry.'

      b. i-kʊ-fw-a
           1-PRS-die-FV

          'S/he is dying.'

(39) a. a-lɪ pa-kʊ-kalal-a
           1-COP 16-15-be(come)_angry-FV

          'S/he is about to be angry.'

      b. a-lɪ pa-kʊ-fw-a
           1-COP 16-15-die-FV

          'S/he is about to die.'

Some transitional achievements can be used with the simple present as the complement of the persistive aspect auxiliary, but not all (40). In this case, what is referred to is the continuation of the resultant state. This behaviour is shared with resultative achievements (§5.3.5) but not transitional accomplishments (§5.3.3). However, those language assistants that accepted these readings were either hesitant at first or considered these readings to be less natural than the use of the persistive plus perfective aspect, which makes this look like a clear case of coercion; see Michaelis (2004) for a theory of coercion.

(40) a. a-kaalɪ i-kʊ-fugam-a
           1-PERS 1-PRS-kneel-FV

          1. 'S/he still kneels.'
          2. 'S/he is still kneeling.'

      b. * a-kaalɪ i-kʊ-fw-a
           1-PERS 1-PRS-die-FV

          (intended: 'S/he is still being dead.')

As with all inchoative verbs, the perfective form of transitional achievements is licensed as the complement of the persistive aspect auxiliary (41).

(41) a. a-kaalɪ a-kaleele
           1-PERS 1-be(come)_angry.PFV

          'S/he is still angry.'

b. ii-lʊʊka lɪ-kaalɪ lɪ-fw-ile
5-store 5-PERS 5-die-PFV
'The store is still dead (viz. closed).'

The ingressive auxiliary *anda* 'begin, start' refers to the beginning of the development:

(42) a. and-ile ʊ-kʊ-kalal-a
1.begin-PFV AUG-15-be(come)_angry-FV
'S/he has started to become angry.'

b. and-ile ʊ-kʊ-fw-a
1.begin-PFV AUG-15-die-FV
'S/he has started to die.'

Some transitional achievements are compatible with *mala* 'finish', in which case the reference is to the eventuality as a whole. As observed in §5.3.1–5.3.3, this requires the subject to have the semantic role of agent or force, or to be construable as such. Thus compare (43a, 43b) to (43c, 43d):

(43) a. a-mal-ile ʊ-kʊ-kol-a ii-bwe
1-finish-PFV AUG-15-grasp/hold-FV 5-stone
'S/he has finished holding a/the stone.'

b. a-mal-ile ʊ-kʊ-fugam-a
1-finish-PFV AUG-15-kneel-FV
'S/he has finished kneeling.'

c. ? a-mal-ile ʊ-kʊ-kalal-a
1-finish-PFV AUG-15-be(come)_angry-FV
'S/he has finished being angry.'

d. * ii-lʊʊka lɪ-mal-ile ʊ-kʊ-fw-a
5-store 5-finish-PFV AUG-15-die-FV
(intended: 'The store is not closed anymore (i.e. has opened again).')

Likewise, a single event reading with the egressive auxiliary *leka* is available for some, but not all, transitional achievements. In accordance with their meaningful focus on the resultant state, this denotes an interruption or cessation of the latter. It is not entirely clear what the determining semantic factors are. The following examples suggest that at least world knowledge comes into play:

(44) a. a-lek-ile   ʊ-kʊ-fugam-a
          1-cease-PFV AUG-15-kneel-FV
          'S/he has ceased to be kneeling.'

      b. a-lek-ile   ʊ-kʊ-kalal-a
          1-cease-PFV AUG-15-be(come)_angry-FV
          'S/he has ceased to be angry.'

      c. ? ɪɪ-nyumba   jɪ-lek-ile   ʊ-kʊ-nyala-a
          AUG-house(9) 9-cease-PFV AUG-15-be(come)_dirty-FV
          'A/the house has ceased to be dirty.'

      d. * ii-lʊʊka ly-a-fw-ile   looli lɪ-lek-ile   ʊ-kʊ-fw-a
          5-store 5-PST-die-PFV but   5-cease-PFV AUG-15-die-FV
          (intended: 'The store was closed but it is not closed anymore.')

The language assistants commented that examples such as (44a, 44b) are acceptable but not very natural. A more common way to refer to a state, e.g. of anger, that has come to an end, would be the following:

(45) a-a-kaleele,   looli   si-mal-iike
      1-PST-be(come)_angry.PFV now/but 10-finish-NEUT.PFV
      'S/he was angry, but now it is over.'

Last, the time-span phrase 'take X time' refers to the time elapsing before the change-of-state:

(46) eeg-ile   a-ka-balɪlo a-ka-pimba fiijo   ʊ-kʊ-kalala
      1.take-PFV AUG-12-time AUG-12-short INTENS AUG-15-be(come)_angry-FV
      'S/he got angry in a very short time.'

(47) eeg-ile   a-ka-balɪlo a-ka-tali   ʊ-kʊ-fugam-a
      1.take-PFV AUG-12-time AUG-12-short AUG-15-kneel-FV
      'S/he took a lot of time to get on his/her knees.'

5.3.5 Resultative achievements

Resultative achievements encode a change-of-state together with the resultant state. Their phasal structure can thus be schematized as in Figure 5.5 for *hoboka* 'be(come) happy'. Other examples are *benga* 'hate', *gana* 'like, love', *gona ʊtʊlo* 'sleep' and *twala* 'carry, bring'.

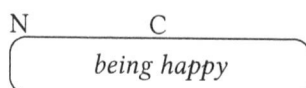

Figure 5.5: Phasal structure of resultative achievement

In the simple present, resultative achievements have a futurate reading as well as a habitual/generic one, but no progressive reading (48).

(48) a. i-kʊ-hobok-a
          1-PRS-be(come)_happy-FV
          1. 'S/he will become happy.'
          2. 'S/he becomes happy (e.g. on each particular occasion).'
      b. i-kʊ-m-beng-a
          1-PRS-1SG-hate-FV
          1. 'S/he will hate me.'
          2. 'S/he hates me (e.g. shows it every time we meet).'

The periphrastic progressive construction with resultative achievements refers to the resultant state (49). This is unlike transitional achivements (§5.3.4), which do encode an Onset state.

(49) a. a-lɪ   pa-kʊ-hobok-a
          1-COP 16-15-be(come)_happy-FV
          'S/he is happy.'
      b. a-lɪ   pa-kʊ-m-beng-a
          1-COP 16-15-1SG-hate-FV
          'S/he hates me (e.g. is acting hostile).'

Some, but not all, resultative achievements can be coerced into a progressive reading with the simple present as the complement of the persistive aspect auxiliary (50). As with transitional achievements, what is referred to in this case is the resultant state.

(50) a. a-kaalɪ i-kʊ-hobok-a
          1-PERS 1-PRS-kneel-FV
          1. 'S/he still becomes happy.'
          2. 'S/he is still being happy.'

b. a-kaalɪ i-kʊ-m-beng-a
    1-PERS 1-PRS-1SG-hate-FV

    1. 'S/he still hates me (e.g. still shows it every time we meet).'
    2. 'S/he is still hating me (e.g. acting hostile).'

c. a-kaalɪ i-kʊ-twal-a   ɪ-kɪ-kapʊ
    1-PERS 1-PRS-carry-FV AUG-7-basket

    'S/he still carries a/the basket (regularly).'
    not: 'S/he is still carrying a/the basket.'

As with all inchoative verbs, the common way to refer to the resultant state is with the use of the perfective aspect, which is licensed as the complement of the persistive aspect auxiliary (51), a combination that denotes the persistence of the resultant state.

(51) a. a-kaalɪ a-hobwike
          1-PERS 1-be(come)_happy.PFV

          'S/he is still happy.'

      b. a-kaalɪ a-m-beng-ile
          1-PERS 1-1SG-hate-PFV

          'S/he still hates me.'

The time-span phrase 'take X time' refers to the time elapsing before the entry into the new state:

(52) a. eeg-ile   a-ka-balɪlo a-ka-tali   ʊ-kʊ-hobok-a
          1.take-PFV AUG-12-time AUG-12-long AUG-15-be(come)_happy-FV

          'S/he took a long time to become happy.'

      b. eeg-ile   a-ka-balɪlo a-ka-pimba ʊ-kʊ-m-beng-a
          1.take-PFV AUG-12-time AUG-12-short AUG-15-1SG-hate-FV

          'S/he came to hate me within a short time.'

Related to the behaviour of resultative achievements with the simple present and periphrastic progressive, the auxiliary *anda* 'begin, start' in the single event reading refers to an initial subphase of the resultant state:

(53) a. and-ile   ʊ-kʊ-hobok-a
          1.begin-PFV AUG-15-be(come)_happy-FV

          'S/he has begun to be happy.'

b. and-ile   ʊ-kʊ-m-beng-a
   1.begin-PFV AUG-15-1SG-hate-FV
   'S/he has begun to hate me.'

Parallel to what has been observed for transitional achievements, at least some resultative achievements can be coerced into a progressive reading of the resultant state in the syntactic frame of the simple present as the complement of the persistive aspect auxiliary.

(54)   a-kaalɪ i-kʊ-hobok-a
        1-PERS 1-PRS-be(come)_happy-FV

        1. 'S/he still becomes happy (e.g. on each certain occasion).'
        2. 'S/he is still being (behaving) happy.'

(55)   a-kaalɪ i-kʊ-m-beng-a
        1-PERS 1-PRS-1SG-hate-FV

        1. 'S/he still hates me (generally speaking).'
        2. 'S/he is still hating me (i.e. acting hostile).'

The auxiliary *mala* 'finish' refers to the resultant state. As has been observed in the preceding sections, *mala* requires its subject to have the semantic role of agent or force:

(56)   a-mal-ile   ʊ-kʊ-twal-a   ɪ-kɪ-kapʊ
        1-finish-PFV AUG-15-cary-FV   AUG-7-basket
        'S/he has finished carrying a/the basket.'

(57)   a-mal-ile   ʊ-kʊ-gon-a   ʊ-tʊ-lo
        1-finish-PFV AUG-15-rest-FV   AUG-12-sleep
        'S/he has finished sleeping.'

(58) * a-mal-ile   ʊ-kʊ-hobok-a
        1-finish-PFV AUG-15-be(come)_happy-FV
        (intended: 'S/he is not happy anymore.')

(59) * a-mal-ile   ʊ-kʊ-m-beng-a
        1-finish-PFV AUG-15-1SG-hate-FV
        (intended: 'S/he does not hate me anymore.')

As is the case with transitional achievements, a single event reading with the egressive auxiliary *leka* is available for at least some resultative achievements:

(60) a. a-lek-ile   ʊ-kʊ-gon-a   ʊ-tʊ-lo
          1-cease-PFV AUG-15-rest-FV AUG-12-sleep

          'S/he has ceased to be sleeping.'

      b. a-lek-ile   ʊ-kʊ-n̩-gan-a
          1-cease-PFV AUG-15-like/love-FV

          'S/he has ceased to love him/her.'

      c. ? a-lek-ile   ʊ-kʊ-hobok-a
          1-cease-PFV AUG-15-be(come)_happy-FV

          'S/he has ceased to be happy.'

One verb in the sample, *manya* 'know', patterns to a large extent with resultative achievements. Unlike the latter, however, *manya* is incompatible with the periphrastic progressive:

(61) * a-lɪ   pa-kʊ-many-a ɪ-kɪ-ngelesa
        1-COP 16-15-know-FV AUG-7-English

      (intended: 'S/he is learning English.' or 'S/he knows English.')

In all other respects, *manya* 'know' behaves no differently from the verbs discussed so far in this section. Thus in the simple present it has a generic (62) as well as a futurate reading (63). To refer to the state of having knowledge, the perfective aspect is employed (64) and its compatibility with persistive aspect shows that this state forms part of its lexical meaning (65).

(62) a-baa-sukuulu bi-kʊ-many-a   ɪ-kɪ-ngelesa
      AUG-2-student 2-PRS-know-FV AUG-7-English

      'Students know English.'

(63) lɪlɪno   kʊʊ-many-a,   fiki ʊ-ti-kw-amul-a   bo
      now/today 2SG.PRS.1SG-know-FV why 2SG-NEG-PRS-answer-FV as
      n-gʊ-kʊ-laalʊʊsy-a?
      1SG-PRS-2SG-ask-FV

      'Now you'll get to know me, why don't you answer when I'm asking you?' [Saliki and Hare]

(64) a-meenye   ɪ-kɪ-ngelesa
      1-know.PFV AUG-7-English(<SWA)

      'S/he knows English.'

(65) a-kaalı a-meenye ı-kı-ngelesa
      1-PERS 1-know.PFV AUG-7-English
      'S/he still knows English.'

The time-span verb phrase 'take X time' refers to the time elapsing before entering into the state of knowledge (66). Also note that *manya* in the narrative tense – see §7.3 – normally yields a change-of-state reading (67).

(66) eeg-ile   ı-fy-ınja   f-ingi ʊ-kʊ-many-a   ı-kı-ngelesa
      1.take-PFV AUG-8-year 8-many AUG-15-know-FV AUG-7-English
      'S/he took many years to (get to) know English.' [ET]

(67) ʊ-mw-ene Jesu nakalınga   a-lınkʊ-**many**-a mu-n-dumbula j-aake
      AUG-1-self J. immediately 1-NARR-know-FV 18-9-heart   9-POSS.SG
      ʊkʊtı bi-kw-inogon-a bo ı-si   mu-n-dumbula sy-abo,
      COMP 2-PRS-think-FV as AUG-PROX.10 18-10-heart   10-POSS.PL
      a-lınkʊ-ba-laalʊʊsy-a, a-lınkʊ-tı   ...
      1-NARR-2-ask-FV   1-NARR-say

      'And immediately when Jesus perceived in his spirit that they so reasoned within themselves, he said unto them ...[J. immediately understood in his heart ...he asked them ...]' (Mark 2: 8)

In their discussion of neighbouring Ndali and Sukwa, Botne (2008) and Kershner (2002), respectively, recognize a separate group of purely static verbs, which among others includes the cognates of Nyakyusa *benga* 'hate', *gana* 'love', and, in the case of Sukwa, *manya* 'know'. As seen above, in Nyakyusa the first two pattern with other verbs such as *hoboka* 'be(come) happy' as resultative achievements. It is noteworthy that these putatively stative verbs in Ndali and Sukwa pattern with the other classes of inchoatives with respect to their behaviour with perfective aspect ("completive" in Botne & Kershner's terms; see §6.5.3.2 for discussion), which is unfortunately not further discussed by these authors. The validity of a separate class of states in Nyakyusa remains open to further research. Note that Seidel (2008) does not recognize such a class for Yeyi R41. Concerning the broader Niger-Congo context, Toews (2015: ch. 5.4) finds that Siamou (Kru) entirely lacks state verbs. In order to describe stative situations, other strategies are evoked, namely non-verbal predicates, a stativizing verbal suffix, imperfective aspect with certain non-inchoatives (often as the result of a figurative reading) and perfective aspect with inchoative verbs.

5.3.6 Other achievement classes

Two verbs in the sample, *fika* 'arrive' and *aga* 'find', classify as achievements, but they both differ from the achievements classes discussed in the preceding sections in important ways. These two verbs can be taken as representatives of the classes of inceptive and acute achievements (Kershner's 'inceptive punctives' and 'achievement punctives'), which are well-established classes in neighbouring Ndali and Sukwa. Their scarcity in the sample is most likely due to the limited sample of verbs. As a single verb, however, it is insufficient to justify an achievement class of its own, and this classification thus remains tentative. The two verbs are discussed jointly in this section.

To begin with, *fika* in the simple present has a coming-to-be reading (68) as well as a habitual/generic and a futurate one. Likewise, the periphrastic progressive refers to the coming-to-be (69). This indicates a lexical Onset phase and parallels the transitional achievements (§5.3.4).

(68)	i-kʊ-fik-a	(69)	a-lɪ pa-kʊ-fik-a
	1-PRS-arrive-FV		1-COP 16-15-arrive-FV
	'S/he is arriving.'		'S/he is arriving.'

fika also resembles transitional achievements in that the simple present as the complement of the persistive aspect auxiliary has a habitual/generic reading, but not one of a progressive change-of-state:

(70) a-kaalɪ i-kʊ-fik-a
      1-PERS 1-PRS-arrive-FV
      'S/he still arrives (regularly).'
      not: 'S/he is still arriving.'

Further proof of a lexicalized Onset phase is found in the behaviour of *fika* with *anda* 'begin, start'. This auxiliary has a habitual/generic reading and can also refer to the preliminary phase of a single eventuality with *fika* (71).

(71) and-ile   ʊ-kʊ-fik-a
      1.begin-PFV AUG-15-arrive-FV
      1. 'S/he has begun to arrive (e.g. get to a place regularly).'
      2. 'She has begun to arrive (right now).'

As expected, the time-span verb phrase 'take X time' with *fika* refers to the time elapsing before the change-of-state:

(72) eeg-ile   a-ka-balılo a-ka-tali   ʊ-kʊ-fik-a
1.take-PFV AUG-12-time AUG-12-long AUG-15-arrive-FV
'S/he took a long time to arrive.'

The perfective aspect with *fika* denotes that the eventuality has passed (73). The fact that perfective aspect is not licensed in the complement of the persistive aspect auxiliary (74) provides proof that, unlike transitional and resultative achievements, no Coda state is lexically encoded.

(73) a-fik-ile   (74) * a-kaalı a-fik-ile
      1-arrive-PFV   1-PERS 1-arrive-PFV
      'S/he has arrived.'

Lastly, *mala* 'finish' is not compatible with *fika* (75), while *leka* 'cease, stop' denotes the cessation or interruption of a series or habit, but does not have a single event reading with this verb (76).

(75) * a-mal-ile   ʊ-kʊ-fik-a
      1-finish-PFV AUG-15-arrive-FV
      (intended: 'S/he has arrived completely.')

(76) a-lek-ile   ʊ-kʊ-fik-a   a-pa
      1-cease-PFV AUG-15-arrive-FV AUG-PROX.16
      'S/he no longer gets here.'
      not: 'S/he has ceased to arrive here.'

To summarize, *fika* differs from transitional and resultative achievements in that it does not lexicalize a Coda state. Like transitional, but unlike resultative achievements, it does, however, encode an Onset phase. Its phasal structure can thus be schematized as in Figure 5.6.

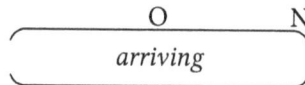

Figure 5.6: Phasal structure of *fika*

As for *aga* 'find', in the simple present this verb has a habitual/generic and a futurate reading, but no progressive one (77), which indicates the lack of a lexical Onset phase. Accordingly, the simple present in the complement of the persistive aspect auxiliary does not have a single event reading (78).

(77) tʊ-kw-ag-a   ɪɪ-fungulo   jɪ-lɪ   paa-meesa
      1PL-PRS-find-FV AUG-key(9)(<SWA) 9-COP 16-table(9)(<SWA)

      1. 'We will find that a/the key is on a/the table (e.g. thus we have been informed).'
      2. 'We find that a/the key is on a/the table (e.g. each time we search for it).'

(78) tʊ-kaalɪ tʊ-kw-ag-a   bi-kʊ-ly-a
      1PL-PERS 1PL-PRS-find-FV 2-PRS-eat-FV

      'We still find them eating (frequently).'
      not: 'We are still finding them eating (sic!).'

Further proof of the lack of an Onset phase is found in the facts that *aga* is incompatible with the periphrastic progressive (79) and that it does not have a single event reading with the ingressive *anda* (80):

(79) tw-and-ile   ʊ-kw-ag-a   bi-kʊ-ly-a
      1PL-start-PFV AUG-15-find-FV 2-PRS-eat-FV

      'We have begun to find them eating (e.g. each time we pass).'
      not: 'We have begun to find them eating (right now).'

(80) * tʊ-lɪ   pa-kw-ag-a bi-kʊ-ly-a
      1PL-COP 16-15-find-FV 2-PRS-eat-FV

      (intended: 'We are about to find them eating.')

The perfective aspect with *aga* denotes that the eventuality has passed (81). The incompatibility of perfective aspect with persistive aspect shows that no Coda phase is encoded (82).

(81) tw-ag-ile   bi-kʊ-ly-a
      1PL-find-PFV 2-PRS-eat-FV

      'We have found them eating.'

(82) * tʊ-kaalɪ tw-ag-ile   bi-kʊ-ly-a
      1PL-PERS 1PL-find-PFV 2-PRS-eat- FV

      (intended: 'We are still informed that they are eating.')

The time-span phrase 'take X time' denotes the time elapsing before the change-of-state:

(83) tw-eg-ile   a-ka-balılo a-ka-tali   ʊ-kw-ag-a
      1PL-take-PFV AUG-12-time AUG-12-long AUG-15-find-FV
      ıı-fungulo   jı-lı   paa-meesa
      AUG-key(9)(<SWA) 9-COP 16-table(9)(<SWA)
      'We took a long time to find that a/the key is on a/the table.'

Lastly, *mala* 'finish' cannot be used with *fika* (84) and *leka* 'cease, stop' does not have a single event reading (85).

(84) * tʊ-mal-ile   ʊ-kw-ag-a   ıı-fungulo jı-lı paa-meesa
      1PL-finish-PFV AUG-15-find-FV AUG-key(9) 9-COP 16-table(9)
      (intended: 'We're done finding that a/the key is on the table (sic!).')

(85) tʊ-lek-ile   ʊ-kw-ag-a   ıı-fungulo jı-lı paa-meesa
      1PL-cease-PFV AUG-15-find-FV AUG-key(9) 9-COP 16-table(9)
      'We no longer find that a/the key is on the table'
      not: 'We have ceased to be finding that a/the key is on the table (sic!).'

To summarize, *aga* differs from the other achievements in that it encodes neither an Onset nor a Coda phase, but only a punctual change-of-state. That is, it corresponds to the Vendlerian definition of achievements; see §1.4.3.1 for discussion. Its phasal structure can be schematized as in Figure 5.7.

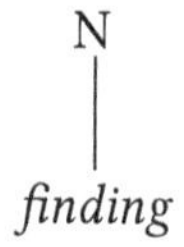

N
|
finding

Figure 5.7: Phasal structure of *aga*

6 Tense and aspect constructions 1: present and past tense

6.1 Introduction

In this and the following two chapters, constructions expressing tense and grammatical aspect will be described. This chapter contains a general overview of tense and aspect in Nyakyusa, followed by a discussion of negation (§6.3) and an investigation into two recurring aspectual suffixes, which show considerable morphophonemic alternation (§6.4.1, 6.4.2). Its main body consists of a description of present and past tense constructions. This description is divided into constructions consisting of just the inflected verb (§6.5) and or compound constructions (§6.6). What is for convenience termed 'present tense' throughout this study can be understood as having non-past reference. This is discussed in §6.7. Note that the dedicated narrative markers, though they have past tense reference, will be dealt with separately in §7.

6.2 Overview of tense aspect in Nyakyusa

A key element of the Nyakyusa TMA system in the present (non-past) and past tense is the opposition between imperfective and perfective aspect. The use of grammatical aspect is closely linked to the lexical opposition between inchoative and non-inchoative verbs (see Chapter 5). A central element here is the completion of the Nucleus phase of an eventuality, which is discussed in §6.5.3.2. As each of the major present and past tense construction are also marked for aspect, neither tense nor grammatical aspect can be considered primary. Instead, when linguistically construing a given state-of-affairs, a speaker of Nyakysa has to decide on both the temporal dimension (§1.4.2.1) as well as the aspectual vantage point (§1.4.2.2) in relation to the verb's inherent aspectual potential (§1.4.3.1).

Concerning constructions with future time reference, which build on the simple present,simple present as well as the subjunctive and desiderative moods, Nyakyusa rather has an opposition between aspectually neutral and imperfective aspect, where the latter frequently also adds modal nuances.

6.3 Negation in Nyakyusa

In §6.5, 6.6, 9.3, the description of each affirmative construction will be followed by its negative counterpart. As has been pointed out by Contini Morava (1989), among others, the semantic relationship between affirmative and negative forms is not a straightforward one. Nevertheless, when language assistants were asked for the negative equivalent of a given form, they responded readily and unanimously (see also Nurse 2008: 196). Negation in Nyakyusa shows some uncommon characteristics, however, which deserve a short discussion.

Nyakyusa has three negative prefixes: *ti-*, *ka-* and *nga-*. All three stand in the post-initial slot. Their distribution is delimited along two major lines: mood and temporal reference. The *nga-* negation is limited to the negative subjunctive (§9.3.4). Of the remaining two negative prefixes, *ka-* is used in constructions that make reference to a point of time prior to the moment of speech,[1] while *ti-* occurs solely in the present and in futurates.[2] The apparent exception is the negative copula, which for the non-generic present is *ka-j-a* (§10.2.1). However, this can clearly be attributed to its origin in the negation of 'become', which, depending on the context, is still a possible reading. What has just been outlined is uncommon in two ways. First, in the majority of those Bantu languages having more than one negative marker, these occur in different positions in the verbal word. Second, in those Bantu languages with three negative markers, the typical distribution is main clause vs. subjunctive vs. relative clause (Nurse 2008: 184–191).

A common typological criterion concerning verbal negation is symmetry. As Miestamo (2007: 556) defines it, "symmetric negative constructions do not differ from non-negatives in any other way than by the presence of the negative marker(s)".[3] While negation in Nyakyusa is mostly symmetric, as can be seen from the sample constructions in Table 6.1, there are several cases of asymmetric negation; see Table 6.2. There are also cases of syncretism, where more than one affirmative paradigm shares a common negative counterpart; see Table 6.3. Miestamo (2005) calls the latter "paradigmatic A/Cat asymmetry".

---

[1] The moment of speech is to be understood here as the default reference point.

[2] This contrasts with Ndali, which has *ta-* for non-pasts as well as pasts (Botne 2008; Swilla 1998). The Ngonde varieties described by Kishindo (1999) and Labroussi (1998) seem to exhibit a certain variability and stand between Nyakyusa and Ndali with regards to the negative markers.

[3] More precisely, Miestamo in the quoted section is concerned with 'standard negation', that is, the negation of declarative verbal main clauses, excluding, for instance, existential or copula clauses or non-declarative ones such as the imperative.

Table 6.1: Cases of symmetric negation

	Affirmative	Negative
Simple present	*kʊ*-VB-*a*	*ti-kʊ*-VB-*a*
Past perfective	*a(lɪ)*-VB-*ile*	*ka-a(lɪ)*-VB-*ile*
Past imperfective	*a*-VB-*aga*	*ka-a*-VB-*aga*

Table 6.2: Cases of asymmetric negation

	Affirmative	Negative
Present perfective	*ø*-VB-*ile*	*ka*-VB-*a*
Subjunctive	*ø*-VB-*e(ge)*	*nga*-VB-*a(ga)*
Narrative tense	*lɪnkʊ*-VB-*a*	*lɪnkʊ-sit-a* + infinitive

Table 6.3: Syncretism in negation

Affirmative	Negative
Simple present Present progressive	Negative present
Past imperfective Past progressive	Negative past imperfective
Subjunctive Distal/itive subjunctive	Negative subjunctive

6.4 Morphophonology of common TMA suffixes

6.4.1 Alternations of imperfective -*aga*

The imperfective suffix surfaces as -*aga* in those paradigms characterized by the default final vowel -*a*, and as -*ege* in the affirmative subjunctive. The defective verb *tɪ* (§10.3) occurs as *tɪgɪ*.

(1)   *twajobaga*   'we were speaking'
         tʊjobbege   'we should be speaking'
         twatɪgɪ   'we were saying'

    When one of the clitics (see §3.3.8) =*po*, =*mo* or =*ko* (independent of their specific function) or =*kʊ* 'where' follows, the velar segment is prenasalized (2). With the enclitic form of *ki* 'what', no prenasalization takes place (3).

(2)   *baaswɪlangapo*   (°ba-a-swɪl-aga=ko)   'they were raising there (class 16)'
      biigalangako   (°ba-a-igala-aga=ko)   'they were closing there (class 17)'
      baasookangamo   (°ba-a-sook-aga=mo)   'they were going outside (class 18)'
      ʊswɪlengeko   (°ʊ-swɪl-ege=po)   'you should raise there (class 16)'
      gwigalengeko   (°ʊ-igal-ege=ko)   'you should close there (class 17)'
      ʊsookengemo   (°ʊ-sook-ege=mo)   'you should go outside (class 18)'
      gwabʊʊkangakʊ (°ʊ-a-bʊʊk-aga=kʊ)   'Where were you going?'
      mbʊʊkengekʊ   (°n-bʊʊk-ege=kʊ)   'Where should I go?'

(3)   *gwabombagaki*   (°ʊ-a-bom-aga=ki)   'What were you doing?'

6.4.2 Perfective -*ile* and its variants

Perfective stems in Nyakyusa are subject to complex allomorphic variation. With the widespread Bantu suffix -*ile* as the underlying form, surface forms are diverse and in many cases show characteristics of fusional morphology. Before going into detail with the numerous shapes perfective stems take and the phonological and morphological factors triggering the choice of these, it should be stated that perfective stem formation can be understood as variation on three re-occurring themes. The first and most straightforward is suffixation of -*ile*:

(4)   *nwa*   'drink'   > *nwile*
      gana   'love'   > *ganile*
      nyunyuuta   'whine'   > *nyunyuutile*

The second theme is called *imbrication*, a term coined by Bastin (1983). In its prototypical form, imbrication consists of infixing -*i*- before the last base consonant and suffixing -*e*. The rules of word-internal hiatus solution (§2.2.1.4) apply.

(5) *lwasya*   'nurse the sick, care for'   > *lwa<i>sy-e*   > *lwesye*
    bukuka   'flare'   > *buku<i>k-e*   > *bukwike*
    ambɪlɪla   'receive; entertain guests'   > *ambɪlɪ<i>l-e*   > *ambɪliile*

A third theme will be referred to as *copying*. In its basic form, copying consists of a surface alternation /-CG/ → /-CiiCGe/, where CG stands for the base-final consonant plus a following glide. Although at first this looks like a case of reduplication, the discussion below will show that these forms can best be explained by assuming templatic requirements of certain types of stems.

(6) *busya* 'return (tr.)'   > *busiisye*
    pɔfya 'whistle'   > *pɔfiifye*
    ibwa 'forget'   > *ibiibwe*

The following in-depth description of perfective stem formation will be structured according to the syllable count of the verbal base, as this is a major conditioning factor and each syllable count can be associated with a default process. Some of the regularities outlined have already been recognized by Berger (1938). However, the present data shows a number of deviations from Berger's analysis, which in most cases can be attributed to the greater quantity of data considered.[4] This is based on the examination of some 1600 verbal bases for which perfective stems were available at the time of writing this section.

6.4.2.1 Monosyllabic verbs

With monosyllabic verbs, -*ile* is suffixed. The general rules of vowel juxtaposition apply (§2.2.1.4). Defective *tɪ* (§10.3) yields *tile*, which is often reduced to [tʰi̯ɛ]. Likewise, *jile* is often heard as [ɟi̯ɛ]. In both cases, stress remains on the stem syllable.

(7) *pa* 'give'   > *peele*
    ja 'be(come)'   > *jile*
    tɪ 'say'   > *tile*

---

[4]Berger himself recognizes the limits of his corpus and that the transcription of some of his second-hand data is rather dubious. Nevertheless, his work is a valuable point of departure. Apart from Berger (1938), the forms cited in Felberg (1996) have been taken as an indication of where to look for regularity and variation. All forms stemming from those sources that were felt to be suspicious have been checked in elicitation.

fwa 'die' > fwile
gwa 'fall' > gwile
kwa 'pay dowry' > kwile
lwa 'fight' > lwile
mwa 'shave' > mwile
nwa 'drink' > nwile
swa 'spit; forgive' > swile
twa 'be plenty (esp. fish)' > twile
kya 'dawn; cease to rain' > kiile
lya 'eat' > liile
nia 'defecate' > niile
pya 'be(come) burnt' > piile
sya 'grind' > siile

6.4.2.2 Disyllabic verbs

Disyllabic verbs show by far the most complex variation. Suffixation of -*ile* can be considered the default case:

(8) goga   'kill'   > gogile
     keeta   'watch'   > keetile
     konga   'follow'   > kongile
     ʋla   'buy'   > ʋlile

With disyllabic applicatives (that is, applicatives of monosyllabic roots) -*iile*, with a long morpheme-initial vowel, is suffixed.

(9) peela 'give off'   > peeliile
     jɪɪla 'be in a condition'   > jɪɪliile
     lɪɪla 'eat with/at/for'   > lɪɪliile
     niela 'defecate with/at/for'   > nieliile
     syela 'grind with/at/for'   > syeliile
     gwɪla 'fall with/to/for'   > gwɪliile
     nwela 'drink with/at/for'   > nweliile

With disyllabic fossilized passives (§4.2.8), -*il*- is infixed before the glide and -*e* is suffixed (10). These verbs thus occupy an intermediate position between suffixing and imbrication in the strict sense.[5] The same holds for one of the perfective stem variants of *lɪɪgwa* 'be eaten'. (11)

---

[5]Schumann (1899) and Berger (1938) note that these verbs form their perfective stem with long -*iilwe*. This could not be confirmed and might be due to diatopic variation or confusion with their applicativized forms.

(10)   babwa   'be in pain'   > babilwe
       gogwa   'dream'   > gogilwe
       milwa   'drown'   > mililwe
       nyonywa   'desire'   > nyonyilwe
       syʊkwa   'miss sadly'   > syʊkilwe
       tolwa   'be burdened'   > tolilwe

(11)   lɪɪgwa   'be eaten'   > lɪɪgilwe (also lɪɪgiigwe, see below)

Verbs of the shapes CGal and CGan induce imbrication (12). One exception
to this rule is attested (13). The unusual sequence /ŋw/ indicates that the verb
ng'wala might be a Ndali loan.[6] Berger (1938) further lists nywama > nyweme,
thus CGam. Of the speakers consulted, several did not know this verb at all.
Those familiar with it unanimously gave nywamile as their first answer. Some
accepted nyweme as a variant perfective stem, whereas it was rejected by others
(14). The only other verb of the shape in question is kwama 'be(come) stuck', an
obvious loan from Swahili, which has the perfective stem kwamile not *kweme.
As the examples in (15) illustrate, other CGaC shapes do not induce imbrication.

(12)   fwala   'wear; receive salary'   > fwele
       syala   'remain'   > syele
       fwana   'resemble; be enough'   > fwene
       lwana   'quarrel'   > lwene

(13)   ng'wala 'scratch with claws'   > ng'walile (not *ng'wele)

(14)   nywama 'enlarge (intr.); chase'   > nywamile (also nyweme)

(15)   fyata   'fasten'   > fyatile (not *fyete)
       kwaba   'take'   > kwabile (not *kwebe)

The verb baala 'increase, thrive' shows variation between an imbricating and
a suffixing form (16). This must be considered an idiosyncrasy, as no other verb
of the shape /Caal/ has an imbricating perfective stem (17).

(16)   baala 'increase; thrive'   > beele / baalile

(17)   gaala 'get drunk, be drunk' > gaalile (not *geele)
       paala 'invite'   > paalile (not *peele)
       saala 'be(come) happy'   > saalile (not *seele)

---

[6]Cf. pairs such as Nyakyusa nwa, Ndali ŋwa 'drink' < PB *ɲwó.

Two further disyllabic verbs must be considered irregular: *manya* 'know' and *bona* 'see'. These trigger imbrication although no other regularity can account for this. Further, *bona* does not yield *bwine* as would be expected from the rules of vowel coalescence.

(18) *manya*   'know'   > *meenye*
      bona   'see'   > *bwene*

Disyllabic causatives trigger copying, yielding (C)(G)V*siisye* if the base ends in /sy/ and (C)(G)V*fiifye* if the base ends in /fy/. This holds for causatives of monosyllabic roots formed with the long causative$_2$ *-ısi* (19), as well as for those causatives formed with the short causative$_1$ *-i* on disyllabic verbs (20); see §4.2.4 for a discussion of the two causatives. Causatives with base-final nasals also have a perfective stem of the shape (C)VN*iisye* (21), which shows that synchronically speaking this is not a rule of reduplication, as it might appear at first sight. A historic scenario for this alternation is provided by Hyman (2003). He argues that its origin most probably lies in imbrication plus a cyclic application of spirantization through the causative$_1$ *-i* (§4.2.2), thus yielding (C)(G)V*siisye* for base-final spirantizing oral linguals. This then came to be re-analysed as a process of reduplication, yielding (C)(G)V*fiifye* with base-final oral labials. Lastly, this turned into a phonological pattern requirement for disyllabic causative stems to end in *-ii{s,f}ye*, hence the extension to final nasals (and causatives of monosyllabic verbs, which are not discussed by Hyman).

Note that disyllabic causatives derived from the verbs of the shape CG*a{l, n}* discussed above are excluded from this process. As with their underlying bases, imbrication takes place (22). The causative of *baala, baasya* 'increase (tr.)' shows variation just like its underlying root, and is attested with both imbricating and copying forms (23).

(19) Causatives of monosyllabic roots:
      lw-ısi-a   'make fight'   > *lwısiisye*
      gw-ısi-a   'overturn; throw down'   > *gwısiisye*

(20) Disyllabic causatives with -i:
      bosya   (°bol-i-a)   'cause to rot'   > *bosiisye*
      pyʊfya (°pyʊp-i-a) 'warm, heat up'   > *pyʊfiifye*

(21) Disyllabic causatives with final nasal:
      pon-i-a   'greet; visit'   > *poniisye*
      an-i-a   'ask'   > *aniisye*
      sim-y-a   'put out, switch off' > *simiisye*
      taam-y-a   'trouble, persecute' > *taamiisye*

(22) Disyllabic causatives CGa{l, n}-i:

    lwasya   (°lwal-i-a)   'nurse the sick, care for'   > *lwesye*

    syasya   (°syal-i-a)   'leave over'   > *syesye*

    fwania   (°fwan-i-a)   'match; reconcile'   > *fwenie*

    lwania   (°lwan-i-a)   'confront; make quarrel'   > *lwenie*

(23) Causative of *baala*:

    baasya   (°baal-i-a)   'increase (tr.)'   > *beesye* / *baasiisye*

Some other verbs of the shape (C)VCG form their perfective stems by copying $(C_1)VC_2G \rightarrow (C_1)VC_2\text{-}ii\text{-}C_2G\text{-}e$.[7]

(24) *bɪfwa*   'ripen'   > *bɪfiifwe*

    ibwa   'forget'   > *ibiibwe*

    ikya   'be(come) confident'   > *ikiikye*

    okya   'grill, burn'   > *okiikye*

    lɪɪgwa   'be eaten'   > *lɪɪgiigwe* (also *lɪɪgilwe*; see above)

    peegwa   'be given'   > *peegiigwe*

6.4.2.3 Tri- and polysyllabic verbs

With verbs that have three or more syllables, imbrication is the default.

(25) *aganila*   'meet'   > *aganiile*

    gundamika 'bend over'   > *gundamiike*

    guulɪla   'wait for'   > *guuliile*

    itɪkɪla   'answer; approve'   > *itɪkiile*

    geleka   'thatch, pile'   > *geliike*

    koolela   'call; name; bid'   > *kooliile*

    bagala   'carry on shoulder'   > *bageele*

    fumbata   '(en)close'   > *fumbeete*

    jobana   'converse'   > *jobeene*

    honyoka   'be slackened; give in' > *honywike*

    kosomola   'cough'   > *kosomwile*

    bʊmbʊlʊka 'get well, be healed'   > *bʊmbʊlwike*

---

[7]For *bɪfwa*, Berger (1938) and Felberg (1996) list *bɪfwifwe* as a variant, while for *ibwa* Berger (1938) also has *ibwibwe*; Nurse (1979) has *okya* > *okyokye*, thus $(C_1)(G)VC_2G \rightarrow (C_1)VC_2GV\text{-}i\text{-}C_2G\text{-}e$. All the speakers consulted in the present study rejected these forms, which seems to be a case of diatopic variation (both Felberg's and Berger's main sources stem from more southern varieties). Felberg (1996) further lists a copying stem for *miimwa* 'crave; envy', which was also rejected.

fyʊtʊla	'pull out'	> fyʊtwile
fujula	'humiliate, dishonour'	> fujwile
amula	'answer'	> amwile

With the long allomorph of the reciprocal -aan and its causativized/pluraction-al form -(ɪs)aani, imbrication takes place:

(26)

bʊngaana	'(be) assemble(d)'	> bʊngeene
bʊngaania	'gather'	> bʊngeenie
lʊngaana	'join together (intr.)'	> lʊngeene
lʊngɪsaania	'put together, arrange'	> lʊngɪseenie
ongaana	'be together, mixed'	> ongeene
ongaania	'mix, sum up'	> ongeenie

The verb *ilaamwa* 'disregard, doubt' shows some variation. An imbricating stem *ileemwe*, as well as *ilaamwisye* was observed. Berger (1938) observes a third hybrid variant *ileemwisye*. With the speakers consulted, *ileemwe* is the most frequent form.

All other verbs which have more than two syllables, a long rightmost vowel and that are not causatives form their perfective stems by suffixation of *-ile*:

(27)

jɪgɪɪla	'shake (intr.)'	> jɪgɪɪlile
ogeela	'swim'	> ogeelile
niembeteela	'wrap, conceal'	> niembeteelile
tendeela	'peep, peek'	> tendeelile
kolooma	'grown'	> koloomile

With verbs that feature a base-final prenasalized plosive (recall that these pre-dictably induce lengthening in the preceding vowel), as well as with causatives having a long vowel in the rightmost position (minus those containing the re-ciprocal plus causative, as discussed above), variation is found. Typically, the former trigger suffixing of *-ile* while the latter trigger copying, which yields -Ciisye/-Ciifye. These are the only formations given by Schumann (1899) and Berger (1938) that are attested in the textual data. However, at least for the verbs given in (29, 30), some speakers also have imbricating forms.[8]

---

[8]Given this variation and the variant forms of *ilaamwa*, together with the fact that tri- and polysyllabic verbs ending in -aan(i) induce imbrication, one might suspect a loosening con-straint against imbrication with long and lengthened vowels (in terms of moraic phonology: bimoraic vowels). Felberg (1996) lists *bulunga > bulungile / bulwinge, l[a]alʊʊsya / l[a]alwsiye* (indication of vowel length missing) and *palamaasya > palamaasiisye / palameesye*.

(28) Copying with -VV{s, f}y:

    malɪɪsya   'end, eliminate'   > *malɪɪsiisye*

    eneesya   'inspect, visit'   > *eneesiisye*

    balabaasya   'spread out (tr.); pretend'   > *balabaasiisye*

    syʊngʊʊsya 'rotate (tr.)'   > *syʊngʊʊsiisye*

    nyonyoofya 'attract, rouse desire'   > *nyonyofiifye*

(29) Variation with -VNC:

    onanga   'destroy'   > *onangile* / *onenge*

    tononda   'peck; dot up'   > *tonondile* / *tonwinde*

    kung'unda   shake off; beat up'   > *kung'undile* / *kung'winde*

    bulunga   'roll up, make round'   > *bulungile* / *bulwinge*

(30) Variation with -VVsy:

    palamaasya 'touch; grope'   > *palamaasiisye* / *palameesye*

    tangaasya   'proclaim (<SWA)'   > *tangaasiisye* / *tangeesye*

    laalʊʊsya   'ask'   > *laalʊʊsiisye* / *laalwisye*

Lastly, partially reduplicated that have one of the shapes $C_1V_1C_1V_1V_1C_2$ or $C_1G_1V_1C_1G_1V_1C_2$, where C_2 is an approximant or plosive, are treated as if disyllabic. The same holds for spirantized causatives (§4.2.2) thereof. Although for the first pattern this behaviour could also be motivated by the rightmost long vowel, the second group shows that this is rather a function of the overall phonemic shape. It is a noteworthy fact that all the attested verbs in question can be considered onomatopoetic or de-ideophonic. A similar rule that blocks imbrication holds in Yao P21 (Berger 1938: 112, 120). This suggests itself to be functionally motivated, in order to preserve the sound symbolism. For a discussion of how sound symbolism can motivate exceptions on the diachronic axis, see Dimmendaal (2011: 55f).

(31) Shape $C_1V_1C_1V_1V_1C_2$:

    boboota   'grunt'   > *bobootile*

    hohoola   'jeer'   > *hohoolile*

    ng'ong'oola 'grimace at' > *ng'ong'oolile*

    nyunyuuta   'whine'   > *nyunyuutile*

    nyinyiila   'squint'   > *nyinyiilile*

(32) Shape $C_1G_1V_1C_1G_1V_1C_2$:

    bwabwata   'blab, talk nonsense'   > *bwabwatile*

    bwabwaja   'blab, talk nonsense'   > *bwabwajile*

    mwemweka 'glitter'   > *mwemwekile*

(33)   Shape $C_1G_1V_1C_1G_1V_1C_2\text{-}i_{CAUS}$:
        mwemwesya   'move around light'   > *mwemwesiisye*
        myamyasya   'smoothen out'   > *myamyasiisye*
        i-ng'weng'wesya   'grumble'   > *i-ng'weng'wesiisye*
        ng'wang'wasya   'not do thoroughly'   > *ng'wang'wasiisye*

6.5 Synthetic present and past constructions

In the following, present (non-past) and past tense constructions consisting of solely the inflected verb will be described. These are listed in Table 6.4.

Table 6.4: Synthetic non-past/present and past tense constructions

Label	Shape	Example	
Simple present	SM₂-*kʋ*-VB-*a*	*tʋkʋjoba*	'we speak'
Negative present	SM-*ti-kʋ*-VB-*a*	*tʋtikʋjoba*	'we do not speak'
Present perfective	SM-VB-*ile*	*tʋjobile*	'we have spoken'
Neg. present perfective	SM-*ka*-VB-*a*	*tʋkajoba*	'we have not spoken'
Past perfective	SM-*a(lɪ)*-VB-*ile*	*twajobile*	'we spoke'
Neg. past perfective	SM-*ka-a(lɪ)*-VB-*ile*	*tʋkaajobile*	'we did not speak'
Past imperfective	SM-*a*-VB-*aga*	*twajobaga*	'we were speaking'
Neg. past imperfective	SM-*ka-a*-VB-*aga*	*tʋkaajobaga*	'we were not speaking'

6.5.1 Simple present

The simple present is formed by a subject prefix from the second series (see §3.3.2) followed by a prefix *kʋ-* in post-initial position, together with the final vowel *-a*.

(34)   *tʋkʋjoba* 'we speak / are speaking'

   The familiar label *simple present* is applied to this construction for reasons of convenience. More precisely, this construction can be understood as the imperfective counterpart to the present perfective (§6.5.3). Depending on context and co-text, the simple present can have a continuous/progressive reading (35). For a discussion of this reading vis-à-vis the periphrastic progressive, see §6.6.1.

(35) tʊ-kʊ-fw-a,   jɪ-kʊ-tʊ-gog-a   ɪ-n-galamu
      1PL-PRS-die-FV 9-PRS-1PL-kill-FV AUG-9-lion

'We're dying, the lion is killing us.' [Chief Kapyungu]

The availability of this continuous reading hinges on the availability of a pre-culminative phase, i.e. an extended Onset or Nucleus phase (see Chapter 5), or alternatively, as in (35), the availability of a series reading.

The simple present is found in some further functions that can be related to its continuous reading. These are illustrated in the following examples (terminology following Binnick 1991: 247). For use of the simple present as a narrative present, see §6.7.1.

(36) Reportative:
      ii-peasi   lɪ-mo **li-kʊ-satʊk-a** paa-si. **i-kʊ-sal-a**
      5-pear(<SWA) 5-one 5-PRS-fall-FV 16-down 1-PRS-pick-FV
      n=ʊ-kʊ-pugut-a   n=ɪ-kɪ-tambala. **i-kʊ-bɪɪk-a** kangɪ
      COM=AUG-15-shake_off-FV COM=AUG-7-cloth 1-PRS-put-FV again
      n-kɪ-kapʊ
      18-7-basket

      'One pear falls on the ground. He picks it up and cleans it with a cloth. He puts it back into the basket.' [Elisha Pear Story]

(37) Performative:
      n-gʊ-mm-oosy-a   ʊ-mw-ana ʊ-jʊ   Joni
      1SG-PRS-1-baptize-FV AUG-1-child AUG-PROX.1 J.

      'I baptize [name] this child John.' [ET]

The simple present is further used in habitual and generic statements:

(38) ɪ-n-gambɪlɪ   si-ti-kʊ-j-a   n=ɪ-n-dumbula
      AUG-10-monkey 10-NEG-PRS-be(come)-FV COM=AUG-10-heart
      m-mu-nda.   ɪ-n-gambɪlɪ   **tʊ-kʊ-si-lek-a**   m-mi-piki
      18-3?-inside_of_body AUG-10-monkey 1PL-PRS-10-let-FV 18-4-tree

      'Monkeys don't have their hearts inside the body. Us monkeys, we leave them in the trees.' [Crocodile and Monkey]

(39) po   na   lɪlɪno   **li-kʊ-kol-a**   kʊkʊtɪ ii-sikʊ. looli ɪ-n-gʊkʊ
      then COM now/today 5-PRS-grasp-FV every 5-day but AUG-10-chicken
      kw-ag-a   kʊkʊtɪ ka-balɪlo si-lɪ   paa-si, si-kʊ-lond-a
      2SG.PRS-find-FV every 12-time   10-COP 16-down 10-PRS-search-FV

ıı-sindaano   ı-jı   sy-aly-asiime   kʊ-ly-ebe
AUG-needle(<SWA)(9) AUG-PROX.9 10-PST-borrow.PFV 17-5-crow

'So even now it [Crow] takes them [little chicks] every day. As for the chickens, you find them all the time on the ground, searching for the needle that they had borrowed from Crow.' [Chickens and Crow]

The simple present can also be used to refer to future eventualities, often within the same day. In (40), the speaker, Monkey, angrily soliloquises, announcing that Tortoise will pay back his overdue debts this very same day. In (41), a strange woman has visited the speaker's wife and asked for breast milk. She was told to come back later and now the husband explain his plans to trap her, using the simple present with future reference.

(40)   ii-sikʊ lı-lı-ngı po a-al-iis-ile   mwa=n-gambılı,
       5-day 5-5-other then 1-PST-come-PFV matronym=9-monkey
       a-al-iis-ile   n=ı-ly-ojo   "lılıno   kʊ-m-b-a=ko
       1-PST-come-PFV COM=AUG-5-anger now/today 2SG.PRS-1SG-give-FV=17
       ıı-heela   j-angʊ,   kʊ-m-b-a=ko   ıı-heela
       AUG-money(9) 9-POSS.1SG 2SG.PRS-1SG-give-FV=17 AUG-money(9)
       j-angʊ" i-kʊ-job-a   mu-n-jıla
       9-POSS.1SG 1-PRS-speak-FV 18-9-path

       'Another day Mr. Monkey came, he came with anger. "Today you're giving me my money, you're giving me my money" he is saying on the way.' [Monkey and Tortoise]

(41)   lınga   iis-ile   ʊ-ne   n-gw-i-fis-a   n-gʊ-j-a
       if/when 1.come-PFV AUG-1SG 1SG-PRS-REFL-hide-FV 1SG-PRS-be(come)-FV
       kʊʊ-sofu, ʊ-gwe ʊ-job-ege   nagwe ʊkʊtı a-kʊ-p-e
       17-room.9 AUG-2SG 2SG-speak-IPFV.SUBJ COM.1 COMP 1-2SG-give-SUBJ
       ı-kı-kombe gʊ-n-kam-il-e.   ʊ-ne   n-gʊ-n-kol-a   ʊkʊtı
       AUG-7-cup 2SG-1-milk-APPL-SUBJ AUG-1SG 1SG-PRS-1-hold-FV COMP
       a-m-bʊʊl-e   ı-fi   i-kʊ-bomb-el-a!
       1-1SG-tell-SUBJ AUG-PROX.8 1-PRS-do-APPL-FV

       'When she comes, I'll hide, I'll be in the bedroom, you talk with her so that she gives you the cup so that you can express milk for her. I'll catch her so that she tells me what she does with it!' [Killer woman]

Rather than being a calendaric constraint, the present day is the default for the futurate use of the simple present. However, the simple present can also be used to talk about eventualities later than the same day. This is common with plans

(42) and regular or scheduled eventualities (43). What is more, the simple present can be used to talk about a future eventuality with certainty (44); see also (10) on p. 253.

(42) Context: The household help informs that she will not be present the next day.

kɪ-laabo   n-gʊ-sumuk-a   kʊ-Tʊkʊjʊ
7-tomorrow 1sG-PRs-depart-FV 17-T.

'Tomorrow I am heading to Tukuyu.' [overheard]

(43) kɪ-laabo   n=ʊ-lʊ-bʊnjʊ   fiijo   ii-sʊba li-kʊ-sook-a
7-tomorrow COM=AUG-11-morning INTENS 5-sun   5-PRs-leave-FV

'The sun rises early tomorrow morning.' [ET]

(44) Context: Mbeya FC is playing against Simba SC tomorrow. You are sure that Mbeya FC will win.

tʊ-kʊ-ba-tol-a   kɪ-laabo
1PL-PRs-2-defeat-FV 7-tomorrow

'We are defeating them tomorrow (sic!).' [ET]

Conversely, when specifically evoking a later period of the same day as the reference frame, the future proclitic *aa=* (§8.2) is used. (45) illustrates this. Note that the proclitic is represented as *a=* in this example, as it is followed by a prenasalized plosive and its length is thus predictable. Likewise, addition of the future proclitic changes (44) above to a mere prediction (46).

(45) Context: Talking about the speaker's plans for the evening.

na=a-ma-jolo   a=n-gʊ-j-a   pa-kʊ-bomb-a pa-ky-alo
COM=AUG-6-evening FUT=1sG-PRs-be(come)-FV 16-15-work-FV 16-8-field

'In the evening I will be working in the field.' [ET]

(46) Context: Mbeya FC is playing against Simba SC tomorrow. You think that Mbeya FC will win.

aa=tʊ-kʊ-ba-tol-a   kɪ-laabo
FUT=1PL-PRs-2-defeat-FV 7-tomorrow

'We will defeat them tomorrow.' [ET]

In past narrative discourse, the simple present features as a narrative present and in subordinate contexts; see §6.7. It is also found in the coda section of some narratives, with reference to the speaker-now, as in (39) above.

6.5.2 Negative present

The negative counterpart to the simple present consists of the post-initial negative prefix *ti* followed by the present prefix *kʊ-* and the final vowel *-a*. As the subject prefix is not directly adjacent to the present prefix, the series 1 prefixes are used; see §3.3.2. Diachronically speaking, *ti-kʊ-* most likely goes back to the fusion of *ta-* and *ikʊ-*; see §3.3.2 on the vowel /i/ preceding the present prefix. The negative prefix is *ta-* in all indicative constructions in neighbouring Ngonde (Kishindo 1999: 77), as well as in Ndali (Botne 2008: 108–116) and Sukwa (Kershner 2002: 45–51).

(47) *tʊtikʊjoba* 'we do not speak / we are not speaking'

   Like its affirmative counterpart, the negative present has a continuous reading (48), which also serves as the negative counterpart to the present progessive (§6.6.1). It is also used for negative habituals and generics (49, 50).

(48) bʊle, a-lɪ   pa-kʊ-ly-a? – mma, **a-ti-kʊ-ly-a**
      Q   1-COP 16-15-eat-FV no   1-NEG-PRS-eat-FV

   'Is s/he eating?' – 'No, s/he is not eating.' [ET]

(49) ʊ-gʊʊso   m-oolo. **a-ti-kʊ-bomb-a**   n=ɪ-m-bombo
      AUG-your_father(1) 1-lazy   1-NEG-PRS-work-FV COM=AUG-9-work
      na=jɪ-mo. i-kʊ-syʊngʊʊtɪl-a itolo
      COM=9-one 1-PRS-surround-FV just

   'Your father is lazy. He doesn't do any work. He just wanders around.'
   [Monkey and Tortoise]

(50) n=ɪɪ-swi   ɪ-si   si-li=mo n-kɪ-siba mu-la,
      COM=AUG-fish(10) AUG-PROX.10 10-COP=18 18-7-pond 18-DIST
      a-b-eene   ka-aja   a-ba   ba-lɪ kɪfuki **ba-ti-kʊ-ly-a**,
      AUG-2-owner 12-homestead AUG-PROX.2 2-COP near   2-NEG-PRS-eat-FV
      paapo a-ba-ndʊ   ba-al-iibiile   ba-a-jongiile
      because AUG-2-person 2-PST-sink.PFV 2-PST-disappear.PFV
      paa~po
      REDUPL~REF.16

   'And as for the fish in that pond, the people living near do not eat them, because people sank and disappeared there.' [Selfishness kills]

   The following examples illustrate the use of the negative present in negative futurates.

(51) n-sulumeenie fiijo   paapo ʊlʊ n-iis-ile   n-kʊ-kw-eg-a
      1SG-afflict.PFV INTENS because now 1SG-come-PFV 18-15-2SG-take-FV
      ʊ-ti-kʊ-gomok-a   kaŋɪ
      2SG-NEG-PRS-return-FV again
      'I'm very sad, because this time that I've come to pick you up you won't
      return.' [Crocodile and Monkey]

(52) Context: According to contract we do not work the next day.
      kɪ-laabo   **tʊ-ti-kʊ-bomb-a**   ɪ-m-bombo
      7-tomorow 1PL-NEG-PRS-work-FV AUG-9-work
      'Tomorrow we do not work.' [ET]

6.5.3 Present perfective

6.5.3.1 Formal makeup and overview of meaning

The present perfective is formed with the perfective final suffix *-ile* or one of its
allomorphs; see §6.4.2.

(53) *tʊjobile* 'we have spoken'

The meaning of the present perfective depends on the aspectual class of the
lexical verb. When used with non-inchoative verbs, it refers to a completed act
(54). With inchoative verbs, the default reading of the present perfective is one
of a present state (55).

(54) mu-keet-ile   leelo,   mu-keet-ile   leelo!   n-iis-ile   ne
      2PL-watch-PFV now/but 2PL-watch-PFV now/but 1SG-COME-PFV 1SG
      malafyale
      chief(1)
      'You have seen now! You have seen now! I have come as a king.' [Hare
      and Hippo]

(55) a-kaleele
      1-be(come)_angry.PFV
      (Default reading:) 'S/he is angry.' [ET]

Accordingly, the present perfective is used with inchoative verbs in a number
of cases that translate as a simple present or present progressive in English. The
following are a few examples; for narrative present uses see §6.7.1.

(56) Stative:
      ee, nalooli **n-dʊ-gan-ile**
      yes really 1SG-11-love-PFV
      'Yes, I really love him [spider].' [Hare and Spider]

(57) Stative:
      a-tʊʊgeele   pa-kɪ-kota, a-lɪ   pa-kw-ɪmb-a ɪ-kɪ-tabʊ
      1-get_seated/sit.PFV 16-7-chair 1-COP 16-15-read-FV AUG-7-book(<SWA)
      'He is sitting in a chair, reading a book.' [ET]

(58) Reportative:
      i-kʊ-kɪnd-a   ʊ-n-nyambala n=ɪ-m-bene.   **a-kol-ile**
      1-PRS-pass-FV AUG-1-man   COM=AUG-9-goat 1-grasp/hold-PFV
      ɪɪ-kamba
      AUG-rope(9)(<SWA)
      'A man with a goat passes. He holds a rope.' [Elisha Pear Story]

Although a present state reading is more common with inchoative verbs, the present perfective also allows for a change-of-state reading (59).[9] However, to express that the resultant state of an inchoative verb held at a certain time in the past, the past perfective has to be used (60).

(59) Context: How did your father react when he heard the news this
      morning?
      pa-bw-andɪlo   a-kaleele   fiijo, ʊlʊ si-maliike
      16-14-beginning 1-be(come)_angry.PFV INTENS now 10-finish.PFV
      'First he got angry, but now the anger is gone.' [ET]

(60) a-a-kaleele
      1-PST-be(come)_angry.PFV
      (Default reading:) 'S/he was angry.' [ET]

---

[9]Crane (2011: 127) gives a pragmatic explanation as to why the stative reading is the default for inchoative verbs: "With change-of-state verbs [inchoatives, BP], the implicature of continued resultant state is particularly salient. This implicature is easy to derive from general conversational principles of relevance. Use of a verb describing entry into a state, in general, is most relevant if the state holds at perspective time. For example, [in Totela K41, BP] a verb like -taba 'become happy', requires no direct reference to the situation resulting in happiness, although the context may provide such information. Thus, when uttering ndataba without much other context, a speaker is less likely to be referring to the rather ethereal process of obtaining happiness than to the ensuing happy state."

Like all present tense paradigms, the present perfective can be used with relative time reference in a number of subordinate contexts and as a narrative present (§6.7). Given the right context, it can also be used to refer to a completed eventuality situated in future time. In (61) the future reference anchor established by the adverbial clause is re-introduced through a stressed form of the class 14 referential demonstrative *bo*. In (62), context plus *tajalı* 'already' (a Swahili loan) licenses a future reading. Note that in many cases this is the only way of depicting a future state without referring to its inception.

(61) ʋ-lı   n-sekele fiijo,   kangı lınga   ga-kınd-ile a-ma-sikʋ ma-nandı,
      2SG-COP 1-thin   INTENS again if/when 6-pass-PFV AUG-6-day 6-little

      ʋ-gwe   bo   ʋ-fw-ile
      AUG-2SG REF.14 2SG-die-PFV

      'You are very tiny, also, when few days have passed, then you'll be dead.'
      [Mosquito and Ear]

(62) Context: Your brother is late for dinner.
      lınga   a-fik-ile   ı-fi-ndʋ   **tajalı**   **fi-talaliile**
      if/when 1-arrive-PFV AUG-8-food already(<SWA) 8-cool.PFV

      'When he arrives, the food will be cold.' [ET]

6.5.3.2 Perfectivity as completion of the Nucleus

The question now arises as to whether there is a common semantic core to the different readings and uses of the present perfective. Botne (2010: 43) defines perfectivity in Bantu as "an assertion about a time of the event subsequent to the endpoint of the event nucleus". Recall from §1.4.3.1 that Nucleus in Botne & Kershner's framework is the characteristic act encoded in the verb. With inchoative verbs this is the change-of-state; with most types of non-inchoatives it is the eventuality as such.

Botne's definition of perfectivity obviously differs from the more widespread one in theories of grammatical aspect, according to which "perfectivity indicates the view of a situation as a whole, without distinction of the various separate phases that make up the situation" (Comrie 1976: 16). It does, however, correspond to what Botne & Kershner (2000) call "completive" for the Zulu S42 suffix *-ile*, a label that is also employed by Botne (2008) and Kershner (2002) for *-ite* (allomorphs i.a. *-ile*) in Nyakyusa's neighbours Ndali and Sukwa. A comparable use of *completive* is already found in Welmers (1974). Crane (2011: 118–142), in a lengthy discussion of the subject in Totela K41, speaks of "nuclear completion".

Botne's definition also comes close to Johanson's (2000: 29) "postterminal view-point", that "envisag[es] the event after the transgression of its relevant limit". Johnson's "relevant limit", however, hinges upon a conception of Aristotelian aspect similar to Sasse & Breu's (see §1.4.3.1). In the present study, the term *perfective* is preferred over *completive*, as the latter is commonly used with a sense of "to do something thoroughly and to completion, e.g. *to shoot someone dead, to eat up*" (Bybee et al. 1994: 318). What is more, the term *perfective* stresses the opposition to a clearly imperfective category, opposition which is central to the Nyakyusa TMA system.

Adopting the above definition of perfectivity, the different readings of the perfective in Nyakyusa find a unified explanation.[10] With non-inchoatives, a post-Nucleus vantage point equals a vantage point following the situation as a whole. This is depicted in Figure 6.1 for the activity verb *moga* 'dance'. As for inchoative verbs, both the stative and the change-of-state reading can be explained by a post-Nucleus vantage point. In the more common stative reading, the vantage point falls within the stative coda phase. For the present perfective used in main clauses this normally coincides with the time of speech, thus giving a present state reading. A change-of-state reading arises from a vantage point following the eventuality as a whole. That is to say, the perfective selects a time as following the Nucleus as the vantage point, but is vague as to the exact position of the eventuality. Figure 6.2 depicts the two perspectives for the transitional achievement *kalala* 'be(come) angry'.

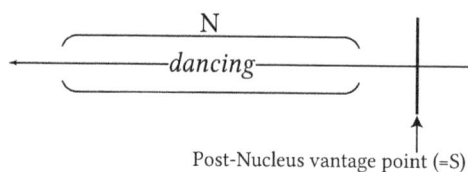

Figure 6.1: Perfective with activity verb

---

[10]The following argumentation owes much to Crane's (2011) ample discussion of the concept of completion of the Nucleus phase in Totela K41, which shares a number of similarities with Nyakyusa.

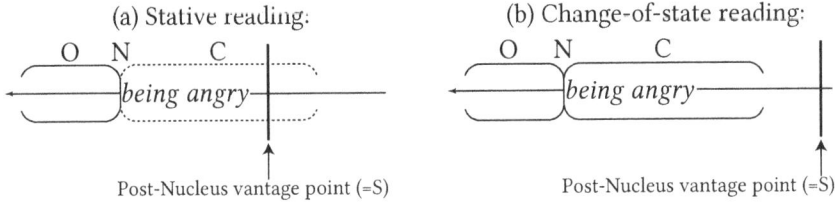

Figure 6.2: Perfective with an inchoative verb

6.5.3.3 Present perfective vs. anterior

It is opportune at this point to consider an alternative analysis of present perfective construction. At first glance, the Nyakyusa configuration ø-VB-*ile* resembles an *anterior* or *perfect*.[11] This is how it has been labelled in some of the previous accounts of Nyakyusa: Schumann (1899) speaks of a "Perfectum" and Endemann (1914) of a "Perfekt". Likewise, Mwangoka & Voorhoeve (1960c) use the label "recent perfect". The anterior (perfect) is also how this construction is in many cases conveniently translated into English. In fact, the Nyakyusa present perfective covers all of the sentences in Dahl's (1985) tense and aspect questionnaire that are identified as prototypical for the employment of the crosslinguistic category of anteriors.

An analysis as an anterior is also suggested by the criteria proposed in Nurse's pan-Bantu study of tense and aspect, in which he identifies the configuration ø-VB-*ile* as the most common marker of anteriors in his sample of Bantu languages (Nurse 2008: 156). More importantly, Nurse (2008: 95–99) proposes a number of criteria specific to the morphosyntactic make-up of Bantu languages in order to distinguish between anteriors on the one hand and near past perfectives on the other. Two of these criteria can readily be applied to Nyakyusa. The first one concerns the interaction of grammatical aspect with the aspectual potential of the lexical verb. Drawing on the concepts of consequent state and relevance, which are widely considered core components of anteriors, Nurse states:

> For an action verb, for example, anterior represents a situation that is completed but relevant, whereas for a stative verb anterior represents the continuing state resulting from an action initiated in the past. (Nurse 2008: 73)

---

[11] The term *anterior*, as used by among others Bybee et al. (1994), is synonymous with the traditional *perfect*, but has the advantage of not being easily confused with *perfective*.

As has been seen in §6.5.3.1, while a resultant state reading is indeed the default for the Nyakyusa present perfective with inchoative verbs (Nurse's statives), a dynamic change-of-state reading is also available. More example cases are given in the following. In (63) the resultant state is explicitly cancelled for utterance time, leaving only the dynamic reading. In (64), the question is about a previous event of turning angry, not a present state.[12] Lastly, in (65) the event time adverbial phrase 'last year' allows only for a change-of-state reading. While 'to die' in English is often considered a punctual achievement (e.g. Dowty 1979: 54), its Nyakyusa equivalent *fwa* is an inchoative verbinchoative verbs best translated as 'to be moribund/die/be dead'; see §5.3.4. Also note that lexical verbs which are non-inchoative but suggest entry into a state do not depend upon a result persisting at utterance time, as with *isa* 'come' in (67) below.

(63) ii-treni   ly-ɪm-ile,   lɪno li-kw-end-a   kangɪ
      5-train(<SWA) 5-stand/stop-PFV now 5-PRS-walk/travel-FV again

      'The train stopped, but now it is moving again.' [ET]

(64) a-kaleele=mo   sikʊ baaba   gw-ako?
      1-be(come)_angry.PFV=some ever father(<SWA) 1-POSS.2SG

      'Has your father ever become angry?' [ET]

(65) a-fw-ile ɪ-ky-ɪnja   ɪ-kɪ   kɪ-kɪnd-ile
      1-die-PFV AUG-7-year AUG-PROX.7 7-pass-PFV

      'He died last year.' [ET]

What is more, the present perfective does not feature a strong relevance component. Instead it is the default paradigm for relating recent non-progressive states-of-affairs. In doing so it can be freely used with sequential eventualities, which is a negative criterion for anteriors (Dahl 1985: 138; Bybee et al. 1994: 54; Lindsted 2000: 371). The following examples illustrate both points. In (66) Tortoise asks his child for the whereabouts of a grindstone. Tortoise's child's answer consists of three clauses. In the first, the past perfective with inchoative *kalala* 'be(come) angry' refers to Mr. Monkey's previous state of mind, which has not only passed but is background information. In the two following clauses, the eventualities affecting the discourse topic (the grindstone) are summarized in the form of a minimal narrative using the present perfective. In (67) a woman reports to her husband the recent happenings, again using two narrative clauses with the present perfective.

---

[12] See §3.3.8.4 on the enclitic =*mo*.

(66) mw-anangʊ, lʊ-lɪ koo=kʊʊgʊ ʊ-lw-ala lw-angʊ?
1-my_child 11-COP REF.17=where AUG-11-grindstone 11-POSS.1SG

'[Tortoise:] My child, where is my grindstone?'

aah, mwa=n-gambɪlɪ a-a-kaleele fiijo.
INTERJ matronym=9-monkey 1-PST-be(come)_angry.PFV INTENS

eeg-ile ʊ-lw-ala lʊ-la, **a-taag-ile** m-mi-syanjʊ
1.take-PFV AUG-11-grindstone 11-DIST 1-throw-PFV 18-4-bush

'[Tortoise's child:] Aah, Mr. Monkey was very angry. He took that grindstone, he threw it into the bush.' [Monkey and Tortoise]

(67) **iis-ile=po** ʊ-mu-ndʊ jʊ-mo, a-a-sʊʊm-aga a-ma-beele.
1.come-PFV=16 AUG-1-person 1-one 1-PST-beg-IPFV AUG-6-breast_milk

leelo **n-um-bʊʊl-ile** ʊkʊtɪ iis-e na=a-ma-jolo
now/but 1SG-1-tell-PFV COMP 1.come-SUBJ COM=AUG-6-evening

'Somebody came by, she was asking for breast milk. I told her to come back in the evening.' [Killer woman]

To sum up so far, the Nyakyusa present perfective neither necessarily brings about a persistent result, nor does it feature a strong relevance component. Now, recall from §1.4.2 that Botne & Kershner define tense in terms of inclusion and exclusion of the deictic locus. Being a present tense construction, not only does the vantage point evoked by the present perfective by default coincide with the time of speech, but the eventuality depicted is also situated within the same reference frame. Any notion of prevailing effects can thus be understood as a mere function of the eventuality being included within the here-and-now reality of the speech event, particularly when taking into consideration the opposition to its past tense counterpart a(lɪ)-VB-*ile*. There is thus no need to assume any of the further components of meaning commonly assumed in the literature on anteriors such as the introduction of a "perfect state" (Moens 1987; Moens & Steedman 1988), "result state" (Kamp & Reyle 1993) or a modal presupposition (Portner 2003);[13] see Ritz (2012) for an overview of common theories of anteriors.

Nurse's second criterion concerns compound verb constructions. Anteriors, but not perfectives, should be found in these. The present perfective with inchoative verbs can serve as the complement of the persistive aspect auxiliary (§6.6.2), which would speak in favour of a classification as an anterior. However,

---

[13] Also note that these authors, in drawing on Reichenbach (1947), take as a starting point the temporal ordering of an eventuality relative to a reference point (which for a present anterior equals time of speech), as in Reichenbach's famous formalisation "E–R,S". As seen in §6.5.3.2, the vantage point evoked rather follows the characteristic act (Nucleus) which may be followed by a resultant state phase (Coda).

the same combinatory possibility also holds for the past perfective, which itself is most likely derived historically from a compound verb construction consisting of the copula plus the present perfective (§6.5.5).

Furthermore, the notion of 'still', as expressed through the persistive in Nyakyusa, is typically incompatible with anteriors (see Nedjalkov & Jaxontov 1988, among others). To combine with 'still' is instead said to be a hallmark of resultatives. These are grammatical constructions that express a state brought about by a past situation. In this they differ from anteriors, which focus on the past situation itself (Dahl 1985: 134; Bybee et al. 1994: 69). The Nyakyusa perfective in its stative reading asserts that the subject is in the resultant state of the act lexically encoded as the Nucleus, and thus comes closer to a resultative than to an anterior. As seen in §6.5.3.2 above, this resultative-like reading falls out naturally from the analysis of -ile as a marker of nuclear completion.

Lastly, consider the organization of the Nyakyusa TAM system. Within the present tense, the perfective contrasts primarily with the simple present. While the perfective selects a time posterior to the right edge of the Nucleus phase, the simple present denotes the unfolding or future occurrence of a single eventuality. That is, it denotes a time before the endpoint of the Nucleus. In the past tense, the very same opposition is found between the past perfective – which shows the same interaction with the lexical dimension – and the past imperfective.

In sum, an analysis of the configuration ø-VB-ile as an anterior is contradicted by its semantics and distribution. Instead, its meaning and use, including any overlap with the crosslinguistic category of anterior, are readily explained by the aspectual notion of a post-Nucleus vantage point, together with the present tense "denoting a primary, prevailing [...] perspective" (Botne & Kershner 2008: 153). What is more, postulating an analysis of ø-VB-ile as an anterior would preclude a compositional analysis of its past-marked counterpart a(lɪ)-VB-ile.[14] It would also miss the systematic parallel between the aspectual oppositions in the present and past tenses.

6.5.3.4 Summary

To sum up, the Nyakyusa present perfective depicts the completion of an eventuality's Nucleus without dissociation to a distant reference frame. In this it forms part of a coherent grammatical system, centred around the notions of perfectiv-

---

[14]Unless both are analysed as anteriors, which would not only render this label vacuous, but is contradicted by the negative criteria of their compatibility with sequential events and persistive aspect.

ity as completion of thc Nucleus phase in the dimension of grammatical aspect, and association vs. dissociation in the dimension of tense.

Consistent with this analysis, in past tense narrative discourse the present perfective is found in a few clearly determined environments: first, as a narrative present, where it provides information ancillary to the storyline and patterns with the simple present and present copula; and second, with relative time reference in subordinate clauses. These two kinds of uses are discussed separately in §6.7. Lastly, it features in the coda section of some narratives (68), where it refers to the speaker-now and is again in predictable alternation with the other present-tense paradigms.

(68) a-ka-pango ka-mal-iike
      AUG-12-story 12-finish-NEUT.PFV
      'The story is over.' [Monster with Guitar]

6.5.4 Negative present perfective

The negative counterpart to the present perfective consists of the negative post-initial prefix *ka-* and the default final vowel *-a*.

(69) *tʊkajoba* 'we have not spoken'

With inchoative verbs, this construction typically negates the resultant state (70), while with non-inchoatives, the eventuality is typically understood not to have occurred (71).

(70) **ba-k-ii-gan-a**   ʊ-kʊ-bomb-el-a   ɪ-fy-ombo ɪ-fy-a
      2-NEG-REFL-like-FV AUG-15-work-APPL-FV AUG-8-tool AUG-8-ASSOC
      kw-asim-a   kʊ-ba-palamani
      15-borrow-FV 17-2-neighbour
      'They do not like to work with tools borrowed from neighbours' [Types of tools in the home]

(71) mma, **a-ka-job-a**   bo ʊ-lʊ.   a-t-ile   "kalʊlʊ ʊ-jʊ
      no,   1-NEG-speak-FV as AUG-PROX.11 1-say-PFV hare(1) AUG-PROX.1
      n-heesya   gw-ɪtʊ"
      1-foreigner 1-POSS.1PL
      'No, he didn't speak like that. He said "This hare's our guest."' [Saliki and Hare]

Examples such as (72, 73) constitute a variation on Dowty's (1979) "imperfective paradox". These were judged redundant but not contradictory. This suggests that what is actually negated is the completion of the Nucleus phase.

(72) a-ka-fik-a,   leelo   a-lɪ pa-kʊ-fik-a
      1-NEG-arrive-FV now/but 1-COP 16-15-arrive-FV

      'He has not arrived (yet), but he is arriving.' [ET]

(73) a-ka-kalal-a,   leelo   a-lɪ pa-kʊ-kalala-a
      1-NEG-be(come)_angry-FV now/but 1-COP 16-15-be(come)_angry-FV

      'He is not angry (yet), but he is about to get angry.' [ET]

6.5.5 Past perfective

6.5.5.1 Formal makeup

The past perfective consists of a prefix *a-* and the suffix *-ile* (74); see §6.4.2 on the allomorphs of *-ile*. Preceding a vowel, i.e. in vowel-initial stems (75) or the reflexive object marker (76), the prefix of the past perfective has the allomorph *alɪ-*. The usual rules of pre-stem vowel contact apply; see §2.2.1.4.

(74) *twabombile* (°tʊ-a-bomb-ile) 'we worked'
      twakeetile   (°tʊ-a-keet-ile)   'we watched'

(75) *twaliisile*   (°tʊ-alɪ-is-ile)   'we came'
      twalyɪmile   (°tʊ-alɪ-ɪm-ile)   'we stopped'
      twalyegile   (°tʊ-alɪ-eg-ile)   'we took'
      twalyagile   (°tʊ-alɪ-ag-ile)   'we found'
      twalyogile   (°tʊ-alɪ-og-ile)   'we bathed'
      twalyʊmile (°tʊ-alɪ-ʊm-ile) 'we dried'

(76) *twaliikeetile* (°tʊ-alɪ-i-keet-ile) 'we looked at ourselves'
      twaliipakile (°tʊ-alɪ-i-pak-ile) 'we painted ourselves'

The same allomorph *alɪ-* also surfaces preceding the object markers of the first person singular (77) and noun class 1 (78), regardless of their respective allomorphs.[15]

(77) *mwalɪndaagile* (°mu-alɪ-ny-taag-ile) 'you (pl.) threw me'
      mwalɪmbʊʊlile (°mu-alɪ-ny-bʊʊl-ile) 'you (pl.) told me'

---

[15]See §3.3.4.1, 3.3.4.2 on the morphophonemics of these prefixes.

mwalɪɪmetile	(°mu-alɪ-ny-met-ile)	'you (pl.) shaved me'
mwalɪɪsalile	(°mu-alɪ-ny-sal-ile)	'you (pl.) chose me'
mwalɪɪnyaagile	(°mu-alɪ-ny-ag-ile)	'you (pl.) found me'

(78)

twalɪntaagile	(°tʊ-alɪ-mu-taag-ile)	'we threw him/her'
twalɪmbʊʊlile	(°tʊ-alɪ-mu-bʊʊl-ile)	'we told him/her'
twalɪmmetile	(°tʊ-alɪ-mu-met-ile)	'we shaved him/her'
twalɪnsalile	(°tʊ-alɪ-mu-sal-ile)	'we chose him/her'
twalɪmmwagile	(°tʊ-alɪ-mu-ag-ile)	'we found him/her'
twalɪmmootile	(°tʊ-alɪ-mu-ot-ile)	'we invited him/her'

The sequence /lɪ/ indicates that diachronically the longer form of the prefix is derived from a serial construction involving the copula *lɪ* (see Botne 1986). From a synchronic perspective, this allomorphy finds a functional explanation: due to the rules of vowel coalescence (§2.2.1.4), a prefix *a-* would assimilate to the vowel of vowel-initial stems and the reflexive prefix, resulting in forms homophonous with the present perfective. Similarly, any vowel preceding the first person singular object prefix surfaces as long (§3.3.4.1), while any vowel preceding the class 1 object prefix surfaces as short (§3.3.4.2). Again, without the alternation *a-/alɪ-* this would result in formal identity of the present and past perfective with subjects of 1, 2, 6, 12 and 16. Note that classes 1 and 2 include all human beings. Thus the alternation between *a-* and *alɪ-* serves to avoid a high degree of ambiguity.[16]

6.5.5.2 Overview of meaning

The past perfective construes a state-of-affairs as situated in the conceptual past (i.e. past D-domain in Botne & Kershner's framework; see §1.4.2.1) with its Nucleus phase completed. The aspectual notion of completion is discussed in more detail in §6.5.3.2. As (77, 78) show, with non-inchoative verbs this gives a typical posterior reading. With inchoative verbs, the default reading is one of a state holding at some contextually defined past moment:

(79) a-a-kaleele
      1-PST-be(come)_angry.PFV
      (Default reading:) 'S/he was angry.' [ET]

However, a posterior, holistic perspective is also possible with inchoative verbs. In the opening of a given in (80), the past perfective with the inchoative verb *lambalala* 'lie down, sleep' depicts the eventuality as a whole, rather than the state

---

[16]Interestingly, where Nyakyusa has ø-VB-*ile* vs. *a(lɪ)*-VB-*ile*, the Ngonde variety described by Kishindo (1999: 76f) has an opposition between *a*-VB-*ile* and *alɪ*-VB-*ile*.

of being asleep at a certain point in time. The same holds for the inchoative verb *gona* 'rest, sleep' in (81).

(80) po leelo   ɪ-n-galamu j-aa-lɪ   m-bine. **j-aa-lambaleele**
     then now/but AUG-9-lion 9-PST-COP 9-ill   9-PST-lie_down.PFV
     a-ma-sikʊ ma-tatʊ n-nyumba
     AUG-6-day 6-three 18-house(9)

     'Lion was ill. He slept for three days in his house.' [Lion and Tortoise]

(81) bo a-fik-ile   kʊ-ka-aja   **a-a-gon-ile.** n=ʊ-lʊ-bʊnjʊ
     as 1-arrive-PFV 17-12-homestead 1-PST-rest-PFV COM=AUG-11-morning
     a-lɪnkʊ-bʊʊk-a m-ma-tengele
     1-NARR-go-FV   18-6-bush

     'When she arrived home, she slept. In the morning she went into the
     bush.' [Mfyage turns into a lion]

Note that the past perfective by itself does not denote sequential events. Consider the following plot summary of a story, which was given subsequent to the itself; Hare's running alone, mentioned for the first time in (82a), only takes place after Tugutu's preparations (82c, 82d). The flowchart in Figure 6.3 illustrates the relative order of events. The shunt to the right symbolizes that the negative verb in (82b) remains outside the sequence as a function of its negative polarity.

(82) a. a-a-bop-ile   mw-ene, a-a-bop-ile   mw-ene kalʊlʊ
        1-PST-run-PFV 1-self   1-PST-run-PFV 1-self   hare(1)

        'He ran alone, Hare ran alone.'

     b. mwa=n-dugutu   a-ka-a-bop-ile=po
        matronym=9-type_of_bird 1-NEG-PST-run-PFV=PART

        'Mr. Tugutu did not run at all.'

     c. a-a-ba-paal-ile   a-ba-nine
        1-PST-2-invite-PFV AUG-2-colleague

        'He had gathered companions.'

     d. bo   a-ba   a-a-ba-bɪɪk-ile ʊ-kʊ-tɪ   maelɪ   jɪ-mo,
        REF.2 AUG-PROX.2 1-PST-2-put-PFV AUG-15-say mile(9)(<EN) 9-one
        maelɪ jɪ-mo, maelɪ jɪ-mo
        mile(9) 9-one mile(9) 9-one

        'Those are the ones he placed, like one mile, one mile, one mile.'

e. po kalʋlʋ a-a-bop-ile   ɩɩw-ene
   then hare(1) 1-PST-run-PFV 1-self
   'So Hare ran alone.' [Hare and Tugutu]

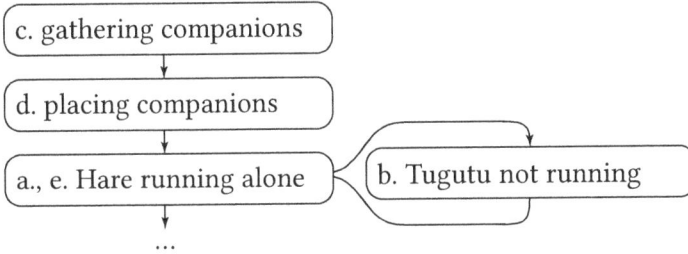

Figure 6.3: Relative event order of (82)

6.5.5.3 The past perfective in narrative discourse

6.5.5.3.1 Introduction   While in many languages a perfective form is the principle paradigm for relating the storyline in narrative discourse (see i.a. Hopper 1979; Fleischman 1990), this does not hold for Nyakyusa.[17] As discussed in §7.2.2, none of the narrative texts in the corpus exclusively features the past perfective in the recollection of storyline eventualities. Instead, Nyakyusa possesses two dedicated narrative markers – see §7.2 for an introduction – which are employed in a collaborative manner together with the past perfective to fulfil this function.

As was observed in the discussion of (82) above, the past perfective may be used with sequential events, but does not inherently encode any chronological ordering. Further, what is construed with the past perfective has an independent existence in discourse, quite contrary to the narrative tense an subsecutive, which are pragmatically dependent and thus embedded in a situation established by other means, usually through the use of a preceding past tense verb (§7.2.2). A series of mere past perfectives, such as the plot summary in (82) above, thus results in a loose enumeration of discrete events rather than forming a coherent narrative discourse of its own.

In the following, the usage of the past perfective in Nyakyusa narrative discourse will be outlined. In order to identify patterns of usage, it is necessary to

---

[17]For a recent discussion of the relationship between TMA constructions and narrating in African languages see Payne & Shirtz (2015).

first take a look at the typical composition of Nyakyusa narratives (§6.5.5.3.2–
6.5.5.3.4). Considering a set of occurrences not readily explained by notions of
textual macro-structure (§6.5.5.3.5), it will then be shown that the various uses of
the past perfective in discourse form part of a larger coherent pattern of tense usage, whose common denominator is the notion of thematic continuity (§6.5.5.3.6).
The following analysis is based mainly on the oral narratives in the corpus, but
some additional examples were taken from written texts.

6.5.5.3.2 Opening a narrative   A narrative in Nyakyusa typically opens with
an orientation section of varying length. By definition – see §1.4.4.2 – the orientation section depicts states-of-affairs that hold throughout the whole text and
orient the listener in respect to the setting. In the expected division of labour with
the other past tense paradigms, the past perfective is used here with inchoative
verbs, giving a stative reading (83), as well as with non-inchoatives, which have
a pluperfect reading (84).

(83)   a-a-li=ko   kalʊlʊ n=ɪɪ-fubu.   **ba-a-many-eene**   fiijo.
       1-PST-COP=17 hare(1) COM=AUG-hippo(9) 2-PST-know-RECP.PFV INTENS
       kangɪ b-angal-aga   pamopeene ʊ-bʊ-sikʊ   b-oosa
       again 2-PST.be_well-IPFV together   AUG-14-time 14-all

   'Once upon a time, Hare and Hippo were very much friends. And they
   used to be together the whole time.' [Hare and Hippo]

(84)   ijolo   ky-a-li=ko   ɪ-ky-amba.   pa-mwanya pa-ky-amba
       old_times 7-PST-COP=17 AUG-7-mountain 16-high   16-7-mountain
       pa-a-lɪ   pa-tengaamu itolo. **ba-a-jeng-ile=po** a-ba-ndʊ   ba-tatʊ
       16-PST-COP 16-peaceful   just 2-PST-build-PFV=16 AUG-2-person 2-three

   'Long ago there was a mountain. On top of the mountain it was all
   peaceful. Three people had built there.' [Selfishness kills]

   Following the orientation section, one commonly finds a verb in one of the
past tense paradigms that sets the stage for the first episode. In cases where
there is no orientation section, this constitutes the opening of the text. For an
example of the past perfective in this environment, see (9) on p. 215.

6.5.5.3.3 Textual boundaries   In longer narratives, subsequent major units are
commonly also delimited by one or more past tense verbs. This often implies
a shift away from one of the narrative markers. These verbs depict the state-
of-affairs out of which the following course of events develops. Again, the past

perfective, imperfective and copula pattern together, depending on the aspectual profile of the state-of-affairs and the verb's Aristotelian aspect.

It is important to note at this point that the notions of boundary marking and staging operate within the textual component. An event that forms part of the semantic storyline may additionally be construed as the setting of a unit within the text if it depicts the circumstances under which following eventualities take place (Payne 1992). By virtue of its aspectual semantics, it is the past perfective that is employed in these cases. Further, it is typically not every episode within longer texts that starts out with a past tense. The following examples will illustrate both points.

In the text "Monkey and Tortoise", lazy but witty Tortoise sends his child to Monkey's to get food, pretending to buy it on credit. After obtaining the food, little Tortoise returns home. They enjoy their meals and never make the agreed payment (85). Clause (85a) is the last one in the food-obtaining episode. The following clauses (85b–85e) are all marked for past tense and group together to describe a major discontinuity in action and time. Of these, (85d, 85e), by virtue of the states-of-affairs they depict, as well as the fact that they include two negatives, give information that diverges from the main storyline. The eating in (85b), however, is no less eventive than the preceding walk home. Nevertheless, it is construed as part of the upcoming episode's setting.

(85) a. po   mw-ene jʊ-la gw-a   kajamba   a-lɪnkʊ-bʊʊk-a
          then 1-self   1-DIST 1-ASSOC tortoise(1) 1-NARR-go-FV
          kʊ-ka-aja   n=ɪ-fi-ndʊ   fi-la
          17-12-homestead COM=AUG-8-food 8-DIST

          'Tortoise's child went home with that food.'

      b. po   n=ʊ-gwise   po   **ba-a-l-iile**
          then COM=AUG-his_father(1) then 2-PST-eat-PFV

          'He and his father ate.'

      c. po   ba-a-hobwike   fiijo   a-ma-sikʊ ma-bɪlɪ
          then 2-PST-be(come)_happy.PFV INTENS AUG-6-day 6-two

          'They were very happy for two days.'

      d. leelo   bo gɪ-kɪnd-ile ɪ-mi-lʊngʊ mi-bɪlɪ, kajamba
          now/but as 4-pass-PFV AUG-4-week 4-two   tortoise(1)
          a-ka-a-buj-iisye.   a-ka-a-bʊʊk-ile   kw-a
          1-NEG-PST-return-CAUS.PFV 1-NEG-PST-go-PFV 17-ASSOC

mwa=n-gambılı   kʊ-kʊ-bıık-a ıı-heela
matronym=9-monkey 17-15-put-FV AUG-money(9)

'When two weeks passed, Tortoise had not paid. He had not gone to Monkey's to hand over the money.'

e. gw-a-kınd-ile   ʊ-ṇ-dʊngʊ   gʊ-mo. gy-a-kınd-ile   mi-bılı
    3-PST-pass-PFV AUG-3-week 3-one   4-PST-pass-PFV 4-two
    na=ka-mo   n=ʊ-kʊ-bʊʊk-a   kʊ-kʊ-bıık-a
    COM=12-one COM=AUG-15-go-FV   17-15-put-FV

'One week passed. Two weeks passed, not once going to hand it over.'

f. po mwa=n-gambılı   a-a-tı   "hee. po   m-bʊʊk-e
   as matronym=9-monkey 1-SUBSEC-say INTERJ then 1SG-go-SUBJ
   kw-a   kajamba kʊ-kʊ-mel-a ıı-heela   sy-angʊ"
   17-ASSOC tortoise(1) 17-15-claim-FV AUG-money(10) 10-POSS.1SG

'Then Monkey said "Hee. I shall go to Tortoise to demand my money."'

g. po   a-lınkw-end-a,   a-lınkw-end-a,
   then 1-NARR-walk/travel-FV 1-NARR-walk/travel-FV
   a-lınkw-end-a
   1-NARR-walk/travel-FV

'He walked and walked and walked.' [Monkey and Tortoise]

With (85f, 85g) the storyline continues. Tortoise makes an excuse and Monkey gives up on claiming his money that day. This episode is narrated entirely using the (plus one token of a narrative present). Now, after two more weeks, Monkey returns to Tortoise's only to hear another excuse and to go home again without his money. This episode, whose main events essentially repeat those of the preceding one, is not further delimited by a shift to the past tense (86).

(86)   a. kangı po   bo gı-kınd-ile ı-mi-lʊngʊ   mi-bılı, kangı
       again then as 4-pass-PFV AUG-4-week 4-two   again
       a-lınkʊ-buj-a   kw-a   kajamba
       1-NARR-return-FV 17-ASSOC tortoise(1)

'When two weeks had passed, he returned again to Tortoise's.'

     b. bo i-kʊ-fik-a   i-kʊ-mmw-ani-a ʊ-mw-anaake   "a-li=po
       as 1-PRS-arrive-FV 1-PRS-1-ask-FV   AUG-1-his_child 1-COP=16
       ʊ-gʊʊso   a-pa?"
       AUG-your_father AUG-PROX.16

'As he was arriving he asks his (Tortoise's) child "Is your father here?"' [Monkey and Tortoise]

In contrast, the next episode does start with a shift to the past tense (87). Note how the content of the first two clauses of this episode (87a, 87b) mostly parallels the first clause of the preceding episode (86a). The use of the past perfective instead of the coincides with a change in Monkey's attitude. This entails an important shift in the development of events. Instead of continuing the routine of the preceding two episodes, Tortoise finds himself needing to resort to a more elaborate trick to get away without paying his debts.

(87)   a. ii-sikʊ lɪ-lɪ-ngɪ po **a-al-iis-ile**   mwa=n-gambɪlɪ
         5-day 5-5-other then 1-PST-come-PFV matronym=9-monkey

        'Another day Mr. Monkey came.'

     b. **a-al-iis-ile**   n=ɪ-ly-ojo
         1-PST-come-PFV COM=AUG-5-anger

        'He came with anger.'

     c. "lɪlɪno   kʊ-m-ba=ko   ɪɪ-heela   j-angʊ,
         now/today 2SG.PRS-1SG-give=17 AUG-money(9) 9-POSS.1SG

         kʊ-m-ba=ko   ɪɪ-heela   j-angʊ" i-kʊ-job-a
         2SG.PRS-1SG-give=17 AUG-money(9) 9-POSS.1SG 1-PRS-speak-FV

         mu-n-jɪla
         18-9-path

        '"Today you're giving me my money, you're giving me my money", he is saying on his way.'

     d. a-lɪnkw-a   kʊ-fik-a   pa-a   kajamba
         1-NARR-go.FV 15-arrive-FV 16-ASSOC tortoise(1)

        'He arrived at Tortoise's.' [Monkey and Tortoise]

6.5.5.3.4 Further supportive material   The storyline may be sprinkled with occasional supportive information in the past tense, be it the past perfective, past imperfective or the past copula, or a narrative present (see §6.7.1 on the latter). This may consist of embedded orientations, that is, states-of-affairs that hold throughout all or parts of the text. The past perfective is therefore used with inchoative verbs. This is common with verbs depicting psychological states, as illustrated in (88b). Note that with most inchoative verbs the past perfective is the only paradigm that can denote the resultant state and not merely the change-of-state.

(88)   Context: Monkey is waiting for Tortoise.

   a. a-a-j-ile   kʊ-buj-a.   "Hahaha mwa=n-gambılı
      1-PST-go-PFV 15-return-FV INTERJ matronym=9-monkey
      ʊ-li=po.   gw-is-ile,   pole!   n-gʊ-p-a   lılıno
      2SG-COP=16 2SG-come-PFV sorry(<SWA) 1SG-PRS-give-FV now/today
      ıı-heela   sy-ako"
      AUG-money(10) 10-POSS.2SG

     'He [Tortoise] went and returned. "Hahaha, Mr. Monkey, you are
     here! You have come, sorry! I'm giving you your money now."

   b. po mwa=n-gambılı   **a-a-hobwike**   "haa
      then matronym=9-monkey 1-PST-be(come)_happy.PFV INTERJ
      (clapping hands) mma po   kʊ-m-b-a   ahahaa"
                 no   then 2SG.PRS-1SG-give-FV INTERJ

     'Mr. Monkey was happy "Haa (clapping hands), you are giving me
     [my money], ahahaa." [Monkey and Tortoise]

   The past perfective is also used for flashbacks. It is the only verbal paradigm attested in the case of flashbacks.

(89)   Context: Tortoise's child and Monkey are waiting for Tortoise.

   a. ba-lınkʊ-ṃ-bon-a bo a-fum-ile   bo kʊ-la
      2-NARR-1-see-FV as 1-come_from-PFV as 17-DIST

     'They saw him [Tortoise] as he came from over there.'

   b. ʊ-tı   **ba-alı-n-taag-ile** mu-m-mi-syanjʊ
      2SG-say.SUBJ 2-PST-1-throw-PFV 18-18-4-bush

     'Do you know, they had thrown him into the bush.'

   c. po **a-a-j-ile**   kw-end-a   kʊ-la
      then 1-PST-go-PFV 15-walk/travel-FV 17-DIST

     'He had (gone and) had a walk there.'

   d. **a-a-j-ile**   kʊ-buj-a
      1-PST-go-PFV 17-return-FV

     'He had gone and returned.' [Monkey and Tortoise]

6.5.5.3.5 Further storyline events As has been discussed thus far, the past perfective is frequently employed – together with the other past tense paradigms – in narrative discourse for setting the stage at major episode boundaries and for providing information ancillary to the storyline. In addition, it is commonly found in relating more storyline events, where its employment vis-à-vis the dedicated narrative markers is not readily explained by the patterns described above. A closer examination shows that in these cases it normally depicts eventualities that are unpredictable, pivotal for the development of the plot and/or constitute a major change in the roles of participants.[18] In §6.5.5.3.6 below it will be shown that all these uses of the past perfective form part of one coherent pattern of employment of the past tense paradigms vis-à-vis the narrative markers. It will be shown that this pattern is governed by the notion of thematic continuity.

The uses of the past perfective with further storyline events will be illustrated by walking through the narrative of "Hare and Tugutu". A summary of this story was given in (82) on p. 168 above. (90) presents the first three clauses of the narrative. Instead of featuring a proper orientation section, the two protagonists and the setting are introduced in the opening clause (90a). This is followed by a switch to the in (90b). The use of the past perfective in (90c), however, is conspicuous, as this example neither constitutes an episode boundary nor backgrounded material. However, the proposition given in this clause, Tugutu's challenging of Hare, is a major turning point in the story. It constitutes the raison d'être for the following race, around which the story revolves. Furthermore, apart from Tugutu's answer being somewhat unexpected, there is a major discontinuity in the relative roles of the participants. From this point on, Tugutu is the focal character driving the action. This stands in contrast to the first two clauses which centre around Hare.

(90) a. ii-sikʊ lɪ-mo, kalʊlʊ a-aly-ag-an-iile   n=ii-tugutu
          5-day 5-one hare(1) 1-PST-find-RECP-APPL.PFV COM=5-type_of_bird

          'One day, Hare met with Tugutu (a type of bird).'

     b. a-lɪnkʊ-tɪ   "gwe, tugutu, ʊ-gwe!   ʊ-ka-bagɪl-a
          1-NARR-say   2SG   t.o.bird AUG-2SG 2SG-NEG-be_able-FV

          ʊ-kʊ-n-gɪnd-a   ʊ-ne   ʊ-kʊ-bop-a,   ʊ-ne
          AUG-15-1SG-surpass-FV AUG-1SG AUG-15-run-FV AUG-1SG

          n-gʊ-bop-a   fiijo,   m-bagiile   ʊ-kʊ-kʊ-tol-a"
          1SG-PRS-run-FV INTENS 1SG-be_able.PFV AUG-15-2SG-beat-FV

          'He said "You, Tugutu, you! You can't beat me in running, I run fast, I
          can beat you."'

---

[18] Jones & Jones (1979: 8) define pivotal events as "very crucial or significant events of a narrative [...] when collected together, they form a high-level summary or abstract of the story". This definition is reflected in Tomlin (1985: 90) and Longacre (1990: 5).

    c. ii-tugutu **ly-a-t-ile** "mma. ʊ-ka-bagɪl-a
        5-t.o.bird 5-PST-say-PFV no   2SG-NEG-be_able-FV
        ʊ-kʊ-n-dol-a   kalʊlʊ ʊ-kʊ-bop-a. tʊ-bagiile   pamo
        AUG-15-1SG-beat-FV hare(1) AUG-15-run-FV 1PL-be_able.PFV maybe
        ʊ-kʊ-tol-an-a,   ʊ-kʊ-fwan-a"
        AUG-15-beat-RECP-FV AUG-15-be(come)_equal-FV
        'Tugutu said "No. You, Hare, can't beat me in running. We can maybe have a tie."' [Hare and Tugutu]

The continuation of the story is given in (91). Hare's answer in (91a), using the subsecutive, still forms part of the challenging episode. With (91b–91g) the narrator shifts to the past perfective as he takes up a new line of events: Tugutu invites his companions and places them along the track. Leaving aside the parenthetic insertion in (91d), the events given are preliminary and decisive for the development of the plot. Rather than mere staging for the upcoming race, these can be considered to form a coherent episode of their own.

(91) a. a-a-tɪ   "mma popaa~po   tw-and-e   kɪ-laabo
        1-SUBSEC-say no   REDUPL~then 1PL-start-SUBJ 7-tomorrow
        ʊ-kʊ-bop-a"
        AUG-15-run-FV
        'He (Hare) said "Ok then, tomorrow let's start to run."'

    b. po mwa=n-dugutu   **a-a-bʊʊk-ile**
        then matronym=9-t.o.bird 1-PST-go-PFV
        'Mr. Tugutu went.'

    c. **a-a-ba-paal-ile** a-ba-nine   ba-haano
        1-PST-2-invite-PFV AUG-2-companion 2-five
        'He gathered five companions.'

    d. paapo ba-al-iitɪk-eene   na kalʊlʊ ʊ-kʊ-bop-a
        because 2-PST-agree-RECP.PFV COM hare(1) AUG-15-run-FV
        a-ma-eli   ma-haano
        AUG-6-mile(EN) 6-five
        'Because they had agreed to run five miles.'

    e. bo ii-sikʊ ly-a   kɪ-laabo, bo lɪ-fik-ile,   mwa=n-dugutu
        as 5-day 5-ASSOC 7-tomorrow as 5-arrive-PFV matronym=9-t.o.bird
        a-alɪ-m̩-bɪɪk-ile mwa=n-dugutu   n-nine   pa-bw-andɪlo
        1-PST-1-put-FV matronym=9-t.o.bird 1-companion 16-14-start
        'When the next day arrived, Mr. Tugutu placed a fellow Mr. Tugutu at the start.'

f. ɪɪ-maeli   j-aa   bʊ-bɪlɪ mwa=n-dugutu   ʊ-jʊ-ngɪ   [...]
AUG-mile(9) 9-ASSOC 14-two matronym=9-t.o.bird AUG-1-other

'The second mile another Mr. Tugutu [...]'

g. na kʊ-bʊ-malɪ̃kɪlo, maeli ga-a   bʊ-haano, mwa=n-dugutu
COM 17-14-end   mile 6-ASSOC 14-five   matronym=9-t.o.bird

ʊ-jʊ-ngɪ
AUG-1-other

'At the finish line, the fifth mile, another Mr. Tugutu.' [Hare and Tugutu]

The rest of the story consists of a detailed description of the race itself and the dialogue that takes place throughout the race, which are narrated entirely using the narrative markers, with the exception of one flashback.

6.5.5.3.6 Summary and discussion   The preceding sections have shown a number of recurring contexts in which the past perfective is employed within narrative discourse. It can be seen that it is used, as are the other past tense paradigms, in free and restricted clauses that provide information ancillary to the storyline. These clauses may be contained within a dedicated orientation section or be distributed throughout the text. Consistent with the semantics of the past perfective, this mostly gives a stative reading with inchoative verbs and a posterior one with non-inchoatives. Within the plot proper, the latter can be employed for flashbacks. The past perfective is further used to set the stage at major boundaries within the text, again in a division of labour with the other past tense paradigms. This is common as a 'backdrop' to the first episode of a text, and is also found in major units throughout narratives. Lastly, the past perfective is also found with storyline events that form important turning points. Note that this distribution of the past perfective defies Longacre's approach of storyline ranks, which is widely received in linguistic discourse studies, especially in the SIL tradition. According to Longacre, TMA categories within a given language can be ranked in order of the degree to which the clauses they are found in either belong to the primary storyline, augment the storyline (pivotal events) or depart from it (e.g. secondary storyline, backgrounded actions, setting); also see §7.2.1. The Nyakyusa past perfective figures all over Longacre's storyline ranks: it is used with ancillary material, i.e. below the storyline, with events serve as staging for what follows, as well as with pivotal events, which have the highest degree of saliency in Longacre's framework. That is, the employment of TMA categories in Nyakyusa narrative discourse cannot be explained on the basis of storyline ranks.

Interestingly, in Longacre's own work one finds a case that very much parallels that of Nyakyusa. In a discussion of Avokaya (East Sudanic, Nilo Saharan), Longacre stipulates that the so-called *narrative tense* is a marker of the primary storyline, while the perfect or perfective – his use of the two terms is inconsistent – belongs to a lower rank, the secondary storyline (Longacre 1990: 91–97). The latter paradigm, however, is used not only to stage and re-stage sequences of actions, but also to "show that a particular action is not script-predictable". Longacre goes on to conclude that in the first case we are dealing with events that are "preliminary and preparatory for what follows [...] but this usage grades off into one representing events that are not script-predictable, but rather of themselves shift a sequence of actions/events into the direction of a new script". If not storyline concerns, then what is the conceptual category that governs Nyakyusa narrative discourse? Nurse (2008: 120), in a discussion of narrative markers in Bantu, states that "[u]se of the special [narrative, BP] marker can be suspended and then deliberately reintroduced by the speaker to stress continuity." Put the other way around, use of verbal paradigms other than the narrative markers signals discontinuity. If one states Nurse's vague term of continuity more precisely as thematic continuity, all of the uses of the past perfective, as well as of the other past tense paradigms, find a common denominator. As Givón (1984) describes it, is a conceptual notion that holds within (parts of) a text and is made up of four thematic dimensions: the three dimensions of time, place, action, i.e. the unity well-known from ancient Greek playwrights, plus a fourth one of participants. Languages may employ specific signals that continuity is significantly interrupted in at least one of these four dimensions (Dooley & Levinsohn 2000). Table 6.5 illustrates the dimensions of thematic continuity and their respective continuities and discontinuities.

The opening of a narrative, as well as an initial orientation section, are discontinuous amongst all these dimensions with regard to the discursive context. Ancillary information distributed throughout the text is highly discontinuous with regard to the storyline, by virtue of the type of material it provides (dimension of action), as well as by being outside the temporal sequence (dimension of time). The latter also holds for flashbacks. Episodes and groups of episodes within a text are by definition major thematic groupings that deserve to be delimited by use of a past tense paradigm. Lastly, important turning points in the plot constitute major changes in at least one of the thematic dimensions.

To sum up then, as far as tense and narrative markers are concerned, Nyakyusa narrative discourse is structured around the conceptual notions of thematic continuity in the storyline (employment of the narrative markers) and discontinuity

Table 6.5: Dimensions of thematic continuity/discontinuity (adapted from Dooley & Levinsohn 2000: 19)

	Continuity	Discontinuity
time	events separated by at most only small forward gaps	large forward gaps or events out of order
place	same place or continuous motion	discrete changes of place
action	all material of the same type	changes from one type of material to another
participants	same cast and some general roles vis-à-vis one other	discrete changes of cast or changes in relative roles

(employment of the past tense paradigms). Comparable analyses focusing on thematic continuity as the motivation for the choice of TMA categories in narrative discourse have been put forward by Watters (2002) for Kham (Sino-Tibetan) and by Robar (2014) for Biblical Hebrew. A similar line of reasoning is made by R. Carlson (1992) for a number of West and East African languages. The past perfective occupies a privileged role in this interplay between past tense and narrative markers as it can be employed for discontinuous events. It is important to note at this point that this employment of the TMA categories constitutes a discursive convention, which leaves the narrator with room for stylistic considerations. There is considerable variation across texts concerning how much of the storyline is carried by the past perfective vis-à-vis the narrative markers. This is further discussed and illustrated in §7.2.3.

6.5.6 Negative past perfective

The negative past perfective is formed with the negative prefix *ka-*, the past prefix *a-* and the perfective suffix -*ile* or one of its allomorphs (see §6.4.2). As with the affirmative past perfective, the past prefix surfaces as *alɪ-* preceding vowel-initial stems, the object marker, as well as the object markers of the first person singular and noun class 1; see §6.5.5.

(92) *tʊkaajobile* 'we did not work'

With non-inchoative verbs, this construction gives a negative posterior/holistic reading (93). As such it is by far the most common form used in the corpus to assert the non-occurrence of eventualities. With inchoative verbs, all tokens in the corpus have a negative state reading, as illustrated in (94, 95).

(93) po jɪ-lɪnkʊ-bʊʊk-a ʊ-kʊ-sook-a=po. po leelo
    then 9-NARR-go-FV AUG-15-leave-FV=16 then but/now
    jɪ-ka-a-bʊʊk-ile pa-bʊ-tali
    9-NEG-PST-go-PFV 16-14-long
    'It [snake] went and left. It did not go far.' [Python and woman]

(94) ʊ-mw-ene kalʊlʊ **a-ka-a-meenye** ʊkʊtɪ ʊ-lw-ɪfi
    AUG-1-self hare(1) 1-NEG-PST-know.PFV COMP AUG-11-chameleon
    lʊ-nyeel-iile pa-n-sana paapo lw-a-lɪ lʊ-pepe
    11-jump-APPL.PFV 16-3-waist because 11-PST-COP 11-light
    'Hare himself did not know that Chameleon had jumped at his hip because he was light.' [Hare and Chameleon]

(95) a-a-li=ko kajamba jʊ-mo. a-a-lɪ m-oolo fiijo.
    1-PST-COP=17 tortoise(1) 1-one 1-PST-COP 1-lazy INTENS
    a-ka-al-iigan-ile ʊ-kʊ-bomb-a ɪ-m-bombo
    1-NEG-PST-like-PFV AUG-15-work-FV AUG-9-work
    'There was a certain tortoise. It was very lazy. It did not like to work.' [Monkey and Tortoise]

6.5.7 Past imperfective

6.5.7.1 Formal makeup and overview of meaning

The past imperfective is formed with the past prefix *a-* and the imperfective suffix *-aga*. See §6.4.1 for allomorphs of the latter.

(96) *twajobaga* 'we used to speak / we were speaking'

This construction has the uses typically associated with a past imperfective category (Comrie 1976; Dahl 1985). It can give a past continuous reading (97, 98) and can also give a broad range of past habitual or generic readings (99, 100).

(97) a-pa ʊ-m-b-eele ɪ-fi-ndʊ. ɪ-n-jala
    AUG-PROX.16 2SG-1SG-give-PFV AUG-8-food AUG-9-hunger
    j-a-n-dʊm-aga
    9-PST-1SG-bite-IPFV
    'Here you've given me food. I was hungry [lit. hunger was biting me].' [Lake Kyungululu]

(98) fyobeene **gw-a-job-aga**, nalooli lʊ-kafu
therefore 2SG-PST-speak-IPFV really 11-difficult

'That is why you were speaking, it [the lock] truly is tough.' [Wage of the thieves]

(99) n-kɪ-panga kɪ-la a-a-li=po ʊ-n-kiikʊlʊ ʊ-n-hɪɪji ʊ-jʊ
18-7-village 7-DIST 1-PST-COP=16 AUG-1-woman AUG-1-thief AUG-PROX.1

a-a-bomb-aga ɪ-j-aa kw-ib-a ɪ-fi-ndʊ ɪ-fi
1-PST-work-IPFV AUG-9-ASSOC 15-steal-FV AUG-8-food AUG-PROX.8

ba-pɪɪj-ile a-ba-nine,
2-cook-PFV AUG-2-companion

'In that village there was a thieving woman, who used to steal the food the others had cooked,'

a-a-fyʊl-aga mu-n-deko na muu-sefulɪla
1-PST-remove-IPFV 18-10-earthen_pot COM 18-cooking_pot(9)(<SWA)

'She used to take it out of earthen pots and cooking pots.'

pa-la lɪnga a-bʊʊk-ile n-k-ookol-a ʊ-m-ooto
16-DIST if/when 1-go-PFV 18-15-fetch_fire-FV AUG-3-fire

kʊ-ba-nine, lɪnga ba-lɪ pa-nja, **a-a-kuputul-aga**
17-2-companion, if/when 2-COP 16-outside 1-PST-uncover-IPFV

ɪ-fi-ndʊ n=ʊ-kʊ-fyʊl-a=mo fi-mo, **a-a-bʊʊk-aga** na=fyo
AUG-8-food COM=AUG-15-remove-FV=18 8-one 1-PST-go-IPFV COM=REF.8

kʊ-my-ake
17-4-POSS.SG

'When she went to her neighbours to get fire, if they were outside she would uncover the food, take some out and go home with it.' [Thieving woman]

(100) a-ba-nyambala **ba-a-fwal-aga** ɪ-n-gʊbo j-aa ng'ombe
AUG-2-man 2-PST-dress/wear-IPFV AUG-9-skin 9-ASSOC cow(9)

mu-no mu-n-sana
18-PROX 18-3-waist

'The men wore a skin of a cow here at the waist.' [Clothing long ago]

6.5.7.2 Uses in narrative discourse

Not surprisingly, in past narratives the past imperfective is mainly used in the orientation section, as exemplified in (99) above. To a lesser extent, it is found in free or restricted clauses that constitute embedded orientation. This is illustrated in (101).

(101) kɪ-laabo   ɪ-kɪ-ngɪ   Sokoni a-lɪnkʊ-bʊʊk-a kangɪ kʊ-kʊ-kʊng-ɪl-a
       7-tomorrow AUG-7-other S.   1-NARR-go-FV   again 17-15-tie-APPL-FV
       ɪɪ-ng'ombe
       AUG-10.cow

       'The next day, Sokoni went again to tie the cows.'

       p-oope a-alɪ-mmw-ag-ile ʊ-n-kasi   gw-a   Pakyɪndɪ i-kʊ-bomb-a
       16-also 1-PST-1-find-PFV AUG-1-wife 1-ASSOC P.   1-PRS-work-FV
       bo sila~si-la   ɪ-sy-a   m-ma-jolo
       as REDUPL~10-DIST AUG-10-ASSOC 18-6-evening

       'Again he found Pakyindi's wife doing just like the day before.'

       looli ʊ-ɲ-dʊme   **a-m-bʊʊl-aga   a-a-t-ɪgɪ**   "n-gʊ-bʊʊk-a
       but AUG-1-husband 1.PST-1-tell-IPFV 1-PST-say-IPFV 1SG-PRS-go-FV
       kʊ-kʊ-nyukul-a a-ma-jabʊ"
       17-15-pull_up-FV AUG-6-cassava

       'But to her husband she always said "I am going to harvest cassava."'
       [Sokoni and Pakyindi]

The past imperfective is also used in the staging of episodes within a text, as in (102); see 6.5.5.3) §6.5.5.3.3 on staging in Nyakyusa discourse.

(102) a. ʊ-mu-ndʊ   jʊ-mo **a-a-tiim-aga**   ɪɪ-ng'oosi
          AUG-1-person 1-one 1-PST-herd-IPFV AUG-sheep(10)

          'A man was herding sheep.'

       b. a-a-lɪ   n=ɪ-m-bwa
          1-PST-COP COM=AUG-9-dog

          'He had a dog.'

       c. popaa~po   ʊ-mu-ndʊ   jʊ-la a-lɪnkʊ-bʊʊk-a pa-kɪ-syanjʊ
          REDUPL~then AUG-1-person 1-DIST 1-NARR-go-FV   16-7-thicket
          pa-kʊ-tʊʊsy-a
          16-15-rest-FV

          'That man went into the thicket to rest.'

6.5.7.3 Modal uses

Apart from its basic uses, the past imperfective is also found in the apodoses of counterfactual conditionals.[19] Employed in this way, the past imperfective loses its temporal and aspectual specification. It can be used with a present or future reading (103, 104) and in typical perfective contexts (105).

(103) linga   n-aa-lɪ   ne laɪsi   n-aa-ba-tʊʊl-aga
      if/when 1SG-PST-COP 1SG president(<SWA) 1SG-PST-2-help-IPFV
      a-ba-londo
      AUG-2-poor
      'If I were president, I would help/be helping the poor.' [ET]

(104) linga   n-aa-lɪ   jo   ʊ-ne   n-aa-bʊʊk-aga kɪ-laabo
      if/when 1SG-PST-COP REF.1 AUG-1SG 1SG-PST-go-IPFV 7-tomorrow
      'If it were me, I would go tomorrow.' [ET]

(105) linga   tʊ-ka-aly-ag-ile   ʊ-lw-ɪsi   tw-a-fw-aga
      if/when 1PL-NEG-PST-find-PFV AUG-11-river 1PL-PST-die-IPFV
      'If we had not found the river, we would have died.' [ET]

Another modal use is attested in the following example:

(106) Context: The researcher has asked a language assistant if she is free in
      the following days.
      ee ka-lʊmbʊ   n-dɪ   na=a-ka-balɪlo.   ʊ-gwe
      yes 12-sibling_of_opposite_sex 1SG-COP COM=AUG-12-time AUG-2SG
      gw-a-lond-aga   bo ndɪɪli tw-ag-an-il-e
      2SG-PST-want-IPFV as when 1PL-find-RECP-APPL-SUBJ
      'Yes little brother, I have time. Whenever you want, let's meet.'
      [overheard]

6.5.8 Negative past imperfective

The negative counterpart to the past imperfective consists of the negative prefix *ka-*, the past prefix *a-* and the imperfective suffix *-aga*. See §6.4.1 for allomorphs of the latter.

(107) *tʊkaajobaga* 'we did not use to speak / we were not speaking'

---

[19]For another strategy of marking the apodoses of counterfactuals see §9.6.

The uses of the negative past imperfective parallel those of its affirmative counterpart. It has a continuous/progressive reading (108), which also serves as the negative counterpart to the periphrastic past progressive (§6.6.1). It is further used for negative past habituals and generics (109, 110).

(108) fiki gwe mw-ınıtʋ,   gwe gw-a   bʋ-tatʋ,
why 2SG 1-our_companion 2SG 1-ASSOC 14-three

gw-a-tʋ-bʋʋl-iile   bo ʋ-seng-iigwe,   **ʋ-ka-a-lek-aga**
2SG-PST-1PL-tell-APPL.PFV as 2SG-chop-PASS.PFV 2SG-NEG-PST-let-IPFV

fiki tw-esa tʋ-seng-igw-e?
why 1PL-all 1PL-chop-PASS-SUBJ

'Why, our friend, you the third one, did you tell us when you were cut, why did you not let all of us be cut?' [Wage of the thieves]

(109) ʋ-mw-ana **a-k-end-aga**.   ɪ-fy-ınja
AUG-1-child 1-NEG.PST-walk/travel-IPFV AUG-8-year

a-k-end-aga
1-NEG.PST-walk/travel-IPFV

'The child did not walk. For years it did not walk.' [Pregnant women]

(110) **ba-k-eeg-an-aga**   ʋ-bw-egi   bʋ-la bw-a
2-NEG-PST.marry-RECP-IPFV AUG-14-marriage 14-DIST 14-ASSOC

kʋ-piny-a pamo kw-i-kanisa.   b-aa-lɪ   n=ʋ-bw-egi
15-tie-FV   maybe 17-5-church(<SWA) 2-PST-COP COM=AUG-14-marriage

ʋ-bw-a   kyenyeeji
AUG-14-ASSOC informal_type(<SWA)

'They did not have weddings of that type where they tie the bond maybe at church. They had weddings of an informal type.' [Life and marriage long ago]

6.6 Periphrastic present and past constructions

In the following subsections, periphrastic present (non-past) and past tense constructions will be described. An overview of these is given in Table 6.6. For ease of reading, the present and past forms of each paradigm will be discussed together in single sections (§6.6.1, 6.6.2). Some further infrequent constructions will be discussed in §6.6.3.

Table 6.6: Periphrastic non-past/present and past tense constructions

Label	Shape	Example	
Progressive	SM-*lɪ pa-kʊ*-VB-*a*	*tʊlɪ pakʊjoba*	'we are speaking'
	SM-*a-lɪ pa-kʊ*-VB-*a*	*twalɪ pakʊjoba*	'we were speaking'
Persistive	SM-*kaalɪ* (+ Verb)	*tʊkaalɪ tʊkʊjoba*	'we still speak'
	SM-*a-kaalɪ* (+ Verb)	*twakaalɪ twajobaga*	'we were still speaking'

6.6.1 Progressive

The progressive consists of the copula *lɪ* and an infinitive marked for locative noun class 16. The past progressive is formed with the past prefix *a-* on the copula.

(111) a. *tʊlɪ pakʊjoba* 'we are speaking'

  b. *twalɪ pakʊjoba* 'we were speaking'

There is no counterpart to the progressive. Instead, the negative present (§6.5.2) and the negative past imperfective (§6.5.8) are used.

As the label *progressive* suggests, this construction expresses that an eventuality is ongoing. Unlike the and the past imperfective, no habitual/generic reading is available with the progressive.[20] While frequently heard, use of the periphrastic progressive is far from obligatory. The simple present and the past imperfective can also give a progressive reading (§6.5.1, 6.5.7). In temporal clauses (§6.7.2.1), the progressive is used only infrequently and often retains a locational reading (112, 113). The is the paradigm of choice for an ongoing eventuality in this context.

(112) a-ba-ndʊ   bo a-bo   bi-kʊ-bʊʊk-a kʊ-kw-asim-a ɪ-fi-bombelo
       AUG-2-person as AUG-REF.2 2-PRS-go-FV 17-15-borrow-FV AUG-8-tool
       ɪ-fy-a   kʊ-bomb-el-a   ɪ-m-bombo **bo** a-b-iinaabo
       AUG-8-ASSOC 15-work-APPL-FV AUG-9-work as AUG-2-their_companion

---

[20]Kershner (2002: 168–174) discusses a parallel construction in Sukwa, for which she coins the label "punctuated imperfectivity". Contrasting this with the progressive reading of the Sukwa equivalents of the simple present and past imperfective, she postulates that the periphrastic construes the subject as ""inside the event' or "engaged in the event" in contrast with a mere unfolding of the eventuality. No indication of such a reading was found in the Nyakyusa data.

> ba-lɪ pa-kʊ-tʊʊsy-a
> 2-COP 16-15-rest-FV
>
> 'People like those go to borrow tools to do work with, when their fellows are resting.' [Types of tools in the home]

(113) lɪnga   ba-lɪ pa-kʊ-sanuk-a kʊʊ-nyuma kʊ-no   k-oope
      if/when 2-COP 16-15-alter-FV   17-back(9)   17-PROX 17-also
      ba-a-kyakyatɪl-aga   fiijo   bʊno~bʊ-no
      2-PST-move_back_and_forth-IPFV INTENS REDUPL~14-DEM

'When they were turning back there they would move quickly back and forward like this.' [Custom of dancing]

A further difference between the and the past impefective on the one hand and the (past) progressive on the other concerns the interaction of the progressive with the lexical class of resultative achievements: with these verbs, the and the past impefective are not available in a progressive reading, while the periphrastic progressive may be used with reference to the resultant state (see Chapter 5).[21]

6.6.2 Persistive

Persistive aspect denotes that a state-of-affairs continues to hold from an earlier point until a later point of reference, by default the moment of speech. Grammaticalized constructions for this "still-tense" are common in Bantu, although often overlooked (Nurse 2008: 45). In Nyakyusa, persistive aspect is expressed by a periphrastic construction consisting of the subject prefix and a persistive auxiliary *kaalɪ*.

(114)   tʊ-kaalɪ tʊ-kʊ-job-a
        1PL-PERS 1PL-PRS-speak-FV

'we still speak / we are still speaking'

---

[21]Note that locative noun class 16 commonly denotes proximity (§2.3.1). To summarize the interaction of the periphrastic progressive with different lexical classes as analysed in Chapter 5, one finds an ongoing/pre-change reading with those verbs that feature either an extended Nucleus or an extended Onset phase. Resultative achievements, however, feature a punctiliar Nucleus plus an extended Coda, but lack an Onset phase. One may now interpret the phase selection of the progressive as a metaphoric extension of the erstwhile locative semantics: 'proximity to X' → 'proximity to culmination of the characteristic act (N)'. The post-change reading with resultative achievements can then be understood as a "second-best choice" where no other phase around the right edge of N is available.

The persistive auxiliary takes an infinitive with the augment, an infinitive additionally marked for either of locative classes 16 and 18, or an inflected verb as its complement. It can also be used with nominal predicates and for locative predication. Some of these combinations merit a short discussion.

With an infinitive complement, the persistive denotes that the act encoded in the verb has not yet taken place ('yet to V'):

(115) m-ba-kooliile   ʋkʋtɪ m-ba-lagɪl-e   a-ma-syʋ   bo **n-gaalɪ**
       1SG-2PL-call.PFV COMP 1SG-2PL-dictate-SUBJ AUG-6-word as 1SG-PERS
       ʋ-kʋ-fw-a
       AUG-15(INF)-die-FV
       'I've called you (pl.) to give you instructions before I die.' [Chief
       Kapyungu]

(116) nsyɪsyɪ a-lɪnkʋ-m̩-bʋʋl-a kalʋlʋ a-lɪnkʋ-tɪ "ɪɪ-nyama
       skunk(1) 1-NARR-1-tell-FV hare(1) 1-NARR-say AUG-meat(9)
       jɪ-p-iile,   is-aga   tʋ-ly-ege!"   po kalʋlʋ
       9-be(come)_burnt-PFV come-IPFV 1PL-eat-IPFV.SUBJ then hare(1)
       a-lɪnkʋ-tɪ "taasi. **jɪ-kaalɪ ʋ-kʋ-py-a**"
       1-NARR-say yet   9-PERS AUG-15(INF)-be(come)_burnt-FV
       'Skunk told Hare "The meat is done, come let's eat!" Hare said "Later.
       It's not yet done."' [Hare and Skunk]

This is also the default interpretation for the persistive without an overt complement (117). If a polar question contains the persistive plus a complement, a bare persistive in the answer is understood as being elliptic (118).

(117) ɪ-li-sikʋ   ly-a   kw-and-a   a-a-bʋʋk-ile kʋ-kʋ-keet-a ɪ-fi-lombe
       AUG-5-day 5-ASSOC 15-begin-FV 1-PST-go-PFV 17-15-look-FV AUG-8-maize
       muno   fi-j-ɪɪl-iile   ʋkʋtɪ kalɪ fi-bɪfiifwe   pamo **fi-kaalɪ**
       whether 8-be(come)-APPL-PFV COMP Q   8-ripen.PFV or   8-PERS
       'On the first day he went to look at how the maize was looking to see if
       it had ripened yet or not.' [Thieving monkeys]

(118) bʋle, ʋ-kaalɪ kʋ-manyil-a?   – ee, **n-gaalɪ**
       Q   2SG-PERS 2SG.PRS-learn-FV   yes 1SG-PERS
       'Are you still studying?' – 'Yes, I still am.' [overheard]

Apart from the bare infinitive, verbal nouns additionally marked for locative classes 16 and 18 are attested. It is unclear whether these differ in meaning and in how far speaker preferences and diatopic variation are involved.[22]

(119) i-kʊ-j-a   pa-kʊ-kwel-a kangɪ, paapo ɪ-kɪ-kapʊ   kɪ-mo
       1-PRS-be(come)-FV 16-15-climb-FV again because AUG-7-basket 7-one

       kɪ-kaalɪ pa-kw-isʊl-a
       7-PERS   16-15-be(come)_full-FV

       'He is about to climb up again, because one basket is still empty.' [Elisha Pear Story]

(120) **ga-kaalɪ n-kʊ-kom-a**
       6-PERS   18-15-become_ripe-FV

       'They [the bananas] are still not ripe.' [overheard]

With a simple present (§6.5.1) or past imperfective (§6.5.7) complement, both the continuous and habitual/generic readings are available; see (114) above and (129) below. With inchoative verbs, the persistive can take a complement inflected for perfective aspect. This collocation denotes that the resultant state continues to hold. For further discussion see Chapter 5.[23]

(121) a-ba   ba-ka-j-a   ba-kɪlisiti **ba-kaalɪ b-ʊʊmɪɪliile**
       AUG-PROX.2 2-NEG-be(come)-FV 2-christian 2-PERS   2-stick_to.PFV

       ʊ-lw-iho   ʊ-lw-a   kʊ-lond-a ʊ-kʊ-tiil-igw-a
       AUG-11-custom AUG-11-ASSOC 15-want-FV AUG-15-fear-PASS-FV

       'Those that are not Christians stick to the tradition of wanting to be feared.' [Should she save a life...]

With the negative counterpart to the present perfective (§6.5.4) as a complement, the persistive denotes that the state-of-affairs encoded in the lexical verb still has not occurred.

(122) **a-kaalɪ a-ka-fik-a**   pa-ka-aja
       1-PERS   1-NEG-arrive-FV 16-12-homestead

       'S/he still has not arrived home.' [ET]

---

[22]For a comparable case with phasal verbs see §11.4.1.

[23]This argument is of course circular, as the possible collocation of persistive and perfective is the major criterion for distinguishing inchoative verbs.

(123) taata   ʊ-ne   nalooli ɪ-fy-ʊma   **n-gaalɪ n-ga-kab-a**
       my_father AUG-1SG truely   AUG-8-rich 1SG-PERS 1SG-NEG-get-FV

       ɪɪ-sala   ɪ-jɪ
       AUG-hour(9)(<SWA) AUG-PROX.9

       'Father [honorific], I still haven't obtained the brideprice.' [Man and his
       in-law]

The meaning of this combination ('still not V-ed') is obviously similar to that
of the persistive with an infinitive complement ('yet to V'). One difference can be
found in pragmatics: when the pending state-of-affairs is expressed as counter
to expectation or custom, it is the perfective that is used:

(124) a. m-ma-jolo   n-aa-lambaleele   bo ʊ-n-kʊlʊ   gw-angʊ
          18-6-evening 1SG-PST-lie_down.PFV as AUG-1-elder_sibling 1-POSS.SG

          a-kaalɪ a-ka-fik-a   pa-ka-aja
          1-PERS 1-NEG-arrive-FV 16-12-homestead

          'Yesterday I went to bed when my elder brother still had not come
          home.' (implies: his late arrival is unusual) [ET]

       b. m-ma-jolo   n-aa-lambaleele   bo ʊ-n-kʊlʊ   gw-angʊ
          18-6-evening 1SG-PST-lie_down.PFV as AUG-1-elder_sibling 1-POSS.SG

          a-kaalɪ ʊ-kʊ-fik-a   pa-ka-aja
          1-PERS AUG-15-arrive-FV 16-12-homestead

          'Yesterday I went to bed before my older brother arrived home.' [ET]

The persistive can also take a predicate nominal as a complement with subjects
other than the participants (see §10.2.2 on the use of the zero copula):

(125) ba-kaalɪ ba-fumuke
       2-PERS   2-famous

       'They are still famous.' [ET]

(126) a-ma-tunda ga-kaalɪ ma-nyaafu
       AUG-6-fruit 6-PERS 6-tasty

       'The fruits are still tasty.' [ET]

Interestingly, locative predication, otherwise one of the cases where use of the
copula is obligatory, is also possible with the persistive (127). The copula can be
used here, though in most cases it is optional (128). Also see (65) on p. 284.

(127) po   bo a-kaalı mu-n-jıla po   kajamba   a-a-t-ile
       then as 1-PERS 18-9-path then tortoise(1) 1-PST-say-PFV

'As he [Mr. Monkey] was still on the way, Tortoise said:' [Monkey and Tortoise]

(128) ʊ-n-kiikʊlʊ   a-kaalı (a-lı)   paa-sokoni
       AUG-1-woman 1-PERS (1-COP) 16-market(9)(<SWA)

'The woman is still at the market.' [ET]

The past persistive is formed with the past prefix *a-* following the subject prefix (129, 130). Note that this clearly distinguishes the persistive from the negated past copula, which shares the shape *kaalı* with the present persistive (see §10.2.1).

(129) tw-a-kaalı   tw-a-ly-aga
       1PL-PST-PERS 1PL-PST-eat-IPFV

'We were still eating. / We still used to eat.' [ET]

(130) tw-a-kaalı   tw-a-kateele
       1PL-PST-PERS 1PL-PST-be(come)_tired.IPFV

'We were still tired.' [ET]

6.6.3 Minor constructions

In this subsection, a few less frequent constructions will be discussed. The collocation of the existential construction (§10.2.3) with the locative class 18 enclitic plus the simple present gives a reading of a constantly or consistently occurring eventuality (131). In this, it can itself occur as the complement of the persistive aspect auxiliary, as illustrated in (132); Nurse (1979: 125) lists a comparable example. Its past counterpart is formed with the past imperfective (133).

(131) **a-li=mo i-kw-ib-a**   ı-fi-lombe   fy-angʊ
       1-COP=18 1-PRS-steal-FV AUG-8-maize 8-POSS.1SG

'S/he constantly steals my maize.' [ET]

(132) ʊ-saj-igw-ege   n=ʊ-n-twa   paapo   na   ʊlʊ ʊ-kaalı
       2SG-bless-PASS-IPFV.SUBJ COM=AUG-1-lord because COM now 2SG-PERS

       ʊ-li=mo   kʊ-bomb-a   ı-sy-a   b-ooloolo. kangı lılıno
       2SG-COP=18 2SG.PRS-do-FV AUG-10-ASSOC 14-kind   again now/today

       po   ʊ-bomb-ile ı-n-gınd-ılisi   kʊ-sy-a   kw-and-a
       then 2SG-do-PFV AUG-10-pass-INTS.AGNR 17-10-ASSOC 15-begin-FV

'Blessed be thou of the lord, my daughter: for thou hast shewed more kindness in the latter end than at the beginning [lit. ...because you still continuously do kind things and now you have done things much more kind than those in the beginning]' (Ruth 3:10)

(133) a-a-li=mo   a-a-tʊ-taamy-aga
       1-PST-COP=18 1-PST-1PL-trouble-IPFV
       'S/he constantly annoyed us.' [ET]

A parallel construction is formed with a noun class 16 (but not class 17) existential. This denotes a continuous single event or series of events. The following examples were both suggested during elicitation sessions directed at verb categorization (Chapter 5).

(134) **n-di=po   n-gʊ-ly-a**   (ıı-sala   j-oosa)
       1SG-COP=16 1SG-PRS-eat-FV (AUG-hour(<SWA) 9-all)
       'I have been eating continually (for a whole hour).' [ET]

(135) ıı-nyumba   j-and-ile   ʊ-kʊ-nyal-a,   a-ba-ndʊ
       AUG-house(9) 9-begin-PFV AUG-15-be(come)_dirty-FV AUG-2-person
       b-ingi **ba-li=po bi-kw-ingıl-a**
       2-many 2-COP=16 2-PRS-enter-FV
       'The house has begun to get dirty, many people are entering.' [ET]

Lastly, as discussed in §6.6.1, 8.7, 7.3, the collocations of the copula plus an infinitive marked for locative noun class 16 or 18 have become grammaticalized as the progressive, the prospective/inceptive (both class 16) and the narrative tense (§7.3) (class 18) respectively. An infinitive marked for locative noun class 17, however, is very rare and maintains a primarily locative reading. Schumann (1899: 23) also notes that this is a "very infrequent form" (translated from the original German, BP) and Endemann (1914) mentions it only marginally. The only attested token in the data is (136). Also note (137).

(136) Context: You are asked where your brother is.
       n-gw-ag-a   kʊʊ-sala   ı-si   a-lı kʊ-kʊ-kin-a
       1SG-PRS-find-FV 17-hour(10)(<SWA) AUG-PROX.10 1-COP 17-15-play-FV
       'I think he is playing (= is where they play).' [ET]

(137) leelo   popaa~po   n-aa-meenye   ʊkʊtı taata   a-lı
       now/but REDUPL~then 1SG-PST-know.PFV COMP my_father(1) 1-COP
       kʊ-kʊ-lım-a
       17-15-farm-FV
       'I however knew that Father was farming.' (Busse 1949: 204;
       orthography adapted)

6.7 The present as non-past

Having discussed the individual present tense constructions, it is worth considering a number of cases in which all of the present tense paradigms pattern with references other than the time of speech, including the unmarked copula (§10.2.1) and derived constructions. It is essential here to make a basic distinction between their use in main clauses on the one hand, and in subordinate clauses on the other hand.

With regard to the former, a widespread crosslinguistic phenomenon is the so-called narrative present, which is the employment of a present tense in past discourse. While in a language such as English this may be subsumed under a single category of *present tense* uses, in Nyakyusa, with its pervasive system of aspectuality, this phenomenon encompasses a wider array of verbal paradigms. This will be discussed in §6.7.1.

Regarding use in subordinate clauses, Nurse (2008) exhorts researchers of Bantu languages not to be misled in their analysis by the sequence-of-tense rules commonly found in Western European languages, such as in the English sentence *When he had paid the car, he drove it home*, not *When he (has) paid the car he drove it home*. Discussing these sequence-of-tense rules, he observes that

> No Bantu language with which I am familiar does what English does. Instead of shifting the tenses on the left one step further into the past, as English, Bantu languages would keep the forms on the left in the contexts on the right. (Nurse 2008: 159)

For a more general discussion see Cover & Tonhauser (2015). Tense use in subordinate contexts will be discussed in §6.7.2, where a further distinction will be made between different types of subordinate clauses.

As will become clear from the following discussion, in a number of subordinate contexts the present tense paradigms take their temporal reference from the matrix clause. Further, the simple present (§6.5.1) may be used as a futurate,futurate and can be shifted to a future reference frame by the use of the future enclitic *aa=* (§8.2). What is more, under certain conditions that will be discussed in their appropriate places, other paradigms such as the present perfective (§6.5.3) and the present or zero copula (§10.2.1) may be used with reference to future state-of-affairs. What is termed *present tense* throughout this study can thus well be understood as having non-past reference.[24]

---

[24]Cf. Klein's (1994: 124–128) analysis of the German present tense as expressing non-past.

6.7.1 Narrative present

As Fleischman (1990: 376) defines it, a narrative present is the primarily oral phenomenon of a present tense that is used in narratives, where it refers to the past time of the storyworld. This device "enables particular textual or expressive effects because the meaning 'simultaneous with S' [...] is always open" (p. 54).

In Nyakyusa, given the basic division between inchoative and non-inchoative verbs and its reflection in choice of grammatical aspect, as well as the morphologically divergent copulae, the phenomenon of narrative present encompasses a number of verbal paradigms. (138) illustrates the use of the simple present. Note how the use of a narrative present here forms part of a shift towards drama,[25] characterized by the omission of an otherwise compulsory form of the quotative verb *tɪ* (§10.3). Example (139) illustrates the use of the negative counterpart to the present perfective with the inchoative verb *manya* 'know'.

(138) po   kalʊlʊ a-lɪnkʊ-lembʊk-a. **i-kʊ-kuut-a** "hɪhɪɪ.   ba-n-gom-ile,
then hare(1) 1-NARR-awake-FV 1-PRS-cry-FV of_crying 2-1SG-hit-PFV
ba-n-gom-ile, ba-n-gom-ile." po   nsyɪsyɪ "jw-ani a-kʊ-kom-ile?"
2-1SG-hit-PFV 2-1SG-hit-PFV   then skunk(1) 1-who 1-2SG-hit-PFV

'Then Hare woke up. He cries "Hihii. They've beaten me, they've beaten me, they've beaten me." Skunk: "Who's beaten you?" [Hare and Skunk]

(139) po   ʊ-m-fimba   gw-ake gw-a   n-nyambala jʊ-la, a-lɪnkw-a
then AUG-3-corpse 3-POSS.SG 3-ASSOC 1-man   1-DIST 1-NARR-go.FV
kʊ-syɪl-a. a-lɪnkw-a   kʊ-bɪɪk-ɪl-a   ii-pumba
15-bury-FV 1-NARR-go.FV 15-put-APPL-FV 5-grave
n=ʊ-kʊ-syɪl-a   kʊ-la
COM=AUG-15-bury-FV 17-DIST

'The corpse of that man, he went and buried it. He went and put it in a grave and buried it there.'

ʊ-n-kasi   **a-ka-many-a** ɪ-lɪ   na ɪ-lɪ
AUG-1-wife 1-NEG-know-FV AUG-PROX.5 COM AUG-PROX.5

'His [killer's] wife does not know anything.' [Man and his in-law]

The narrative present is relatively infrequent in the corpus. With the exception of one text, in which nearly the entire peak episode is related in the narrative present, it hardly ever appears in consecutive clauses.

---

[25]Drama, in the sense of Longacre (1996: 43), is "a very vivid style of discourse in which quotation formulas drop out and people speak out in multiple I-thou relations".

Fleischman (1990), following Buffin (1925), distinguishes between two varieties of the narrative present: the "action" variety, used for narrating events, and the "visualizing" variety for descriptions. The majority of instances of the narrative present of the type discussed so far belong to the action variety. (139) above is amongst the few exceptions. Furthermore, all occurrences of the action variety in the corpus feature the imperfective simple present.

Concerning the visualizing variety of the narrative present, there is a reoccurring construction consisting of a present tense paradigm together with the interjection of surprise *ngɪmba* (topolectual variant: *ndɪmba*) 'behold, gosh'. This construction is in fact not limited to narratives, but also found in past expository texts. In the case of narratives, the use of *ngɪmba* plus narrative present often goes along with intrusions of the narrator, who typically foregrounds relevant information that is not transparent for at least one participant or the hearer. This is specifically the case with the secret intentions or attitudes of a protagonist. With this construction, a greater variety of verbal paradigms is encountered. (140–142) illustrate uses of the simple present, the present perfective and the zero copula respectively.

(140)   bo bi-kʊ-gomok-a mu-n-jɪla, kalʊlʊ a-lɪnkʊ-jɪ-bʊʊl-a ɪɪ-fubu
        as 2-PRS-return-FV 18-9-path hare(1) 1-NARR-9-tell-FV AUG-hippo(9)
        a-lɪnkʊ-tɪ "ba-kʊ-tuufiifye fiijo   ʊ-gwe ʊkʊtɪ ʊ-lɪ   n-nunu,
        1-NARR-say 2-2SG-praise.PFV INTENS AUG-2SG COMP 2SG-COP 1-good
        looli fi-fy-ɪma fy-ako   fi-kɪnd-ɪliile   ʊ-bʊ-nywamu, ba-t-ile
        but   8-8-thigh 8-POSS.2SG 8-pass-INTS.PFV AUG-14-big   2-say-PFV
        ʊ-pungusy-e".
        2SG-reduce-SUBJ

        'As they were on the road returning, Hare told Hippo, "They've praised you a lot, that you're a good person, but your thighs are too big, they have said you should lose weight."'

        looli **ngɪmba** kalʊlʊ **i-kʊ-lond-a**   ɪɪ-nyama   ɪ-j-aa   kʊ-ly-a
        but   behold   hare(1) 1-PRS-want-FV AUG-meat(9) AUG-9-ASSOC 15-eat-FV

        'But gosh, Hare wants meat for eating.' [Hare and Hippo]

(141)   kalʊlʊ a-lɪnkw-angal-a   pala~pa-la   kɪsita   kʊ-lʊ-bon-a
        hare(1) 1-NARR-be_well-FV REDUPL~16-DIST without 15-11-see-FV
        ʊ-lʊ-bʊbi.
        AUG-11-spider

        'Hare stayed right there without seeing Spider.'

ngɪmba ʊ-lʊ-bʊbi   lʊ-bʊʊk-ile kʊ-ka aja   kʊ-my-ake
behold AUG-11-spider 11-go-PFV 17-12-homestead 17-4-POSS.SG

'Gosh, Spider has gone home.' [Hare and Spider]

(142) a-a-kalang-ile ii-fumbɪ lɪ-la. ngɪmba ii-fumbɪ (ø)   ly-a   sota
       1-PST-fry-PFV 5-egg   5-DIST behold 5-egg (COP) 5-ASSOC python(9)

'She fried that egg. Gosh, that egg is Python's.' [Python and woman]

The interjection *ngɪmba/ndɪmba* is strongly associated with the present tense. It is otherwise only attested in the corpus as an exclamation of surprise or a question tag in direct speech. It should be noted that exchanging the present tense paradigms in the above examples for their past tense counterparts would lead to a past-in-the-past reading.

6.7.2 Present tense in subordinate clauses

In the following, the use of the present tense in the most common types of subordinate clauses which feature a finite indicative verb will be described. The focus is on past tense discourse.

6.7.2.1 Temporal and conditional adverbial clauses

Temporal adverbial clauses are most commonly introduced by the augmentless noun class 14 referential demonstrative *bo*, which in this use will be glossed as 'as' throughout this study. When it introduces temporal clauses *bo* is unstressed and may be considered a proclitic to the verb phrase.

These clauses introduced by *bo* can occur in either pre-verbal or post-verbal position, although the pre-verbal position clearly predominates in the corpus. The most common paradigms in temporal clauses are the present perfective and the simple present. The present perfective is used when the state-of-affairs it describes is construed as completed before the one expressed in the matrix clause takes place (143). With inchoative verbs this typically gives a stative reading (144). The simple present, on the other hand, is commonly used with a continuous, simultaneous reading (145).

(143) **bo a-mal-ile**   ɪ-m-bombo j-aake   a-a-sook-ile=po,   a-a-bʊʊk-ile
       as 1-finish-PFV AUG-9-work 9-POSS.SG 1-PST-leave-PFV=16 1-PST-go-PFV
       kʊ-my-ake
       17-4-POSS.SG

'When he finished his work, he left and went home.' [Hare and Hippo]

(144) po **bo** ɪ-li-ndʊ   lɪ-la   **lɪ-gon-ile** itolo ba-aly-eg-ile
      then as AUG-5-monster 5-DIST 5-rest-PFV just 2-PST-take-PFV

      a-m-ɪɪsi   ga-la
      AUG-6-water 6-DIST

      'When that monster was deeply asleep they took that water.' [Monster with guitar]

(145) po **bo i-kw-ɪmb-a**   po   jɪ-lɪnkʊ-tup-a
      then as 1-PRS-sing-FV then 9-NARR-become_fat-FV

      'As it [child] was singing, it [snake] became fat.' [Snake and children]

At first glance it may seem that these clauses introduced by *bo* express two conflicting kinds of temporal ordering between the matrix clause and the temporal clause: posteriority (143) vs. simultaneity (144, 145). However, in both cases the time interval for which the matrix clause eventuality is asserted can be understood as concomitant with the state-of-affairs expressed in the adverbial clause. As discussed in §6.5.3, perfective aspect in Nyakyusa introduces a post-Nucleus perspective. With a perfective non-inchoative verb in the temporal clause, as in (143), the main clause eventuality is thus constrained to the post-time of the subordinate one. With an inchoative verb in the temporal clause (144), the main clause eventuality is concomitant with the resultant state. In the same fashion, adverbial clauses of anteriority feature either the persistive (§6.6.2) in its 'still to/not yet' reading (146) or the negative counterpart to the present perfective (147).

(146) po   jʊ-mo ʊ-jʊ   a-lɪnkʊ-mmw-eg-a ʊ-mw-ana **bo a-kaalɪ**
      then 1-one AUG-PROX.1 1-NARR-1-take-FV   AUG-1-child as 1-PERS

      ʊ-kʊ-piny-a   ɪ-ly-ʊndʊ
      AUG-15-bind-FV AUG-5-thatching_grass

      'One of them took her child before binding the grass.' [Throw away the child]

(147) **bo a-ka-fik-a**   pa-la   a-lɪnkw-ag-an-il-a
      as 1-NEG-arrive-FV 16-DIST 1-NARR-find-RECP-APPL-FV

      n=ʊ-mu-ndʊ   pa-n-jɪla
      COM=AUG-1-person 16-9-path

      'Before she arrived there, she met a person on the way.' [Throw away the child]

(148) illustrates the use of the copula in a temporal clause. (149) is an example featuring a negated verb,negative while (150) illustrates reference to a future state-of-affairs.

(148) **bʊ tʊ-lɪ** ba-niini tw a bʊʊk-ile kʊ-dalesalama
as 1PL-COP 2-little 1PL-PST-go-PFV 17-D.

'When we were little we went to Dar es Salaam.' [ET]

(149) po **bo ba-ti-kʊ-j-aag-a** po ɪ-ly-ebe ly-al-iis-ile
then as 2-NEG-PRS-9-find-FV then AUG-5-crow 5-PST-COME-PFV

ʊ-kw-and-a ʊ-kʊ-kol-a ʊ-tw-ana tw-a n-gʊkʊ
AUG-15-begin-FV AUG-15-grasp-FV AUG-12-child 12-ASSOC 10-chicken

'As/while they were not finding it [needle], Crow came, beginning to
catch the little children of the chickens.' [Chickens and Crow]

(150) **bo ga-kɪnd-ile** a-ma-sikʊ a-ma-longo ma-na a-ka-aja
as 6-pass-PFV AUG-6-day AUG-6-ten 6-four AUG-12-village

a-ka-a Ninibe ki-kʊ-pyut-igw-aga
AUG-12-ASSOC N. 12-MOD.FUT-ruin-PASS-MOD.FUT

'Yet forty days, and Nineveh shall be overthrown.' (Jonah 3:4)

A less frequent kind of temporal clauses is introduced by the locative noun
class 17 proximal demonstrative *kʊno*. All occurrences of this in the corpus are
found in post-verbal positions. Again, the present tense paradigms are used, with
temporal reference stemming from the matrix clause. Thus, in (151) the present
perfective with inchoative *kola* 'grasp, hold' induces a stative reading, which is
construed as concomitant with the eventuality of returning. Similarly in (152)
the act of singing, in the simple present, takes place at the same time as the act
of going home.

(151) a-ba-ndʊ ba-la ba-lɪnkʊ-buj-a kʊ-ka-aja, **kʊ-no**
AUG-2-person 2-DIST 2-NARR-return-FV 17-12-homestead 17-PROX

ba-kol-ile a-ma-boko ga-abo m-mi-tʊ ·
2-hold-PFV AUG-6-hand 6-POSS.PL 18-4-head

'Those people returned home with their hands on their heads.' [Thieving
monkeys]

(152) ba-lɪnkʊ-bʊʊk-a na=gyo kʊ-my-abo n=ʊ-lʊ-saalo
2-NARR-go-FV COM=REF.4 17-4-POSS.PL COM=AUG-11-happiness

ʊ-lʊ-nywamu fiijo **kʊ-no bi-kw-ɪmb-a** ɪɪ-nyɪmbo
AUG-11-big INTENS 17-PROX 2-PRS-sing-FV AUG-song(10)

'They went home with them [monkey's tails], very happy and singing
songs.' [Thieving monkeys]

A similar pattern of usage is found with adverbial clauses introduced by *lɪnga* 'if, when'. As the English translation suggests, these can receive a temporal as well as a conditional reading. Again, one of the present paradigms is used, with temporal reference stemming from the main clause:

(153) po lɪnga ba-n-swɪl-ile po ʊ-mw-ana a-a-j-aga
then if/when 2-1-feed-PFV then AUG-1-child 1-PST-be(come)-IPFV
na=a-ma-ka   fiijo
COM=AUG-6-strength INTENS

'When they had fed it, the child would become very strong.' [Clothing long ago]

(154) kangɪ lɪnga kʊ-ga-keet-a   ma-tiitʊ
again if/when 2SG.PRS-6-watch-FV 6-black

'When you look at it [water], it is black' [Selfishness kills]

(155) lɪnga ga-fik-ile   a-ma-jolo   ʊ-ka-suluk-ege
if/when 6–arrive-PFV AUG-6-evening 2SG-ITV-descend-IPFV.SUBJ
paa-si
16-below

'When the evening has come, then you can climb down.' [Mfyage turns into a lion]

However, in the conditional reading of *lɪnga*, overt marking of past tense is possible, if the state-of-affairs in the conditional clause is overtly construed in a past reference frame.

(156) lɪnga   ɪ-fi-ndʊ   fy-a-lɪ   paa-meesa   ba-a-l-iile
if/when AUG-8-food 8-PST-COP 16-table(9)(<SWA) 2-PST-eat-PFV

'If the food was on the table [on that occasion] then they ate it.' [ET]

(157) lɪlɪno   lɪnga ʊ-jo   ʊ-gwise   gw-a n-dʊme
now/today if/when AUG-REF.1 AUG-his_father(1) 1-ASSOC 1-husband
a-ka-alɪ-ṃ-bonwile   ʊ-n-kasi gw-a   mw-anaake, po
1-NEG-PST-1-pay_off.PFV AUG-1-wife 1-ASSOC 1-his_child   then
i-kʊ-bomb-aga   bʊle~bʊle?
1-MOD.FUT-do-MOD.FUT REDUPL~how

'Nowadays, if the father of the husband has not paid the wife of his child, then what will she do?' [Should she save a life...]

Lastly, in adverbial clauses referring to itcratives, habituals or generics, the
temporal reference can be understood as relative to the singular events that make
up these repeated occurrences. These types of adverbial clauses are often introduced by *kʊkʊtɪ* 'every' (158, 159). (160) illustrates a temporal clause of anteriority
relating to a past generic proposition. See also (153) above.

(158) **kʊkʊtɪ m-bomb-ile=po**   panandɪ itolo ɪ-m-bombo n-gw-ag-a
      every 1SG-work-PFV=PART a_little just AUG-9-work 1SG-PRS-find-FV
      n-gateele
      1SG-be(come)_tired.PFV
      'Every time after working just a bit I find myself tired.' [ET]

(159) **kʊkʊtɪ a-sulwike**   paa-si   a-a-j-aga   ɪ-n-galamu
      every 1-descend.PFV 16-down 1-PST-be(come)-IPFV AUG-9-lion
      'Every time she went down to the ground she would become a lion.'
      [Mfyage turns into a lion]

(160) **bo ba-kaalɪ ʊ-kw-and-a**   ʊ-kʊ-mog-a   ba-a-fwal-aga
      as 2-PERS AUG-15-begin-FV AUG-15-dance-FV 2-PST-dress/wear-IPFV
      ɪ-my-enda ɪ-my-elu,   pamo a-ma-golole a-m-eelu
      AUG-4-cloth AUG-4-white or   AUG-6-sheet AUG-6-white
      'Before starting to dance, they would put on white clothes, or white
      sheets.' [Custom of dancing]

6.7.2.2 Complements of PCU verbs

With verbs of perception, cognition and utterance (PCU verbs; terminology following Givón 2001), a pattern parallel to that of temporal adverbial clauses is
found. In the following, verbs of perception and cognition will be discussed before turning to verbs of utterance, specifically information verbs.

The following examples illustrate the use of present tense paradigms in the
clausal complements of perception and cognition verbs, with temporal reference
relative to the state-of-affairs depicted in the matrix clause. Thus, the simple
present in (161) and in the first complement clause of (162) depicts a process unfolding at the same time as its perception. The same holds for the periphrastic
present progressive in the second complement clause of (163). The present perfective is used with inchoative verbs in the second and third complement clauses
of (162) and accordingly gives a stative reading. Use of the present perfective
with non-inchoative verbs is illustrated in (163, 164). Accordingly it denotes a
completed eventuality whose result is perceived.

(161) Sambʊka a-lɪnkʊ-kalal-a   mu-n-dumbula ʊkʊtɪ
       S.   1-NARR-be(come)_angry-FV 18-9-heart   COMP
       i-kʊ-n̩-dek-a mw-ene
       1-PRS-1-let-FV 1-only

       'Sambuka became angry in her heart that she [Asia] was leaving her alone.' [Juma, Asia and Sambuka]

(162) po   a-lɪnkw-ag-a   kajamba **i-kʊ-sook-a,** **a-fwele**
       then 1-NARR-find-FV tortoise(1) 1-PRS-leave-FV 1-dress/wear.PFV
       ɪ-kɪ-tili,   n=ii-koti   ly-ake,   **a-kol-ile**   n=ɪ-n-gili
       AUG-7-hat COM=5-coat(<SWA) 5-POSS.SG 1-grasp-PFV COM=AUG-9-stick
       j-aa   kw-end-el-a,   ɪ-kɪ-ngoti
       9-ASSOC 15-walk/travel-APPL-FV AUG-7-walking_stick

       'He [Monkey] found Tortoise coming out, wearing a hat and his coat, holding a stick for walking, a walking stick.' [Monkey and Tortoise]

(163) bo a-fik-ile   pa-la   a-lɪnkʊ-sy-ag-a   ɪ-n-gambɪlɪ   i-haano
       as 1-arrive-PFV 16-DIST 1-NARR-10-find-FV AUG-10-monkey 10-five
       si-fi-fungamiile   ɪ-fi-lombe   mu-n̩-gʊnda gw-ake, **si-lɪ**
       10-8-put_pressure_on.PFV AUG-8-maize 18-3-field   3-POSS.SG 10-COP
       pa-kʊ-ly-a
       16-15-eat-FV

       'When he arrived there, he found five monkeys had devastated the maize in his field and were eating.' [Thieving monkeys]

(164) ii-sikʊ lɪ-mo kalʊlʊ bo i-kʊ-jaat-a   a-lɪnkʊ-fi-bon-a ɪ-fi-lombe
       5-day 5-one hare(1) as 1-PRS-walk-FV 1-NARR-8-see-FV AUG-8-maize
       mu-n̩-gʊnda **fi-bɪfiifwe**
       18-3-field   8-ripen.PFV

       'One day Hare, while he was taking a walk, saw that the maize in the field was ripe.' [Saliki and Hare]

Sometimes *bo* 'as' (see §6.7.2.1 above) follows a verb of perception:

(165) po   a-a-pɪliike   bo kʊ-kʊ-lɪl-a   "káa!"
       then 1-PST-hear.PFV as 17-PRS-sound-FV of_sickle_swinging

       'Then he heard it as there was a sound "Káa!" [of a sickle swinging]' [Wage of the thieves]

Information verbs also follow the now familiar pattern. They differ however in their preferences as to the syntactic structure of their complement. The complcmcnt most commonly consists of a headless relative clause, as in (166). Alternatively, complementation through the associative plus infinitive of *tɪ* (see §10.3) is attested (167). In both cases, within the relative clause the subject marker typically is of noun class 10. This can be understood as referring to implicit *ɪɪnongwa* 'issue(s) (9/10)', an interpretation that is strengthened by example (168). Note that again the present perfective is used in the relative clause.

(166) a-lɪnkʊ-ba-bʊʊl-a ɪ-si   si-sookiile   pa-ka-aja
       1-NARR-2-tell-FV AUG-PROX.10 10-happen.PFV 16-12-homestead
       pa-my-ake
       16-4-POSS.SG
       'He told them what had happened in his house.' [Killer woman]

(167) bo ba-gomwike kʊ-malafyale gw-abo, ba-alɪ-m-pangiile ɪ-sy-a
       as 2-return.PFV 17-chief(1)   2-POSS.PL 2-PST-1-tell.PFV AUG-10-ASSOC
       kʊ-tɪ ʊ-n-nuguna   a-fug-ile   ɪ-n-galamu
       15-say AUG-1-younger_sibling 1-tame-PFV AUG-9-lion
       'When they returned to their chief, they told him that his younger brother had tamed a lion.' [Chief Kapyungu]

(168) ʊ-n-kʊlʊmba gw-abo ɪɪ-sofu   jɪ-lɪnkw-igʊl-a
       AUG-1-older 1-POSS.PL AUG-elephant(9) 9-NARR-open-FV
       ʊ-lʊ-komaano n=ʊ-kʊ-fi-bʊʊl-a   ɪ-fi-nyamaana ɪɪ-nongwa
       AUG-11-meeting COM=AUG-15-8-tell-FV AUG-8-animal AUG-issue(9)
       ɪ-jɪ   jɪ-m-pel-ile ʊ-kʊ-koolel-a ʊ-lʊ-komaano
       AUG-PROX.9 9-1-make-PFV AUG-15-call-FV AUG-11-meeting
       'Their eldest, Elephant, opened the meeting and told the animals the reason that had made him call the meeting.' [Hare and Chameleon]

Similarly to what was found for temporal clauses, in complements of PCU verbs which relate to an iterative, habitual or generic proposition, the temporal perspective can be understood as relative to the individual sub-events:

(169) po tw-a-many-aga   ʊkʊtɪ kʊ-la ʊ-bw-ite   bʊ-kol-eene
       then 1PL-PST-know-IPFV COMP 17-DIST AUG-14-fight 14-hold-RECP.PFV
       ʊ-bw-a   kʊ-mog-a
       AUG-14-ASSOC 15-dance-FV
       'Then we would know that a dancing competition was being held.' [Custom of dancing]

6.7.2.3 Relative clauses

Relative clauses show a more complex picture. Within past narrative discourse, both present tense verbs and past tense verbs are encountered in relative clauses. In terms of temporal reference, the present tense is found both with its default meaning and with past time reference (present-in-the-past). Likewise, the past tense is encountered both as a concomitant past and as a past-in-the-past.

In the cases discussed in §6.7.1–6.7.2.2 above – that is, relative clauses subordinate to a narrative present, embedded in a temporal clause or modifying the perceived, cognized or uttered proposition of PCU verbs – the use of a present tense paradigm is predictable through syntax and semantics. Further straightforward cases are those relative clauses referring to timeless statements or past iteratives, habituals and generics. These will be discussed further below. Excluding these predictable cases, there remains a number of alternations between present and past tense which are governed by pragmatic consideration, namely the textual and expressive components of meaning. The past tense, however, clearly predominates and is to be considered the default.

For a first approximation of the alternations of tenses, it is worth considering the activation status of the information given in the relative clauses in question; see §1.4.4.2 on the categories of activation status. All relative clauses that feature a present tense predicate with past time reference contain either old information, that is, both their head and the proposition they contain can be classified as either discourse-old/hearer-old, or information that is strongly inferable.

It follows from this generalization that all relative clauses containing brand new information relating to past time (the story-now) feature a past tense verb. A prototypical case is that of explicative relative clauses in the orientation section:

(170) ijolo   n-k-iisʊ ky-a   Tʊkʊjʊ, ba-a-li=ko   a-ba-ndʊ
       old_times 18-7-land 7-ASSOC T.   2-PST-COP=17 AUG-2-person
       a-ba   **ba-a-lɪm-aga**   ɪ-mi-gʊnda gy-abo   kɪfuki
       AUG-PROX.2 2-PST-farm-IPFV AUG-4-farm 4-POSS.PL near
       na=a-ma-tengele
       COM=AUG-6-bush

       'Long ago in Tukuyu there were people who were farming their fields near the forest.' [Thieving monkeys]

This association between information status and tense marking is a one-way conditional. While brand new information invariably comes with the past tense, discourse-old/hearer-old or inferable propositions can also receive past tense marking:

(171) Context: A monster had caught and killed a child.
ba-lınku-pılıkısy-a a-ba-kamu ba-a mw-ana **ju-la**
2-NARR-listen-FV AUG-2-relative 2-ASSOC 1-child 1-DIST
ly-alı-n-kol-ile ı-li-ndu
5-PST-1-grasp-PFV AUG-5-monster
'The relatives of that child that the monster had caught listened.'
[Monster with Guitar]

Before taking a closer look at these tense alternations, the contexts which allow for them need to be narrowed down further. In semantic terms, what allows for the use of the present tense as a present-in-the-past is the lack of tense specification which goes together with the lack of overt morphological tense marking. Fleischman (1990) calls this the "zero interpretation". Consequently, if a relative clause depicts a state or an unfolding process that is situated prior to the state-of-affairs of the matrix clause, an overt past tense is required.[26] This is illustrated in (172–174) for an inchoative verb with perfective aspect a non-inchoative verb with imperfective aspect, and the copula respectively.

(172) Context: A dog had hunted and saved some leftover meat, which in the meantime has been eaten by another dog.
ıı-nine j-oope jı-lınku-kong-a muu-nyuma pa-kı-syanju
AUG-companion(9) 9-also 9-NARR-follow-FV 18-back(9) 16-7-thicket
a-pa **j-aa-syele** ıı-nyama
AUG-PROX.16 9-PST-remain.PFV AUG-meat(9)
'The other dog followed behind to the thicket where the meat had been left.' [Dogs laughed at each other]

(173) Context: Sambuka has deceived Juma by saying that her fiancé does not love her.
Juma a-lınku-swig-a fiijo ku-ma-syu a-ga
J. 1-NARR-wonder-FV INTENS 17-6-word AUG-PROX.6
a-a-job-aga Sambuka
1-PST-speak-IPFV S.
'Juma wondered much about the words that Sambuka had been saying.'
[Juma, Asia and Sambuka]

---

[26] As Smith (1997: 84) notes, both stat(iv)es and progressives depict a state-of-affairs that is stable and extends in time. Another logically possible case, that would be predicted to require a past tense, but which is not attested in the corpus, is that of habitual or generic propositions relating to a previous reference frame, as in *He carved with the same adze that his father had used to carve with.*

(174)   Context: The late chief has split up his chiefdom between his two heirs.
bo ka-kɪnd-ile a-ka-balɪlo ka-nandɪ ʊ-n-kʊlʊmba a-lɪnkʊ-lond-a
as 12-pass-PFV AUG-12-time 12-little AUG-1-older 1-NARR-want-FV
ʊ-bʊ-nyafyale   bo ʊ-bʊ   a-a-lɪ   na=bo
AUG-14-chiefdom as AUG-PROX.14 1-PST-COP COM=PROX.14
ʊ-gwise
AUG-his_father

'After a little while the elder brother wanted a chiefdom just like the one
his father had had.' [Chief Kapyungu]

So far it has been established that the alternations between past and present
tense are found in those relative clauses that act on old or inferred information
and which do not require a preceding reference frame. A look at the relative frequency again reveals a clear preference for the past tense, which dominates by
a factor of approximately 2.5 in the corpus. The present tense is thus to be considered the "deviation from [the] default parameter setting" (Haspelmath 2006:
64f) for which specific pragmatic functions must be assumed.[27]

(175) is a representative example of the alternation between present and past
tense with a concomitant state. Perfective aspect is here employed with an inchoative verb, yielding a stative reading. In (175a) the present perfective is used,
but in (175b) – a few clauses later in same text and depicting essentially the same
state-of-affairs – the past perfective is used. Two things are apparently going
on in this example. First, the act of hiding in (175a) immediately precedes this
eventuality.[28] Second, (175a) depicts a moment of high tension: will the invaders
notice the hidden locals? Note how the narrator employs repetition so as not to
let this moment go unnoticed. The relative clause with the default past tense in
(175b), however, merely serves to identify the patient of the stabbing.

(175)   a. Context: Invaders have come to a certain land. Three of the locals
have run off and hidden below the straw on the fields.
po leelo   bo b-iibɪɪliile   ba-lɪnkw-is-a   a-ba-lʊgʊ.   po
then now/but as 2-hide_at.PFV 2-NARR-come-FV AUG-2-enemy then
ba-lɪnkw-end-a   pa-mwanya pa-my-abo.
2-NARR-travel/walk-FV 16-high   14-4-POSS.PL

---

[27]Haspelmath (2006) discusses the numerous possible uses of the more traditional term *marked-*
ness and suggests abandoning it altogether in favour of a more specific terminology. In the
case discussed here, two uses of markedness are in conflict: "markedness as deviation from the
default parameter setting" vs. "markedness as overt coding".

[28] *biibɪɪliile* may thus be paraphrased as 'have just hidden and are in hiding'. See §6.5.3 for a more
detailed discussion of the semantic interplay between perfective aspect and inchoative verbs.

ba-lɪnkw-cnd-a   pa-my-abo pa-ba-ndʊ **a-ba**
2-NARR-walk/travel-FV 16-4-POSS.PL 16-2-person AUG-PROX.2
b-iibɪɪliile   paa-si
2-hide_at.PFV 16-below

'So when they had hidden, the invaders came. They walked on top of them. They walked on top of the people that were hidden below.'

b. Context: One of the invaders has heard one of the hidden locals speaks.

a-a-las-ile   paa-si.   a-alɪ-n̩-das-ile   **jʊ-la a-al-iibɪɪliile**
1-PST-stab-PFV 16-below 1-PST-1-stab-PFV 1-DIST 1-PST-hide_at.PFV

paa-si
16-below

'He drove the spear downwards. He stabbed that one that was hidden below.' [Invaders]

The preceding examples feature perfective aspect with an inchoative verb. A specifically intriguing case is the alternation between the past and present perfective with non-inchoative verbs. Independent of tense, perfective aspect with these verbs yields a posterior vantage point (see §6.5.3). There is thus the choice of which temporal perspective to apply to the preceding event (§1.4.2.1). Example (176) illustrates the use of the present perfective vis-à-vis the past perfective with a non-inchoative verb. The eating of the remaining meat, construed with the present perfective (176a), takes place in the episode preceding the two dogs' encounter; while the act of hunting, which is construed in the past perfective, is more remote in temporal and textual terms (176c). Further, it is the act of eating that allows the story's central conflict to develop. Lastly, in (176c) the negative counterpart to the present perfective is employed, which as an evaluative device works on the expressive component: it is the second dog's imprudence that will have fatal consequences and that constitutes the story's theme. As Fleischman (1990: 159) points out, negative predicates in narratives are evaluative, as they entail an unrealized alternative scenario.

(176)   Context: A dog has hunted and left some meat uneaten, which in the meantime has been eaten by another dog.

a. jɪ-lɪnkw-ag-an-il-a   n=ɪ-m-bwa   ɪ-jɪ   jɪ-l-iile
    9-NARR-find-RECP-APPL-FV COM=AUG-9-dog AUG-PROX.9 9-eat-PFV

ıı-nyama
AUG-meat(9)

'He met the dog that had eaten the meat.'

b. jı-lınkʊ-jı-laalʊʊsy-a jı-lınkʊ-tı, "mw-inangʊ, ʊ-sumwike
9-NARR-9-ask-FV 9-NARR-say 1-my_companion 2SG-depart.PFV
kʊʊgʊ?"
where

'He [dog who has eaten the meet] asked "My friend, where are you going?"'

c. ı-m-bwa ı-jı j-aa-fwım-ile jı-lınkʊ-tı "n-sumwike
AUG-9-dog AUG-PROX.9 9-PST-hunt-PFV 9-NARR-say 1SG-depart.PFV
kʊ-kʊ-malıısy-a ıı-nyama j-angʊ"
17-15-end-FV AUG-meat(9) 9-POSS.1SG

'The dog that had hunted said "I am going to finish my meat."'

d. ı-m-bwa ı-jı jı-ka-fwım-a=po jı-lınkʊ-tı
AUG-9-dog AUG-PROX.9 9-NEG-hunt-FV=PART 9-NARR-say
"ıı-nyama ı-jı gw-a-syesye n-d-iile
AUG-meat(9) AUG-PROX.9 2SG-PST-remain.CAUS.PFV 1SG-eat-PFV
ʊ-ne"
AUG-1SG

'The dog that had not hunted said "The meat you left over, I ate it."'
[Dogs laughed at each other]

Immediateness as well as evaluation also appear to be relevant in the following example:

(177) Context: A woman has cooked chicken for her guests. While she was outside fetching water, a thieving woman stole most of the food.
Ngateele a-al-iinogwine fiijo kangı sy-alı-m̩-bab-ile
N. 1-PST-think.PFV INTENS again 10-PST-1-hurt-PFV
mu-n-dumbula, paapo a-al-iib-ıl-iigwe ı-fi-ndʊ
18-9-heart because 1-PST-steal-APPL-PASS.PFV AUG-8-food
ı-fi a-ba-pııj-ile a-ba-heesya ba-ake
AUG-PROX.8 1-2-cook-APPL.PFV AUG-2-foreigner 2-POSS.SG

'Ngateele thought much and it hurt her in her heart, because she was robbed of the food she had cooked for her guests.' [Thieving woman]

To summarize then, in past tense narrative discourse relative clauses that refer to the story-now and that introduce new information invariably feature a past tense verb. In relative clauses that contain old or inferred information, the past tense is the default. The present tense may however be employed to foreground and evaluate.[29] In the case of stative predicates or continuous/progressive aspect, this requires the depicted state-of-affairs to be concomitant with the one expressed in the matrix clause. With perfective aspect, the preceding event or entrance into a new state is typically close by and/or of direct relevance to the storyline.

Other instances of present tense relative clauses in a past tense environment are subject- and object-relative clauses of past iteratives, habituals and generics. This patterns with what has been found for temporal clauses and complements of PCU verbs. In (178) there are a present tense copula and a simple present in the subject- and object-relative clauses respectively. These describe states-of-affairs concomitant with the one expressed in the main clause. In (179), the present perfective in the object-relative clause construes the occurrences of cooking as taking place before the occurrences of stealing.

(178) **a-ba**   **ba-lɪ** kɪfuki n=ii-tengele ba-a-tumul-aga
AUG-PROX.2 2-COP near   COM=5-bush 2-PST-cut-IPFV

n=ʊ-kʊ-b-ʊʊl-ɪkɪsy-a   **a-ba**   **bi-kʊ-ga-lond-a**
COM=AUG-15-2-buy-CAUS.APPL-FV AUG-PROX.2 2-PRS-6-want-FV

'Those who were near to the bush would cut it [grass] and sell it to those who wanted it.' [Nyakyusa houses of long ago]

(179) n-kɪ-panga kɪ-la a-a-li=po   ʊ-n-kiikʊlʊ   ʊ-n-hɪɪji   ʊ-jʊ
18-7-village 7-DIST 1-PST-COP=16 AUG-1-woman AUG-1-thief AUG-PROX.1

a-a-bomb-aga   ɪ-j-aa   kw-ib-a   ɪ-fi-ndʊ   **ɪ-fi**
1-PST-work-IPFV AUG-9-ASSOC 15-steal-FV AUG-8-food AUG-PROX.8

---

[29] One may object that relative clauses are inherently backgrounded as a function of their syntactic status. However, as shown i.a. by Fleischman (1985; 1990: ch. 6) among others, grounding is best understood as a cluster concept. It follows that salience within a text constitutes a spectrum or continuum rather than a binary opposition. What is more, the syntactic status of a clause is only one amongst various factors determining the relative salience of the state-of-affairs it describes. Information provided in a relative clause thus possesses a relative salience, which can be modulated by the choice of TMA paradigm among other means. Fleischman further notes a close conceptual connection between grounding as a means of textual organisation and evaluation as an expressive device.

ba-pɪɪj-ile a-ba-nine
2-cook-PFV AUG-2-companion

'In that village there was a thieving woman, who used to steal the food the others had cooked.' [Thieving woman]

Lastly, the present tense paradigms feature with their default meaning in relative clauses that depict timeless states-of-affairs. Thus, in (180), the referential demonstrative serves as an emphatic copulative (see §10.2.2) and in (181) the simple present has a reading.

(180) ɪɪ-sofu   j-aa-jɪ-kooliile ɪ-n-galamu **ɪ-jɪ**   **jo**   j-a
       AUG-elephant(9) 9-PST-9-call.PFV AUG-9-lion AUG-PROX.9 REF.9 9-ASSOC
       kɪ-bɪlɪ
       7-two

       'Elephant called Lion, who is the second [in rank].' [Hare and Chameleon]

(181) kangɪ ga-a-li=ko   na=a-ma-laasi   **a-ga**   **bi-kʊ-tem-a**
       again 6-PST-COP=17 COM=AUG-6-bamboo AUG-PROX.6 2-PRS-tap-FV
       ʊ-bw-alwa   **ʊ-bʊ**   **bi-kʊ-tɪ** ʊ-bʊ-laasi
       AUG-14-alcohol AUG-PROX.14 2-PRS-say AUG-14-bamboo_beer

       'Also there was bamboo from which they tap this beer they call bamboo beer.' [Nyakyusa houses of long ago]

7 Tense and aspect constructions 2: narrative markers

7.1 Introduction

This chapter deals with two verbal paradigms whose use is essential for understanding coherent narrative discourse in Nyakyusa: the narrative tense (§7.3) and the subsecutive (§7.4). Table 7.1 shows the formal composition of the two.

Table 7.1: Narrative markers

Label	Shape	Example	
Narrative tense	SM-*lınkʊ*-VB-*a*	*tʊlınkʊjoba*	'we spoke'
Subsecutive	SM-*a*-VB-*a*	*twajoba*	'(then) we spoke'

In the following sections, first a short approximation to the concept of narrative markers will be given, together with an overview over the commonalities and differences between Nyakyusa's two narrative markers (§7.2). This is followed by an in-depth examination of the the narrative tense and the subsecutive (§7.3, 7.4).

7.2 The two narrative markers: a comparison

Dedicated narrative markers are a common device in African languages (Dahl 1985: 113f). Concerning Bantu, Nurse (2008) gives a rough description of what makes up this wider category:

> The time of the situation is first established, either explicitly in the first verb in a string, or implicitly [...] All following verbs in the sequence are then marked by a special narrative marker, which replaces the tense marker

appropriate to the time established by the first verb. Just because most sequences deal with past events, this special marker is most frequent in past
narratives, less frequent in timeless events, followed by futures. It also occurs across sentences and utterances, in which case the context most often
crosses sentence boundaries and characterizes a long utterance. Use of the
special marker can be suspended and then deliberately reintroduced by the
speaker to stress continuity. (Nurse 2008: 120)

Nurse's description will serve as a valuable starting point for an understanding
of the function of narrative markers in Bantu. Nevertheless, it contains a number
of points that require further scrutiny as they relate to the Nyakyusa narrative
tense and subsecutive. Before turning to a closer examination of these points for
each of the two narrative makers, some more general points about the Nyakyusa
inventory of narrative markers are worth a discussion.

To begin with, Nurse (2008: 120) goes on to generalize that "most [Bantu]
languages have only one narrative marker and the number of narrative markers
never exceeds that of past tense markers." Nyakyusa, having two narrative markers, thus not only runs counter to a strong tendency within the language family,
but contradicts Nurse's second generalization, as Nyakyusa does not make remoteness distinctions in the past.[1]

In the following sections, common typologies of narrative markers will be
discussed (§7.2.1), to then take a closer look at the pragmatic factors that license
the employment of the Nyakyusa narrative markers (§7.2.2). This is followed by
a discussion of their distribution in the macro-structure of narrative discourse
(§7.2.3) and their quantitative distribution (§7.2.4). Lastly, §7.2.5 summarizes the
functional differences between the two narrative markers.

7.2.1 On typologies of narrative markers

Given Nyakyusa's inventory of two narrative markers, the question arises as
to how far they differ in meaning and use. In discussions of narrative markers,
especially for African languages, two typologies are commonly encountered. The
first one has a syntactic basis and distinguishes narrative markers according to
the subject of the verb thus marked (Rose et al. 2002: 19). Narrative markers
that are used with the same subject as that of the initial verb then classify as
consecutive or *narrative*. A narrative marker used with different subjects, on the
other hand, is termed a *subsecutive/sequential*. However, (dis-)continuity of the

---

[1] Unless one classifies the present perfective as a near past, an attribute that rather derives from
its more general aspectual meaning (§6.5.3).

grammatical subject is not a delimiting parameter in Nyakyusa. Firstly, both the Nyakyusa narrative tense and the subsecutive can co-occur in the same stretch of a narrative, as in (34) below. Secondly, the subject of both the narrative tense and the subsecutive may be the same as that of the initial verb within a span; see e.g. (19) below for the narrative tense and (37) for the subsecutive. Both are, however, also found with different subjects; see e.g.(19) below for the narrative tense and (38) for the subsecutive. Another dichotomous typology of narrative markers has been proposed by Longacre (1990), who focuses on pragmatic factors. He distinguishes a *narrative tense*, defined as marking only storyline events (i.e. only those events that advance the narrative) and possibly used from the first clause of a text onwards, from a *consecutive tense*, which is "either dependent on a special initial form and/or is rank-shifted in sequence with non-storyline initials" (Longacre 1990: 109). The first criterion, dependency on an initial form, will be examined in §7.2.2.

Longacre's second criterion, rank-shifting, deserves a short excursion. In his work on narrative discourse, Longacre stipulates that in any given language there is a verbal construction associated with those clauses that advance the progress of a story. Once this construction is identified, the remaining verbal paradigms or constructions used in narrative discourse can be ranked. This ranking is based on the degree that the clauses they are found in depart from the main storyline (e.g. secondary storyline > backgrounded actions > setting). Some languages may also posses a construction that is used in those clauses that rank higher than the main storyline (pivotal events).

7.2.2 Licensing and dependency

As discussed in §7.2.1, Longacre's (1990) typology distinguishes between those narrative markers that can be used from the first clause of a narrative on and those that require the employment of an initial verb form.

An examination of the text corpus shows that all narratives open with at least one past tense verb, typically in the form of an orientation section that may vary in length. Thus in (1a), not only the protagonists are introduced, but the situation is established by the use of the past imperfective. The onset of the storyline here coincides with the use of the narrative tense (1b, 1c).

(1) a. po leelo ɪ-m-bwele **j-aa-lond-aga** ʊkʊtɪ
        then now/but AUG-9-mosquito 9-PST-want-IPFV COMP

ɟɪ-j-eeg-e   ɪ-m-bʊlʊkʊtʊ
9-9-marry-SUBJ AUG-9-ear

'So, Mosquito wanted to marry Ear.'

b. po leelo   ɪ-m-bwele   **ɟɪ-lɪnkʊ-bʊʊk-a** kʊ-m-bʊlʊkʊtʊ
then now/but AUG-9-mosquito 9-NARR-go-FV 17-9-ear

'So Mosquito went to Ear.'

c. **ɟɪ-lɪnkʊ-tɪ** "gwe, m-bʊlʊkʊtʊ, ʊ-ne   n-gʊ-gan-ile   fiijo   ..."
9-NARR-say 2SG 9-mosquito AUG-1SG 1SG-2SG-love-PFV INTENS

'It said "You, Ear, I love you very much ..."' [Mosquito and Ear]

Note that while in the case of (1) the onset of the storyline coincides with a shift from a past tense verb to the narrative tense, this is not true for all texts. This will be discussed in detail in §7.2.3.

To continue, negative data corroborates the observation that neither the narrative tense nor the subsecutive can by themselves open a text. Constructed mini-narratives that open with a verb in the narrative tense, such as (2), were unanimously rejected by the language assistants and corrected so as to start with a past tense verb (3). Note that this example does feature the frame adverb *mma-jolo* 'yesterday'.

(2) a. # m-ma-jolo   **n-dɪnkʊ-lembʊk-a** n=ʊ-lʊ-bʊnjʊ   fiijo
18-6-evening 1SG-NARR-awake-FV COM=AUG-11-morning INTENS

b. n-dɪnkʊ-nw-a   ɪɪ-tʃai
1SG-NARR-drink-FV AUG-tea(9)(<SWA)

c. bo n-nw-ile   ɪɪ-tʃai   n-dɪnkʊ-bʊʊk-a kʊ-kʊ-kam-a
as 1SG-drink-PFV AUG-tea(9) 1SG-NARR-go-FV 17-15-milk-FV
ʊ-lʊ-kama ...
AUG-11-milk

(intended: 'Yesterday I got up very early. I had breakfast (lit. 'drank tea'). When I finished breakfast, I went to milk the cows ...') [ET]

(3) Correction of (2):

a. m-ma-jolo   **n-aa-lembwike**   n=ʊ-lʊ-bʊnjʊ   fiijo
18-6-evening 1SG-PST-awake.PFV COM=AUG-11-morning INTENS

b. n-dɪnkʊ-nw-a   ɪɪ-tʃai   ...
1SG-NARR-drink-FV AUG-tea(9)

Constructed texts whose opening sentence consists of a temporal clause referring to a specific situation, such as (4), however, were accepted.

(4) a. m-ma-jolo, **bo n-gʊ-pɪlɪk-a**   ɪɪ-ng'ombe si-kʊ-jweg-a
         18-6-evening as 1SG-PRS-hear-FV AUG-cow(10) 10-PRS-shout-FV
         fiijo   **n-dɪnkʊ-lembʊk-a**
         INTENS 1SG-NARR-awake-FV
         'Yesterday, when I heard the cows making a lot of noise, I got up.'

    b. n-dɪnkʊ-bʊʊk-a kʊ-kʊ-kam-a ʊ-lʊ-kama   …
        1SG-NARR-go-FV 17-15-milk-FV AUG-11-milk
        'I went to milk the cows …' [ET]

The same can be observed for the subsecutive: constructed mini-narratives such as (5) were rejected by the language assistants and corrected so as to start with a past tense verb (6).

(5) a. # m-ma-jolo **n-aa-lembʊk-a**   n=ʊ-lʊ-bʊnjʊ   fiijo
         18-6-evening 1SG-SUBSEC-awake-FV COM=AUG-11-morning INTENS

    b. n-aa-nw-a   ɪɪ-tʃai
        1SG-SUBSEC-drink-FV AUG-tea(9)(<SWA)

    c. bo n-nw-ile   ɪɪ-tʃai   n-aa-bʊʊk-a   kʊ-kʊ-kam-a
        as 1SG-drink-PFV AUG-tea(9) 1SG-SUBSEC-go-FV 17-15-milk-FV
        ʊ-lʊ-kama
        AUG-11-milk
        (intended: 'Yesterday I got up very early. I had breakfast (lit. 'drank tea'). When I finished breakfast, I went to milk the cows …') [ET]

(6) Correction of (5):
    a. m-ma-jolo **n-aa-lembwike** n=ʊ-lʊ-bʊnjʊ   fiijo
        18-6-evening 1SG-PST-awake.PFV COM=AUG-11-morning INTENS

    b. n-aa-nw-a   ɪɪ-tʃai   …
        1SG-NARR-drink-FV AUG-tea(9)

To conclude, neither of Nyakyusa's narrative markers can on their own open a text. Instead, they are pragmatically dependent on an otherwise established context. In this, they come close to encoding a dependent *taxis*, as originally defined by Jakobson (1957: 46): "taxis characterizes the narrated event in relation to another narrated event and without reference to the speech event". Its temporal semantics, however, preclude the application of this term. Contini Morava (1987; 1989), in a discussion of Swahili, speaks of a "contingency" relation. Seidel (2015), in a wider perspective, employs the term "notional dependency".

In Nyakyusa narrative discourse the function of providing a context on which
the narrative tense elaborates is normally fulfilled by a preceding independent
clause. As will be shown in §7.3.2, 7.4.3, the semantics of both the narrative tense
and the subsecutive include past time reference. Examples (2–6) above indicate
that what is required for the employment of the narrative markers in Nyakyusa
is not so much a preceding independent clause, nor a narrowed-down time frame,
but rather the establishment of a specific situation.

7.2.3 Distribution in narrative discourse

Having discussed the principle pragmatic requirements for the employment of
Nyakyusa's narrative markers, in this section their distribution will be discussed
in regards to the macro-structure of narratives and the discourse conventions
governing their use in alternation with other verbal paradigms.

The narrative tense and the subsecutive are found essentially only within the
complicating action, evaluation and resolution sections of the text, that is within
the plot proper (Fleischman 1990: ch. 5). The only exceptions are endings of the
type illustrated in the following examples:[2]

(7) gʊ-lɪnkʊ-j-a   mw-iʃo   gw-ake   papaa~pa
     3-NARR-be(come)-FV 3-end(<SWA) 3-POSS.SG REDUPL~PROX.16
     'Right here it ended.' [Throw away the child]

(8) ka-a-j-a   ka-mpyenyule
     12-SUBSEC-be(come)-FV 12-closing_formula
     'The story is over' [Man and his in-law]

Note that this association of the narrative markers with the plot, however, is a
one-way conditional. Unlike what has been reported for other African languages
such as Supyire (Senufo), where a narrative marker is used "in all but the initial
main line clause" (R. Carlson 1994: 34), in the Nyakyusa corpus there are few
narratives in which the entire storyline is told using the narrative tense and subsecutive. To varying degrees, events that clearly form part of the storyline are
construed in the past perfective.

To begin with, the onset of the plot does not always equal a switch to the
narrative markers. In many texts, following the orientation section, one finds a
verb in one of the past tense paradigms setting the stage for the first episode. In

---

[2] *kampyenyule* as a nominal predicate without a copula is a common closing formula in the folk
tales collected by Berger (1933) and Busse (1942). (8) is the only token in the present corpus.

cases where there is no orientation section, this constitutes the opening of the text. With eventive material, the past perfective is the paradigm of choice. This is illustrated in (9), where the narrative tense is employed only from (9d) onwards; see Appendix B.1 for the full text.

(9) a. Orientation section:

ɪ-n-gwina   n=ɪ-n-gambɪlɪ   ba-a-lɪ   bʊ-manyaani fiijo
AUG-9-crocodile COM=AUG-9-monkey 2-PST-COP 14-friendship INTENS

a-ka-balɪlo a-k-a   ijolo.   ba-a-jaat-an-il-aga
AUG-12-time AUG-12-ASSOC old_times 2-PST-walk-RECP-APPL-IPFV

n=ʊ-kw-angal-a   pamopeene. ɪ-n-gwina
COM=AUG-15-be_well-FV together   AUG-9-crocodile

j-iis-aga   n-kʊ-j-eeg-a   ɪ-n-gambɪlɪ   n=ʊ-kʊ-bʊʊk-a
9-PST.come-IPFV 18-15-9-take-FV AUG-9-monkey COM=AUG-15-go-FV

na=jo   pa-lʊ-sʊngo pa-kw-angal-a.   ii-sikʊ lɪ-mo
COM=REF.9 16-11-island 16-15-be_well-FV 5-day 5-one

ʊ-n-na   gw-a   n-gwina   a-a-lɪ   m̩-bine
AUG-1-his_mother 1-ASSOC 9-crocodile 1-PST-COP 1-ill

'Monkey and Crocodile were good friends long ago. They visited and accompanied each other. Crocodile used to come to pick up monkey and go with him to an island to spend time together. One day, Crocodile's mother was sick.'

b. Begin of complicating action:

po   ɪ-n-gwina   **j-aa-bʊʊk-ile** n-kʊ-jɪ-bʊʊl-a ɪ-n-gambɪlɪ
then AUG-9-crocodile 9-PST-go-PFV 18-15-9-tell-FV AUG-9-monkey

ʊkʊtɪ "jʊʊba   gw-angʊ m̩-bine. tʊ-bʊʊk-e
COMP my_mother 1-POSS.1SG 1-ill   1PL-go-SUBJ

ʊ-ka-n-keet-e."
2SG-ITV-1-look-SUBJ

'So Crocodile went to tell Monkey, "My mother is sick. Let's go, you should see her."'

c. ɪ-n-gambɪlɪ   **j-aal-iitiike**
AUG-9-monkey 9-PST-agree.PFV

'Monkey agreed.'

d. **ba-lɪnkʊ-bʊʊk-a**
2-NARR-go-FV

'They went.' [Crocodile and Monkey]

In the same vein, eventive material that occurs at the beginning of a subsequent major textual unit is commonly expressed in the past perfective. In addition, the past perfective rather than the narrative tense or subsecutive is often employed for storyline events that are highly unpredictable, pivotal and/or constitute a major change in the roles of participants. In §6.5.5.3.6 it is shown that the central conceptual notion that governs the linguistic construal of narrative discourse in Nyakyusa is thematic continuity. These mentioned cases of the employment of the past perfective form part of a larger coherent pattern, in which past tense paradigms are employed at significant interruptions to thematic continuity. Employment of the narrative tense and subsecutive, on the other hand, is a linguistic signal of maintained thematic continuity. In this the narrative markers and their alternation with the past tense paradigms work mainly on the textual component of meaning (§1.4.4.2), in that they serve to structure the hearer's mental representation. As will be seen in (10, 11), these alternations also seem to serve to control the information flow.

While the conceptual notion of thematic continuity allows for a coherent explanation of the employment of the narrative markers vis-à-vis the past tense paradigms, it has to be kept in mind that this is a discoursive convention. There is significant variation across texts concerning how much of the storyline is carried by the narrative markers on the one hand and the past perfective on the other. The opposite poles of this continuum can be illustrated by two stories in the corpus. In the text "Throw away the child" two women with young children go to pluck thatching grass. Having gathered enough, they tie it into bundles. One of the two women hides her child in the grass. Instead of the child, she then carries a stone on her back. On their way home, she convinces the other woman to throw her child into a ravine, claiming to have done so with her own child. During a pause, she then takes out her child to breastfeed it and thus the second woman understands she has been deceived. She sets off and magical beings give her directions to a place where she is finally given a child more beautiful than her own one. Nearly the entire storyline is carried by the narrative tense plus a few occurrences of the narrative present. The only exception is the past perfective in (10c), which delimits the deception episode.

(10) a. ba-lınkw-i-twık-a   ɪ-ly-ʊndʊ
          2-NARR-REFL-lift_to_head-FV   AUG-5-thatching_grass
          'They loaded the grass on their heads.'

b. ba-lɪnkw-end-a
   2-NARR-walk/travel-FV

   'They went.'

c. po   bo bi-kw-end-a   bi-kw-end-a   po
   then as 2-PRS-walk/travel-FV 2-PRS-walk/travel-FV then
   ba-a-fik-ile   pa-mo a-pa   b-end-aga
   2-PST-arrive-PFV 16-one AUG-PROX.16 2-PST.walk/travel-IPFV

   'As they were going and going they arrived at some place where they
   were going.'

d. ba-lɪnkʊ-ky-ag-a ɪ-k-iina   ɪ-kɪ   ki-kʊ-job-igw-a   ʊkʊtɪ
   2-NARR-7-find-FV AUG-7-cave AUG-PROX.7 7-PRS-speak-PASS-FV COMP
   kɪ-sooko, ɪ-kɪ-tali   fiijo
   7-ravine AUG-7-long INTENS

   'They found a cave which is called a ravine, a deep one.'

e. po   ʊ-jʊ   **a-lɪnkʊ-n-syob**-a   ʊ-n-nine
   then AUG-PROX.1 1-NARR-1-deceive-FV AUG-1-companion

   'This one betrayed her friend.' [Throw away the child]

The text "Hare and Skunk", of comparable length, shows the very opposite
distribution of the past perfective vis-à-vis the narrative markers. The story goes
as follows. The two protagonists go hunting and get hold of a guinea fowl. They
put it on a fire and roast it. While Skunk repeatedly claims that it is done, Hare
each time replies "Not yet". This leads to Skunk getting tired of waiting and
dozing off. Hare seizes the chance and eats up all the meat. When Skunk wakes
up, Hare claims to have also been asleep and that the meat has burnt on the
fire. Another day, Skunk takes revenge while Hare is asleep. He covers him with
leaves and beats him hard with a stick. Then he steals off again. When Hare
wakes up crying, Skunk appears and acts as if he has no idea what has happened.
Some days later, both go to a festivity where drums are played. First Hare, then
Skunk plays the drum and while singing they confess their deeds. This leads to a
fight (resulting in Hare's ears being stretched and Skunk's nose being squeezed),
which is stopped by Dog.

Within each episode of this second text, all of the essential actions and developments are depicted in the past perfective (plus some ancillary information
with inchoative verbs). Verbs with the narrative tense and subsecutive mainly
depict the communication between the two protagonists and amplify their actions (e.g. 'They fought and fought and fought'). This gives the impression of

the narrator sharply delimiting the sets of predications that depict the 'outline' of the story from elaboration upon these circumstances. In quantitative terms, this employment of the verbal categories leads to nearly twice as many verbs in the past perfective as in the narrative tense and subsecutive combined. As an example, the third episode is given in (11); see Appendix B.2 for the full text.

(11) a. po   nsyɪsyɪ a-a-kateele
         then skunk(1) 1-PST-be(come)_tired.PFV

         'Then Skunk became tired.'

      b. a-aly-and-ile   ʋ-kʋ-sipʋk-a
         1-PST-begin-PFV AUG-15-doze-FV

         'He began to doze.'

      c. po   bo i-kʋ-sipʋk-a, bo a-gon-ile ʋ-tʋ-lo   po   kalʋlʋ
         then as 1-PRS-doze-FV as 1-rest-PFV AUG-13-sleep then hare(1)
         a-aly-eg-ile   ɪɪ-nyama   j-oosa
         1-PST-take-PFV AUG-meat(9) 9-all

         'As he was dozing, as he was asleep, Hare took all the meat.'

      d. a-a-l-iile   pyʋ́,   a-a-l-iile   pyʋ́
         1-PST-eat-PFV of_consuming_completely 1-PST-eat-PFV O.C.C.

         'He ate it up, he ate it up.'

      e. bo i-kʋ-lembʋk-a   nsyɪsyɪ a-lɪnkw-ag-a   kalʋlʋ a-l-iile
         as 1-PRS-wake_up-FV skunk(1) 1-NARR-find-FV hare(1) 1-eat-PFV
         j-oosa ɪɪ-nyama
         9-all AUG-meat(9)

         'When Skunk woke up, he found that Hare had eaten all of the meat.'

      f. po   a-lɪnkʋ-mmw-ani-a kalʋlʋ a-lɪnkʋ-tɪ "ɪɪ-nyama   jɪ-bʋʋk-ile
         then 1-NARR-1-ask-FV   hare(1) 1-NARR-say AUG-meat(9) 9-go-PFV
         kʋʋgʋ?"
         where

         'So he asked Hare "The meat, where has it gone?"'

      g. po   kalʋlʋ a-lɪnkʋ-tɪ "hee. n-aa-gon-eliile   niine
         then hare(1) 1-NARR-say INTERJ 1SG-PST-rest-INTS.PFV COM.1SG
         ʋ-tʋ-lo.   keet-a,   jɪ-p-iile   j-oosa, jɪ-bwes-ile.
         AUG-13-sleep watch-FV 9-be_burnt-PFV 9-all   9-be_burnt_down-PFV

jɪ-bwes-ile,   hee"'
9-be_burnt_down-PFV INTERJ

'Hare said "Hee, I was also asleep. Look, it all burnt to ashes. It burnt, hee."

h. po   nsyɪsyɪ a-a-kaleele   fiijo
   then skunk(1) 1-PST-be(come)_angry.PFV INTENS

'Skunk was very angry.'

i. a-a-tɪ   "haya!"
   1-SUBSEC-say OK(<SWA)

'He said "OK!"' [Hare and Skunk]

Interestingly, Contini Morava (1989: 118–120) observes a similar variability for Swahili and points out the extensive use of the simple past by the author Shabaan Robert, which goes along with a "leisurely, didactic, even pedantic" (p. 119) style, whereas fast-spaced, fluent discourse is characterized by greater reliance on the so-called 'consecutive'.

To sum up, in Nyakyusa, narrative texts are construed around the notion of thematic continuity and discontinuity. The narrative markers are here confined to the plot (complicating action, resolution, evaluation sections) and contrast with the past perfective. It has been seen that the narrator nevertheless possesses a considerable degree of freedom as to the degree to which s/he explicitly signals (dis-)continuity in the storyline by alternating between the narrative markers and the past perfective. A discussion of two texts in the corpus has shown the opposite poles of this continuum. In one, all of the essential developments are related in the past perfective and contingent elaboration is depicted through the narrative markers. In the other text, once sufficient orientation has been given, the storyline is 'allowed to flow' almost entirely through the use of the narrative markers.

7.2.4 Quantitative distribution

In the preceding subsections, it has been seen that the narrative tense and the subsecutive show equal behaviour in regards to subject continuity (§7.2.1) as well as in regards to Longacre's criteria of textual dependency and storyline ranks (§7.2.2, 7.2.3). It has also been seen that both markers have the same distribution in regards to the macro-structure of narrative discourse (§7.2.3). With neither of these allowing for a functional differentiation of Nyakyusa's two narrative markers, it is necessary to take a closer look.

A striking difference between Nyakyusa's narrative markers can be found in their quantitative distribution. As an approximation to the latter, Table 7.2 lists the number of clauses marked with the narrative tense versus the subsecutive in 17 narratives. All of these come from recordings of oral renditions, apart from "The one who eats ...", which is the only written story in the corpus that features the subsecutive. Sequences of a verb of speech followed by an inflected form of the quotative verb *tɪ* (see §10.3) have been conflated into a single clause. Elliptical verbless clauses – see (82) in §6.5.5.2 for an example – as well as each turn within drama (renditions of dialogue without overt quotation formulae) are counted as one independent clause.

As can be gathered from Table 7.2, in all oral narratives in the corpus, the narrative tense is employed. The narrative tense further clearly predominates over the subsecutive in the total number of tokens (it is also used in all of the written narratives). The subsecutive, however, does not feature at all in a number of texts. Within those texts in which both narrative markers are employed, either the narrative tense clearly predominates or both markers are roughly equal. Furthermore, the subsecutive, but not the narrative tense, is subject to certain sociolinguistic constrictions (see §7.4.2).

Table 7.2: Frequency distribution of narrative tense and subsecutive

	HaS	LaT	MaE	MaI	PaD	PW	HaT	EoF	MaT
Clauses	77	19	9	98	10	41	34	9	96
Narrative tense	21	11	5	56	2	20	19	5	21
Subsecutive	2	0	0	24	2	2	4	1	21

	CaM	INV	CaC	SaC	TaC	LK	MwG	PaW	$\sum$
Clauses	27	29	21	59	90	92	66	142	918
Narrative tense	17	6	6	30	72	54	8	34	387
Subsecutive	0	0	1	10	0	0	10	22	99

HaS = Hare and Skunk; LaT = Lion and Tortoise; MaE = Mosquito and Ear; MaI = Man and his in-law; PaD = Pig and Duck; PW = Pregnant women; HaT = Hare and Tugutu; EoF = The one who eat's ...; MaT = Monkey and Tortoise; CaM = Crocodile and Monkey; INV = Invaders; CaC = Chickens and Crow; SaC = Snake and children; TaC = Throw away the child; LK = Lake Kyungululu; MwG = Monster with guitar; PaW = Python and woman

7.2.5 Functional differences

As the detailed examination of the two narrative markers in §7.3, 7.4 will show, the two markers do not only differ in regards to their quantitative distribution, but also in their diachronic sources, their semantics and their micro-patterns of employment. To anticipate these findings, Nyakyusa's two narrative markers most likely constitute two former present tense paradigms contrasting in grammatical aspect. In the present-day language, their opposition can be understood as one between the narrative tense as the aspectually unspecified, all-purpose narrative marker on the one hand and the subsecutive as the more restricted, specifically perfective marker of a narrative development on the other.

7.3 Narrative tense

This section deals with the narrative tense, the more frequent of Nyakyusa's two narrative markers. In this section, its formal makeup will be discussed first (§7.3.1). Building on this, a number of semantic features will be examined (§7.3.2, 7.3.3).

7.3.1 Formal makeup

The narrative tense consists of the non-tensed copula *lɪ* with an infinitive complement marked for locative class 18.

(12)   *tʊlɪ nkʊjoba* 'we spoke'

The familiar label *narrative tense* is applied to this construction for reasons of convenience. Note, however, that this construction does not constitute a tense in the sense of §1.4.2.1. Earlier studies referred to the Nyakyusa narrative tense as the *historical tense* or *tempus historicum* (Schumann 1899; Endemann 1914; Mwangoka & Voorhoeve 1960a).

Throughout the rest of this study the left-of-the-stem portion of the narrative tense will be considered one unanalysed morpheme. While its composition is still transparent, the fact that no material can intervene between what corresponds to the copula and its complement suggests that synchronically this construction should be analysed as consisting of a prefix *lɪnkʊ-* plus the default final vowel.

(13)   a.   m-ma-jolo   tʊ-lɪnkʊ-job-a
              18-6-evening 1PL-NARR-speak-FV
              'Yesterday we spoke.'

    b.   tʊlɪnkʊjoba mmajolo

    c. * tʊlɪ mmajolo nkʊjoba

In its composition the Nyakyusa narrative tense corresponds to a periphrastic progressive construction that is widespread in Bantu and in many languages has grammaticalized further to a simple present tense (Bastin 1989a; 1989b); also see de Kind et al. (2015) for numerous cases in the Kikongo H16 cluster.[3] This correspondence vis-à-vis its present-day uses point to a former simple present (i.e. present imperfective), whose use as a narrative present has become conventionalized up to the point of losing its original meaning and becoming restricted to the "narrative mode" (Smith 2003) of discourse. As a syntactic correlate, the narrative tense is attested exclusively in independent clauses. In all probability, this specialization as a narrative marker took place parallel to the rise of the new simple present (§6.5.1). As Haspelmath (1998) points out, in many languages old present tense paradigms that have been replaced by newer construction persist in specialized functions, e.g. as futurates, subjunctives or narrative markers; this functional shift is discussed in more detail in Persohn (2016). For a Bantu language, however, this originally periphrastic construction is a very uncommon source for a narrative marker. It does not figure as such in the neighbouring languages, nor in any of the around 140 languages for which Nurse (2008) provides tense and aspect matrices.

To conclude the discussion of the narrative tense's formal makeup, note that there is no morphologically negated counterpart to the narrative tense, instead a negative auxiliary *sita* is used, which takes an augmentless infinitive as its complement:

(14)   tʊ-lɪnkʊ-sit-a   kʊ-job-a
        1PL-NARR-NEG.AUX-FV 15-speak-FV
        'We did not speak.'

7.3.2 Temporal and aspectual semantics

Taking up Nurse's (2008) description of narrative markers in Bantu, recall that he points out that "just because most sequences deal with past events, this special [narrative, BP] marker is most frequent in past narratives, less frequent in timeless events, followed by futures" (p. 120). Concerning the Nyakyusa narrative tense, despite its source in a present tense construction, it is attested only

---

[3]In fact, Lusekelo (2008b; 2013) does not distinguish the narrative tense from the periphrastic progressive construction (§6.6.1), and lists it under the heading of progressive aspect.

with past time reference. This was already observed by Endemann (1914: 61), who notes that "[i]n its original meaning, this is thus a present tense form, but it serves as a Tempus historicum with a preterite meaning" (translated from the original German, BP). Negative evidence from elicitation shows that the narrative tense is not licensed in timeless generic (15) nor future (16) contexts.

(15) Context: Describing the process of preparing stiff porridge.

    a. bi-kʊ-kosy-a ʊ-m-ooto
       2-PRS-light-FV AUG-3-fire

    b. # ba-lɪnkʊ-suk-a ɪ-fy-a   kʊ-pɪɪ-jɪl-a
       2-NARR-wash-FV AUG-8-ASSOC 15-cook-APPL-FV

    c. # ba-lɪnkʊ-bɪɪk-a a-m-ɪɪsi   pa-m-ooto ...
       2-NARR-put-FV AUG-6-water 16-3-fire

       (intended: 'They light the fire. They wash the cooking utensils. They put the water on the fire.')

(16) Context: A young man's plans for the future.

    a. bo n-gʊl-ile   a=n-gʊ-jeng-a   ɪɪ-nyumba   ɪɪ-nywamu
       as 1SG-grow-PFV FUT=1SG-PRS-build-FV AUG-house(9) AUG-big(9)

    b. # n-dɪnkʊ-tim-a   ɪɪ-ng'ombe pa-ka-aja
       1SG-NARR-herd-FV AUG-cow(10) 16-12-homestead

       (intended: 'When I am grown up, I will build a big house. Then I will herd cows at home.')

As described in §6.7.2, temporal adverbial clauses feature present tense (non-past) predicates, which take their temporal reference from the matrix clause. The narrative tense here patterns with the past tense paradigms (and the subsecutive). What is more, with an intervening narrative present, past time reference need not be re-established (17). The latter has also been observed before by Eaton (2013).[4]

(17) a. Asia a-lɪnkʊ-sʊʊbɪl-a ʊkʊtɪ Juma aa=i-kʊ-j-a   ŋ-dʊme
     A. 1-NARR-expect-FV COMP J.   FUT=1-PRS-be(come)-FV 1-husband
     gw-ake
     1-POSS.SG

    'Asia expected that Juma would become her husband.'

---

[4]See §6.7.1 on the interjection ngɪmba.

b. ngɪmba **a-saam-iile**   kw-a   Sambʊka kɪsita   kʊ-many-a
   behold 1-migrate-APPL.PFV 17-ASSOC S.   without 15-know-FV

   'Gosh, he has moved to Sambuka's, without knowing [that Sambuka has lied to him].'[5]

c. Juma na   Sambʊka **ba-lɪnkw-eg-an-a**
   J.   COM S.   2-NARR-marry-RECP-FV

   'Juma and Sambuka married.' [Juma, Asia and Sambuka]

To conclude, the temporal semantics of the narrative tense includes past time reference. This leads to the question of its aspectual meaning. In (15) above it was shown that the narrative tense is incompatible with timeless generic statements. Apart from temporal semantics, this is further linked to the fact that the narrative tense is attested only in episodic sentences. As Krifka et al. (1995: 36) define them, "[e]pisodic sentences are those whose main predicate has a situation argument bound by existential closure; they report a specific event or occasion" as opposed to the generalizations that characterize generic and habitual statements. Note that this definition includes cases of plural participants or events (see G. N. Carlson 2009). (18) illustrates such a case, where the narrative tense apparently serves to individuate the single, asserted occurrences.[6] This interpretation is strengthened by the fact that the past imperfective in its non-episodic habitual/generic reading (see §6.5.7) was considered infelicitous in this context.

(18)   Context: Children have killed a snake that was laying in front of them on the path. Now they try to pass the snake's dead body.
       bo bi-kʊ-lond-a ʊ-kʊ-kɪnd-a   kʊkʊtɪ bi-kʊ-tɪ   ba-jɪ-tambʊk-e
       as 2-PRS-try-FV AUG-15-pass-FV every 2-PRS-say 2-9-cross-SUBJ
       ba-kɪnd-e   **jɪ-lɪnkʊ-tup-a**   kangɪ **jɪ-lɪnkʊ-j-a**   n-dali
       2-pass-SUBJ 9-NARR-become_fat-FV again 9-NARR-be(come)-FV 9-long

       'As they tried to pass, each time they wanted to cross and pass it [snake], it became fat and long.' [Children and Snake]

Apart from its restriction to episodic sentences, the narrative tense can be considered unspecified for grammatical aspect. With inchoative verbs and other types of verbs that include a change-of-state or inherent endpoint (see §5), it typically refers to the passing of this endpoint. This is illustrated in (19, 20) with the inchoative verbs *hoboka* 'be(come) happy' and *ɪma* 'stand, stop'.

---

[6]For the projective/conative construction consisting of *tɪ* followed by a verb in the subjunctive, see §9.3.2.

(19) Juma a-lɪnkʊ-m̩-bʊʊl-a Sambʊka a-lɪnkʊ-tɪ   "Po
      J.   1-NARR-1-tell-FV S.   1-NARR-say then
      n-gw-eg-ege   jʊ~jʊʊ-gwe, bʊle, paapo gʊ-n-gan-ile.
      1SG-2SG-marry-IPFV.SUBJ REDUPL~2SG Q   because 2SG-1SG-love-PFV
      ʊ-jʊ   a-ka-n-gan-a   n-dek-e."
      AUG-PROX.1 1-NEG-1SG-love-FV 1SG-let-SUBJ

      Juma told Sambuka "Then I'll marry you, because you love me. The one
      who doesn't love me, I'll leave him."'

      Sambʊka **a-lɪnkʊ-hobok-a**   fiijo   paapo ɪ-si
      S.   1-NARR-be(come)_happy-FV INTENS because AUG-PROX.10
      a-a-lond-aga   a-a-sy-ag-ile
      1-PST-want-IPFV 1-PST-10-find-PFV

      'Sambuka became very happy because she had achieved what she
      wanted.' [Juma, Asia and Sambuka]

(20) po leelo   bo a-fik-ile   kɪfuki pa-k-iina pamo paa-sofu j-aa
      then now/but as 1-arrive-PFV near   16-7-cave or   16-room(9) 9-ASSOC
      n-galamu kajamba **a-lɪnkw-ɪm-a**   pa-nja
      9-lion   tortoise(1) 1-NARR-stand/stop-FV 16-outside

      'When it arrived near the cave or the bedroom of Lion, Tortoise stopped
      outside.' [Lion and Tortoise]

With activity-type verbs the reading depends on the context and co-text. To
begin with, the narrative tense can give a reading of an eventuality as a discrete
whole. This is most obvious in those cases where the discourse environment
clearly delimits the occurrence, as in (21b).

(21) a. po ba-lɪnkʊ-bʊʊk-a kʊ-kw-ip-a   ɪ-ly-ʊndʊ   kʊ-la
          then 2-NARR-go-FV   17-15-pluck-FV AUG-5-thatching_grass 17-DIST
          'They went to pluck grass there.'

      b. po **ba-lɪnkw-ip-a**   ɪ-ly-ʊndʊ
          then 2-NARR-pluck-FV AUG-5-thatching_grass
          'They plucked grass.'

      c. po bo b-iip-ile   ɪ-fi-kose,   kʊkʊtɪ mu-ndʊ ɪ-fi-kose,
          then as 2-pluck-PFV AUG-8-bundle every 1-person AUG-8-bundle
          ba-lɪnkʊ-j-a   ba-ndʊ ba-a kʊ-piny-a
          2-NARR-be(come)-FV 2-person 2-ASSOC 15-bind-FV
          'When they had plucked bunches, each one bunches, they began to
          tie [the grass].' [Throw away the child]

Unlike the subsecutive (§7.4.3), a progressive reading, however, is also possible with the narrative tense. The following two examples will illustrate this. In (22) a woman has deceived her friend by asking her to throw her child into a ravine and claiming to have done so with her own child. Now she takes it from its hiding place and begins to breastfeed it (22a, 22b). (22d) serves not only to express her lack of reaction to the deceived woman's indignation, as expressed in (22c), but explicitly depicts the act of breastfeeding as ongoing without interruption.[7] The flow chart in Figure 7.1 gives a graphic illustration of the relative order of events.

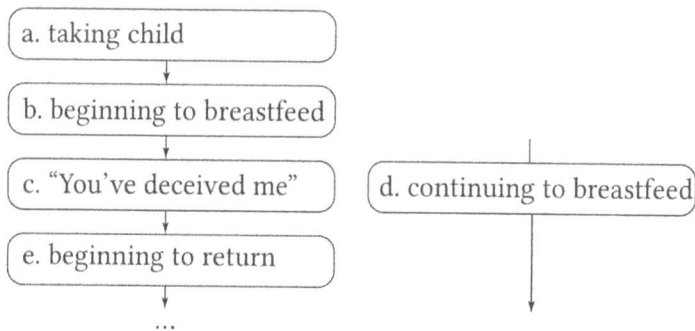

Figure 7.1: Relative event order of (22)

(22) a. a-lɪnkʊ-mmw-eg-a ʊ-mw-anaake
1-NARR-1-take-FV AUG-1-his_child
'She took her child.'

b. a-lɪnkw-end-a n=ʊ-kʊ-tɪ fi, ʊ-kw-and-a
a-NARR-walk/travel-FV COM=AUG-15-say what AUG-15-begin-FV
ʊ-kʊ-mm-ongesya
AUG-15-1-breastfeed-FV
'She then did what, began to breastfeed it.'

c. bo ʊ-kʊ-mm-ongesy-a a-lɪnkʊ-tɪ "Haa! keet-a
as 1-PRS-1-breastfeed-FV 1-NARR-say INTERJ watch-FV
ʊʊ-syob-ile, gwe mw-inangʊ. ʊ-t-ile
2SG.1SG-deceive-PFV 2SG 1-my_companion 2SG-say-PFV

---

[7]This story was told by a speaker of one of the northernmost varieties of Nyakyusa, hence the less common shape ʊ- of the noun class 1 subject prefix in (22c); see §3.3.2.2.

"n-daag-ile   ʋ-mw-ana""
1SG-throw-PFV AUG-1-child

'As she was breastfeeding it, she [the other woman] said "Haa! Look,
you've deceived me, my friend. You said "I've thrown away the
child.""'

d. po   jʋ-la **a-lɪnkw-endelel-a** ʋ-kʋ-mm-ongesy-a   ʋ-mw-ana
then 1-DIST 1-NARR-continue-FV AUG-15-1-breastfeed-FV AUG-1-child
'That one continued to breastfeed the child.'

e. jʋ-la a-lɪnkw-and-a   ʋ-kʋ-buj-a   ʋ-kʋ-bʋʋk-a
1-DIST 1-NARR-begin-FV AUG-15-return-FV AUG-15-go-FV
kʋ-kʋ-n-keet-a ʋ-mw-anaake
17-15-1-look-FV AUG-1-child

'That one began returning, going to look for her child.' [Throw away
the child]

Example (23) depicts the beginning of a race between Hare and Tugutu, a type
of bird. While Tugutu remains at the start (23d), Hare does run (23b, 23e). Hare's
act of running is construed as an ongoing activity contemporaneous with his acts
of speaking (23c) and completing the first mile (23f). Figure 7.2 illustrates this as
a flow chart.

(23)   Context: Hare and Tugutu are running a race.

a. a-lɪnkʋ-tɪ "oko   kalʋlʋ! tʋ-bop-ege   leelo!"
1-NARR-say INTERJ hare(1) 1PL-run-IPFV.SUBJ now/but

'He [Tugutu] said "Here we go, Hare! Let's run now!"'

b. po   kalʋlʋ **a-lɪnkʋ-bop-a**
then hare(1) 1-NARR-run-FV

'Hare ran/was running.'

c. a-lɪnkʋ-tɪ "lɪnga   tʋ-bop-ile   a-ma-elɪ   jɪ-mo
1-NARR-say if/when 1PL-run-PFV AUG-6-mile(<EN) 9-one
n-gʋ-kʋ-koolel-a   ʋkutɪ "bʋle, mwa=n-dugutu,
1SG-PRS-2SG-call-FV COMP Q   matronym=9-type_of_bird
ʋ-li-po?" gw-itɪk-e   ʋ-tɪ   "ee, n-di=po""
2SG-COP=16 2SG-agree-SUBJ 2SG-say.SUBJ yes 1SG-COP=16

'He said "When we've run one mile, I'll call you saying "Mr. Tugutu
are you there?" You shall answer "Yes, I'm here.""'[8]

---

[8]The narrator oscillates between placing the loanword for 'mile' in noun class 6, thus re-
analyzing /ma/ as a prefix, and placing it in noun class 9a, the default for loans.

d. po bo b-and-ile   ʊ-kʊ-bop-a   jʊ-la mwa=n-dugutu
   then as 2-begin-PFV AUG-15-run-FV 1-DIST matronym=9-t.o.bird
   a-a-syeele   pala~pa-la
   1-PST-remain.PFV REDUPL~16-DIST

   'When they had started to run that Mr. Tugutu had remained right
   there.'

e. po   kalʊlʊ **a-lɪnkʊ-bop-a** mw-ene
   then hare(1) 1-NARR-run-FV 1-only

   'So Hare ran/was running alone.'

f. a-lɪnkʊ-mal-a   a-ma-elɪ   ga-mo
   1-NARR-finish-FV AUG-6-mile 6-one

   'He completed one mile.' [Hare and Tugutu]

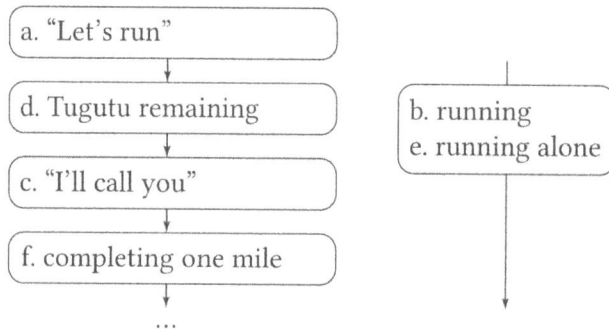

Figure 7.2: Relative event order of (23)

To summarize, the semantics of the Nyakyusa narrative tense include past
time reference. Further, it is closely linked to episodic events and unspecified for
grammatical aspect.

Considering that historically the narrative tense constituted a present tense
construction, likely one carrying imperfective aspect, this indicates that its employment as a narrative present has led to a profound re-adjustment of its semantics. For discussion see Persohn (2016), where this shift in meaning is attributed to
Fleischman's (1990) "plus interpretation", by which a simple present as the least
specific TMA construction takes over the temporal (i.e. past tense) and aspectual
meaning appropriate to context, as well as to a cross-Bantu tendency to have aspectually underspecified forms as narrative markers. Robar (2014) convincingly

argues that the so-called *wayyiqtol*-construction in Biblical Hebrew underwent a comparable change, starting out as a simple present whose extensive use as a narrative present with the pragmatic function of signalling continuity has led to a bleaching of its original semantic content. In the case of Biblical Hebrew this has gone even further, allowing for the construction in question to take over any kind of tense, aspect or mood.

7.3.3 Sequentiality of events

Closely linked to the question of aspectual semantics is that of sequential ordering. At first the very concept of a narrative marker may suggest that the Nyakyusa narrative tense denotes sequential ordering of events. Moreover, on the basis of a Swahili example taken as typical for Bantu, Nurse (2008: 121) generalizes that "the narrative explicitly sequences events [...] and says that [...] the second situation is later than the first". Cover (2010: 111) cautions againt prematurely accepting such an assumption and observes that sequentiality is not part of the semantics of the narrative paradigms in Badiaranke (Northern Atlantic). Similar observations have been made for the *narrative/consecutive tense* in the Senufo language Supyire (R. Carlson 1994) and the so-called *wayyiqtol*-construction in Biblical Hebrew (Cook 2004). Concerning Bantu, Morrison (2011: 277), in her grammar of Bena G63, notes that "[the narrative tense] is *often* best translated as 'and then X' [emphasis added]", while Seidel (2015) makes a similar observation for Yeyi R41. Even for Nurse's model example, Swahili, a detailed examination shows that not all instances of the paradigm in question feature sequential ordering (Contini Morava 1987: 112f).

Labov & Waletzky's (1967) framework of narrative analysis – see §1.4.4.2 – provides us with a valuable tool to check whether the Nyakyusa narrative tense inherently encodes sequentiality. Assuming that it does encode an ordering of events would predict that no clause containing it can be displaced without changing the underlying order of events. That is, the narrative tense should only figure in those clauses that are classified as *narrative clauses*. The discussion of its aspectual semantics, however, has already shown that the narrative tense can have a progressive reading. As a function of being ongoing, the eventualities in question overlap with other eventualities. That is, they can be displaced throughout a determined part of the text without changing the underlying order of events and can therefore be classified as *restricted clauses*. A few additional examples will illustrate the Nyakyusa narrative tense outside of narrative clauses.

Another representative example of the narrative tense appearing in a restricted clause is given in (24). (24a) contains a husband's orders to his wife and (24b, 24c) her carrying out these orders. Each step is dependent on the previous one. That is, these three clauses describe eventualities that happen in sequential order. The eventuality described in (24d), however, takes place simultaneously to the ones described in (24b, 24c). This means that (24d) could be anticipated without changing the relative order of events, and is hence a restricted clause. This becomes clear from the wider context of the story – he goes on to clandestinely kill her father – and is also signaled by spatial deixis: his actions take place at the deictic centre (*kʊno* 'here') while hers is viewed against the ground of an associated motion event (see §10.4.1 on the movement gram (*j*)*a*). Figure 7.3 is a visualization of the relative order of events.

(24) a. a-lɪnkʊ-n-koolel-a ʊ-n-kasi,   a-lɪnkʊ-tɪ "n-kasi gw-angʊ, bʊʊk-e
         1-NARR-1-call-FV   AUG-1-wife 1-NARR-say 1-wife 1-POSS.1SG, go-SUBJ
         lɪlɪno   ʊlʊ, k-ʊʊl-e   ɪ-fi-lombe,   ʊ-ka-sy-e
         now/today now ITV-buy-SUBJ AUG-8-maize 2SG-ITV-grind-SUBJ
         ʊ-bʊ-fu,   kʊ-ma-lʊʊka"
         AUG-14-flour 17-6-store
         'He called his wife and said "My wife, go right now, go buy maize, go grind flour, in the stores."'

     b. nalooli ʊ-n-kiikʊlʊ   a-lɪnkw-a   k-ʊʊl-a   ɪ-fi-lombe
         really AUG-1-woman 1-NARR-go.FV 15-buy-FV AUG-8-maize
         'She went and bought maize.'

     c. a-lɪnkw-a   kʊ-sy-a   ʊ-bʊ-fu   kʊ-ma-lʊʊka
         1-NARR-go.FV 15-grind-FV AUG-14-flour 17-6-shop
         'She went and ground flour at the stores.'

     d. kʊ-no ʊ-ŋ-dʊme   a-lɪnkʊ-tendekesy-a ʊ-tʊ-ndʊ,
         17-PROX AUG-1-husband 1-NARR-prepare-FV   AUG-13-thing
         ɪ-fi-lwɪlo   fy-a   kʊ-ŋ-gog-el-a   ʊ-gwise
         AUG-8-poison 8-ASSOC 15-1-kill-APPL-FV AUG-his_father(1)
         'Here her husband prepared things, poison to kill her father with.'

     e. a-a-gomok-a   ʊ-mw-anike   jʊ-la
         1-SUBSEC-return-FV AUG-1-young_person 1-DIST
         'Then that young woman returned.' [Man and his in-law]

The narrative tense also features in iconic repetitions that express a single extended eventuality (25). What is depicted in the three clauses in (25a) is not internally ordered. These clauses are thus classified as *co-ordinate clauses*. The

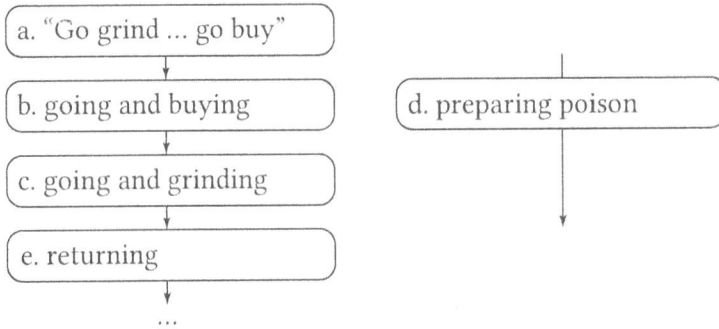

Figure 7.3: Relative event order of (24)

case of (25b) presents more difficulties: it is not entirely clear if the speech act depicted takes place during the protagonists' walking or if it is preceded by a stop.

(25)   a. po   ba-lınkw-end-a,   ba-lınkw-end-a,
            then 2-NARR-walk/travel-FV 2-NARR-walk/travel-FV
            ba-lınkw-end-a
            2-NARR-walk/travel-FV
            'They walked, they walked, they walked.'

       b. ba-lınkʊ-tı "eh   tʊ-kateele"
           2-NARR-say INTERJ 2PL-be(come)_tired.PFV
           'They said "Eh, we're tired."' [Throw away the child]

Another case of the narrative tense featuring in co-ordinate clauses is given in (26). Clauses (26a, 26b) describe eventualities that happen in sequence: the pepper only comes out of the bottles after the monkeys catch them. Clauses (26c–26e) however, describe various facets of one and the same eventuality. They can be freely swapped with each other, but are ordered relative to (26b).

(26)   Context: People try to get rid of a group of thieving monkeys that devastate their fields. To fight them, they throw small bottles filled with pepper.

       a. si-lınkw-angıl-a   m-mwanya
           10-NARR-catch-FV 18-high
           'They caught (the bottles) in mid air.'

    b. ɪ-m-bilipili   jɪ-lɪnkʊ-sunyunduk-a   n-tʊ-supa mu-la
        AUG-9-pepper(<SWA) 9-NARR-come_out_of-FV 18-13-bottle 18-DIST
        n=ʊ-kʊ-nyeel-el-a   m-maa-so na m-mi-lomo
        COM=AUG-15-jump-APPL-FV 18-6-eye   COM 18-4-lip
        'The pepper came out of the little bottles and flew into their eyes and mouths.'

    c. popaa~po   ɪ-n-gambɪlɪ   **si-lɪnkʊ-gw-a** paa-si   paapo
        REDUPL~then AUG-10-monkey 10-NARR-fall-FV 16-below because
        j-aa-lɪ   n-galɪ fiijo
        9-PST-COP 9-fierce INTENS
        'And so the monkeys fell down because it was very hot.'

    d. **si-lɪnkʊ-kuut-a** si-lɪnkʊ-tɪ, "Ho!   Ho!   Ho!"
        10-NARR-cry-FV 10-NARR-say INTERJ INTERJ INTERJ
        'They cried and said, "Ho! Ho! Ho!"'

    e. si-mo **si-lɪnkʊ-gw-a** paa-si,   "puu!"
        10-one 10-NARR-fall-FV 16-below of_falling_down
        'Some fell down, "Splat!"' [Thieving monkeys]

To conclude, the Nyakyusa narrative tense appears in narrative clauses as well as in restricted and co-ordinate clauses. This shows that sequential order is not one of its semantic features. The fact that most eventualities depicted in this paradigm stand in sequence is a mere correlate of the predominantly iconic ordering of narrative discourse.

However, it is important to note that while in examples (22–26) not all the eventualities depicted in the narrative tense are ordered relative to each other, no out-of-sequence uses are attested. The narrative tense does not feature in free clauses. Although it does feature in certain restricted clauses, this is limited to clearly defined episodic situations; see also §7.3.2. That is, the narrative tense does not feature in clauses that serve as orientation; see also §7.2.3. Lastly, flashbacks in narrative discourse are exclusively expressed by means of the past perfective (§6.5.5.3.4).

7.3.4 Summary

To summarize, the Nyakyusa narrative tense goes back to a simple present or present progressive used as a narrative present. In the present-day language, it is the most common dedicated narrative marker (see §7.2.4), whose semantics include reference to the past time. It is unspecified for grammatical aspect, but restricted to episodic situations and thus the narrative storyline. The narrative tense by itself does not encode sequential ordering. Instead it is attested with sequential as well as simultaneous eventualities. The employment of the narrative tense, like the subsecutive, is dependent on an otherwise established situation and forms part of a larger pattern, in which narrative discourse is constructed around the notion of thematic continuity and discontinuity. Given that the narrative tense is a dedicated marker of narrative discourse, the narrative tense can further be understood as a metalinguistic signal of narrativity.

7.4 Subsecutive

This section deals with the subsecutive, Nyakyusa's second dedicated narrative marker. In the following sub-sections, first its formal makeup and possible diachronic source will be discussed (§7.4.1), then some restrictions on the use of the subsecutive will be broached (§7.4.2). This is followed by an overview of its semantics together with its basic textual function (§7.4.3), as these two facets are inseparably linked. The latter are then illustrated by a number of common uses (§7.4.4) before going on to discuss a number of examples of the subsecutive without strict temporal progression (§7.4.5).

7.4.1 Formal makeup

The subsecutive is formed by a prefix *a-* in the post-initial slot, together with the default final vowel *-a*.

(27) *twajoba* 'then we spoke'

There is no negative counterpart to the subsecutive. In elicitation, negation of the subsecutive through the negative auxiliary *sita* plus an augmentless infinitive, parallel to what is found for the narrative tense (see §7.3.1), was accepted. This pattern is, however, not attested in the text corpus. Like the narrative tense, the subsecutive is attested only in independent clauses.

Schumann (1899) and Endemann (1914) consider the subsecutive a simple past,[9] an analysis that is, however, not corroborated by its usage in text collections from the chronolect described by them (Berger 1933; Busse 1942; 1949). The term *subsecutive* has been adopted from Mwangoka & Voorhoeve's (1960c) grammatical sketch. Some of the uses of this construction found in Meyer's (1989) ethnological notes, originally gathered at the turn of the twentieth century, indicate that

---

[9]They refer to it as *Imperfektum*. In the German tradition this term is sometimes used as a synonym for *Präteritum* (preterite/simple past), which fits their description.

the subsecutive constitutes a former present perfective or anterior. Such an origin is also indicated by the evidential of report *baatɩ* (§10.3), most likely from 'they (have) said', and the two variants of the courtesy formula *naapela / mbelile* 'please', the former featuring the subsecutive, the latter the present perfective. What is more, as the following discussion will show, a diachronic source along the lines of a present perfective or anterior is consistent with the meaning and use of the subsecutive in the present day language.

7.4.2 Restrictions on use

As discussed in §7.2.4, the subsecutive is the less frequent of Nyakyusa's two narrative markers, considering the absolute frequency within a given text as well as across the entire corpus of oral narratives. Unlike the narrative tense, which no narrative in the corpus can do without, the subsecutive is completely absent from nearly half of all oral narratives. What is more, the subsecutive is subject to normative restrictions.

To begin with, the subsecutive does not appear in written narratives, with the exception of one sole token. In discussions of examples from oral narratives, some of the language assistants stated that the subsecutive is a common device in storytelling, but followed up by saying that it would be inappropriate in the written medium.[10] Other language assistants rejected any constructed examples containing the subsecutive but then used it themselves in oral texts. A few speakers even considered this construction a Ndali intrusion into their language. This assessment can easily be rejected, given the construction's apparent age, the fact that it is found in the eastern varieties of Nyakyusa (§1.2.5), whereas Ndali is one of Nyakyusa's western neighbours, and its distribution, which does not resemble that of its Ndali cognate as described by Botne (2008).

7.4.3 Semantics and basic textual function

As discussed in §7.3.2, narrative markers across languages differ, among other ways, in their possible temporal reference. The Nyakyusa subsecutive, like the narrative tense, is attested only with temporal reference preceding the time of speech. This is corroborated by negative evidence from elicitation, where it was rejected for future predictions (28, 29) as well as in a timeless generic use (30).

---

[10] A similar phenomenon has been observed in Malila M24, where speakers would use the present perfective, likewise of the shape *a*-VB-*a*, in the storyline of oral narratives, but insisted that it would be inappropriate for a written story (Eaton 2015: 24).

(28) Context: A young man's plans for the future.

    a.   bo n-gʊl-ile   a=n-gʊ-jeng-a   ɪɪ-nyumba   ɪɪ-nywamu
        as 1SG-grow-PFV FUT=1SG-PRS-build-FV AUG-house(9) AUG-big(9)

    b. # n-aa-tim-a   ɪɪ-ng'ombe pa-ka-aja
        1SG-SUBSEC-herd-FV AUG-cow(10) 16-12-homestead

        (intended: 'When I am grown up, I will build a big house. Then I will herd cows at home.')

(29) Context: Talking about the speaker's plans for tomorrow.

    a.   kɪ-laabo   a=n-gʊ-kin-a   ʊ-m-pɪla
        7-tomorrow FUT-1SG-PRS-play-FV AUG-3-ball

    b. # bo m-mal-ile   pa-kʊ-kin-a   n-aa-bʊʊk-a
        as 1SG-finish-PFV 16-15-play-FV 1SG-SUBSEC-go-FV

        kʊ-n-nuguna   gw-angʊ kʊ-kʊ-ly-a nagwe
        17-1-younger_sibling_of_same_sex 1-POSS.1SG 17-15-eat-FV COM.1

        ɪ-fi-ndʊ   fy-a   pa-muu-si
        AUG-8-food 8-ASSOC 17-3-daytime

        (intended: 'Tomorrow I will play football. When I am done playing, I will go to my younger brother to have lunch with him.')

(30) Context: Describing the process of preparing stiff porridge.

    a.   bi-kʊ-kosy-a ʊ-m-ooto
        2-PRS-light-FV AUG-3-fire

    b. # b-aa-suk-a   ɪ-fy-a   kʊ-pɪɪj-ɪl-a
        2-SUBSEC-wash-FV AUG-8-ASSOC 15-cook-APPL-FV

    c. # b-aa-bɪɪk-a   a-m-ɪɪsi   pa-m-ooto ...
        2-SUBSEC-put-FV AUG-6-water 16-3-fire

        (intended: 'They light the fire. Then they wash the cooking utensils. Then they put the water on the fire ...')

Like the narrative tense, the subsecutive is only attested in episodic sentences, that is reports of specific events or occasions; see §7.3.2 for discussion. Negative evidence from elicitation shows that even within the past it cannot continue habituals or generics:

(31) a.   ijolo   ba-a-mog-aga   fiijo
           old_times 2-PST-dance-IPFV INTENS

      b.   ba-a-fwal-aga   kanunu fiijo
           2-PST-dress/wear-IPFV well   INTENS

    c. # b-oog-a
        2-SUBSEC.bathe-FV

    d. # ba-a-sanjʊl-a   n=ıı-nywili   ...
        2-SUBSEC-comb-FV COM=AUG-hair(10)

        (intended: 'Long ago they used to dance a lot. They dressed well.
        They bathed. They combed their hair ...')

Concerning its aspectual semantics, the subsecutive, unlike the narrative tense, always has a perfective reading; see §6.5.3.2 for a discussion of perfectivity. What is more, the subsecutive explicitly marks a step forward in the text. In this it can be understood as a verbal variety of what Dooley & Levinsohn (2000) call a "developmental marker", which "indicate[s] that the material so marked represents a new development in the story or argument, as far as the author's purpose is concerned" (p. 48). This function will become clear when looking at its common uses in §7.4.4. In the majority of cases, the narrative development goes along with an advancement of narrative time. Thus, the subsecutive nearly exclusively occurs in narrative clauses, i.e. those clauses that stand in fixed sequence; see §1.4.4.2 for Labov & Waletzky's (1967) classification of independent clauses within narratives. Unlike the narrative tense, the subsecutive is not attested in restricted clauses. A few cases of the subsecutive in co-ordinate clauses will be examined more closely in §7.4.5. Closely linked to this distribution, the only type of temporal adverbials the subsecutive is attested with is adverbials referring to a subsequent time span. (32b) illustrates the latter for a temporal clause, (32e) for the adverbial *kɪlaabo* 'tomorrow, next day'.

(32)   Context: A girl has eloped with a man. Her father has found out where they are.

    a. po   piitaasi ʊ-n-nyambala jʊ-la a-lınkʊ-j-a   mu-ndʊ
        then later   AUG-1-man   1-DIST 1-NARR-be(come)-FV 1-person
        gw-a   kʊ-fung-a ıı-safalı   j-aake   j-aa
        1-ASSOC 15-tie-FV AUG-journey(9)(<SWA) 9-POSS.SG 9-ASSOC
        kʊ-bʊʊk-a kʊ-no   ba-li=ko ba-la, kʊ-kʊ-mel-a ı-fy-ʊma
        15-go-FV   17-PROX 2-COP=17 2-DIST 17-15-claim-FV AUG-8-rich

        'Then later that man started to set out for where they were, in order to claim the brideprice.'

    b. **bo a-fik-ile**   kʊ-la **b-a-mmw-ambılıl-a** kanunu
        as 1-arrive-PFV 17-DIST 2-SUBSEC-1-receive-FV well

        'When he arrived there, they received him well.'

c. a-a-ly-a
1-SUBSEC-eat-FV
'He ate.'

d. a-a-gon-a
1-SUBSEC-rest-FV
'He slept.'

e. po **kɪ-laabo**   **a-mmw-eg-a**   ʊ-n-kyameni
then 7-tomorrow 1.SUBSEC-1-take-FV AUG-1-chairman(<EN)

n=ʊ-kʊ-m-bʊʊl-a   ɪ-si   si-n-twele   pa-la
COM=AUG-15-1-tell-FV AUG-PROX.10 10-1-carry.PFV 16-DIST

'The next day he contacted a chairman and told him what brought him there.' [Man and his in-law]

Consecutive clauses featuring the subsecutive are generally understood as depicting an ordered sequence of completed eventualities building on each other, as in (§32a–32e). A few exceptions, in which a sequence of clauses featuring the subsecutive group together, will be examined in §7.4.5.

Note at this point that the opposition between the narrative tense and the subsecutive in the present-day language cannot be reduced merely to one of grammatical aspect. As discussed in §7.3.2, the narrative tense is best understood as unspecified for aspect and allows for a perfective-like reading, too. Rather, these two paradigms form an opposition between the default, all-purpose narrative tense on the one hand and the subsecutive as the more restricted, specifically perfective marker of a narrative development on the other.

7.4.4 Common occurrences

Many tokens of the subsecutive in the corpus are found in discernible, reoccurring environments. To begin with, it is found in pairings with the narrative tense, as in (33b, 33c) and (33e, 33f), in which a situation is depicted first in its inception or preparation and then in its culmination.

(33) a. po ba-lɪnkw-and-a b-oope bo bʊ-k-iile   n=ʊ-lʊ-bʊnjʊ
then 2-NARR-begin-FV 2-also as 14-dawn-PFV COM=AUG-11-morning

'Early in the morning they started.'

b. ba-lɪnkʊ-j-a   b-andʊ ba-a   k-oog-a   b-ooga
2-NARR-be(come)-FV 2-person 2-ASSOC 15-bathe-FV 14-bath

'They began to bath.'

    c. **ba-a-fwal-a**   kanunu
        2-SUBSEC-dress/wear-FV well

        'They got dressed up.'

    d. ba-lınkʊ-j-a   b-andʊ ba-a   kʊ-piny-a ı-mi-sigo
        2-NARR-be(come)-FV 2-person 2-ASSOC 15-bind-FV AUG-4-burden
        gy-abo   n=ʊ=kʊ-bʊʊk-a
        4-POSS.PL COM=AUG-15-go-FV

        'They began to bind their things and go.'

    e. a-lınkʊ-pimb-a ʊ-bʊ-fu   bw-ake   ŋgoosi
        1-NARR-load-FV AUG-14-flour 14-POSS.SG N.

        'Ngoosi lifted that flour.'

    f. **ii-twɪk-a**   pa-n-tʊ
        1.SUBSEC.REFL-lift_to_head-FV 16-3-head

        'She loaded it on her head.' [Man and his in-law]

Interestingly, Fleischman (1990: ch. 6) notes a mostly parallel pattern in Old French epics, which consists of depicting certain eventualities through an alternation of a narrative present followed by the present anterior (*passé composé* in the francophone tradition). The latter in that early romance variety came close to a present perfective. She goes on to observe that

> the first situation is presented in its inception [...] and the second as completed [...], it is as if the first precipitates the second to its conclusion, uniting the two into a global event [...] Tense switches of this type, which operate to split a macro-event into its constituent phases, are a common device for establishing cohesion. The distinct phases reported by verbs in individual clauses are bound together into complex predicates (Fleischman 1990: 196f)

Recall from §7.4.1 that there are a number of independent indications that the subsecutive constitutes a former present anterior or present perfective, while the source of the narrative tense is doubtless a former imperfective present (§6.7.1). Pairings such as (33b, 33c) and (33e, 33f) can thus be understood as another case in point and may well be the source of the present-day functions of the subsecutive.

In a fashion similar to the preceding example, the movement gram (*j*)*a* (§10.4.1) is commonly found in the subsecutive with *fika* 'arrive' as its complement and following iconic repetitions of *enda* 'walk, travel' in the narrative tense (34). This can be understood as closing the macro-event of motion on the one hand, while

on the other advancing the text by indicating the conclusion of a prolonged journey. Note also how temporal and spatial progression in this case go together
in one complex predicate. A variation of this theme is found in (35), where the
subsecutive follows *endelela* 'continue (the journey)'.

(34) a. b-oosa ba-bɪlɪ ba-lɪnkʊ-j-a   ba-ndʊ   ba-a   kʊ-bʊʊk-a
       2-all   2-two 2-NARR-be(come)-FV 2-person 2-ASSOC 15-go-FV
       m̩-bʊ-ganga
       18-1-doctor
       'The two of them set out to go to a healer.'

      b. boo=bʊno∼bʊ-no   ba-lɪnkw-end-a,
       REF.14=REDUPL∼14-DEM 2-NARR-walk/travel-FV
       ba-lɪnkw-end-a,   ba-lɪnkw-end-a,
       2-NARR-walk/travel-FV 2-NARR-walk/travel-FV
       ba-lɪnkw-end-a   n=ʊ-kw-end-a
       COM=AUG-15-walk/travel-FV COM=AUG-15-walk/travel-FV
       'Thus they travelled, travelled, travelled and travelled.'

      c. **ba-a-j-a**   kʊ-**fik**-a   n-k-iisʊ kɪ-mo
       2-SUBSEC-go-FV 15-arrive-FV 18-7-land 7-one
       'Finally they arrived in some land.' [Pregnant women]

(35) a. ba-alɪnkw-endelel-a n=ɪɪ-safalɪ
       2-NARR-continue-FV COM=AUG-journey(9)(<SWA)
       'They continued their journey.'

      b. po balɪnkw-endelel-a   bʊbʊʊ∼bʊ
       then 2-NARR-continue-FV REDUPL∼PROX.14
       'Thus they continued.'

      c. **ba-a-j-a**   kʊ-**fik**-a   n-ky-eni   kangɪ
       2-SUBSEC-go-FV 15-arrive-FV 18-7-forehead again
       'They got further ahead.' [Man and his in-law]

This use of the subsecutive to conclude a macro-event and at the same time
advance the story is also found on a bigger scale. (36) is an abridged version of a
narrative episode in which Tugutu, a type of bird, prepares a racetrack in order
to outwit Hare. The subsecutive in (36f) concludes the preparation episode and
leads over to the next episode, the race itself. See (24) on p. 230 for a comparable
example of the subsecutive concluding an extensive macro-event.

(36) Context: Tugutu (a type of bird) has challenged Hare to a race. He has
gathered five companions.

    a. mwa=n-dugutu   a-a-bʊʊk-ile
       matronym=9-type_of_bird 1-past-go-PFV

       'Mr. Tugutu went.'

    b. a-a-ba-paal-ile   a-ba-nine   ba-haano ...
       1-PST-2-invite-PFV AUG-2-companion 2-five

       'He gathered five companions ...'

    c. bo ii-sikʊ ly-a   kɪ-laabo,   bo lɪ-fik-ile,   mwa=n-dugutu
       as 5-day 5-ASSOC 7-tomorrow as 5-arrive-PFV matronym=9-t.o.bird
       a-alɪ-m̩-bɪɪk-ile mwa=n-dugutu   n-nine   pa-bw-andɪlo
       1-PST-1-put-PFV matronym=9-t.o.bird 1-companion 16-14-start

       'When the next day arrived, Mr. Tugutu placed a fellow Mr. Tugutu at
       the start.'

    d. kangɪ maelɪ   jɪ-ngɪ jɪ-mo a-alɪ-m̩-bɪɪk-ile
       again mile(9)(<EN) 9-other 9-one 1-PST-1-put-PFV
       mwa=n-dugutu   n-nine   ...
       matronym=9-t.o.bird 1-companion

       'Another mile, he placed a fellow Mr. Tugutu ...'

    e. na kʊ-lʊ-malɪɪkɪlo, ma-elɪ ga-a   bʊ-haano mwa=n-dugutu
       COM 17-11-end   6-mile 6-ASSOC 5-five   matronym=9-t.o.bird
       ʊ-jʊ-ngɪ
       AUG-1-other

       'At the finish line, the fifth mile, another Mr. Tugutu.'

    f. po mwa=n-dugutu   ʊ-jʊ-ngɪ,   jʊ-la ba-a-job-aga   na
       then matronym=9-t.o.bird AUG-1-other 1-DIST 2-PST-speak-IPFV COM
       kalʊlʊ **a-a-j-a**   pa-bw-andɪlo pa-la
       hare(1) 1-SUBSEC-be(come)-FV 16-14-start   16-DIST

       'The other Mr. Tugutu, the one who had been talking with Hare, he
       then was at the start.' [Hare and Tugutu]

Interestingly, Crane (2011: 143ff) observes that, in Totela K41, a hodiernal perfective – she speaks of a marker of "nuclear completion"; see §6.5.3.2 for discussion – is similarly employed at the boundary of scenes or episodes within
narratives, where it marks the "completion of one set of activities and the commencement of another". The situation in that particular language, however, dif-

fers from Nyakyusa in that the verbal paradigm in question is fully operative outside of narrative discourse.

Another recurring device in the narrative corpus consists of a past imperfective verb followed by one in the subsecutive. In these pairs, the imperfective depicts a setting, while the subsecutive verb constitutes a progression that evolves out of, and ruptures, the preceding situation. (37) gives the opening four sentences of a short narrative. (37a) constitutes the orientation section, while (37b) sets the stage for the upcoming event. Duck's pecking for food is a continuous activity and accordingly it is depicted in the past imperfective. With (37c), the complicating action of the narrative begins. Duck's search ends with the sight of Pig's food, which is marked by use of the subsecutive plus *enda* 'walk/travel' as an ingressive auxiliary. This sets the ball rolling and leads to the ultimately fatal act described in (37d).

(37) a. ɪ-li-sikʊ lɪ-mo, ɪ-n-gʊlʊbe j-aa-bɪɪk-ɪl-iigwe ɪ-fi-ndʊ
    AUG-5-day 5-one AUG-9-pig 9-PST-put-APPL-PASS.PFV AUG-8-food
    fy-ake
    8-POSS.SG
    'One day, Pig was given its food.'

   b. po leelo ɪ-li-seekwa **ly-a-salaga~sal-aga**
    then now/but AUG-5-pig 5-PST-REDUPL~choose-IPFV
    ʊ-kʊ-lond-a ɪ-fi-ndʊ fy-a kw-i-swɪl-a ly-ope
    AUG-15-search-FV AUG-8-food 8-ASSOC 15-REFL-feed-FV 5-also
    'Duck was pecking for food to feed itself.'

   c. po ɪ-ly-ene **ly-end-a** n=ʊ-kʊ-fi-bon-a
    then AUG-5-self 5-SUBSEC.walk/travel-FV COM=AUG-8-see-FV
    ɪ-fi-ndʊ fy-a n-gʊlʊbe
    AUG-8-food 8-ASSOC 9-pig
    'Then it saw Pig's food.'

   d. lɪ-lɪnkw-ingɪl-a mw-i-tembe ly-a n-gʊlʊbe
    5-NARR-enter-FV 18-5-stable 5-ASSOC 9-pig
    n=ʊ-kw-and-a ʊ-kʊ-ly-a ɪ-fi-ndʊ fi-la
    COM=AUG-15-begin-FV AUG-15-eat-FV AUG-8-food 8-DIST
    'It entered the pigshed and started to eat that food.' [The one who eats others' food]

While the preceding example constitutes the opening of a short narrative, (38) is an excerpt close to the end of a longer text. (38a) depicts a crucial moment in the development of the plot. With tension at the maximum, the past imperfective verb in (38b) demarcates and sets the stage for the peak episode, while at the same time depicting the husband's attempt at flight, which is impeded immediately (38c). All four following narrative clauses, the first of which is given in (38d), likewise feature the subsecutive, and, in clearly delimited steps that built on each other, they advance the story towards resolution.

(38) Context: The protagonist's husband has killed his father-in-law, whose chopped-off head is hidden in a sack of flour. People have become suspicious.

    a. ba-lınkw-abʊl-a, ba-lınkʊ-gw-ag-a ʊ-n-tʊ   gw-a   gwise
        2-NARR-open-FV 2-NARR-3-find-FV AUG-3-head 1-ASSOC his_father(1)

        gw-a   ngoosi gʊ-li=ko kʊ-bʊ-fu bʊ-la
        1-ASSOC N.   3-COP=17 17-14-flour 14-DIST

        'They opened it [sack], they found that Ngoosi's father's head was in that flour.'

    b. ʊ-n-nyambala jʊ-la **a-a-lond-aga** ʊ-kʊ-bop-a,   ʊ-n-dʊme
        AUG-1-man   1-DIST 1-PST-try-IPFV AUG-15-run-FV AUG-1-husband

        gw-a   ngoosi
        1-ASSOC N.

        'That man, Ngoosi's husband, was trying to run away.'

    c. **b-a-n-kol-a**   pala~pa-la
        2-SUBSEC-1-grasp-FV REDUPL~16-DIST

        'They caught him right there.'

    d. **b-a-n-gog-a**
        2-SUBSEC-1-kill-FV

        'They killed him.' [Man and his in-law]

A similar case of advancement towards the resolution is found in (39), which is taken from a second version of the fable of Pig and Duck, whose commencement was discussed in (37) above. Note how the storyteller creates a crescendo in that he first depicts, in the narrative tense, two eventualities that are ongoing and simultaneous with what follows (39c, 39d), and thereafter employs the subsecutive to lead the story to its dramatic end in two concise steps (39e, 39f).

(39) Context: Pig sees Duck feeding on his food.

    a. j-aa-bop-ile
       9-PST-run-PFV
       'He [Pig] ran.'

    b. j-aa-kat-ile   ʊ-n-tʊ   gw-a   ii-seekwa
       9-PST-break(<SWA)-PFV AUG-3-head 3-ASSOC 5-duck
       'He broke Duck's head.'

    c. po   ii-seekwa lɪ-lɪnkw-i-pʊʊl-a   "po po po po po"
       then 5-duck   5-NARR-REFL-thresh-FV of_cackling
       'Duck fluttered around "po po po po po".'

    d. ʊ-mw-ene   fi-tiimigwa a-lɪnkʊ-bop-a
       AUG-1-owner 8-livestock 1-NARR-run-FV
       'The livestock owner ran.'

    e. **eeg-a**   ʊ-m-mage
       1.SUBSEC.take-FV AUG-3-knife
       'He took a knife.'

    f. **a-a-lɪ-buut-a**   ii-seekwa
       1-SUBSEC-5-slaughter-FV 5-duck
       'He slaughtered Duck.' [Pig and Duck]

7.4.5 Tokens without strict temporal progression

In §7.4.3 it has been observed that the subsecutive is attested mainly in narrative clauses, that is those clauses that cannot be displaced without changing the inferred sequence of eventualities (see §1.4.4.2). In a few tokens, however, the subsecutive is attested in co-ordinate clauses, i.e. clauses that can be freely swapped with each other. These belong to two types: first, the copula *ja* in the subsecutive preceded by a past imperfective (see §10.2.1 on Nyakyusa's two copulae) and second, a series of subsecutives depicting various components of one and the same eventuality.

    Concerning the first, the stative description provided by a copula seems to be essentially incompatible with the notion of narrative development. Three tokens of the copula *ja* in the subsecutive preceded by a past imperfective are attested in the corpus. Two of these pairs are given in (40a, 40b) and (40c, 40d) respectively. These four clauses stand at the beginning of a crucial episode within this story, in which a man clandestinely kills his father-in-law at night, chops off his head and hides it in a sack of flour.

(40)   a. ʊ-gwise   gw-a   ŋgoosi, ʊ-n-nyambala jʊ-la,
           AUG-his_father(1) 1-ASSOC N.   AUG-1-man   1-DIST
           a-a-tʊʊgal-aga n-ky-umba   ky-ake   pasima
           1-PST-stay-IPFV 18-7-room(<SWA) 7-POSS.SG different

       'Ngoosi's father, that man's father in-law, he was staying in a
       separate room.'

       b. po   n-ky-umba mu-la **a-a-j-a**   mw-ene itolo
           then 18-7-room   18-DIST 1-SUBSEC-be(come)-FV 1-self   just

       'In that room he was all alone.'

       c. po   mw-ene ŋgoosi na   jʊ-n-dʊme ba-a-j-aga
           then 1-self   N.   COM 1-1-husband 2-PST-be(come)-IPFV
           n=ɪ-ky-umba   ky-abo
           COM=AUG-7-room 7-POSS.PL

       'Ngoosi and her husband, they had their own room.'

       d. po   p-ii-balasi   pa-la **j-aa-j-a=po**
           then 16-5-veranda 16-DIST 9-SUBSEC-be(come)-FV=16
           ɪɪ-meesa   a-pa   paa~pa   ŋgoosi
           AUG-table(9)(<SWA) AUG-PROX.16 REDUPL~PROX.16 N.
           a-a-tʊʊl-ile   ʊ-bʊ-fu   bw-ake
           1-PST-take_from_head-PFV AUG-14-flour 14-POSS.SG

       'On the veranda there was a table where Ngoosi had put the flour.'
       [Man and his in-law]

Recall from the discussion of (37, 38) in §7.4.4 that the same pattern of a past
imperfective followed by the subsecutive is employed with verbs other than the
copula to relate the setting of an episode within a narrative, plus an ensuing
disruptive development. One may assume that the narrator is resorting to this
convention in order to promote the states of the father-in-law's aloneness and the
presence of the table with the sack of flour to an event-like status (see Longacre
1996: 25). Such an interpretation matches with the dramatic effect that is created
in both (40a, 40b) and (40c, 40d), in that the scene of the upcoming killing is
first depicted broadly, to then 'aim the camera' first at the victim and then at the
essential prop. All other tokens of the copula in the subsecutive contain locative
predicates, giving a change-of-location reading as in (36f) above.

Concerning the subsecutive in co-ordinate clauses, a first example is given in
(41). Note that what is depicted in (41b, 41c) does not constitute two separate subsequent eventualities, but provides different components, namely manner and

goal, of one and the same motion eventuality; see Talmy (1985) on the semantics of motion. In Nyakyusa, the different components of motion are mostly encoded in separate lexical verbs. In narrating a motion event, the speaker thus has to resort either to infinitives (§11.4.2) or, as in this case, to separate independent clauses. The hearer unequivocally understands these two clauses as one single event subsequent to the one depicted in (41a).

(41)   a. a-a-nyak-ile   ʊ-lw-ala
           1-PST-snatch-PFV AUG-11-grindstone
           'He [Monkey] snatched the grindstone.'

      b. **a-a-bop-a**   na lw-ala   lʊ-la
           1-SUBSEC-run-FV COM 11-grindstone 11-DIST
           'He ran with that grindstone.'

      c. **a-a-bʊʊk-a**   m-mi-syanjʊ
           1-SUBSEC-go-FV 18-6-bush
           'He went [=ran] into the bush.' [Monkey and Tortoise]

(42) is another representative example of the subsecutive in co-ordinate clauses. Clauses (42c, 42d) again describe different components of one and the same eventuality of taking food, which is then summarized in (42e). Note that the acts depicted in these clauses close off a longer chain of eventualities about Tortoise sending his son to Monkey to get food, similar to the cases discussed in §7.4.4 above.

(42)   Context: Tortoise has sent his son to buy food from Monkey on credit. Monkey has agreed.

      a. po kajamba ʊ-n-nine   a-lınkʊ-tı "ndaga"
           then tortoise(1) AUG-1-companion 1-NARR-say thanks
           'Tortoise's child said "Thanks."'

      b. po b-ingıl-a   mu-n-gʊnda
           then 2-SUBSEC.enter-FV 18-3-field
           'They entered the farm.'

      c. **b-eeg-a**   a-ma-sımbı
           2-SUBSEC.take-FV AUG-6-cocoyam
           'They took cocoyam.'

      d. **b-eeg-a**   ii-seeke
           2-SUBSEC.take-FV 5-sidedish
           'They took a side dish.'

e. **b-eeg-a**   fy-osa
   2-SUBSEC.take-FV 8-all

   'They took all sorts of food.' [Monkey and Tortoise]

Unlike the narrative tense, the subsecutive does not figure in iconic repetitions. The only apparent case is given in (43). Discussion of this example in elicitation, however, shows that (43b–43d) can only be understood as a sequence of eventualities performed by different subsets of the subject *abanyambala* '(the) men'. Thus, examples (41–43) share a common denominator in that a single eventuality is broken down into its constituent components and that these are clearly identifiable as such, either through the convention of how motion eventualities are depicted (41), or by featuring identical verbs (42, 43).

(43)   Context: Python has devoured a woman's children.

   a.   a-lınku-koolel-a a-ba-nyambala "a-mil-ile   a-ba-ana!"
        1-NAR-call-FV   AUG-2-man   1-devour-PFV AUG-2-child

        'She called to the men, "She's devoured the children!"'

   b.   po   a-ba-nyambala **b-and-a**   ʊ-kʊ-bop-a
        then AUG-2-man   2-SUBSEC.begin-FV AUG-15-run-FV

        '[Some of the] men began to run.'

   c.   **b-and-a**   ʊ-kʊ-bop-a
        2-SUBSEC.begin-FV AUG-15-run-FV

        'They [some other men] began to run.'

   d.   **b-and-a**   ʊ-kʊ-bop-a
        2-SUBSEC.begin-FV AUG-15-run-FV

        'They [some other men] began to run.' [Python and woman]

7.4.6 Summary

To summarize, the subsecutive most likely goes back to a former present perfective or anterior. In the present-day language, it is the less frequent and more specific of Nyakyusa's two narrative markers. Its semantics include reference to the past time and, unlike the narrative tense, it is specified for perfective aspect and marks an advancement in the story. This usually, but not always, goes along with an advancement of narrative time. The use of the subsecutive often serves a textual function of creating cohesion, in that it closes off one set of eventualities while advancing the text towards the next one. Just like the narrative tense, the subsecutive is pragmatically dependent on an otherwise established context and its employment forms part of the same larger discourse convention, according to which narratives are built around the notion of thematic continuity and discontinuity (see §7.2.3). Being a dedicated narrative marker, the subsecutive can be understood to also work on the metalingistic component by signalling this specific type of discourse. Lastly, it is the subject of normative considerations and a marker of an informal, oral style.

8 Tense and aspect constructions 3: futurates

8.1 Introduction

It is a common feature of languages to have several constructions with future time orientation. This synchronic multiplicity of forms arises through historical layering of grammaticalization processes from different sources as well as from similar sources at different periods (Bybee et al. 1991; Bybee et al. 1994). Not all of these constructions can be considered to encode future tense in the sense of §1.4.2. Therefore FUTURATE will be used as an umbrella term, following Binnick (1991).

From a wider Bantu perspective, Nyakyusa is unusual in having more constructions for future states-of-affairs than for the past (cf. Nurse 2008: 89). All of these are grammaticalized from two sources. On the one hand, there are paradigms featuring reflexes of Proto-Bantu *gɪ 'go', which is found in the present day language as a movement gram (§10.4.1) as well as a copula 'be(come)' (see §10.2.1). On the other hand, there are constructions featuring *isa* 'come' (§10.4.2). Leaving aside the copula, one finds a parallel distribution of the two movement verbs: both are found with their bare stems as proclitics to the inflected verb (§8.2, 8.3) and both are found in constructions that originate in their use as auxiliaries in the simple present (§8.5, 8.6).

An intriguing feature of futurates in Nyakyusa is the possibility of combining them into a single complex predicate. The following examples illustrate these possibilities:

(1)   a. tʊ-kw-a   kʊ-kin-a
            1PL-PRS-go.FV 15-play-FV
            'We will go and play.'

       b. aa=tʊ-kw-a   kʊ-kin-a
            FUT=1PL-PRS-go.FV 15-play-FV
            'We will go and play (at some distant time).'

    c. tw-isakw-a   kʊ-kin-a

       1PL-INDEF.FUT-go.FV 15-play-FV

       'We might go and play.'

    d. aa=tw-isakw-a   kʊ-kin-a

       FUT=1PL-INDEF.FUT-go.FV 15-play-FV

       'We might go and play (at some distant time).' [ET]

As can be seen in (1), the meaning of these complex futurates arises through the composition of its constituent parts. In the following discussion, each futurate construction will thus be dealt with separately.

    Lastly, it has often been noted (Dahl 1985: 103 among others) that there is a close conceptual tie between future orientation and modality. In the case of Nyakyusa, this becomes clearest in the cases of constructions that are on the threshold between futurate and modality (§8.6,9.4, 9.5). These have been classified as either futurates or modals according to which meaning component prevails in the present-day language.

8.2 Proclitic *aa=*

A clitic *aa=* can be added to all constructions that have future, namely the simple present (§6.5.1), the other futurates-isfuturate (§8.5–8.7), the subjunctive (§9.3), the desiderative (§9.4) and the modal future construction (§9.5). It can also attach to conditional *ngalɪ* (§9.6). Concerning the pre-initial position in Bantu, Güldemann observes:

> For pre-initial forms one can say that they are most likely the result of concatenation and truncation of a binary predicate structure. The first part is a finite auxiliary or non-finite predicator while the second part is a dependent finite form comprising the content verb. In the first case, the auxiliary is subject to phonetic truncation and the initial of the content verb continues to encode the subject. (Güldemann 2003: 186)

The clitic's shape, its future semantics and its opposition to a proclitic form of *isa* 'come' in some varieties of Nyakyusa (§8.3) all give evidence that the first part of this former binary structure included the auxiliary (*j*)*a* 'go'.

    As for its semantics, *aa=* localizes the eventuality described in its host verb to a future reference frame – or temporal domain, in Botne & Kershner's (2008) terminology. Nurse (2008: 316) calls this kind of marker a "shifter", which is defined as "a clitic, which, added to an existing tensed form, shifts its reference further away from the reference point". This notion of shifting will become more tangible when looking at some uses of *aa=*.

A very common collocation consists of *aa=* and the simple present. This collocation covers many of the prototypical uses ascribed to a future tense (Dahl 1985; 2000b). It is the default form for pure predictions about the future (2, 3) and can also be used when intention is involved (4, 5).

(2) Context: What will happen if I eat this mushroom?
     lınga   ʊ-l-iile,   aa=kʊ-fw-a
     if/when 2SG-eat-PFV FUT=2SG.PRS-die-FV

     'If you eat it, you will die.' [ET]

(3) Context: It's no use trying to swim in the lake tomorrow.
     komma ʊ-kʊ-bʊʊk-a, a-m-ıısi   aa=gi-kʊ-j-a   ma-talalıfu
     PROH   AUG-15-go-FV AUG-6-water FUT=6-PRS-be(come)-FV 6-cold

     'Don't go, the water will be cold.' [ET]

(4) Context: A young man is speaking about his plans for the future.
     lınga   n-gʊl-ile   a=n-gʊ-jeng-a   ıı-nyumba   ıı-nywamu
     if/when 1SG-grow-PFV FUT=1SG-PRS-build-FV AUG-house(9) AUG-big(9)

     'When I am grown up, I will build a big house.' [ET]

(5) Context: Talking about the speaker's plans for the evening.
     na=a-ma-jolo   a=n-gʊ-j-a=po   pa-ka-aja
     COM=AUG-6-evening COM=1SG-PRS-be(come)-FV=16 16-12-homestead

     'In the evening I will be at home.' [ET]

Interestingly, Lusekelo (2007; 2013) lists *aa=* plus simple present under "future tense" and states that "there is only one future tense in Kinyakyusa" (Lusekelo 2013: 109), while a century earlier Schumann (1899: 32) listed it under "rarely used constructions" (Translated from the original German, BP.) and Endemann (1914) did not discuss it at all. This coincides with the chronolect (and topolect) described by the latter authors having the de-ventive indefinite future (§8.6) as the primary construction for predictions. For a short discussion of the diachronic scenario see §8.6.3. Also note that unlike the indefinite future, the collocation of *aa=* plus the simple present does not allow for a purely epistemic reading without future time reference:

(6) Context: You are asked where your brother is.

#aa=i-kʊ-kin-a   ʊ-m-pɪla

FUT=1-PRS-play-FV AUG-3-ball

(intended: 'He will be [=presumably he is] playing football.')

(7) Context: The cows are mooing. You are asked why they are making so much noise.

#aa=si-kʊ-j-a   n=ɪ-n-jala

FUT=10-PRS-be(come)-FV COM=9-hunger

(intended: 'They will be [=presumably they are] hungry.')

Some further examples from discourse will illustrate the shifting function of *aa=*. In (8) Tortoise answers Monkeys's demand for payment by making an excuse and promising to pay at another time. Monkey in turn accepts and announces that he will come again. Both Tortoise's promise in (8a) and Monkey's announcement in (8c) feature the future proclitic, with the modal future construction and the simple present as the respective hosts. Omission of *aa=* was judged inadequate in discussion of these examples. Note also how this contrasts with the use of the simple present in (40) on p. 154, which is taken from an earlier episode of the same narrative and describes Monkey's demand to be paid on that very day.

(8) Context: Monkey has come to Tortoise's in order to collect debts.

    a. po   kajamba a-a-tɪ   "hee.

       then tortoise(1) 1-SUBSEC-say INTERJ

       gʊʊ-hobok-el-ege.   lɪlɪmo   n-dɪ

       2SG.1SG-be(come)_happy-APPL-IPFV.SUBJ now/today 1SG-COP

       n=ɪ-n-jɪla.   n-sumwike   kw-a   ɗaaɗa   gw-angʊ. a-lɪ

       COM=9-path 1SG-depart.PFV 17-ASSOC sister(1)(SWA) 1-POSS.1SG 1-COP

       n=ɪ-fy-ɪnja   mia   mooja.   po a-bɪɪk-ile

       COM=AUG-8-year one(SWA) hundred(SWA). then 1-put-PFV

       ʊ-bʊ-fumbwe

       AUG-14-concern

       'Tortoise said "Hee. Forgive me. Now I am travelling. I'm heading to my sister's. She is a hundred years old. She has made an invitation.'

    b. po   lee   koo=kʊ-no   n-gʊ-bʊʊk-a. po   leelo

       then now/but REF.17=17-PROX 1SG-PRS-go-FV then now/but

       ɪɪ-heela   j-aako   aa=kw-eg-aga   kangɪ bo

       AUG-money(9) 9-POS.2SG FUT=2SG.MOD.FUT-take-MOD.FUT again as

n-iis-ile"
1SG-come-PFV

"There I'm going. Your money you shall take when I've come back.'"

c. po   mwa=n-gambılı   a-a-tı   "ee, haya!   mma po
then matronym-9-monkey 1-SUBSEC-say yes OK(<SWA) no   then

a=n-gw-is-a   kangı". a-lınkʊ-bʊʊk-a kʊ-ka-aja
FUT=1SG-PRS-come-FV again   1-NARR-go-FV   17-12-homestead

'Mr. Monkey said "Yes, OK. I'll come again." He went home.' [Monkey
and Tortoise]

In (9) the trickster Hare asks Spider's prospective wife, rhetorically, if she is
willing to draw eight buckets of water each time her future husband bathes. The
reference frame evoked here is the time of being married, which is not only situated in the future, but also constitutes an entirely new situation.

(9) ee, a-lı   na=go   lwele kʊkʊtı kı-lʊndı ki-k-oog-a   ı-n-dobo
yes, 1-COP COM=REF.6 eight every 7-leg   7-PRS-bathe-FV AUG-9-bucket

jı-mo. ʊ-gwe   kʊ-lond-a   ʊ-neg-ege
9-one AUG-2SG 2SG.PRS-want-FV 2SG-draw_liquid-IPFV.SUBJ

ı-n-dobo   lwele, bʊle **aa=kʊ-bwesy-a?**
AUG-10-bucket eight Q   FUT=2SG.PRS-overcome-FV

'Yes, it [Spider] has eight legs, every leg bathes in one bucket. You, do you
want to draw eight buckets full, will you bear that?' [Hare and Spider]

Similarly, in (10) the speaker, an anthropomorphized python, first employs the
simple present as a generic futurate. In the following sentence, *aa=* serves to shift
to a specific reference frame which is characterized by a change in conditions,
namely that the children are locked in.

(10) Context: A python wants to devour a woman's children. She has
announced that she will lock them in. Python answers.
mma, n-gʊ-ba-ag-a.   p-oope **a=n-gʊ-ba-ag-a**
no   1SG-PRS-2-find-FV. 16-also FUT=1SG-PRS-2-find-FV

'No, I'm finding them (sic!). Even then I'll find them.' [Python and
woman]

The first sentence of (10) illustrates another important fact about the organization of the future in Nyakyusa. While the collocation of *aa=* with the simple
present is the common form for making predictions, the bare simple present may

be employed to convey a high degree of certainty. Thus (11) contrasts with (2) above in its epistemicmodality value. See also (44) on p. 155.

(11) Context: What will happen if I eat this mushroom?
      lɪnga   ʊ-l-iile,   kʊ-fw-a
      if/when 2SG-eat-PFV   2SG.PRS-die-FV

      'If you eat it, you die (i.e. this is a known fact).' [ET]

The employment of *aa=* with a number of other future-orientated paradigms is illustrated in the following examples. In (12), the subjunctive verb carries *aa=* because the reference frame is shifted to the time after the chief's death. (13–15) illustrate the use of *aa=* with the periphrastic progressive,[1] the de-itive prospective/movement construction and the indefinite future respectively. For an example featuring the desiderative, see (89) on p. 290.

(12) Context: A moribund chief gives his sons instructions for the time after his death.
      looli ɪ-si   n-gʊ-ba-bʊʊl-a,   **aa=mu-si-kol-ege**   fiijo
      but   AUG-PROX.10 1SG-PRS-2PL-tell-FV FUT=2PL-10-grasp-IPFV.SUBJ INTENS
      lɪnga   m-fw-ile
      if/when 1SG-die-PFV

      'The things I tell you, you must stick to when I'm dead.' [Chief Kapyungu]

(13) **aa=i-kʊ-j-a**   pa-kʊ-jeng-a
      FUT=1-PRS-be(come)-FV 16-15-build-FV

      'He will be building.' [ET]

(14) **aa=tʊ-kw-a**   kʊ-kin-a ʊ-m-pɪla
      FUT=1PL-PRS-go.FV 15-play-FV AUG-3-ball

      'We will go and play football (at some distant time).' [ET]

(15) pa-lʊ-bʊnjʊ   **aa=tw-isakʊ-kin-a**   ʊ-m-pɪla
      16-11-morning FUT=1PL-INDEF.FUT-play-FV AUG-3-ball

      'The day after tomorrow we might play football.' [ET]

The future proclitic can also attach to a simple present that stands as the complement of the persistive aspect auxiliary (§6.6.2). This is illustrated in (16). Lastly, for a discussion of *aa=* together with the conditional marker *ngalɪ*, see §9.6.

---

[1]While the present and past progessives feature the copula *lɪ*, for future reference *ja* 'be(come)' has to be used. See §10.2.1 on the two copulae.

(16) na=a-ma-jolo   ba-kaalı aa–bi-kʊ-mog-a
      COM=AUG-6-evening 2-PERS   FUT=2-PRS-dance-FV
      'In the evening they will still be dancing.' [ET]

8.3 Proclitic (*i*)*sa=*

Parallel to the de-itive future proclitic *aa=* (§8.2), some varieties of Nyakyusa feature a de-ventive clitic *(i)sa=*. Though this form is not found in the varieties on which this description is based, it merits a short discussion for the sake of completeness.

Schumann (1899: 31) and Endemann (1914: 54) both list the combination of a proclitic *isa=* and the simple present without further discussions of meaning and use. Two tokens of this construction are found in the text collection by Berger (1933), one of which is given in (17). All three sources are based on the topolect (and respective chronolect) of the lake-shore plains.

(17)   Context: a discussion of how a group of people may cross a river.
       leelo   ʊ-ne   ni-kʊ-laalʊʊsy-a ni-kʊ-tɪ: kalı
       now/but AUG-1SG 1SG-PRS-ask-FV   1SG-PRS-say Q
       b-isakʊ-lobok-a   bʊle∼bʊle   pa-lw-ısi? namanga
       2-INDEF.FUT-cross_over_water-FV REDUPL∼how 16-11-river because
       ʊ-lw-ısi   lʊlʊʊ∼lʊ   kı-siba, kangı ı-n-gwina   ny-ingi
       AUG-11-river REDUPL∼PROX.11 7-pond again AUG-10-crocodile 10-many
       fiijo;   mw-ene mu-ṃ-bwato   mo   bi-kʊ-sʊʊbıl-a
       INTENS 18-only 18-18-boat(1)(<EN) REF.18 2-PRS-hope-FV
       ʊ-kw-end-a
       AUG-15-walk/travel-FV
       'Now I ask and say: How will they cross the river? Because this river is very deep and the crocodiles are many. Only in a boat they can travel.'
       bʊle gwe mw-inangʊ,   gwe kʊ-bal-a   ıı-nongwa
       Q   2SG 1-my_companion 2SG 15-read-FV AUG-issue(10)
       sisii∼si,   kʊ-tı   fi-ki,   kw-inogon-a
       REDUPL∼PROX.10 2SG.PRS-say 8-what 2SG.PRS-think-FV
       sa=bi-kʊ-lobok-a   bʊle∼bʊle?
       come=2-PRS-cross_over_water-FV REDUPL∼how
       'You, my friend, who you are reading these words, how do you think that they will cross over?' (Berger 1933: 150; orthography adapted)

In a current draft of a Bible translation by SIL International, which is also based on the lake-shore-plains variety, the proclitic is found with host verbs inflected for the simple present,simple present the modal future construction (§9.5) and the subjunctive (§9.3). Example (18) again features a host verb inflected for the simple present. Note that, unlike what these examples may suggest, the proclitic is found in both questions and declarative sentences.

(18) Context: Jesus speaks about the Kingdom of Heaven.

ʊ-n-twa a-lɪnkʊ-job-a a-lɪnkʊ-tɪ "mu-sy-ag-an-i-e
AUG-1-lord 1-NARR-speak-FV 1-NARR-say 2PL-10-find-RECP-CAUS-SUBJ

ɪ-si i-kʊ-job-a ʊ-n̩-dongi ʊ-n-niongafu!" bʊle, Kyala
AUG-PROX.10 1-PRS-speak-FV AUG-1-judge AUG-1-twisted Q God(1)

a-ti-kʊ-ba-longel-a kanunu a-ba-sʊngʊligwa ba-ake, a-ba
1-NEG-PRS-2-judge-FV well AUG-2-selected 2-POSS.SG AUG-PROX.8

bi-kʊ-n̩-dɪlɪl-a pa-muu-si na pa-kɪ-lo? bʊle,
2-PRS-1-lament-FV 16-3-daytime COM 16-7-night Q

isa=i-kʊ-kaabɪl-a ʊ-kʊ-ba-tʊʊl-a?
come=1-PRS-be_late-FV AUG-15-2-help-FV?

'And the Lord said, Hear what the unjust judge saith. And shall no God avenge his own elect, which cry day and night unto him, though he bear long with them?'

n-gʊ-ba-bʊʊl-a ʊkʊtɪ, Kyala i-kʊ-ba-longel-a m̩bɪbɪ~m̩bɪbɪ
1SG-PRS-2PL-tell-FV COMP God 1-PRS-2-judge-FV REDUPL~fast

ɪ-fi bi-kʊ-lond-igw-a ʊ-kʊ-kab-a. looli bo i-kw-is-a
AUG-PROX. 2-PRS-want-PASS-FV AUG-15-get-FV but as 1-PRS-come-FV

n-nya-mu-ndʊ, bʊle, **isa=i-kʊ-ba-ag-a** a-ba-ndʊ a-ba
1-kinship-1-person Q come=1-PRS-2-find-FV AUG-2-person AUG-PROX.2

bi-kʊ-mmw-itɪk-a?
2-PRS-1-believe-FV

'I tell you that he will avenge them speedily. Nevertheless when the Son of man cometh, shall he find faith on earth?' (Luke 18: 6–8)

In elicitation, all speakers consulted for the present study rejected this kind of construction. When presented with examples from Berger (1933) and the translation of the Bible, they similarly considered these to be erroneous. Some would "correct" them to feature the indefinite future (§8.6).

Given that the de-ventive proclitic does not occur in the varieties in focus here, a functional characterization clearly lies outside the scope of the present study. In a first examination of its uses in the Bible translation a vague pattern, however, emerges, in which the proclitic is mostly used in the last verb in a paragraph, more often than not in the context of prophecies. Thus both tokens in (18) do not only deal with judgement day, but also close the respective utterances of God and Jesus. This observation must, of course, be taken with a grain of salt, given the peculiarities of religious material. But it does fit the fact that in (17), the author, after an exposition of the subjects' situation, turns towards the reader to ask for his evaluation of how their dilemma will eventually be solved.

8.4 Proclitic *naa=*

In the southern topolects of Nyakyusa, a further proclitic *naa=* with a future or futurate meaning is found. Its shape indicates that this proclitic might be a portmanteau of comitative *na* and the future proclitic *aa=* (§8.2). See p. 272 in §9.3.1.1 for *na* together with the subjunctive mood. The only token in the text corpus is (19), which is taken from a narrative told by a speaker of the lake-shore-plains varieties. See also (20), which is based on the same variety.

In elicitation, speakers of the Selya variety knew this construction, although the difference between this and proclitic *aa=* remains unclear. Speakers from the village of Lwangwa – at the transition between Selya to the south and Mwamba (Lugulu) to the north (§1.2.5) – and speakers of the Mwamba/Lugulu variety either rejected it or considered it a feature of more southern varieties.

(19) po   p-ii-balasi   j-aa-j-a=po   II-meesa
      then 16-5-veranda(<SWA) 9-SUBSEC-be(come)-FV=16 AUG-table(9)(<SWA)

      a-pa   paa~pa   Ngoosi a-a-tʊʊl-ile
      AUG-PROX.16 REDUPL~PROX.16 N.   1-PST-take_from_head-PFV

      ʊ-bʊ-fu   bw-ake, bʊ-la ba-j-ile kʊ-sy-a,   ʊ-bʊ
      AUG-14-flour 14-POSS.SG 16-DIST 2-go-PFV 15-grind-FV AUG-PROX.4

      naa=i-kʊ-bʊʊk-a na=bo   ʊ-gwise
      FUT=1-PRS-go-FV COM=REF.14 AUG-his_father(1)

      'On the veranda there was a table where Ngoosi had put the flour that they had gone to grind, the one that her father would go with.' [Man and his in-law]

(20) po   ʊ-mu-ndʊ   jʊ-la ʊ-gw-a   kɪ-lɪngo   a-lɪnkw-amul-a,
      then AUG-1-person 1-DIST AUG-1-ASSOC 7-inheritance 1-NARR-answer-FV

      a-lɪnkʊ-tɪ "a-pa   bo si-lɪ bʊno~bʊ-no,   ʊ-ne   n-dek-ile,
      1-NARR-say AUG-PROX.16 as 10-COP REDUPL~14-DEM AUG-1SG 1SG-let-PFV

n-ga-bagıl-a   ʊ-kʊ-ʊl-a   paapo   na=n-gw-is-a
1SG-NEG-be_able-FV AUG-15-buy-FV because FUT=1SG-PRS-come-FV
k-oonang-a   ı-kı-lıngo   ky-a   ba-anangʊ a-ba-a
15-destroy-FV AUG-7-inheritance 7-ASSOC 2-my_child AUG-2-ASSOC
kw-is-a   kw-ingıl-a=po pa-my-angʊ"
15-come-FV 15-enter-FV=16 16-4-POSS.1SG

'And the kinsman said "I cannot redeem it for myself, lest I mar mine
own inheritance [lit. ...I cannot buy it because I will come to destroy the
inheritance of my children who will come to succeed me]') (Ruth 4:6)

8.5 Prospective/movement *kwa* INF

The simple present form of the movement gram *(j)a* (§10.4.1), together with an
augmentless infinitive, serves as a marker of prospective aspect.

(21)   *tʊkwa kʊjoba* 'we are going to (go and) speak'

As Comrie (1976: 76) defines it, prospective aspect expresses that "a state is
related to some subsequent action, for instance when someone is in a state of
being about to do something". This is further refined by Fleischman (1982: 18f),
who characterizes 'go-futures' as having a set of closely related and partly over-
lapping uses, denoting present relevance, imminence, intentionality, inception
or assumed eventualities. In Nyakyusa, there are two constructions that each
cover some of these uses: the de-itive constuction discussed in this section and
the prospective/inceptive construction discussed in §8.7.

The following examples will illustrate the use of prospective/movement *kwa*.
In (22), the first occurrence of the construction denotes the speaker's intention to
throw pepper at the thieving monkeys. Apart from intentionality, the notion of
movement remains intact. The second occurrence presents the assumed reaction
of those monkeys, which is also situated away from the speaker's current location. Similarly, in (23) Hare begs local people to help him descend from a tree
where he is trapped, thus present relevance, and presents his intended action.
Again, the original sense of the movement gram remains intact, as Hare's action
is situated away from his initial location. Lastly, in (24) Hare declares his coming back to a group of girls who have just rebuffed him, thus there is an overlap
between intentionality and present relevance.

(22) tʊ-tik-e   ɪ-m-bilipili   tʊ-bɪɪk-e   n-tʊ-supa. **tʊ-kw-a**
      1PL-pound-SUBJ AUG-9-pepper 1PL-put-SUBJ 18-13-bottle 1PL-PRS-go.FV
      kʊ-si-sop-el-a   paapo ɪ-sy-ene   **si-kw-a**   kʊ-t-ɪgɪ
      15-10-throw-APPL-FV because AUG-10-self 10-PRS-go.FV 15-say-IPFV
      "bi-kʊ-tʊ-p-a   ɪ-fi-ndʊ"
      2-PRS-1PL-give-FV AUG-8-food

      'We should pound pepper and put it in little bottles. Then we will go
      throw them at them [monkeys], for they'll think "they're throwing food."'
      (Thieving Monkeys)

(23) n-gʊ-sʊʊm-a mw-eg-e   ʊ-lʊ-goje, mu-m-biny-e
      1SG-PRS-beg-FV 2PL-take-SUBJ AUG-11-rope 2PL-1SG-bind-SUBJ
      ɪ-m-bʊlʊkʊtʊ. mu-kol-e   fiijo,   mu-sulusy-ege
      AUG-10-ear   1PL-grasp-SUBJ INTENS 2PL-lower-IPFV.SUBJ
      panandɪ~panandɪ. lɪnga   m-fik-ile   **n-gw-a**   kʊ-jɪgɪsy-a
      REDUPL~a_little   if/when 1SG-arrive-PFV 1SG-PRS-go.FV 15-shake-FV
      ʊ-lʊ-goj-e, ʊ-mwe   mu-kʊ-lek-esy-aga
      AUG-11-rope AUG-2PL 2PL-MOD.FUT-let-CAUS-MOD.FUT

      'I beg you (pl.) to take a rope and tie it to my ears. Hold it tight, lower it
      step by step. When I arrive [at the ground] I will shake the rope and you
      shall let go of it.' [Hare and Spider]

(24) **n-gw-a**   kw-is-a   n=ʊ-n-kamu   gw-angʊ ʊ-n-nywamu
      1SG-PRS-go.FV 15-come-FV COM=AUG-1-relative 1-POSS.1SG AUG-1-big
      fiijo
      INTENS

      'I will come with my very big relative.' [Hare and Hippo]

Note that the simple present form of (j)a only serves this function as a prospec-
tive/movement futurate. It does not have a habitual/generic reading (see §10.4.1),
nor does it have a progressive one and nor does it denote motion with purpose:

(25) n-gw-a   kʊ-kin-a ʊ-m-pɪla
      1SG-PRS-go.FV 15-play-FV AUG-3-ball

      'I will (go and) play football.'
      not: 'I am going (in order) to play football.'
      not: 'I am going to (the place that we) play football.'

In its use as a futurate, the complement of (j)a can take the imperfective final
suffix -aga. To begin with, this gives a continuous/progressive reading, which

can shade into an emphatic one (26). The imperfective can also add the epistemic flavour of an assumed eventuality, as in (27) and in the second token in (22) above. Lastly, *-aga* can also give a habitual/generic reading (28).

(26) lɪlɪno   tʊ-kw-a   kʊ-kin-aga ʊ-m-pɪla
     now/today 1PL-PRS-go.FV 15-play-IPFV AUG-3-ball

    1. 'Today we will (go and) be playing football (i.e. not stop).'
    2. 'Today we will (go and) be playing (no matter what).' [ET]

(27) i-kw-a   kʊ-jeng-aga kʊ-Tʊkʊjʊ
     1-PRS-go.FV 15-build-IPFV 17-T.

    1. 'He will (go and) be building in Tukuyu (continuously).'
    2. 'He will (go and) build in Tukuyu (assumedly).' [ET]

(28) kʊkʊtɪ ky-ɪnja bi-kw-a   kʊ-mog-aga ii-ng'oma
     every 7-year 2-PRS-go.FV 15-dance-IPFV 5-type_of_dance

    'Every year they will go and dance the *ng'oma* dance.' [ET]

8.6 Indefinite future

8.6.1 Formal makeup

The indefinite future consists of a pre-initial prefix *isakʊ* and the final vowel *-a* or imperfective *-aga*.

(29) *twisakʊjoba* 'we will possibly speak'

    The indefinite future constitutes an advanced stage of grammaticalization of *isa* 'come' as an auxiliary in the simple present (§10.4.2). While its source construction is still mostly transparent, no material can intervene between what corresponds to the original auxiliary and its infinitive complement.

(30) a. tw-isakʊ-kin-a   ʊ-m-pɪla m̩-bʊ-sikʊ bʊla~bʊ-la
       1PL-INDEF.FUT-play-FV   AUG-3-ball 18-14-time REDUPL~14-DIST

       'We might play football some day.' [ET]

    b. * twisa m̩bʊsikʊ bʊlabʊla kʊkina mpɪla

Furthermore, juxtaposition with the subject prefix yields the expected output concerning glide formation and vowel quality (§2.2.1.4), but does not result in a long vowel (31). This also holds for the prefix of the first person singular (32).

(31) *isakʊjoba* (°a-isakʊ-job-a) 'he will possibly speak'
      bisakʊjoba (°ba-isakʊ-job-a) 'they will possibly speak'
      jisakʊjoba (°jɪ-isakʊ-ly-a) 'it (9) will possibly eat'
      sisakʊjoba (°si-isakʊ-ly-a) 'they (10) will possibly eat'

(32) *nisakʊjoba* (°n-isakʊ-job-a) 'I will possibly speak'

The indefinite future is negated with the negative prefix *t(i)* following the subject marker. As the indefinite future is derived from the simple present of auxiliary *isa*, it is assumed that the underlying negation is *ti* (§6.5.2). Again, the vowel remains short (33):

(33) *tʊtisakʊjoba* 'we will not possibly speak'

In the following discussion, the meaning and uses of the indefinite future will be described as they are found synchronically in the varieties that are in the focus of this study. After that, a diachronic perspective will be applied, which will help us to understand the position of the construction in question in the present-day Nyakyusa TMA system.

8.6.2 Meaning and use

While older grammatical sketches consider the construction in question Nyakyusa's main future tense, it was hardly ever spontaneously offered by speakers in this study. In elicitation, language assistants unanimously rejected the use of this construction for prototypical predictions (34, 35) or intention-based future eventualities (36, 37). In these typical future tense contexts, the collocation of *aa=* and the simple present would be used; see (2–5) on p. 251. The examples are based on Dahl's (1985; 2000b) questionnaires.

(34) Context: What will happen if I eat this mushroom? – You will die.
      #lɪnga   ʊ-l-iile   gw-isakʊ-fw-a
      if/when 2SG-eat-PFV 2SG-INDEF.FUT-die-FV

(35) Context: It's no use trying to swim in the lake tomorrow. The water will be cold.
      #a-m-ɪɪsi   g-isakʊ-j-a   ma-talalɪfu
      AUG-6-water 6-INDEF.FUT-be(come)-FV 6-cold

(36) Context: A young man's plans for the future. He intends to build a big house then.
      #lɪnga   n-gʊl-ile   n-isakʊ-jeng-a   ɪɪ-nyumba   ɪɪ-nywamu
      if/when 1SG-grow-PFV 1SG-INDEF.FUT-build-FV AUG-house(9) AUG-big(9)

(37) Context: Talking about the speaker's plans for the evening. He will be at home.

#n-isakʊ-j-a itolo pa-ka-aja
1SG-INDEF.FUT-be(come)-FV just 16-12-homestead

Examples containing the indefinite future that were constructed by the researcher were interpreted as describing events that are less probable and/or contingent on other circumstances.

(38) tw-isakʊ-kin-a ʊ-m-pɪla
1PL-INDEF.FUT-play-FV AUG-3-ball

'We might play football (unsure or dependent on circumstances).' [ET]

(39) tw-isakʊ-fik-a kʊ-ka-aja k-ɪɪnʊ
1PL-INDEF.FUT-arrive-FV 17-12-homestead 12-POSS.2PL

'We might arrive at your place some day (i.e do not overdo your bragging about it, we might come and check).' [ET]

Examples (40, 41) are typical of the few cases in which speakers themselves offered uses of the indefinite future within the wider elicitation context. Again, a future-oriented epistemic reading lies at the heart of these examples, apparently with some persistent ingressive flavour.

(40) mu-nga-bʊʊk-aga kʊ-m-ɪɪsi mwibeene, ɪ-n-joka
2PL-NEG.SUBJ-go-IPFV 17-6-water 2PL.self AUG-9-snake
j-isakʊ-ba-mil-a
9-INDEF.FUT-2PL-swallow-FV

'Don't go to the water by yourselves, a snake might devour you.' [ET]

(41) a-ka-pɪɪj-a=mo ɪ-m-balaga, kangɪ
1-NEG-cook-FV=some AUG-9-banana_stew again
a-t-isakʊ-pɪɪj-a=mo
1-NEG-INDEF.FUT-cook-FV=some

'She has never cooked banana stew and she won't likely ever do so.' [ET]

Concerning uses of the indefinite future in a more spontaneous context, consider the following example. The researcher was standing on a path leading away from the village of Lwangwa and having a chat with some of the local inhabitants. A motorcycle taxi came rushing by and the researcher only jumped aside in the last moment. After it had passed, (42) was uttered, giving the researcher to understand that such unalert behaviour might at some point lead to an accident.

(42)   b-isakʊ-kʊ-tik-a
       2-INDEF.FUT-2SG-pound-FV
       'They might (eventually) knock you over.' [overheard]

These readings of the indefinite future are probably the reason that Nurse (1979) considers this construction a "distant future". Rather than a question of temporal remoteness, this interpretation apparently derives from the strongly modal semantics of the construction. To begin with, even in predictions of a temporally very distant time, the collocation of future proclitic *aa=* plus the simple present (§8.2) is normally used:

(43)   lɪnga   fi-kɪnd-ile ɪ-fy-ɪnja   f-ingi ɪ-fi   fi-kw-is-a
       if/when 8-pass-PFV AUG-8-year 8-many AUG-PROX.8 8-PRS-come-FV
       aa=bi-kʊ-mal-a   ɪ-n-jɪla   j-aa   kʊ-bʊʊk-a kʊ-Tʊkʊjʊ
       FUT=2-PRS-finish-FV AUG-9-path 9-ASSOC 15-go-FV   17-T.
       'In many years, they will finish the road to Tukuyu.' [ET]

Furthermore, the indefinite future itself can be combined with the future proclitic *aa=* (44). In fact, when checking in elicitation how far this construction can be combined with definite temporal adverbials, speakers nearly always added *aa=* when repeating the constructed examples.

(44)   aa=tw-isakʊ-fik-a   kɪ-laabo
       FUT=1PL-INDEF.FUT-arrive-FV 7-tomorrow
       'We will probably arrive tomorrow.' [ET]

The indefinite future can further be used to express epistemic modality without future time reference (45, 46). As Bybee et al. (1991) point out, epistemic uses other than future prediction are typical of old future forms. Indeed, as (47) shows, this use was already available in the nineteen-forties.

(45)   Context: You are asked where your brother is. You assume he is playing
       football.
       isakʊ-kin-a   ʊ-m-pɪla
       1.INDEF.FUT-play-FV AUG-3-ball
       'He will be [=presumably he is] playing football.' [ET]

(46) Context: The cows are mooing loudly. You are asked why they are
      making so much noise. You assume they are hungry.
      s-isakʊ-j-a   n=ɪ-n-jala
      10-INDEF.FUT-be(come)-FV COM=AUG-9-hunger
      'They will be [=presumably they are] hungry.' [ET]

(47) ʊ-mw-ana i-kʊ-lɪl-a   n-nyumba. **isakʊ-bunguluk-ɪl-a**
      AUG-1-child 1-PRS-cry-FV 18-house(9) 1.INDEF.FUT-toss_and_turn-APPL-FV
      m-m-ooto
      18-3-fire

      'The chid is crying in the house. It'll have [=presumably it has] fallen into
      the fire.' (Busse 1949: 199; orthography adapted)

Lastly, imperfective *-aga* adds a continuous or reading:

(48) n-isak-ʊʊl-aga   ɪ-fi
      1SG-INDEF.FUT-buy-IPFV AUG-PROX.8
      'I will (probably or eventually) buy these things (habitually).' [ET]

(49) isakʊ-jeng-aga   papaa~pa
      1.INDEF.FUT-build-IPFV REDUPL~PROX.16
      'He will (probably or eventually) be building right here.' [ET]

8.6.3 A diachronic perspective

In the introduction to this section it was commented that the indefinite future
constitutes an advanced stage of grammaticalization of *isa* 'come' as an auxiliary
in the simple present. While the phonetic attrition is self-evident, the construction's meaning and use suggest a more complex chain of developments. As discussed in §10.4.2, the de-ventive auxiliary *isa* has an ingressive reading and in
its futurate use contrasts with the de-itive prospective/movement construction
(§8.5).Only the latter of the two allows a component of intentionality. Now, in
the first grammatical sketches of Nyakyusa (Schumann 1899; Endemann 1914),
the indefinite future construction is listed as the main future tense. Correspond-
ingly it is relatively frequent in the text collections from that time (Berger 1933;
Busse 1942; 1949), where it is found with future predictions that do not necessarily involve an ingressive component. One can thus assume a semantic generalization from an assertion about reaching a certain condition in the future towards a prediction about a future state-of-affairs. This is precisely what has been

documented for de-ventive futures in Swedish (Christensen 1997) and Rhaeto-Romance (Ebneter 1973). Such a grammaticalization path is also suggested by Traugott (1978).

While at the turn of the twentieth century the indefinite future apparently constituted a core construction in Nyakyusa's TMA system, the above discussion has shown that this does not hold for the present-day language. Note also that Lusekelo (2007; 2013) in his discussion of tense and aspect in Nyakyusa, does not list the indefinite future at all, but states that the collocation of the future clitic *aa=* plus the simple present (§8.2) is the only future tense in this language. Nurse (1979), as noted above, considers the construction in question a "distant future" in contrast to the "intermediate future" expressed through *aa=* plus simple present.

The history of the indefinite future as attested in the first descriptions of Nyakyusa and its usage in earlier text collections, its strongly modal flavour in the present-day language plus the fact that it allows for a non-temporal epistemic reading, as well as its distribution and combinatory possibilities, all point towards an old future construction that has mainly been displaced into the modal dimension. This most likely went along with the future proclitic *aa=* (§8.2), especially in collocation with the simple present, occupying the former territory of the construction.[2]

8.7 Prospective/Inceptive *ja pa*-INF

This construction consists of the copula verb *ja* 'be(come)' plus an infinitive marked for locative noun class 16.

(50)   *tʋkʋja pakʋjoba* 'we are about to speak'

Formally this construction constitutes the inceptive counterpart to the periphrastic progressive (§6.6.1). As for its semantics, it construes a future eventuality as very near or imminent to a point of reference, by default the time of speech. This often goes along with a sense of intention. Unlike the de-itive construction described in §8.5, this construction does not have a possible reading of physical motion. The following examples illustrate the use of this construction in the present tense.

---

[2]Note also that some language assistants commented on the use of the indefinite future in typical prediction contexts: "Maybe you would use that in the written language. But in speaking, we don't say it like that". The only more widely known written materials in Nyakyusa are translations of the Bible, which are based on the variety described by Schumann (1899) and Endemann (1914).

(51) ʊ-n-kiikʊlʊ   n-ummw-ag-ile, **tʊ-kʊ-j-a**
AUG-1-woman 1SG-1-find-PFV   1PL-PRS-be(come)-FV
pa-kw-eg-an-a   kɪfuki
16-15-marry-RECP-FV near

'I've found a woman, we'll marry soon.' [Hare and Spider]

(52) bo **kʊ-j-a**   **pa-kʊ-nw-a** ʊ-n-kota   ʊ-gʊ   taasi
as 2SG.PRS-be(come)-FV 16-15-drink-FV AUG-3-medicine AUG-PROX.3 first
ʊ-ka-bʊʊk-ege   n=ʊ-lʊ-bʊnjʊ   m-ma-tengele
2SG-ITV-go-IPFV.SUBJ COM=AUG-11-morning 18-6-bush

'When you plan to drink this portion, first go into the bush in the morning.' [Mfyage turns into a lion]

(53) ɪɪ-fula   **jɪ-kʊ-j-a**   **pa-kʊ-tim-a**
AUG-rain(9) 9-PRS-be(come)-FV 16-15-rain-FV

'It is about to rain.' [ET]

While the prospective/movement construction discussed in §8.5 only has a prospective reading when used in the simple present, the prospective/inceptive construction can be used in the past tense:

(54) bo m-fik-ile   pa-ka-aja,   ʊ-n-nuguna   gw-angʊ
as 1SG-arrive-PFV 16-12-homestead AUG-1-younger_sibling 1-POSS.1SG
a-a-j-aga   **pa-kʊ-sook-a=po**
1-PST-be(come)-IPFV 16-15-leave-FV=16

'When I arrived at home my younger brother was about to leave.' [ET]

9 Mood and modal categories

9.1 Introduction

In this chapter, mood and modal constructions will be described, starting with the imperative (§9.2), then the subjunctive mood (§9.3). The latter shows a broad variety of meanings and uses, as is common in Bantu languages. The treatment of the subjunctive includes a discussion of its negative counterpart and the distal/itive *ka-*. Following this, two modal constructions will be described, which are rather uncommon for a Bantu language, namely the desiderative (§9.4) and the modal future construction (§9.5). Lastly, there is a section on the conditional marker (§9.6).

An overview of mood and modal constructions and their composition is given in Table 9.1. The terminology in this chapter follows Palmer (2007), unless indicated otherwise.

Table 9.1: Mood and modal constructions

Label	Shape	Example	
Imperative	vb-a(*ga*)	*joba*	'Speak!'
Subjunctive	sm-vb-*e*(*ge*)	*tʊjobe*	'we should speak'
Distal subjunctive	sm-*ka*-vb-*e*(*ge*)	*tʊkajobe*	'we should go speak'
Neg. subjunctive	sm-(*lɪ*)-*nga*-vb-a(*ga*)	*tʊngajoba*	'we should not speak'
Desiderative	sm-*lɪ*-vb-a(*ga*)	*tʊlɪjoba*	'we would like to speak'
Modal future	sm2-*kʊ*-vb-*aga*	*tʊkʊjobaga*	'we shall speak'
Conditional	*ngalɪ* verb	*ngalɪ tʊkʊjoba*	'we would speak'

9.2 Imperative

Direct orders in the second person singular are expressed by the imperative, which can consist of the bare stem:

(1)   *bʊʊk-a!* 'Go!'
       kin-a!   'Play!'
       mog-a! 'Dance!'

The prosody of imperatives requires any vowel in initial position of the verbal word to be short (2). This holds even for vowels followed by a prenasalized plosive (3).[1]

(2)   *igala!*   'Open!'
       ɪma!   'Stand up!'
       ega!   'Take!'
       amula! 'Answer!
       okya!   'Roast!'
       ʊlɪsya! 'Sell!'

(3)   *ingɪla!*   [i.ᵑgɪr.a]   'Enter!'
       ɪmba!   ['ɪ.ᵐba]   'Sing!'
       endesya   [ɛ.ⁿdɛ.sʸa]   'Drive!'
       anda!   ['a.ⁿda]   'Start!'
       ongelapo! [ɔ.ᵑgɛ.'la.pʰɔ] 'Continue a bit!'

Verbs in the imperative can carry an object marker. With object prefxies other than the first person singular the final vowel changes to -*e*. This also holds for the reflexive object prefix.[2] When the object prefix of the first person singular precedes a plosive or approximant and thus the resultant word would be monosyllabic, the prefix surfaces as a syllabic nasal. This is discussed in §3.3.2.1.

(4)   a. m-b-a=ko   ʊ-n-katɪ
           1SG-give-FV=17 AUG-3-bread

           'Give me the bread!'

       b. m-p-e=ko   ʊ-n-katɪ
           1-give-IMP=17 AUG-3-bread

           'Give him the bread!'

       c. i-kom-e
           REFL-hit-IMP

           'Hit yourself!'

---

[1]No imperative of the shape /ʊNC.../ is attested in the data and no Nyakyusa verb features initial /u/ (§3.2).

[2]The resulting forms can thus be considered to be hybrid forms between the imperative and the subjunctive; see Devos & van Olmen (2013: 17-22) for a discussion of such forms across Bantu. Also see p. 271 in §9.3 for a similarly hybrid imperative-like subjunctive.

Likewise, monosyllabic verbs in their bare stem form cannot be used as imperatives. They have to be augmented by either a meaningless prefix *i-* or carry the imperfective suffix *-aga* (5). This has also been observed by Schumann (1899: 69). Monosyllabic verbs are, however, acceptable as imperatives when they carry an enclitic (6).

(5) *ilwa!* / *lwaga!* 'Fight!' (not **lwa*)
     ilya! / *lyaga!* 'Eat!'   (not **lya*)
     inwa! / *nwaga!* 'Drink!' (not **nwa*)

(6) *lwapo!* 'Fight a bit!'
     lyapo! 'Eat a bit!'
     nwapo! 'Drink a bit!'

Direct orders addressed to the second person plural are expressed by the subjunctive (§9.3). The only attested cases of formal imperatives directed to the second person plural are *keeta* 'look' and *isaga* 'come', which serve as invariable discourse markers. The imperfective suffix *-aga* adds a range of meanings. Depending on the context, it can express a demand for an action to be carried out habitually/regularly (7). Further, the imperfective imperative can express a demand to continuously perform an action, which can shade over into an urge to initialize or continue the said action (8). Lastly, the imperfective suffix can also serve to mitigate the imperative appeal, yielding phrases that range from weaker commands to invitations (9). Nurse (2008: 192) notes that this mitigating function of the imperfective imperative is found across Bantu.

(7) bomb-aga bwila~bwila!
     work-IPFV REDUPL~always
     'Always work! [ET]

(8) job-aga!
     speak-IPFV
     'Be / get / continue speaking!' [ET]

(9) ingɪl-aga
     enter-IPFV
     'Come in!' [overheard]

Note that imperatives can be used not only for verbs featuring a volitional agent, but also for non-volitional change-of-state verbs; Seidel (2008: 320) observes the same for Yeyi R41.

(10) nyop-a!
      be(come)_soaked-FV
      'Get sweating! (e.g. do the hard work yourself)' [ET]

(11) katal-a!
      be(come)_tired-FV
      'Act tired!' [ET]

(12) Context: The plumber is claiming an excessive price.
      hobok-a!
      be(come)_happy-FV
      'Stop exaggerating!' [overheard]

While in some Bantu languages, such as Yeyi K41 (Seidel 2008) and Zulu S42 (Ziervogel et al. 1981), the subjunctive and not the imperative has to be used in a sequence of commands from the second verb on, sequences of imperatives are allowed in Nyakyusa:

(13) bɪık-a ʊ-lw-igi   lʊ-mo lw-ene saam-il-a   bʊbʊʊ~bo
      put-FV AUG-11-door 11-one 11-only migrate-APPL-FV REDUPL~REF.14
      'Put one door in, so you can move in.' [How to build modern houses]

There is no formal negative counterpart to the imperative. Instead, two different strategies are available for forming negative orders (prohibitives). First, the prohibitive elements *komma* or *somma* followed by the infinitive may be used (see §11.3). This is very common and bears the strongest directive force. A second strategy is the use of the negative subjunctive (§9.3.4).

9.3 Subjunctive

The final vowel -*e* (imperfective -*ege)* marks a modal category that is commonly labelled *subjunctive* in the Bantuist tradition (Doke 1935: 203f; Rose et al. 2002: 83f). Endemann (1914: 62f) speaks of the *final* mood in his description of Nyakyusa. In the case of defective *tɪ* (§10.3), no change in final vowel takes place. The subjunctive in Nyakyusa gives a wide array of readings and comes close to what Timberlake (2007: 326), from a typological perspective, characterizes as "an all-purpose mood used to express a range of less-than-completely real modality".

In the following description, first the uses of the subjunctive as such will be outlined, distinguishing between independent and subordinate clauses. This is followed by a description of some complex verbal constructions that include a subjunctive verb and a section on the distal/itive prefix *ka-*. Lastly, the negative counterpart to the subjunctive paradigm will be discussed.

9.3.1 Uses of the subjunctive

9.3.1.1 Subjunctive uses in main predication

The subjunctive can be used performatively for directives, where it is considered milder than the imperative.

(14) ʊ-m-fis-e   kʊʊ-sofu tʊ-m̩-buut-e
      2SG-1-hid-SUBJ 17-room(9) 1PL-1-slaughter-SUBJ

      'Hide him [Hare] in the room, we shall slaughter him.' [Saliki and Hare]

When the subjunctive is used in a directive, the of the second person singular can be omitted.[3]

(15) igʊl-e   ʊ-lw-igi
      open-SUBJ AUG-11-door

      'Open the door!' [overheard]

(16) bʊʊk-a k-ʊʊl-e   ʊ-bʊ-meme
      go-FV ITV-buy-SUBJ AUG-14-electricity(<SWA)

      'Go buy [vouchers for] electricity!' [overheard][4]

The subjunctive is also used as a counterpart to the imperative for the second person plural (17). Negative commands to the second person plural are formed by the use of either *somma/komma* plus the infinitive (§11.3), or the negative subjunctive (§9.3.4).

(17) ʊ-malafyale a-a-ba-bʊʊl-ile a-a-t-ile   "mu-bʊʊk-e nuumwe
      AUG-chief(1) 1-PST-2-tell-PFV 1-PST-say-PFV   2PL-go-SUBJ COM.2PL

      mu-ka-kol-e   ii-boole ɪ-ly-ʊmi   mu-lɪ-twal-e   kʊ-no!"
      2PL-ITV-grasp/hold-SUBJ 5-leopard AUG-5-live 2PL-5-carry-SUBJ 17-PROX

      'The chief told them "You (pl.) too go, catch a live leopard and bring it
      here!"' [Chief Kapyungu]

---

[3]This is frequent in natural speech and also attested in the textual data. In elicitation, however, speakers were hesitant to use this form. Given the constraint on monosyllabic imperatives and subjunctives (see p. 269 in §9.2 and p. 56 in §3.3.2.1), it is very probable that dropping the subject prefix is not possible with monosyllabic roots. Optionality of the subject marker also holds for Yeyi (Seidel 2008: 323). Devos & van Olmen (2013: 21f) indicate more such cases in other Bantu languages.

[4]See §9.3.3 for the distal/itive prefix *ka-*.

9 Mood and modal categories

The subjunctive is also used in jussives, including hortatives (directions to the first person plural):

(18) ʊ-jʊ   lɪnga   i-kʊ-m-boni-a,   **aa-seng-ege**   taasi
AUG-PROX.1 if/when 1-PRS-1SG-greet-FV 1.1SG-chop-IPFV.SUBJ first

n=ɪ-n-dwanga pa-kɪ-kosi po **a-m-boni-ege**
COM=AUG-9-axe 16-7-neck then 1-1SG-greet-IPFV.SUBJ

'Whoever greets me shall first hit me with an axe in the neck, then he shall greet me.' [Chief Kapyungu]

(19) po   nsyɪsyɪ a-lɪnkʊ-tɪ "gwe jɪ-p-iile.   is-aga
then skunk(1) 1-NARR-say 2SG 9-be(come)_burnt-PFV come-IPFV

tʊ-ly-ege!"
2PL-eat-IPFV.SUBJ

'Then Skunk said "You, it [meat] is done. Come, let's eat!"' [Hare and Skunk]

A pre-initial *a=* is sometimes used in directives and hortatives, which apparently provides the request with a summoning or encouraging character (20, 21). This is not to be confused with the future proclitic *aa=* (§8.2).

(20) mwe a=mu-pɪlɪkɪsy-e
2PL   HORT=2PL-listen-SUBJ

'Hey, listen up!' [ET]

(21) a=tʊ-tʊʊsy-e
HORT=1PL-rest-SUB

'Come, let's rest!' [ET]

A pre-initial form of comitative *na=* with directives and jussives strengthens the coercive force and typically gives a reading of urgency (22–24). Nicolle (2013: 89) uses the label "emphatic subjunctive" for the same construction in Digo E73.

(22) na=tʊ-bʊʊk-e
COM=1PL-go-SUBJ

'Let's go! (urging and/or annoyed)' [ET]

(23) po   leelo   j-aal-iis-ile   ɪ-m-bwa. j-aa-t-ile   "ʊ-mwe
then now/but 9-PST-come-PFV AUG-9-dog 9-PST-say-PFV AUG-2PL

na=mu-lek-e   ʊ-kʊ-lw-a!"
COM=2PL-let-SUBJ AUG-15-fight-FV

'Then Dog came. He said "You (pl.), now stop fighting!"' [Monkey and Tortoise]

(24) a-lɪ   koo=kʊʊgʊ   kajamba? kɛɛt-a, n-ga-m̩-bon-a
      1-COP REF.17=where tortoise(1) look-FV 1SG-NEG-1-see-FV

      ʊ-kw-is-a   ◦   kʊ-kʊ-n-geet-a.   **na=mu-bʊʊk-e,**
      AUG-15-come-FV 17-15-1SG-watch-FV COM=2PL-go-SUBJ

      mu-ka-n-koolel-e, mu-ka-n̩-dond-e!   iis-e   a-n-geet-e
      2PL-ITV-1-call-SUBJ 2PL-ITV-1-search-SUBJ 1.come-SUBJ 1-1SG-watch-SUBJ

      'Where is Tortoise? Look, I haven't seen it coming to see me. Go (pl.)
      right now, call it, find it! It must come and see me.' [Lion and Tortoise]

The subjunctive is also used for expressing obligation, which ranges from a
weaker notion of necessity to recommendations.

(25) j-oope ʊ-n-kiikʊlʊ   **a-j-ege**   n=ɪ-n-dwanga ɪ-j-aa
      1-also AUG-1-woman 1-be(come)-IPFV.SUBJ COM=AUG-1-axe AUG-9-ASSOC

      kʊ-meny-el-a   n=ʊ-kʊ-tumul-ɪl-a   ɪ-mi-piki
      15-chop-APPL-FV COM=AUG-15-cut-APPL-FV AUG-4-tree

      'And a woman should have an axe for splitting with and cutting trees
      with.' [Types of tools in the home]

(26) a-ka-a   bʊ-bɪlɪ a-ma-pamba a-ga-a   kʊ-jeng-el-a
      AUG-12-ASSOC 14-two AUG-6-brick AUG-6-ASSOC 15-build-APPL-FV

      gw-ijʊʊl-e   ʊ-kʊ-fyatʊl-a   jʊ∼jʊʊ-gwe
      2SG-work_hard-SUBJ AUG-15-make_bricks-FV REDUPL∼1-2SG

      n=ʊ-kʊ-kosy-a
      COM=AUG-15-set_on_fire-FV

      'Secondly, you should try yourself to make bricks to build with and bake
      them.' [How to build modern houses]

Conceptually close to expressing obligation, the subjunctive is found in delib-
erative and permissive interrogation:

(27) tʊ-tɪ=bʊle   na=a-ba-anɪɪtʊ!
      1PL-say.SUBJ=how COM=AUG-2-our_child

      'What should we do with our children!' [Thieving monkeys]

(28) lɪlɪno   kʊʊ-many-a,   fi-ki   ʊ-ti-kw-amul-a   bo
      now/today PRS.1SG-know-FV 8-what 2SG-NEG-PRS-answer-FV as

      n-gʊ-kʊ-laalʊʊsy-a? bʊle **n-gʊ-kom-e**   n=ɪ-kɪ-buli?
      1SG-PRS-2SG-ask-FV Q   1SG-2SG-hit-SUBJ COM=AUG-7-fist

      'Now you'll get to know me, why don't you answer when I'm asking
      you? Should I hit you with the fist?' [Saliki and Hare];

The subjunctive is also used for volitives (29, 30) and, closely related, to announce what one is about to do (31).

(29) kyala **a-kʊ-tʊʊl-e**
      God   1-2SG-help-SUBJ

      'May God help you.' [overheard]

(30) ʊ-n-nino   iibiibwe   fi-mo kʊ-no   mw-a-jaat-aga,
      AUG-1-your_companion 1.forget.PFV 8-one 17-PROX 2PL-PST-walk-IPFV
      a-t-ile   **n-ummw-ag-ege**   papaa~pa
      1-say-PFV 2SG-1-find-IPFV.SUBJ REDUPL~PROX.16

      'Your friend has forgotten something while you were talking a walk, he
      said "I want to meet him right here."' [Hare and Spider]

(31) po   mwa=n-gambɪlɪ   a-a-tɪ   "hee.   po   **m-bʊʊk-e**
      then matronym=9-monkey 1-SUBSEC-say INTERJ then 1SG-go-SUBJ
      kw-a   kajamba kʊ-kʊ-mel-a   ɪɪ-heela   sy-angʊ". po
      17-ASSOC tortoise(1) 17-15-claim-FV AUG-money(10) 10-POSS.1SG then
      a-lɪnkw-end-a,   a-lɪnkw-end-a,   a-lɪnkw-end-a
      1-NARR-walk/travel-FV 1-NARR-walk/travel-FV 1-NARR-walk/travel-FV

      'So Mr. Monkey said "I'll go to Tortoise to claim my money". He walked
      and walked and walked' [Monkey and Tortoise]

Following *mpaka* 'no matter what', the subjunctive expresses that the eventuality will or must be fulfilled under all conditions. Thus, in (32) it is used in a promise, while in (33), an excerpt from a procedural text, it marks the denoted instruction as a necessity, whereas a bare subjunctive could be understood as just one step amongst various others.

(32) n-gʊ-bʊʊl-a   ʊkʊtɪ **mpaka**   **n-iis-e**   kɪ-laabo
      1SG-PRS-tell-FV COMP no_matter_what 1SG-come-SUBJ 7-tomorrow

      'I promise that I will come tomorrow.' [ET]

(33) kangɪ **mpaka**   **ʊ-si-keet-e**   taasi ɪ-n-dalama   ɪ-si
      again no_matter_what 2SG-10-look-SUBJ first AUG-10-money AUG-10
      ʊ-lɪ   na=syo   muu-nyambɪ, pamopeene n=ʊ-tʊ-ndʊ
      2SG-COP COM=REF.10 18-pocket   together   COM=AUG-13-thing
      ʊ-tʊ-ngɪ   ʊ-tʊ   tʊ-bagiile   ʊ-kʊ-kʊ-tʊʊl-a
      AUG-13-other AUG-PROX.13 13-be_able.PFV AUG-15-2SG-help-FV

kʊ-m-bombo ɪ-jo
17-9-work   AUG-REF.9

'Again, you should look first at the money which you have in your
pocket, together with other things which can help you in this work.'
[How to build modern houses]

Finally, the subjunctive is also sometimes used to elaborate on states-of-affairs
construed with the past imperfective in its habitual/generic reading (§6.5.7), as
well as with futurates (§8).[5] This is extremely rare in the present data, the only
clear case being given in (34). The additional example in (35) is taken from HIV
prevention materials created by SIL International (orthography adapted). A few
more instances are found in older text collections (Berger 1933; Busse 1942; 1949),
but even there this usage seems far from obligatory. Botne (2008: 130), for neighbouring Ndali, lists a number of examples of subjunctive uses under the label
'coincident future'. Two of his examples are to all appearances also continua-
tions of past generics.

(34)   po ly-a-pɪmb-aga   ii-pango   po~p-oosa   pa-la
      then 5-PST-carry-IPFV 5-type_of_guitar REDUP~-16-all 16-DIST
      li-kʊ-bʊʊk-a. po ly-and-aga   ʊ-kʊ-kʊb-a   ii-pango
      5-PRS-go-FV then 5-PST.begin-IPFV AUG-15-beat-FV 5-type_of_guitar
      lɪ-la. po a-ba-ndʊ   **ba-mog-ege**
      5-DIST then AUG-2-person 2-dance-IPFV.SUBJ

      'It (the monster) carried the guitar wherever it went. It would begin to
      play that guitar. People would then dance.' [Monster with guitar]

(35)   paapo mwe ba-ana ʊ-mwe mu-lɪ   ba-pɪɪna, ba-li=ko a-ba-nyambala
      because 2PL   2-child AUG-2PL 2PL-COP 2-orphan 2-COP=17 AUG-2-man
      ba-mo a-ba   b-isakʊ-ba-syob-aga   n=ʊ-kʊ-peefy-a
      2-one AUG-PROX.2 2-INDEF.FUT-2PL-cheat-IPFV COM=AUG-15-tempt-FV.

      'Because your are orphans, there are some men who might try to
      persuade you.'

      ba-ba-p-ege   ɪ-fi-ndʊ   n=ʊ-tʊ-ndʊ   ʊ-tʊ-ngɪ   ʊkʊtɪ
      2-2PL-give-IPFV.SUBJ AUG-8-food COM=AUG-13-thing AUG-13-other COMP

---

[5]R. Carlson (1992) observes this kind of dual function for categories often labelled 'subjunctive'
in a number of West and East African languages. However, in the languages discussed by
Carlson, these uses are commonly more generalized and fulfil the functions covered by the
Nyakyusa narrative tense (§7.3) and subsecutive (§7.4).

mu-logw-ege   na=bo
2PL-copulate-IPFV.SUBJ COM=REF.2

'They will give you food and presents so that you have sex with them.'
[Kande's Story][6]

Lastly, imperfective -*ege* is highly sensitive to context and yields a range of readings including general or habitual (36, 37) and continuous (38). It also has a mitigating function, thus marking a recommendation in (39).

(36)   gwe n-kiikʊlʊ **ʊ-ɲ-jab-ɪl-ege**   ʊ-ɲ-dʊmego
      2SG 1-woman 2SG-1-divide-APPL-IPFV.SUBJ AUG-1-your_husband
      ɪ-kɪ-jabo   kɪ-nywamu fiijo
      AUG-7-share 7-big   INTENS

      'You, woman must always [while pregnant] give your husband a good share [of the food].' [Pregnant women]

(37)   ɪɪ-fubu   j-aal-iitiike   looli jɪ-lɪnkʊ-n-sʊʊm-a jɪ-lɪnkʊ-tɪ,
      AUG-hippo(9) 9-PST-agree.PFV but 9-NARR-1-beg-FV 9-NARR-say
      "gw-is-enge=ko   kʊ-my-angʊ kʊ-kʊ-m-band-a
      2SG-come-IPFV.SUBJ=17 17-4-POSS.1SG 17-15-1SG-heal_wound-FV
      ɪ-fi-londa
      AUG-8-wound

      'Hippo agreed, but asked him [Hare], "You should come (regularly) to my home to put hot compresses on my sores."' [Hare and Hippo]

(38)   a-ka-a   kw-and-a   **g-ʊʊl-ege**   a-ma-lata
      AUG-12-ASSOC 15-begin-FV 2SG-buy-IPFV.SUBJ AUG-6-corrugated_iron
      manandɪ~ma-nandɪ, mpaka ga-fik-ɪl-e   ɪ-m-balɪlo
      REDUPL~6-little   until   6-arrive-APPL-SUBJ AUG-9-number
      ɪ-jɪ   kʊ-jɪ-lond-a
      AUG-PROX.9 2SG.PRS-9-want-FV

      'To start with, you should be buying corrugated iron, little by little, until you have enough.' [How to build modern houses]

(39)   n-gʊ-kʊ-bʊʊl-a   mu-ndʊ ʊ-gwe, **gw-eg-ege**   fy-osa
      1SG-PRS-2SG-tell-FV 1-person AUG-2SG 2SG-take-IPFV.SUBJ 8-all
      ɪ-fy-ako   ɪ-fi   ʊ-lɪ   na=fyo   pamopeene
      AUG-8-POSS.2SG AUG-PROX.8 2SG-COP COM=REF.8 together

---

[6]http://www.nyakyusalanguage.com/nyy/mlsp-dl/334/12876/42227?r=0 (05 February, 2016). The Swahili version of this texts, on which the translation to Nyakyusa is based, uses an infinitive-based construction instead of the subjunctive mood.

n=ʊ-n-kasigo   na=a-ba-anaako   n=ɪ-fi-nyamaana
COM=AUG-1-your_wife COM=AUG-2-your_child COM=AUG-8-animal
fy-ako   fy-osa.
8-POSS.2SG 8-all

'I'm telling you, you should take all your belongings together with your wife and children and all your animals.'

ʊ-bʊʊk-ege   kʊ-bʊ-tali komma ʊ-kʊ-buj-a   kangɪ kʊ-no,
2SG-go-IPFV.SUBJ 17-14-long PROH   AUG-15-return-FV again 17-PROX
ʊ-nga-ba-bʊʊl-aga   na=a-ba-palamani   ba-ako
2SG-NEG.SUBJ-2-tell-IPFV COM=AUG-2-neighbour 2-POSS.2SG

'You should go far and never return here, you shouldn't tell not even your neighbours.' [Selfishness kills]

9.3.1.2 Subjunctive uses in subordinate clauses

The subjunctive features in the complements of modality and manipulation verbs, where it alternates with the infinitive. If the subject of the main verb is co-referential with the subject of the complement verb, the infinitive is the more common form. The subjunctive is also possible however (40); also see (1a) on p. 211, (9) on p. 253 and (65) on p. 284. Subjunctive complements are sometimes introduced by the complementizer ʊkʊtɪ, but this is optional in most cases. If the subjects of the two verbs differ, the subjunctive is most commonly used (41); this includes partly disjunctive reference; see (89) on p. 290. Alternatively, the complement verb figures as an oblique infinitival clause and its notional subject as the object of the main verb (42).

(40) i-kʊ-lond-a   **eeg-e**   ii-peasi   lɪ-mo
      1-PRS-want-FV 1.take-SUBJ 5-pear(<SWA) 5-one

      'He wants to take one pear.' [Elisha pear story]

(41) gwe ŋ-ganga n-gʊ-sʊʊm-a **ʊ-ŋ-dʊʊl-e**   ʊ-m-b-e=po
      2SG 1-healer 1SG-PRS-beg-FV 2SG-1SG-help-SUBJ 2SG-1SG-give-SUBJ=16
      ʊ-n-kota   ʊ-gw-a   lʊ-gano
      AUG-3-medicine AUG-3-ASSOC 11-love

      'You, witch doctor, I beg you to help me, give me a love portion.' [Mfyage turns into a lion]

(42) ʊ-malafyale a-ba-lagiile   b-oosa **ʊ-kw-is-a**   kʊ-my-ake
      AUG-chief(1) AUG-2-order.PFV 2-all   AUG-15-come-FV 17-4-POSS.SG
      'The chief ordered everybody to come to his place.' [ET]

Related to the preceding examples, the subjunctive is also used in indirect orders:

(43) ɪ-n-galamu jɪ-lɪnkʊ-fi-bʊʊl-a ɪ-fi-nyamaana fy-osa ʊkʊtɪ **f-iis-e**
      AUG-9-lion 9-NARR-8-tell-FV AUG-8-animal 8-all   COMP 8-come-SUBJ
      kʊ-lʊ-komaano
      17-11-meeting
      'Lion told all the animals to come to the meeting.' [Hare and Chameleon]

The subjunctive further alternates with the infinitive after predicative expressions of disapproval, approval or preference when reference is made to eventualities that are either not actualized (44, 45) or are potential (46). These clauses are sometimes introduced by the complementizer ʊkʊtɪ. For an example featuring the infinitive, see (12) on p. 326.

(44) kanunu **ʊ-pungusy-e=po**   ɪ-fy-ɪma   fy-ako   bʊle?
      well   2SG-reduce-SUBJ=PART AUG-8-thigh 8-POSS.2SG Q
      'Isn't it good that you should lose weight [lit. reduce a bit] from your thighs?' [Hare and Hippo]

(45) kyajɪpo   **tʊ-bʊʊk-ege**
      preferable 1PL-go-IPFV.SUBJ
      'We'd better get going.' [ET]

(46) l-oope lʊ-ka-a   lʊ-sumo lʊ-nunu ʊkʊtɪ ʊ-n-kiikʊlʊ
      11-also 11-NEG.be(come)-FV 11-custom 11-good COMP AUG-1-woman
      a-bomb-ege   ɪ-m-bombo n-gafu   bo ʊ-ɲ-dʊme   a-li=ko
      1-work-IPFV.SUBJ AUG-10-work 10-difficult as AUG-1-husband 1-COP=17
      m-ʊʊmi
      1-live
      'Also it is not good manners for a woman to do hard work while the husband is alive.' [Division of labour]

Similarly, it is used in a variety of subordinate clauses with reference to non-actualized eventualities:

(47) iijʊʊl-ege   ʊ-kʊ-fi-lond-a   **mpaka a-fy-ag-e**
      1.work_hard-IPFV.SUBJ AUG-15-8-search-FV until   1-8-find-SUBJ

      'He should try hard to get them (tools) until he gets them.' [Type of tools
      in the home]

(48) po kangɪ po a-lɪnkʊ-buj-a   ʊ-kw-is-a   pa-ka-aja
      then again then 1-NARR-return-FV AUG-15-come-FV 16-12-homestead

      pa-kʊ-ṇ-guul-ɪl-a   kajamba **ʊkʊtɪ iis-e**
      16-15-1-wait-APPL-FV tortoise(1) COMP 1.come-SUBJ

      'Then he [Monkey] returned to the home and waited for Tortoise to
      come.' [Monkey and Tortoise]

Lastly, the subjunctive is also used in purpose clauses (49) and result clauses
(50), which are introduced by the complementizer *ʊkʊtɪ*.

(49) popaa~po   kalʊlʊ a-lɪnkʊ-bop-a fiijo   **ʊkʊtɪ a-lʊ-kɪnd-e**
      REDUPL~then hare(1) 1-NARR-run-FV INTENS COMP 1-11-pass-SUBJ
      ʊ-lw-ifi
      AUG-11-chameleon

      'Hare ran fast to beat Chameleon.' [Hare and Chameleon]

(50) ba-ka-a-fi-lek-aga   panja **ʊkʊtɪ fi-nyop-ege**   n=ɪɪ-fula
      2-NEG-PST-8-let-IPFV outside COMP 8-get_wet-IPFV.SUBJ COM=AUG-rain(9)

      'They would not leave them [animals] outside so that they [animals]
      would get wet in the rain.' [Nyakyusa houses of long ago]

9.3.2 Complex constructions involving the subjunctive

A number of formally biclausal constructions contain subjunctive verbs as the
second element. What is common to all of them is that the first element is a form
of the versatile verb *tɪ* 'say' (§10.3).

A construction featuring an inflected form of *tɪ* together with a co-referential
subjunctive gives projective and conative readings.[7] This is often understood as
a frustrated intent:

---

[7]This construction is fairly common in south-eastern Bantu (Güldemann 1996: 153) and has
   grammaticalized to future tense marking in a number of languages of Bantu zones M and N
   (Botne 1998).

(51) bo i-kʊ-tɪ   a-kol-ege   ʊ-lw-igi   a-lʊ-kab-e
     as 1-PRS-say 1-grasp/hold-IPFV.SUBJ AUG-11-door 1-11-get-SUBJ
     kw-a-t-ile   "kóo".   a-a-kuut-ile   a-a-t-ile
     17-PST-say-PFV of_sickle_swinging 1-PST-cry-PFV 1-PST-say-PFV
     "ɪɪtaata!   m-fw-ile   hɪhɪhɪɪ"
     oh_father 1SG-die-PFV of_crying

     'When he tried to grab the door and get hold of it, there was the sound "kóo!" [of a sickle]. He cried "Oh father! I am dead, hihihii!"' [Wage of the thieves]

This, however, turns out to be an implicature rather than part of the meaning of the construction. This is illustrated in (52, 53). In (52), the referential demonstrative *syo* serves as the copulativecopula of the cleft sentence and refers to the information Hare has just given the woman and which has caused her to change her mind. In (53) the intended action is carried out in the following sentence.

(52) kalʊlʊ a-a-hobwike   fiijo   paapo ʊ-n-kiikʊlʊ
     hare(1) 1-PST-be(come)_happy.PFV INTENS because AUG-1-woman
     a-sambwike, Kalʊlʊ a-lɪnkʊ-tɪ "syo   ɪ-si   **n-d-ile**
     1-rebel.PFV, hare(1) 1-NARR-say REF.10 AUG-PROX.10 1SG-say-PFV
     n-gʊ-bʊʊl-e   ʊkʊtɪ ʊ-many-e"
     1SG-2SG-tell-SUBJ COMP 2SG-know-SUBJ

     'Hare was very happy because the woman had changed her mind, he said "That's what I wanted to tell you so that you know it."' [Hare and Spider]

(53) po leelo a-lɪnkw-is-a   ʊ-gw-a   bʊ-haano [...] po j-oope
     then but   1-NARR-come-FV AUG-1-ASSOC 14-five   then 1-also
     a-lɪnkʊ-tɪ ɪmb-ege   ʊ-lw-ɪmbo. j-oope a-lɪnkw-ɪmb-a
     1-NARR-say 1.sing-IPFV.SUBJ AUG-11-song 1-also 1-NARR-sing-FV
     a-lɪnkʊ-tɪ
     1-NARR-say

     'Then the fifth (child) came. It also wanted to sing the song. It also sang:' [Children and Snake]

The collocation of *fikʊtɪ*, which is the simple present of *tɪ* with a noun class 8 subject, together with a subjunctive verb as its complement denotes various kinds of dynamic and deontic necessity. Only one token of this collocation is attested in the data (54). Speakers accepted this construction in elicitation, but considered it somewhat archaic. It is frequent in older text collections. (55, 56) illustrate this (orthography adapted).

(54) kʊkʊtɪ mu-ndʊ **fi-kʊ-tɪ** a-j-ege   n=ʊ-tʊ-ndʊ
every 1-person 8-PRS-say 1-be(come)-IPFV.SUBJ COM=AUG-13-thing
t-oosa ʊ-tʊ   tʊ-kʊ-lond-igw-a   ʊ-kʊ-bomb-el-a
13-all AUG-PROX.13 13-PRS-want-PASS-FV AUG-15-work-APPL-FV
ɪ-m-bombo sy-ake
AUG-10-work 10-POSS.SG

'It is appropriate for every person to have all the things which are needed to do their work with.' [Types of tools in the home]

(55) lɪnga a-li=po ʊ-mu-ndʊ ʊ-jʊ i-kʊ-job-a na Kyala,
if/when 1-COP=16 AUG-1-person AUG-PROX.1 1-PRS-speak-FV COM god
po **fi-kʊ-tɪ** g-oope ʊ-m-piki gʊ-mo **gʊ-j-e=po**
then 8-PRS-say 3-also AUG-3-tree 3-one 3-be(come)-SUBJ=16

'When there is a person speaking with God, there must also be a tree.' (Busse 1949: 210)

(56) mwe ba-anangʊ, lɪlɪno a-pa ʊ-n-kiikʊlʊ ʊ-jʊ
1PL 2-my_child now/today AUG-PROX.16 AUG-1-woman AUG-PROX.1
a-a-lond-aga ʊ-kʊ-ba-gog-a, po **fi-kʊ-tɪ** na=nuuswe
1-PST-want-IPFV AUG-15-2PL-kill-FV then 8-PRS-say COM=COM.1PL
tʊ-ṇ-gog-e
1PL-1-kill-SUBJ

'My children, now that this woman has tried to kill you, it is up to us to kill her.' (Berger 1933: 143)

Lastly, the subjunctive of *tɪ* itself, together with a subjunctive complement, expresses obligation.[8] Interestingly, in this case the subjunctive of *tɪ* can be marked for past tense (58).

(57) **ba-tɪ b-iis-e** **m-ba-p-e=po** ɪɪ-heela
2-say 2-come-SUBJ 1SG-2-give-SUBJ=16 AUG-money(10)

'They must come so that I give them the money.' [ET]

(58) kʊʊ-nongwa j-aa kʊ-tɪ ɪɪ-ny-iiho sy-a ba-Nyakyʊsa
17-issue(9) 9-ASSOC 15-say AUG-10-custom 10-ASSOC 2-Ny.
si-kʊ-lond-a ʊkʊtɪ a-a-tɪ **a-ṃ-bonol-e** taasi po
10-PRS-want-FV COMP 1-PST-say.SUBJ 1-1-pay_brideprice-SUBJ yet then

---

[8]The lack of a simple present prefix is evidence for this form not belonging to the indicative paradigms.

bi-kʊ-keet-an-aga   n=ʊ-kʊ-ponani-a   kɪsita
2-MOD.FUT-look-RECP-MOD.FUT COM=AUG-greet.RECP-FV without
kʊ-tiil-an-a
15-fear-RECP-FV

'Because the traditions of the Nyakyusa people require that he should have paid her off first, then they shall look at each other and greet each other without fearing.' [Should she save a life...]

9.3.3 Distal/itive *ka-*

The subjunctive can be combined with a prefix *ka-*, which is commonly labelled *distal* or *itive*. This morpheme *ka-* is glossed as ɪTV throughout this study, with DIST being reserved for the distal demonstrative. Other common labels in the Bantuistic literature include *andative* or *ka movendi* (Nurse 2008: 242). Note that the distal/itive does not constitute a mood of its own, but rather a deictic category that in Nyakyusa is limited to the subjunctive mood. As the name suggests, distal/itive *ka-* locates the state-of-affairs away from the deictic centre (see also Botne 1999).[9] This often goes together with a sense of physical motion (59). Accordingly, it is commonly found after *bʊʊka* 'go (to)' (60, 61).

(59)   (ʊ-)**ka-sy-e**   ɪ-fi-lombe!
       (2SG-)ɪTV-grind-SUBJ AUG-8-maize

       'Go grind maize!' [ET]

(60)   po   leelo   ʊ-bʊʊk-e   kw-a   mwa=n-gambɪlɪ
       then now/but 2SG-go-SUBJ 17-ASSOC matronym=9-monkey
       ʊ-ka-m̩-bʊʊl-e   ʊkʊtɪ "taata   i-kʊ-sʊʊm-a a-m-ungu,
       2SG-ɪTV-1-tell-SUBJ COMP   my_father 1-PRS-beg-FV AUG-6-pumpkin
       n=ɪ-m-bilipili   na=a-ma-sɪmbɪ   n=ii-seeke."
       COM=AUG-10-pepper COM=AUG-6-cocoyam COM=5-sidedish

       'Go to Mr. Monkey and tell him "Father begs for pumpkins, peppers, cocoyam and a sidedish."'

---

[9]Lusekelo (2013: 106–109) lists this as "narrative ka-" on the sole basis that in other Bantu languages a segmentally identical prefix is used for several kinds of past time reference, only to then state (p. 108) that it "represents future tense as well in Kinyakyusa". All examples listed by Lusekelo include subjunctive final -*e(ge)* and, although they sometimes appear in past contexts, from his own translation as well as from the distribution of the morpheme it is clear that all these cases belong to the subjunctive paradigm.

ʊ-ka-tɪ   ɪɪ-heela   n-gʊ-twal-aga
2SG-ITV-say.SUBJ AUG-money(10) 1SG-MOD.FUT-carry-MOD.FUT

ʊ-ṇ-dʊngʊ ʊ-gʊ   gʊ-kw-is-a
AUG-3-week AUG-PROX.3 3-PRS-come-FV

'Say that the money I will bring next week.' [Monkey and Tortoise]

(61)   mu-bʊʊk-e mwe ba-ndʊ b-angʊ   nuumwe **mu-ka-kol-e**
2PL-go-SUBJ 2PL 2-person 2-POSS.1SG COM.2PL 2PL-ITV-grasp/hold-SUBJ

ɪ-n-galamu **mu-ka-twal-e**   ɪɪ-ny-ʊʊmi!
AUG-9-lion 2PL-ITV-carry-SUBJ AUG-9-live

'You, my people, you too go catch a lion and bring it alive!' [Chief Kapyungu]

While distal/itive *ka-* often goes together with a sense of physical motion of the subject, this is not always the case. In (62), people plan to take a guitar string, which is made from the dead body of a child, to a witch doctor, who will then bring the child back to life. It is thus not the subject of the distal/itive-marked subjunctive (the witch doctor) that moves, but his actions happen at a place other than the deictic centre. See also (52) on p. 266 for an example of a motion event that is displaced elsewhere.

(62)   baatɪ po ɪ-li-ndʊ   ɪ-lɪ   tʊ-lɪ-gog-e   ʊkʊtɪ
INTERJ then AUG-5-monster AUG-PROX.5 1PL-5-kill-SUBJ COMP

tw-eg-e   ɪ-kɪ-sipa   kɪ-la mw-i-pango, tʊ-twal-e
1PL-take-SUBJ AUG-7-string 7-DIST 18-5-guitar   1PL-carry-SUBJ

kʊ-ṇ-ganga. **a-ka-ṃ-buj-ɪsy-e**   ʊ-mw-ana
17-1-healer 1-ITV-1-return-CAUS-SUBJ AUG-1-child

'Look, that monster, we should kill it so that we take that string in the guitar and bring it to the witch doctor. [So that] he'll make the child return.' [Monster with guitar]

The following examples illustrate some more uses of *ka-* in environments other than directives and requests.

(63)   Volitive:
po ɪɪ-sota   bo jɪ-fum-ile   n-kʊ-jaat-a   jɪ-lɪnkʊ-tɪ
then AUG-python(9) as 9-come_from-PFV 18-15-walk-FV 9-NARR-say

"**n-ga-keet-e**   ii-fumbɪ ly-angʊ"
1SG-ITV-watch-SUBJ 5-egg   5-POSS.1SG

'Python, when it had come from taking a walk, said "I'll go look after my egg."' [Python and woman]

(64) Hortative:

is-aga   tʊ-bʊʊk-e   **tʊ-ka-m̩-bʊʊl-e**   ʊ-n-kʊlʊmba gw-ɪtʊ
come-IPFV 1PL-go-SUBJ 1PL-ITV-1-tell-SUBJ AUG-1-older   1-POSS.1PL

gw-a   fi-nyamaana fy-osa ɪɪ-sofu   ʊkʊtɪ a-koolel-e
1-ASSOC 8-animal   8-all   AUG-elephant(9) COMP 1-call-SUBJ

ʊ-lʊ-komaano
AUG-11-meeting

'Come, let's go and tell our eldest among all animals, Elephant, that he should call a meeting.' [Hare and Chameleon]

(65) Subordinate clause, modality verb:

m-bagiile   ʊ-kʊ-kʊ-tol-a   ʊ-gwe ʊ-kʊ-bop-a   ʊ-lʊ-bɪlo,
1SG-be_able.PFV AUG-15-2SG-beat-FV AUG-2SG AUG-15-run-FV AUG-11-race

paapo kw-end-a   panandɪ~panandɪ. m-bagiile   ʊkʊtɪ
because 2SG.PRS-walk/travel-FV REDUPL~a_little   1SG-be_able.PFV COMP

n-ga-fik-e   kʊ-bʊ-malɪŋkɪsyo n=ʊ-kʊ-gomok-a   bo ʊ-kaalɪ
1SG-ITV-arrive-SUBJ 17-14-finish   COM=AUG-15-return-FV as 2SG-PERS

ʊ-lɪ   pala~pa-la   n-gʊ-lek-ile
2SG-COP REDUPL~16-DIST 1SG-2SG-let-PFV

'I can beat you in running, because you walk slowly. I can [go] reach the end and return while you are still there where I left you.' [Hare and Chameleon]

(66) Subordinate clause of purpose:

a-a-bʊngeenie   a-ma-tunda ʊkʊtɪ lʊmo **a-k-ʊʊl-ɪsy-e**
1-PST-gather.PFV AUG-6-fruit COMP maybe 1-ITV-buy-CAUS-SUBJ

'He gathered the fruits to maybe go and sell them.' [Nicholaus Pear Story]

The distal/itive subjunctive can be combined with desiderative *lɪ-*, yielding *ka-lɪ-VB-e-(ge)*. This is discussed in §9.4. Note that distal/itive *ka-* is only found in affirmative forms. As with the bare subjunctive, it is negated by the negative counterpart to the subjunctive.

9.3.4 Negative Subjunctive

The negative counterpart to the subjunctive consists of *nga-* in the post-initial slot and the default final vowel *-a* or imperfective *-aga*. Contrary to the directive use of the affirmative subjunctive, the use of a subject marker is obligatory in this construction.

(67)   *tʊngajoba* 'we should not speak'

The negative subjunctive prefix is also attested with a variant form *ngɪ-*. This is much less frequent in the data and seems to be typical of the more northern variants of Nyakyusa. With the first person singular, the combination of subject prefix and negative prefix yields *ndɪnga-* (68). Schumann (1899: 34f) and Endemann (1914: 73f) have *n-anga-*. The speakers consulted considered this typical of the variety of the lake-shore plains.

(68)   *ndɪngajoba* 'I should not speak'

The uses of the negative subjunctive essentially parallel those of its affirmative counterpart. Some of these are illustrated in the following examples.

(69)   Prohibitive:
       ʊ-nga-gel-a   ʊ-kʊ-ly-a   ɪ-fi-ndʊ   ɪ-fi!
       2SG-NEG.SUBJ-try-FV AUG-15-eat-FV AUG-8-food AUG-PROX.8
       'Don't you dare eat that food!' [ET]

(70)   Prohibitive plural:
       n-gʊ-ba-asim-a,   looli **aa=mu-nga-sob-esy-a**
       1SG-PRS-2PL-lend-FV but   FUT=2PL-NEG.SUBJ-get_lost-CAUS-FV
       ɪɪ-sindaano   j-angʊ
       AUG-needle(9)(<SWA) 9-POSS.1SG
       'I'm lending it to you, but don't lose my needle.' [Chickens and crow]

(71)   Indirect prohibitive:
       a-m-bʊʊl-ile ʊkʊtɪ **n-dɪnga-bomb-a**
       1-1SG-tell-PFV COMP 1SG-NEG.SUBJ-work-FV
       'He told me not to work.' [ET]

(72)   Negative Hortative:
       tʊ-nga-j-aga   n=ɪ-fi-nyonyo   bo ɪɪ-fubu
       1PL-NEG.SUBJ-be(come)-IPFV COM=AUG-8-desire as AUG-hippo(9)
       ɪ-jɪ   j-aa-fw-ile   kʊʊ-nongwa ɪ-j-aa   fi-londa bo
       AUG-PROX.9 9-PST-die-PFV 17-issue(9)   AUG-9-ASSOC 8-wound as
       jɪ-kʊ-lond-a   ʊ-bʊ-nunu
       9-PRS-search-FV AUG-14-beauty
       'We should not have desire like Hippo, who died because of his sores, when he was looking for beauty.' [Hare and Hippo]

(73) Negative Jussive:

ŋ-dʊme   gw-angʊ, tʊ-lond-e   fi-mo ɪ-fy-a
1-husband 1-POSS.1SG 1PL-search-SUBJ 8-one AUG-8-ASSOC
kʊ-n-teg-el-a   kalʊlʊ ʊkʊtɪ ii-kol-e   tʊ-n-gog-e.
15-1-trap-APPL-FV hare(1) COMP 1.REFL-grasp/hold-SUBJ 1PL-1-kill-SUBJ
a-ng-and-ɪsy-a   ʊ-kʊ-ly-a   ɪ-fi-lombe   fy-ɪtʊ
1-NEG.SUBJ-begin-CAUS-FV AUG-15-eat-FV AUG-8-maize 8-POSS.1PL
paapo   i-kʊ-mal-a
because 1-PRS-finish-FV

'My husband, let's look for something to trap Hare, so that he gets caught and we kill him. He mustn't eat our maize again, because he's finishing it.' [Saliki and Hare]

(74) Negative purpose clause:

ba-lɪnkw-inogon-a ʊ-kʊ-tɪ   "tʊ-bʊʊk-e   tʊ-k-iip-e
2-NARR-think-FV   AUG-15-say 1PL-go-SUBJ 1PL-ITV-pluck-SUBJ
ɪ-ly-ʊndʊ   ɪ-ly-a   kʊ-gelek-el-a   kʊ-mwanya" ʊkʊtɪ
AUG-5-thatching_grass AUG-5-ASSOC 15-thatch-APPL 17-up   COMP
ba-ngɪ-toony-el-igw-aga
2-NEG.SUBJ-drip-APPL-PASS-IPFV

'They thought "We should go pluck grass for thatching the roof with", so that they would not get wet.' [Throw away the child]

Like its affirmative counterpart, the negative subjunctive is also used together with modality and manipulation verbs, where it alternates with the infinitive. Verbs with an inherently negative meaning, such as *kaaniysa* 'forbid' and *sigɪla* 'prevent', only take the negative subjunctive:

(75) a. a-ba-ganga   ba-n-kaniisye ʊkʊtɪ a-nga-kin-a   ʊ-m-pɪla
         AUG-2-healer 2-1-forbid.PFV COMP 1-NEG.SUBJ-play-FV AUG-3-ball

         'The doctors have forbidden him/her to play football.' [ET]

   b. * a-ba-ganga   ba-n-kaniisye ʊkʊtɪ a-kin-e   ʊ-m-pɪla
         AUG-2-healer 2-1-forbid.PFV COMP 1-play-SUBJ AUG-3-ball

As is the case in the affirmative subjunctive, the imperfective suffix -*aga* has a general or habitual reading; see (72, 74) above. It also has a continuous reading (76), as well as a mitigating one with directives (77).[10]

(76) n-uɱ-bʊʊl-ile ʊkʊtɪ a-nga-nw-aga   fiijo
      1SG-1-tell-PFV COMP 1-NEG.SUBJ-drink-IPFV INTENS

      'I have told him that he should not be drinking too much.' [ET]

(77) ʊ-nga-paasy-aga
      2SG-NEG.SUBJ-worry-IPFV

      'Don't worry!' [overheard]

Lastly, a prefix *lɪ-*, homophonous or identical to the desiderative (§9.4) is sometimes found preceding negative *nga-* (78, 79). The fact that it is only attested in the written material and was not spontaneously offered suggests that the employment of this prefix constitutes a case of stylistic variation.

(78) lɪnga   a-agiilwe fi-mo **a-lɪ-nga-asim-aga**   bwila,
      if/when 1-lack.PFV 8-one 1-?-NEG.SUBJ-borrow-IPFV always

      iijʊʊl-ege   ʊ-kʊ-fi-lond-a
      1.work_hard-IPFV.SUBJ AUG-15-8-search-FV

      'If he lacks something, he should not always borrow, he should try hard
      to get them.' [Types of tools in the home]

(79) ijolo   ɲ-dw-iho   lw-a   ba-Nyakyʊsa ba-a-lɪ
      old_times 18-11-custom 11-ASSOC 2-Ny.   2-PST-COP

      na=a-ka-jɪɪlo   k-a   n-kiikʊlʊ ʊ-kʊ-n-tiil-a
      COM=AUG-12-custom 12-ASSOC 1-woman AUG-15-1-fear-FV

      ʊ-gwise   gw-a   ɲ-dʊme,   ʊ-jʊ   tʊ-kʊ-tɪ
      AUG-his_father(1) 1-ASSOC 1-husband, AUG-PROX.1 1PL-PRS-say

      n-kamwana.
      1-in_law

      'Long ago in the tradition of the Nyakyusa people they had a custom of
      the woman fearing the father of her husband, whom we call Nkamwana.'

---

[10]Schumann (1899: 34), concerning the negative subjunctive, observes that -*aga* "is very common with this form" (translated from the original German, BP). According to Nurse (1979), with verbs of movement in the imperative as well as with its negative counterpart -*aga* is obligatory; however, this could not be confirmed. Mwangoka & Voorhoeve (1960c) states that -*aga* is obligatory in the negative subjunctive, but this is contradicted by the data, see i.a (73) above.

mpaka pa-la   lɪnga   a-m̩-bonwile   ʋkʋtɪ a-lɪ-nga-n-tiil-aga
until   16-DIST if/when 1-1-pay_off.PFV COMP 1-?-NEG.SUBJ-1-fear-IPFV

'Until the moment that he has paid her off so that she need not fear him any more.' [Should she save a life...]

9.4 Desiderative

The desiderative construction consists of a prefix *lɪ-* and the final vowel *-a*.

(80)   *tʋlɪjoba* 'we'd like to speak'

The desiderative is hardly attested at all in the text corpus. Much of the following discussion is therefore based on elicitation. As the label *desiderative* and example (80) above suggest, this construction expresses a desire or preference for a state-of-affairs. Discussions of modality in language have come to include a concept of *bouletic* (also *boulemaic*) modality, which concerns "what is possible or necessary, given a person's desires" (von Fintel 2006: 2), or, as Nuyts (2005: 12) puts it, "indicates the degree of the speaker's (or someone else's) liking or disliking of the state of affairs". This type of modality to all appearances lies at the semantic core of the desiderative construction.[11] In this the desiderative – like the subjunctive, with which some overlaps on the paradigmatic level are found (see below) – is confined to states-of-affairs that are not actualized.

In declaratives sentences with a first or second person subject, the desiderative expresses the speaker's desire or preference. Thus the first person singular desiderative in (81) denotes the speaker's preference for a future act of his/her own, while in (82) the speaker desires that the act be performed by the hearer, the second person singular subject. For examples of the first and second person plural respectively, see (83, 84) below.

(81)   n-dɪ-syal-a   pa-ka-aja
       1SG-DESDTV-remain-FV 16-12-homestead

       'I'd rather stay at home (e.g. than join you in your activity).' [ET]

---

[11]Interestingly, for Nyika M23, spoken northwest of Nyakyusa, and Nyikas's western neighbour Namwanga M22 Busse (1940: 70; 1960: 45) gives a future prefix *li-*. Malila M24, according to Kutsch Lojenga (2007: 85), has a future prefix *lɪ(ɪ)-*. Given the well-known path of grammaticalization from desire to future (Bybee et al. 1994), these prefixes might have a common source.

(82) ʊ-lɪ-tem-a=po   ii-bɪfu   ɪ-lɪ
      2SG-DESDTV-2PL-cut-FV=PART 5-banana AUG-PROX.5

      'I would like you to [i.e. please] cut off this banana.' [ET]

The preceding example (82) represents the most common use of the desiderative, namely in polite requests. In fact, it is only in this use that the desiderative was spontaneously offered during elicitation sessions. Polite requests are also the only use attested in older text collections, as well as in a recent draft of a Bible translation. The following two examples will illustrate this (orthography adapted):[12]

(83) Context: Children see guineafowls scarifying each other.
      mwe ma-kanga   ʊ-mwe, **mu-lɪ-tʊ-tem-a=po**   nuuswe
      2PL   6-guineafowl AUG-2PL 2PL-DESDTV-cut-FV=PART COM.1PL

      'You guineafowls, please cut us a bit, too.' (Berger 1933: 116)

(84) Context: A group of children are looking for a place to spend the night.
      They call at a stranger's house.
      ʊ-n-kangale a-a-t-ile: "eena, mu-gon-ile! mwe ba-ani?"
      AUG-1-old   1-PST-say-PFV   yes   2PL-rest-PFV 2PL   2-who

      a-ba-anike   ba-a-t-ile: "jo   ʊ-swe, tʊ-sob-ile
      AUG-2-young_person 2-PST-say-PFV   REF.1 AUG-1PL 1PL-be_lost.PFV

      ɪ-n-jɪla   j-ɪɪtʊ,   **tʊ-lɪ-gon-a=mo**"
      AUG-9-path 9-POSS.1PL 1PL-DESDTV-rest-FV=18

      'The old woman said: "Hello! Who are you?" The chidren said: "It's us, we've lost our way and would like to sleep."' (Berger 1933: 137)

During discussions of examples such as (82 – 84), the language assistants remarked on various occasions that a request formulated in the desiderative specifically leaves the choice to the hearer, who may accept or decline. Similarly, in hortatives the desiderative is considered more of a suggestion (85a) than the subjunctive, which has a stronger character of a prompt or appeal (85b).

(85) a. tʊ-lɪ-ly-a=mo
          1PL-DESDTV-eat-FV=some

          'I'd like us to eat something.' [ET]

---

[12] *mugonile* 'lit. you (pl.) have rested', as in (84), sg. *ʊgonile* is the most common greeting formula amongst the Nyakyusa people.

b. tʊ-ly-e=mo
   1PL-eat-SUBJ=some
   'Let's eat something!' [ET]

With third person subjects, the interpretation depends on context and co-text. With a non-agentive subject the issuer of the modality is the speaker (86). With an agentive subject both the speaker and the subject are available as the source of the desire or preference (87).

(86) ʊ-mw-enda ʊ-gʊ   gʊ-lɪ-j-a   mw-elu
      AUG-3-cloth AUG-PROX.3 3-DESDTV-be(come)-FV 3-white

      'I'd prefer it if this cloth were white.' [ET]

(87) ıı-ng'ombe   si-lɪ-jong-a
      AUG-cow(10) 10-DESDTV-run_away-FV

      1. 'The cows would like to escape (uttered e.g. as a warning).'
      2. 'I wish that the cows would run away (e.g. malicious thinking).' [ET]

In questions with a first or second person subject, the modal assessment shifts to the hearer (see Lehmann 2012 on the role of the modal assessor). With a first person subject, this is typically understood as a request for approval, as in (88). Likewise in (89) – the sole token of the desiderative in the text corpus – Hare asks Hippo whether the latter likes or dislikes the plan of visiting girls in town. Also note the paraphrasis in the last clause. With a second person as the subject, the desiderative in questions is often understood as a request (90).

(88) Context: parent to child.
      ka-kam-e   ıı-ng'ombe! **n-dɪ-kin-a=po**   taasi ʊ-m-pɪla?
      ITV-milk-SUBJ AUG-cow(10) 1SG-DESDTV-play-FV=PART yet   AUG-3-ball

      'Go milk the cows!' – 'May I first play football for a bit?' [ET]

(89) gw-ıtʊ   n-ka-aja   ka-la ba-a-li=ko   a-ba-lındwana a-ba-nunu
      1-POSS.1PL 18-12-village 12-DIST 2-PST-COP=17 AUG-2-girl   AUG-2-good
      fiijo.   **aa=tʊ-lɪ-jaat-a=ko?**
      INTENS FUT=1PL-DESDTV-walk-FV=17

      'Friend, in that town there were very beautiful girls. Should we go and visit them?'

      m-ba-bʊʊl-ile ʊkʊtı a=n-gw-is-a   n=ʊ-m-manyaani gw-angʊ.
      1SG-2-tell-PFV COMP FUT=1SG-PRS-COME-FV COM=AUG-1-friend 1-POSS.SG

bʊle gw-igan-ile ʊkutɪ tʊ-bʊʊk-e tw-esa?
Q 2SG-like-PFV COMP 1PL-go-SUBJ 1PL-all

'I have told them that I will come with my friend. Hey, would you like it, if we both go?' [Hare and Hippo]

(90) **ʊ-lɪ-m-b-a=ko** ɪ-fi-ndʊ?
2SG-DESDTV-1SG-give-FV=17 AUG-8-food

'Will you give us food?' [ET]

In questions with a third person subject, as with declaratives, the source of the modality may be either the hearer or the subject:

(91) a-ba-ndʊ ba-la ba-l-ingɪl-a n-nyumba?
AUG-2-person 2-DIST 2-DESDTV-enter-FV 18-house

1. 'Do you wish that those people go inside?'
2. 'Will those people go inside?'[ET]

The desiderative can take the imperfective suffix -*aga*. This can be used to add a continuous reading, which can shade into an emphatic one (92). It is also used to express a desire or preference for a regular/habitual occurrence. (93).

(92) tʊ-lɪ-bʊʊk-aga
1PL-DESDTV-go-IPFV

'I'd like us to g̀et going.' [ET]

(93) ʊ-lɪ-m-b-aga ɪ-fi-ndʊ kʊkʊtɪ ii-sikʊ
2SG-DESDTV-1SG-give-IPFV AUG-8-food every 5-day

'I'd like you to give me food every day.' [ET]

The desiderative can also be augmented by the distal/itive prefix *ka-* (§9.3.3), in which case the quality of the final vowel changes to -*e*, as is the case in the subjunctive.[13]

(94) ʊ-lɪ-k-iigʊl-e
2SG-DESDTV-ITV-open-FV

'Please go open the door.' [ET]

Unlike the subjunctive, the affirmative desiderative is excluded from subordinate clauses:

---

[13]One might take this as evidence for a circumfix *ka-...-e*, as Nicolle (2002) assumes for Digo E72.

(95) * n-aalɪ-ɳ-dagiile   ʊkʊtɪ a-lɪ-jeng-a   ɪɪ-nyumba
     1SG-PST-1-order.PFV COMP 1-DSDTV-build-FV AUG-house(9)
     (intended: 'I told him/her to please build a house.')

(96) * n-gʊ-lond-a   ʊkʊtɪ ʊ-l-iigʊl-a   ʊ-lw-igi
     1SG-PRS-want.FV COMP 2SG-DSDTV-open-FV AUG-11-door
     (intended: 'I wish you to please open the door.')

(97) * n-aalɪ-m-peele   ɪ-n-dalama   ʊkʊtɪ a-ly-ʊl-a   ɪ-fi-ndʊ
     1SG-PST-1-give.PFV AUG-10-money COMP 1-DSDTV-buy-FV AUG-8-food
     (intended: 'I gave him money so that he could buy food.')

(98) * kyajɪpo / paakipo   / kanunu tʊ-lɪ-bʊʊk-a
     better   preferable well   1PL-DESDV-go-FV
     (intended: 'It is better/preferable/good that we go.')

Lastly, the desiderative is negated with the negative counterpart to the subjunctive, which is discussed in (§9.3.4).

9.5 Modal future

The last modal paradigm to be discussed constitutes an interesting case of constructionalization. As the simple present (§6.5.1), in the affirmative it is formed with a subject prefix from the second series (§3.3.2) and a prefix *kʊ-*, while the negative consists of a subject prefix from the first series and the negative prefix *ti-* preceding *kʊ-*. Unlike the simple present, however, the final slot is filled by the imperfective suffix *-aga* and its allomorphs; see §6.4.1.

In contrast with what would be expected from the composition of this construction, it cannot have a present continuous or habitual/generic reading. Instead it expresses a future-oriented type of modality. The same situation is found in neighbouring Kinga G65 and Vwanji G66 (Eaton, to appear). The following example illustrates this:

(99) tʊ-kʊ-ly-aga   ʊ-m-pʊnga
     1PL-PRS-eat-IPFV AUG-1-rice

     'We shall eat rice. (e.g. announcing the next meal or a change in diet)'
     not: 'We are eating rice.'
     not: 'We eat rice.' [ET]

This construction, which will be labelled MODAL FUTURE throughout this study, depicts a future state-of-affairs as a settled fact; that is, it expresses various kinds of modal necessity.

While this semantics may at first seem odd given the composition of the modal future, this apparent mismatch of form and function may be explained by taking a comparative and diachronic perspective. In various languages of the wider area, e.g. the Tanzanian variety of neighbouring Ndali (Swilla 1998), Kisi G67 (Gray n.d.) and Malila M24 (Helen Eaton, p.c.) the imperfective suffix -*aga* narrows down the possible readings of the simple present to an explicitly habitual one. As Ziegeler (2006: 21) states, habitual or generic aspect – note that not all authors distinguish between these two, and while some consider habituality a special case of genericity, others use the terms interchangeably – is a "prime candidate for [...] categories residing on the aspect-modality interface"; see also Givón (1994). In formal semantics, generic sentences are commonly understood as law-like generalizations about the *most normal* cases (Krifka et al. 1995), a qualification necessary to account for the possibility of exceptions. Stating such a regularity implies a prediction that, all things being normal, the eventuality in question will continue to occur in the future. A similar observation has been made by Brinton (1988: 140f). Assuming that at an earlier stage the situation in Nyakyusa paralleled the one found in Tanzanian Ndali, Kisi and Malila, the present-day semantics of the modal future can be understood as the semanticization of this future-oriented implicature. For a more detailed elaboration of this reconstruction see Persohn (2016).

A verbal construction with a number of striking functional similarities is found in Yucatec Maya *he-...-e'*. Lehmann (2012) calls this a "commissive modality" construction, while Bohnemeyer (2002) speaks of "assurative". As both these labels feature notions which rather belong to the realm of pragmatics, the more neutral, albeit vague label *modal future* is preferred.

The following exposition of its uses will illustrate the meaning of the modal future. To begin with, the modal future is employed in generic contexts to depict consequences and sequences of eventualities. In (100), an excerpt from an expository text is given. The modal future construction is found to express determined consequences of specific behaviour in (100a, 100f, 100g). In (100d) it is used to depict the next step in a series of acts.

(100) Context: Discussing men who do not own tools.

    a. kʊʊ-nongwa ɪ-jo   lɪnga   ʊ-n-nyambala a-bagiile
       17-issue   AUG-REF.9 if/when AUG-1-man   1-be_able.PFV

ʊ-kʊ-tol-igw-a   ʊ-kʊ-mmw-ag-a ʊ-n-kiikʊlʊ   ʊ-gw-a
AUG-15-defeat-PASS-FV AUG-15-1-find-FV AUG-1-woman AUG-1-ASSOC
kʊ-mmw-eg-a, a-ba-ndʊ   **bi-kʊ-mmw-inogon-aga**
15-1-marry-FV AUG-2-person 2-MOD.FUT-1-think-MOD.FUT
ʊ-mu-ndʊ   ʊ-jo   ʊkʊtɪ m-oolo pa-kʊ-bomb-a ɪ-m-bombo
AUG-1-person AUG-REF.1 COMP 1-lazy   16-15-work-FV AUG-9-work

'Because of this, if a man is unable to get a woman to marry, people (will) think that this person is lazy in doing work.'

b. a-ba-ndʊ   bo a-bo   bi-kʊ-bʊʊk-a kʊ-kw-asim-a
AUG-2-person as AUG-REF.2 2-PRS-go-FV   17-15-borrow-FV
ɪ-fi-bombelo ɪ-fy-a   kʊ-bomb-el-a   ɪ-m-bombo bo
AUG-8-tool   AUG-8-ASSOC 15-work-APPL-FV AUG-9-work as
a-b-iinaabo   ba-lɪ pa-kʊ-tʊʊsy-a
AUG-2-their_companion 2-COP 16-15-rest-FV

'People like those go to borrow tools to do work with, when their fellows are resting.'

c. bo ba-m-peele ɪ-fi-bombelo, a-ka-bagɪl-a
as 2-1-give.PFV AUG-8-tool   1-NEG-be_able-FV
ʊ-kʊ-bomb-el-a   a-ka-balɪlo a-ka-tali
AUG-15-work-APPL-FV AUG-12-time AUG-12-long

'When they have given him tools, he cannot work with them for a long time.'

d. lʊmo bo a-bomb-ile=po   panandɪ **kw-ag-aga**
maybe as 1-work-PFV=PART a_little   2SG.MOD.FUT-find-MOD.FUT
a-b-eene   na=fyo   b-iis-ile   kʊ-kw-eg-a
AUG-2-owner COM=REF.8 2-come-PFV 17-15-take-FV

'Or when he has worked for a little while, you will find they have come to take them back.'

e. ʊ-ka-bagɪl-a   ʊ-kʊ-kaan-il-a   paapo
AUG-12-be_able-FV AUG-15-refuse-APPL-FV because
fi-ka-j-a   fy-ako,   kʊ-gomosy-a
8-NEG-be(come)-FV 8-POSS.2SG 2SG.PRS-return.CAUS-FV

'You cannot refuse, because they are not yours, you return them.'

f. lɪnga   kʊ-kaabɪl-a   ʊ-kʊ-gomosy-a
if/when 2SG.PRS-be_late-FV AUG-15-return.CAUS-FV

> **bi-kʊ-kw-im-aga**   bwila
> 2-MOD.FUT-2SG-deprive-MOD.FUT always
>
> 'If you delay in returning, they will withhold them always.'

   g. po   **kʊ-kʊbɪlw-aga**   n=ɪ-n-jala
>   then 2SG.MOD.FUT-suffer-MOD.FUT COM=AUG-9-hunger
>
>   n=ʊ-kʊ-j-a   n-kunwe bwila
>   COM=AUG-15-be(come)-FV 1-poor   always
>
>   'And so you will be troubled by hunger and always be poor.' [Types
>   of tools in the home]

As was observed earlier, the modal future does not allow for a timeless reading. Likewise, it is infeliticious in contexts expressing scheduled eventualities (101, 102). (101) could however be said of a new train that does not yet run but is announced to leave in the afternoon. Likewise, (102) is felicitous as a resolution about a new work schedule.

(101)   Context: According to schedule.
>   #ii-treni   li-kʊ-sook-anga=po   pa-muu-si
>   5-train(<SWA) 5-MOD.FUT-leave-MOD.FUT=16 16-3-daytime
>
>   (intended: 'The train leaves in the afternoon.')

(102)   Context: According to contract.
>   #pa-kɪ-tatʊ tʊ-ti-kʊ-bomb-aga   ɪ-m-bombo
>   16-7-three 1PL-NEG-MOD.FUT-work-MOD.FUT AUG-9-work
>
>   (intended: 'We do not work this Wednesday/on Wednesdays.')

Closely related to the preceding examples, the modal future is very common in commissive speech acts. These are utterances which "commit the speaker to a certain cause of events" (Austin 1962: 156). The following examples illustrate prototypical cases: (103) features a promise, (104) an assurance and (105) an announcement. In all of these the speaker vouches that the future state-of-affairs will occur.

(103)   Context: A girl has eloped with a man. Her father has tracked them
>   down.
>   taata ʊ-ne   nalooli ɪ-fy-ʊm-a   n-gaalɪ n-ga-kab-a
>   father AUG-1SG really   AUG-8-bride_price 1SG-PERS 1SG-NEG-get-FV
>
>   ɪɪ-sala   ɪ-jɪ.   looli **n-gw-i-pʊʊl-aga**.
>   AUG-hour(9) AUG-PROX.9 but   1SG-MOD.FUT-REFL-thresh-MOD.FUT

n-gʊ-homb-a   ɪ-fy-ʊma   fi-la   bo ʊlʊ n-iitiike
1SG-PRS-pay-FV AUG-8-bride_price 8-DIST as   now 1SG-agree.PFV
m̩-ba-ndʊ
18-2-person

'Father [honorific], I still haven't obtained the brideprice. But I'll go after
it. I'm paying that brideprice, just as I've now agreed to in front of
people.' [Man and his in-law]

(104) Context: Hare and Spider want to climb up a tree.
looli kalʊlʊ a-ka-a-meenye   ʊ-kʊ-kwel-a m-mwanya,
but   hare(1) 1-NEG-PST-know.PFV AUG-15-climb 18-up
a-lɪnkʊ-lʊ-bʊʊl-a ʊ-lʊ-bʊbi   a-lɪnkʊ-tɪ "ʊ-ne   n-ga-many-a
1-NARR-11-tell-FV AUG-11-spider 1-NARR-say AUG-1SG 1SG-NEG-know-FV
ʊ-kʊ-kwel-a   m-mwanya"
AUG-15-climb-FV 18-up

'But Hare could not climb up there, he told Spider "I can't climb up
there."'

ʊ-lʊ-bʊbi   lʊ-lɪnkʊ-job-a   ʊkʊtɪ "ʊ-nga-paasy-aga.
AUG-11-spider 11-NARR-speak-FV COMP 2SG-NEG.SUBJ-worry-IPFV
ʊ-ne   n-dɪ   na=bo   ʊ-bʊ-ʊsi   ʊ-bʊ
AUG-1SG 1SG-COP COM=REF.14 AUG-14-thread AUG-PROX.14
bʊ-kʊ-n-dwal-a   ʊ-ne,   mo
14-PRS-1SG-carry-FV AUG-1SG REF.18
kw-end-anga=mo   nungwe"
2SG.MOD.FUT-walk/travel-MOD.FUT=18 COM.2SG

Spider said "Don't worry. I have a thread that carries me, you too will go
on it."' [Hare and Spider]

(105) Context: Elephant, in his function as the eldest of animals, has called a
meeting.
ɪɪ-sofu   jɪ-lɪnkʊ-tɪ   "lɪlɪno
AUG-elephant(9) 9-NARR-say   now/today
tʊ-kʊ-ba-keet-aga   kalʊlʊ n=ʊ-lw-ifi
1PL-MOD.FUT-2-watch-MOD.FUT hare(1) COM=AUG-11-chameleon
bi-kʊ-j-a   pa-kʊ-tol-an-a   ʊ-lʊ-bɪlo"
2-PRS-be(come)-FV 16-15-win-RECP-FV AUG-11-race

'Elephant said "Today we shall see how Hare and Chameleon are going
to compete in a race."' [Hare and Chameleon]

The modal future is also found with a certain directive force. This use is especially common when describing the target procedure of a plan involving the hearer, as in the following example:

(106)   Context: Tortoise explains to his child how to make Monkey believe he is absent.

po   a-pa   n-dʊʊgeele. po   a-n-gw-i-sanusy-a.
then AUG-PROX.16 1SG-stay.PFV then FUT=1SG-PRS-REFL-alter.CAUS-FV

a-ma-lʊndɪ gi-kʊ-keet-a   kʊ-mwanya. po   ʊ-gwe
AUG-6-leg   6-PRS-watch-FV 17-high   then AUG-2SG

kʊ-lond-a   ii-bwe, kʊ-kol-a.   kʊ-bɪɪk-a
2SG.PRS-search-FV 5-stone 2SG.PRS-grasp/hold-FV 2SG.PRS-put-FV

ɪ-fi-lombe   pa-mwanya pa-my-angʊ.
AUG-8-maize 16-high   16-4-POSS.1SG

'Here I stay, I'll turn myself over. The legs will look up. You'll search for a stone and grasp it. You'll put maize on top of me.'

po   **lʊ-kʊ-fwan-aga**   lw-ala.   po
then 11-MOD.FUT-resemble-MOD.FUT 11-grindstone then

kʊ-sy-aga
2SG.MOD.FUT-grind-MOD.FUT

'It'll resemble a grindstone. Then you shall grind.' [Monkey and Tortoise]

Interestingly, all tokens of the modal future within interrogatives in the text corpus constitute rhetorical questions. Thus, in (107), the question is raised as to what it is that a woman will necessarily do when she sees her father-in-law in danger of dying and whether this will involve letting him drown. The answers – to help and not let him drown – are implied in the co-text of this behavioural text, which criticizes the tradition of in-law avoidance. In (108) the narrator employs a dramatic ruse by letting the trapped protagonist ask himself if his death in a pit constitutes his inevitable fate, only to let him answer to the contrary with the actions that follow.

(107)   Context: Discussing the tradition of in-law avoidance.

leelo   lɪnga   ʊ-gwise   gw-a   n-nyambala ɳ-gaala
now/but if/when AUG-his_father(1) 1-ASSOC 1-man   1-drink

bw-alwa   kʊ-lʊ-sako ʊ-lʊ-nunu   lɪnga   ʊ-n-kasi   gw-a
14-alcohol 17-11-luck   AUG-11-good if/when AUG-1-wife 1-ASSOC

mw-anaake i-kʊ-kɪnd-a   pa-la   ʊ-gwise   gw-a   ɳ-dʊme
1-his_child 1-PRS-pass-FV 16-DIST AUG-his_father(1) 1-ASSOC 1-husband

i-kʊ-milw-a   m-m-ıısi jı-kʊ-j-a   n-gafu   kʊʊ-nongwa
1-PRS-drown-FV 18-6-water 9-PRS-be(come)-FV 9-difficult 17-issue(9)
j-aa   bʊ-gaala bw-alwa bw-ake.
9-ASSOC 14-drink 14-alcohol 14-POSS.SG

'But if the father of the man is a drunkard and if by chance the wife of his child passes by while the father of her husband is drowning in the water, it is difficult because of his drinking.'

bʊle ʊ-n-kiikʊlʊ   ʊ-jo   **i-kʊ-bomb-aga**   fi-ki?   [...] kalı
Q   AUG-1-woman AUG-REF.1 1-MOD.FUT-do-MOD.FUT 8-what?   Q
i-kʊ-ṇ-dek-aga   a-fw-ege   m-m-ıısi kʊʊ-nongwa
1-MOD.FUT-1-let-MOD.FUT 1-die-SUBJ.IPFV 18-6-water 17-issue(9)
j-aa   kʊ-tiil-a ʊ-kʊ-kilani-a   ı-m-baatıko   paapo
9-ASSOC 15-fear-FV AUG-15-break_custom-FV AUG-10-procedure because
a-ka-ṃ-bonol-a?
1-NEG-1-pay_off-FV

'What will the woman do? [...] Will she really let him die in the water because of fearing to break the customs because he has not paid her off?' [Should she save a life ...]

(108)   Context: Hare has fallen into a pit. He is afraid a man is waiting to kill him.

kalʊlʊ a-aly-and-ile   ʊ-kw-i-laalʊʊsy-a ʊkʊtı, "lılıno   ʊ-ne
hare(1) 1-PST-begin-PFV AUG-15-REFL-ask-FV COMP   now/today AUG-1SG
n-gʊ-fw-aga   mu-n-k-iina mu-no? po
1SG-MOD.FUT-die-MOD.FUT 18-18-7-cave 18-PROX then
n-ga-bagıl-a.   lınga   jo   mu-ndʊ ʊ-jʊ   a-li=po
1SG-NEG-be_able-FV if/when REF.1 1-person AUG-PROX.1 1-COP=16
pa-mwanya n-dek-e   a-n-gog-ege."
16-high   1SG-let-SUBJ 1-1SG-kill-IPFV.SUBJ

'Hare started to ask himself "Am I to die now in this pit? I can't. If that's a person up there I'll let him kill me."' [he goes on to jump out of the pit] [Saliki and Hare]

In elicitation, the modal future was also accepted in interrogatives when asking the hearer to make a promise, as in (109), the interrogative counterpart to (103) above. In compliance with its semantics of a settled future, it was considered infelicitous when asking for a prediction (110).

(109) Context: The hearer owes you money.

kw-i-pʊʊl-aga?

MOD.FUT-REFL-thresh-MOD.FUT

'Will you [promise me to] go after it?' [ET]

(110) Context: A field has been devastated by monkeys. The owner has just arrived and is shocked by the sight.

#bʊle, i-kʊ-bomb-aga   sy-a   fi-ki   lɪno?

Q   1-MOD.FUT-do-MOD.FUT 10-ASSOC 8-what now

(intended: 'What will s/he do now?')

9.6 Conditional *ngali*

A conditional particle *ngalɪ* serves to introduce the apodosis (consequent clause) of counterfactual conditionals.[14] The protasis (antecedent) is normally introduced by *lɪnga* 'if, when' and features a past tense verb (111, 112).[15]

(111) lɪnga   n-aa-meenye   **ngalɪ** n-ga-lɪm-a   ɪ-ky-ɪnja

if/when 1SG-PST-know.PFV COND 1SG-NEG-farm-FV AUG-7-year

ɪ-kɪ,   paapo si-n-gʊfiifye   fiijo ɪ-n-gambɪlɪ

AUG-PROX.7 because 10-1SG-cause_trouble.PFV INTENS AUG-10-monkey

ɪ-si

AUG-PROX.10

'If I had known, I would not have farmed this year, because these monkeys have very much hurt me.' [Thieving monkeys]

(112) lɪnga   fy-a-li=po   ɪ-fi-ndʊ   paa-meesa   **ngalɪ** tʊ-l-iile

if/when 8-PST-COP=16 AUG-8-food 16-table(<SWA) COND 1PL-eat-PFV

'If there had been food on the table, we would have eaten it.' [ET]

In this use, conditional *ngalɪ* can be combined with the future proclitic *aa=* (§8.2). It is as yet unclear how far this changes the meaning of the clause. The following two textual examples, taken from a draft of a Bible translation and HIV prevention materials by SIL International, suggest that the addition of *aa=* emphasizes the dissociation between the unfulfilled condition on the one hand and the divergent reality on the other.

---

[14]Some information on conditional clauses is also given in Lusekelo (2016).

[15]See §6.5.7.3 for another means of introducing counterfactional apodoses.

(113) a-ba-ndʊ   a-bo   ba-a-fum-ile   kʊ-my-ɪtʊ, looli
AUG-2-person AUG-REF.2 2-PST-come_from-PFV 17-4-POSS.1PL but
ba-ka-a-lɪ   b-iinɪɪtʊ,   paapo **lɪnga** ba-a-lɪ   b-iitɪki
2-NEG-PST-COP 2-our_companion because if   2-PST-COP 2-believer
b-iinɪɪtʊ   **a=ngalɪ**   tʊ-lɪ   na=bo,
2-our_companion FUT=COND 1PL-COP COM=REF.2

'They went out from us, but they were not of us [lit: ...because if they had been of us they would be with us],'

fyobeene ba-a-tʊ-lek-ile, lɪnga ba-a-lɪ   b-iitɪki   b-iinɪɪtʊ
therefore 2-PST-1PL-let-PFV if   2-PST-COP 2-believer 2-our_companion
ngalɪ ba-a-syele   na=nʊʊswe. looli bo ba-a-sook-ile=po
COND 1-PST-remain.PFV COM=COM.1PL but   as 2-PST-leave-PFV=16
ba-a-nangiisye ʊkʊtɪ b-oosa ba-ka-a-lɪ   b-iinɪɪtʊʊ
2-PST-show.PFV COMP 2-all   2-NEG-PST-COP 2-our_companion

'but they went out, that they might be made manifest that they were not all of us' [lit: 'therefore they left us, if they had been believers like us, they would have remained with us ...'] (1 John 2: 19)

(114) Context: An orphan is speaking.
n-gʊ-ba-syʊkw-a   jʊʊba   na   taata,   looli
1SG-PRS-2-miss_sadly-FV my_mother(1) COM my_father(1) but
n-gʊ-sʊʊbɪl-a   ʊkʊtɪ **lɪnga** ba-a-j-anga=po   ʊlʊ, **a=ngalɪ**
1SG-PRS-expect-FV COMP if   2-PST-be(come)-IPFV=16 now FUT=COND
bi-kw-i-tuukɪfy-a   ʊ-swe
2-PRS-REFL-praise.APPL-FV AUG-1PL

'I miss Mama and Papa, but I think if they were here they would be proud of us now.' [Kande's story][16]

Lastly, conditional *ngalɪ* is also found outside of conditional clauses, again giving a hypothetical reading:

(115) **ngalɪ** tʊ-kʊ-ly-a   (looli tʊ-kaalɪ tʊ-kʊ-ba-guul-ɪl-a
COND 1PL-PRS-eat-FV but   1PL-PERS 1PL-PRS-2-WAIT-APPL
a-ba-heesya)
AUG-2-foreigner

'We would be eating (but we are still waiting for the guests).' [ET]

---

[16] http://www.nyakyusalanguage.com/nyy/mlsp-dl/334/12876/42227?r=0 (05 February, 2016).

(116) **ngalɪ** tʊ-l-iile   (looli tʊ-kaalɪ tʊ-kʊ-ba-guul-ɪl-a
       COND 1PL-eat-PFV but 1PL-PERS 1PL-PRS-2-wait-APPL-FV

a-ba-heesya)
AUG-2-foreigner

'We would have eaten (but we are still waiting for the guests).' [ET]

10 Defective verbs, copulae and movement grams

10.1 Introduction

In this chapter, a number of verbs and verbal constructions will be discussed, beginning with a description of Nyakyusa's two copula verbs (§10.2.1). The description will include the syntactic and semantic conditions that govern copula use, copula-based existential constructions and the expression of predicative possession. This is followed by a description of the versatile defective verb *tɪ* 'say' (§10.3). Lastly, two verbs of motion that have grammaticalized into auxiliaries of (figurative) movement will be examined (§10.4).

10.2 The copulae

10.2.1 Copula verbs

Nyakyusa has two copula verbs: defective *lɪ* 'be' and *ja* 'be(come)'. The former must be considered defective because it does not take the default final vowel and only occurs in three paradigms: a zero-marked present, the affirmative past (formed with the prefix *a-*) and the negative past (formed with the prefixes *ka-a-*).

(1) a. *tʋ-lɪ bakafu*   'We are healthy.'
     b. *tw-a-lɪ bakafu*   'We were healthy.'
     c. *tʋ-ka-a-lɪ bakafu* 'We were not healthy.'

The two copulae are in near complementary distribution: in all contexts other than the three mentioned above, *ja* is used.[1] This includes the infinitive and the

---

[1] Interestingly, the distribution of the two copulae in principle corresponds to the distribution of the reflexes of Proto-Bantu *bá* 'dwell, be, become' and *dì* 'be' in other languages of the Corridor, among them Ndali (Botne 2008: 104). *ja* most likely stems from a verb of motion *gì* 'go'; note the contextually triggered loss of the consonantal segmental for both the copula and the motion verb (§10.4.1).

negative counterpart to the present (non-past) copula, which is formed with the negative prefix *ka-* and the final vowel *-a.* In this context the consonantal segment often drops out, yielding *kaa* with a long final vowel. Note that stress remains on *kaa* and is not shifted to the new penultimate syllable.

(2)   *tʋkaja bakafu* ~ *tʋkaa bakafu* 'We are not healthy.'

Further, *ja* is used in the present and past for generic statements:

(3)   ɪ-n-gambɪlɪ   ɪ-si,   boo=bʋ-no   **si-kʋ-j-a**
      AUG-10-monkey AUG-PROX.10 REF.14=14-DEM 10-PRS-be(come)-FV

      'These monkeys, this is how they are!' [Thieving monkeys]

(4)   ba-a-kitɪk-aga   ɪ-m-banda ɪɪ-nunu   ɪ-n-golofu
      2-PST-stick_in_ground-IPFV AUG-9-POST AUG-good(9) AUG-9-straight
      pa-katɪ   paa-nyumba, ɪ-j-aa   kw-ɪm-a=po   ʋ-n-talɪko.
      16-middle 16-house(9),   AUG-9-ASSOC 15-stand/stop-FV=16 AUG-3-beam
      lɪnga   ɪɪ-nyumba   nywamu **j-aa-j-aga**   n=ɪ-m-banda
      if/when AUG-house(9) big(9)   9-PST-be(come)-IPFV COM=AUG-10-post
      i-bɪlɪ   pamo i-tatʋ
      10-two or   10-three

      'They would erect a good straight post in the middle of the house, on which lay the ridge pole. If the house was big, it would have two or three posts.' [Nyakyusa houses of long ago]

Note that the use of *ja* is obligatory for future time reference; that is, the unmarked present of *lɪ* cannot normally be used as a futurate:

(5)   * kɪ-laabo   a-lɪ   kʋ-Tʋkʋjʋ
      7-tomorrow 1-COP 17-T.

      (intended: 'Tomorrow he will be at Tukuyu.')

There is one exception, however: copula *lɪ* is licensed with reference to the future if a temporal anchor is introduced by a stressed form of the augmentless class 14 referential demonstrative *bo* (6); see §10.2.4 for the expression of predicative possession through the use of the copula plus the comitative *na.* Likewise, a zero copula (see §10.2.2) is attested in this environment with reference to a future/hypothetical state-of-affairs (7). See p. 159 in §6.5.3.1 for a comparable case with the present perfective.

(6) lɪnga   fi-kɪnd-ile ɪ-fy-ɪnja   a-ma-longo ma-bɪlɪ, ɪɪ-nyumba   sy-osa
    if/when 8-pass-PFV AUG-8-year AUG-6-ten   6-two   AUG-house(10) 10-all
    n-ka-aja   a-ka   **bo si-lɪ**   n=ʊ-bʊ-meme
    18-12-homestead AUG-PROX.12 as 10-COP COM=AUG-14-electricity(<SWA)

    'In twenty years, all houses in this village will have electricity.' [ET]

(7) lɪnga   mu-sob-iisye,   **bo lw-ɪnʊ**
    if/when 2PL-be_lost-CAUS.PFV as 11-POSS.2PL

    'If you lose it, grief will be yours.' [Chickens and Crow]

10.2.2 Copula use

As described in the previous section, the choice between the two copula verbs *lɪ* and *ja* depends mainly on temporal reference and polarity. In the affirmative present (non-past), certain environments further license a zero copula or copulative use of the augmentless substitutives (§2.3.3); see Stassen (2005) for a discussion of the term *zero copula*.

With third person (noun class) subjects, nominal predication without any overt linking element is the common case (8a, 8b). The predicate never carries an augment. An augmentless substitutive may be added, which seems to be related to focus (8c). Note that copulative use of the substitutive also features in cleft sentences; see e.g. (43; p. 49) and (46; p. 313).

(8) a. ʊ-m-piki   n-nywamu
        AUG-3-tree 3-big

        'The tree is big.' [ET]

     b. ɪ-mi-piki   mi-nywamu
        AUG-4-tree 4-big

        'The trees are big.' [ET]

     c. ɪ-mi-piki   ɪ-gɪ   gyo mi-nywamu
        AUG-4-tree AUG-PROX.4 REF.4 4-big

        'These trees, they are big.' [ET]

Associatives and possessives are also normally used without an overt copula:

(9) gw-a   ba-palamaani
     3-ASSOC 2-neighbour

     'It (the tree) is the neighbours'.' [ET]

(10) gw-aŋgʊ
      3-POSS.1SG
      'It (the tree) is mine.' [ET]

With certain types of predicates, however, the use of a copula verb is obligatory even with noun class subjects in the affirmative present. In some of these, an augmentless substitutive may replace the copula. First, numerals require either the copula or the augmentless substitutive:

(11) a. a-ba-ana   ba-bılı
          AUG-2-child 2-two
          'two children' not: 'The children are two.'
      b. a-ba-ana   ba-lı ba-bılı
          AUG-2-child 2-COP 2-two
          'The children are two.'
      c. a-ba-ana   bo   ba-bılı
          AUG-2-child REF.2 2-two
          'The children are two.'

Note that this does not hold for the quantifiers *nandı* 'little, few' and *ingi* 'much, many', which are treated as nominals:

(12) ʊ-lw-ısi   ʊ-lʊ   lʊ-sisya.   a-m-ıısi   ma-tiitʊ kangı
      AUG-11-river AUG-PROX.1 11-frightening AUG-6-water 6-black again
      ı-n-gwina   **ny-ingi**
      AUG-10-crocodile 10-many
      'This river is frightening. The water is dark and the crocodiles are many.'
      [ET]

(13) ʊ-n-tondolo mw-ingi, leelo   a-ba-tondol-i   **ba-nandı**
      AUG-3-harvest 3-many   now/but AUG-2-harvest-AGNR 2-little
      'The harvest truly is great, but the labourers are few.' (Luke 10: 2)

When adverbials (14, 15) or ideophones (16, 17) are used predicatively, use of a copula verb is compulsory.

(14) a. ʊ-mw-ana a-lı   nnoono
          AUG-1-child 1-COP so_much
          'The child is too much.'
      b. * ʊmwana jo nnoono
      c. * ʊmwana nnoono

(15)   a.   ɪ-m-bwa   jɪ-lɪ   kanunu
            AUG-9-dog 9-COP well

            'The dog is fine.'

       b.   * ɪmbwa jo kanunu[2]

       c.   * ɪmbwa kanunu

(16)   a.   n-nyumba   mu-lɪ   kée
            18-house(9) 18-COP vast

            'The house is empty.'

       b.   * nnyumba mo kée

       c.   * nnyumba kée

(17)   a.   ɪ-my-enda   gɪ-lɪ   swée
            AUG-4-cloth 4-COP intense_white

            'The clothes are white.'

       b.   * ɪmyenda gyo swée

       c.   * ɪmyenda swée

Locative predicates also require a copula verb (18). This includes locative question words (19). (20) illustrates that the locative semantics are responsible for this rather than belonging to one of the locative noun classes.

(18)   a.   ʊ-mw-ana a-lɪ   mu-m-piki
            AUG-1-child 1-COP 18-3-tree

            'The child is in a/the tree.'

       b.   * ʊmwana jo mumpiki

       c.   * ʊmwana mumpiki

(19)   a.   ʊ-mw-ana a-lɪ   kʊʊgʊ   / pooki   / mooki?
            AUG-1-child 1-COP where(17)   where(16)   where(18)

            'Where / Wherein is the child?'

       b.   * ʊmwana jo kʊʊgʊ / pooki / mooki?

       c.   * ʊmwana kʊʊgʊ   / pooki / mooki?

(20)   a.   ʊ-mw-ana a-lɪ   kɪfuki n=ʊ-m-piki
            AUG-1-child 1-COP near   COM=AUG-3-tree

            'The child is near the tree.'

---

[2]This sentence would be acceptable with the meaning 'This dog's name is Kanunu.'

b. *ʊmwana jo kɪfuki nʊmpiki

c. *ʊmwana kɪfuki nʊmpiki

With first and second person subjects, the use of either the copula or a substitutive is obligatory for nominal predicates in the affirmative present. (21–23)
illustrate this for the second person singular. With other types of predicates, the
same regularities as for noun class subjects hold.

(21)   (ʊ-gwe)   ʊ-lɪ   n-nandɪ
       AUG-2SG 2SG-COP 1-small

       'You are small.'

(22)   (ʊ-gwe)   gwe n-nandɪ
       AUG-2SG 2SG 1-small

       'You are small.'

(23)   *ʊ-gwe   n-nandɪ
       AUG-2SG 1-small

Lastly, the copula also forms a compulsory part of existential constructions
and expressions of predicative possession, which are the topics of the following
sections.

10.2.3 Existential construction

The presence or existence of an entity is expressed by a copula plus a locative
enclitic. With the copula *lɪ*, the vowel segment is raised to /i/. Noun class 16
po expresses proximity to the deictic centre or more definite locations, class 17
ko distance from the deictic centre or general existence and class 18 *mo* inside
locations.

(24)   **ga-a-li=po**   a-ma-syabala,   **sy-a-li=po**   ɪ-n-jʊgʊ.
       6-PST-COP=16 AUG-6-groundnut 10-PST-COP=16 AUG-10-jugo_bean
       ba-a-li=po   baa-mwembe, **ga-a-li=po**   a-m-ungu.   fy-osa
       2-PST-COP=16 2-mango   6-PST-COP=16 AUG-6-pumpkin 8-all
       fy-a-li=po   pa-ka-aja pa-n-gambɪlɪ
       8-PST-COP=16 16-12-home 16-9-monkey

       'There were groundnuts, there were jugo beans. There were mangoes,
       there were pumpkins. There was all sorts of food at Monkey's' [Monkey
       and Tortoise]

(25) jɪ-kʊ-tɪ   bo m-fw-ile   ʊ-ne   lɪnga   ga-kɪnd-ile a-ma-sikʊ
9-PRS-SAY as 1SG-die-PFV AUG-1SG if/when 6-pass-PFV AUG-6-day
ma-nandɪ.
6-little

'It says I'm dead when few days have passed.'

po   lɪlɪno   n-gʊ-bʊʊk-aga   kʊkʊtɪ na=a-ma-jolo
then now/today 1SG-MOD.FUT-go-MOD.FUT every COM=AUG-6-evening
kʊ-no   ɪ-m-bʊlʊkʊtʊ jɪ-lambaleele   kʊ-kʊ-jɪ-bʊʊl-a ʊkʊtɪ "ʊ-ne
17-PROX AUG-9-ear   9-lie_down-PFV 17-15-9-tell-FV COMP AUG-1SG
n-gaalɪ   **n-dɪ=ko**,   n-dɪ   n=ʊ-bʊ-ʊmi"
1SG-PERS 1SG-COP=17 1SG-COP COM=AUG-14-live

'So now I shall go every evening when Ear has laid down, to tell it "I'm
still around, I'm alive."' [Mosquito and Ear]

When the copula is negated, non-existence or absence is expressed:

(26) i-kʊ-suluk-a   paa-si   mu-m-piki n=ʊ-kʊ-keet-a   ʊkʊtɪ
1-PRS-descend-FV 16-below 18-3-tree   COM=AUG-15-watch-FV CMPL
kɪ-kapʊ kɪ-mo **kɪ-ka-j-a=po**
7-basket 7-one 7-NEG-be(come)-FV=16

'He climbs down the tree and sees that one basket is missing.' [Elisha
Pear Story]

(27) ka-a-li=ko   a-ka-aja   ka-mo a-ka   a-m-ɪɪsi
12-PST-COP=17 AUG-12-village 12-one AUG-PROX.12 AUG-6-water
ga-ka-a-li=mo
6-NEG-PST-COP=18

'There was a village in which there was no water.' [Water and toads]

When locative marking on the copula co-occurs with an overt locative noun
phrase, both often reference the same locative noun class (28), but mixing of two
locative classes is also found (29).

(28) a-ma-keeke   **ga-a-li=mo** m-ingi **mw-ene mw-i-tengele**
AUG-6-type_of_grass 6-PST-COP=18 6-many 18-only 18-5-bush
ɪ-ly-a   n-ky-amba   Rungwe
AUG-5-ASSOC 18-7-mountain R.

'There was a lot of a certain type of grass only in the bush on mount
Rungwe.' [Nyakyusa houses of long ago]

(29) **n-k-iisʊ** kɪ-mo, **a-a-li=ko**   ʊ-malafyale jʊ-mo. ɪ-n-gamu   j-aake
      18-7-land 7-one 1-PST-COP=17 AUG-chief(1) 1-one AUG-9-name 9-POSS.SG
      a-a-lɪ   jo   Kapyungu
      1-PST-COP REF.1 K.

      'In some land there was a chief. His name was Kapyungu.' [Chief
      Kapyungu]

Note that in examples (24–29) the grammatical subject follows the existential
copula. This is a common presentational construction. In fact, (27, 29) are typical
of the orientation sections of Nyakyusa narratives.

10.2.4 Expression of predicative possession

Ownership is expressed by using the copula together with an enclitic form of the
comitative *na* on the possessee.

(30) ʊ-malafyale ʊ-jʊ   a-a-lɪ   n=ɪ-fi-panga   fi-tatʊ
      AUG-chief(1) AUG-PROX.1 1-PST-COP COM=AUG-8-village 8-three

      'This chief had three villages.' [Chief Kapyungu]

(31) ɪlnga   ʊ-ka-j-a   n=ʊ-bʊ-jo   bw-a
      if/when 2SG-NEG-be(come)-FV COM=AUG-14-place 14-ASSOC
      kʊ-gon-a=mo kʊ-gon-a   muu-nyumba ɪ-sy-a   kʊ-pang-a
      15-sleep-FV=18 2SG.PRS-sleep-FV 18-house(9)   AUG-10-ASSOC 15-rent-FV

      'If you do not have a place to sleep in, you sleep in a rented house.' [How
      to build modern houses]

Typically, the noun expressing the possessee carries the augment, though use
without the augment was also encountered:

(32) n-ga-a   na=m-bombo, n-ga-a
      1SG-NEG.be(come)-FV COM=9-work   1SG-NEG.be(come)-FV
      na=heela
      COM=money(10)

      'I don't have a job, I don't have money.' [overheard]

The possessee can be referred to by a referential demonstrative without the
augment. This is the case with anaphoric reference (33). The referential demonstrative can also be used cataphoricly together with the overt noun phase it in-
dexes (34).

(33) kangɪ mpaka   ʊ-si-keet-e   taasi ɪ-n-**dalama**
      again no_matter_what 2SG-10-watch-SUBJ yet   AUG-10-money
      ɪ-si   ʊ-lɪ   **na=syo**   muu-ny-ambɪ, pamopeene
      AUG-PROX.10 2SG-COP COM=REF.10 18-9-pocket   together
      n=ʊ-tʊ-ndʊ   ʊ-tʊ   tʊ-bagiile   ʊ-kʊ-kʊ-tʊʊl-a
      COM=AUG-13-thing AUG-PROX.13 13-be_able.PFV AUG-15-2SG-help-FV
      kʊ-m-bombo ɪ-jo
      17-9-work   AUG-REF.9

      'Again, you should first look at the money which you have in your
      pocket, together with other things which can help you with this work.'
      [How to build modern houses]

(34) lɪlɪno   tʊ-ka-a   **na=fyo**   na=fi-mo   ɪ-fi-ndʊ
      now/today 1PL-NEG.be(come)-FV COM=REF.8 COM=8-one AUG-8-food
      ɪ-fy-a   kʊ-ly-a   n-nyumba
      AUG-8-ASSOC 15-eat-FV 18-house(9)

      'Today we don't have anything to eat at home.' [Monkey and Tortoise]

10.3 *tɪ* 'say; think; do like'

The verb *tɪ* 'say' must be considered defective for a number of reasons. First, its
stem does not carry the final vowel *-a*. Consequently, it does not change its shape
in the subjunctive. In other respects, its vocalic segment, however, behaves much
like the final vowel of regular verbs: in the imperfective *tɪ* takes the shape *tɪgɪ*,
resembling the *-VCV* shape of the regular imperfective suffix (see §6.4.1). Second,
the vocalic segment is dropped when perfective *-ile* is suffixed, yielding *tile* (not
*tiile). Last, *tɪ* does not accept any derivational suffixes.

    For reasons of space and convenience, *tɪ* is glossed as 'say' throughout this
study. However, as the following discussion will show, this versatile verb shows
uses and functions that go far beyond that of a simple verb of speech. Güldemann
(2000) convincingly argues that the use of *tɪ* as a verb of speech across Bantu has
arisen out of a more abstract cataphoric function.

    Its use as a verb of speech is illustrated in (35). To render speech or sound with
verbs other than *tɪ* itself, a form of *tɪ*, either the infinitive (36) or an inflected verb
in a chaining construction (37), is also required.

(35) po **ly-a-t-ile**   "n-gʊ-lond-a   ɪɪ-sindaano   j-angʊ"
      then 5-PST-say-PFV 1SG-PRS-want-FV AUG-needle(<SWA)(9) 9-POSS.1SG
      'It [Crow] said "I want my needle."' [Chickens and Crow]

(36) a-lɪnkʊ-ba-bʊʊl-a a-ba-ndʊ   **ʊ-kʊ-tɪ**
      1-NARR-2-tell-FV   AUG-2-person AUG-15-say
      'He told the people:' [Chief Kapyungu]

(37) kalʊlʊ a-lɪnkw-amul-a   kʊ-m-manyaani gw-ake   **a-lɪnkʊ-tɪ**
      hare(1) 1-NARR-answer-FV 17-1-friend   1-POSS.SG 1-NARR-say
      'Hare answered to his friend:' [Hare and Chameleon]

   The only attested examples in the corpus of illocutionary verbs of speech without a form of *tɪ* are sections of narratives that move to drama; see p. 193 in §6.7.1.
Apart from speech in the strict sense, *tɪ* is also used for rendering inner speech
or thought:

(38) ngɪmba mu-n-dumbula **i-kʊ-tɪ**   "n-gʊ-tosiisye"
      behold 18-9-heart   1-PRS-say 1SG-2SG-pay_back.PFV
      'But in his heart he [Skunk] is thinking "I've paid you back."' [Hare and
      Skunk]

(39) ɪ-m-bwa   jɪ-lɪnkʊ-j-a   n-galɪ fiijo, **j-aa-t-ɪgɪ**   pamo
      AUG-9-dog 9-NARR-be(come)-FV 9-strict INTENS 9-PST-say-IPFV perhaps
      ɪ-li-paatama   li-kʊ-j-a   pa-kʊ-pok-a   ɪɪ-nyama
      AUG-5-cheetah 5-PRS-be(come)-FV 16-15-plunder-FV AUG-meat(9)
      j-aake
      9-POSS.SG
      'The dog became very angry, it was thinking that maybe the cheetah
      would seize his meat.' [Dogs laughed at each other]

   The verb *tɪ* also serves to introduce ideophones. All cases in the data feature
onomatopoeia. It is unclear if this is a restriction on the use of *tɪ* or an artefact
of the data at hand.

(40) ʊ-gw-a   kɪ-bɪlɪ a-a-lʊ-kol-ile   ʊ-lw-igi   m-ma-ka
      AUG-2-ASSOC 7-two 1-PST-11-grasp/hold-PFV AUG-11-door 18-6-strength
      ma-tupu. looli j-oope kw-a-lɪl-ile   **kw-a-t-ile**   "káa"
      6-sudden but   1-also 17-PST-cry-PFV 17-PST-say-PFV of_sickle_swinging
      'The second one grabbed the door with all his strength. But also with him,
      there was the sound "káa!" [of a sickle swinging]' [Wage of the thieves]

The subjunctive (§9.3) of *tı* is formed by prefixing the subject prefix, without any change in the final vowel (41). When the interrogative *bʋle* 'how' follows *tı*, they optionally merge into one word, with the vocalic segment of the verb assimilating (42). The imperfective suffix in this case is attached to the right of the compound stem and accordingly takes the shape *-ege* (43).

(41) gw-itık-e   ʋ-tı   "ee, n-di=po"
      2SG-agree-SUBJ 2SG-say.SUBJ   yes 1SG-COP=16
      'You shall answer "Yes, I'm here."' [Hare and Tugutu]

(42) *tʋtı bʋle? ~ tʋtʋbʋle?*
      'What should we say/do?'

(43) *tʋtıgı bʋle? ~ tʋtʋbʋlege?*
      'What should we be saying/doing?'

As can be gathered from (42, 43), apart from introducing (inner) speech and sound, *tı* can be understood to have a broader meaning of acting in a certain manner. Thus its subjunctive is also used as a prompt to imitate a certain action (44) (also cf. Felberg 1996: 97). Also note the related uses in (45, 46).

(44) **ʋ-tı**   bʋ-no
      2SG-say.SUBJ 14-DEM
      'Do like this!' [ET]

(45) po jʋ-la ʋ-gw-a   pa-lʋ-ʋlʋ **a-lınkʋ-tı** fi-ki,
      then 1-DIST AUG-1-ASSOC 16-11-north 1-NARR-say 8-what
      a-lınkʋ-kaan-a
      1-NARR-refuse-FV
      'The one from the north did what? He refused.' [Lake Kyungululu]

(46) mwa=n-dugutu   a-ka-a-bop-ile=po.   a-a-ba-paal-ile
      matronym=9-type_of_bird 1-NEG-PST-run-PFV=PART 1-PST-2-invite-PFV
      a-ba-nine.   bo   a-ba   a-a-ba-bıık-ile **ʋ-kʋ-tı**
      AUG-2-companion REF.2 AUG-PROX.2 1-PST-2-put-PFV AUG-15-say
      maelı   jı-mo, maelı jı-mo, maelı jı-mo
      mile(9)(<EN) 9-one mile(9) 9-one mile(9) 9-one
      'Mr. Tugutu did not run at all. He had gathered companions. Those are the ones he placed, like one mile, one mile, one mile.' [Hare and Tugutu]

The infinitive *ʋkʋtı* is further grammaticalized as a complementizer (47). It also serves to introduce clauses of purpose and result; see §9.3.1.2.

(47) ʊ-meenye   ʊkʊtɪ Asia a-ka-kʊ-gan-a?
     2SG-know.PFV COMP A.   1-NEG-2SG-love-FV

'Do you know that Asia doesn't love you?' [Juma, Asia and Sambuka]

Similarly, the infinitiveinfinitive of *tɪ* as the dependent element of the associative construction serves to introduce a clause as a nominal complement.[3] This is frequently used in the collocation *kʊʊnongwa (ɪ)jaa kʊtɪ* 'for the reason that, because'.

(48) kʊʊ-nongwa j-aa   kʊ-tɪ Juma a-a-meenye   ʊkʊtɪ Sambʊka
     17-issue(9)   9-ASSOC 15-say J.   1-PST-know.PFV COMP S.

     m-manyaani gw-a   Asia, po   a-lɪnkw-itɪk-a   ʊ-kʊ-bʊʊk-a
     1-friend   1-ASSOC A.   then 1-NARR-agree-FV AUG-15-go-FV

     kʊ-kʊ-many-a=ko kʊ-my-ake
     17-15-know-FV=17 17-4-POSS.SG

'Because Juma knew that Sambuka was a friend of Asia, he agreed to go and get to know her [Sambuka's] home.' [Juma, Asia and Sambuka]

(49) Mfyage a-a-bʊʊk-ile kʊ-n-ganga ʊ-gw-a   kɪ-tiitʊ, kʊ-kʊ-lond-a
     M.   1-PST-go-PFV 17-1-healer AUG-1-ASSOC 7-black 17-15-search-FV

     ʊ-n-kota   ʊ-gw-a   kʊ-tɪ ba-n-gan-ege   fiijo
     AUG-3-medicine AUG-3-ASSOC 15-say 2-1-love-IPFV.SUBJ INTENS

     a-ba-nyambala
     AUG-2-man

'Mfyage went to a witch doctor to find a medicine that would make men love her very much.' [Mfyage turns into a lion]

The verb *tɪ* also serves as an auxiliary, taking a subjunctive complement in a number of conventionalized constructions; see §9.3.2. It also forms part of the invariable evidential of report *baatɪ*.[4] This particle serves to indicate that the source of information is hearsay. It can be used to distance oneself from what is reported, ascribing responsibility to the original source (50) and is also commonly used to echo what has just been said (51, 52).

---

[3]Following the associative particle, the augment on nouns is banned.

[4]This can doubtless be analyzed as *ba-a-tɪ*. Given that this form is homophonous with the subsecutive with a noun class 2 subject (i.e. 3rd person plural used as impersonal), this might be an indication that the subsecutive configuration has developed diachronically out of a former perfective or anterior, thus 'They (have) said'. Cf. also Ndali *báti*, which apparently fulfils the same function (Botne 2008: 107).

(50) Saliki a-lınkʋ-tı "ʋ-m̩-buut-ile   kalʋlʋ ʋ-jʋ   n-d-ile
     S.   1-NARR-say 2SG-1-slaughter-PFV hare(1) AUG-PROX.1 1SG-say-PFV
     ʋ-buut-ege?"   ʋ-n-kasi   gw-a   Saliki a-lınkʋ-tı "keet-a
     2SG-slaughter-IPFV.SUBJ AUG-1-wife 1-ASSOC S.   1-NARR-say look-FV
     ʋ-t-ile   **baatı**   n-heesya gw-ıtu!? n-um̩-buut-iile
     2SG-say-PFV hearsay 1-guest   1-POSS.1PL 1SG-1-slaughter-APPL.PFV
     ı-n-gʋkʋ.   a-li=mo n-nyumba, a-lı   pa-kʋ-ly-a=mo"
     AUG-9-chicken 1-COP=18 18-house(9) 1-COP 16-15-eat-FV=some

     'Saliki said "Have you slaughtered Hare, whom I told you to slaughter?"
     Saliki's wife said "Look, you said he is our guest!? I slaughtered a chicken
     for him. He's in the house, he's eating."' [Saliki and Hare]

(51) Context: The researcher has asked for a soda at a small shop. The friend of
     the shop owner is surprised by his language skills and repeats his words:
     baatı   "n-gʋ-sʋʋm-a   ıı-kook"
     hearsay 1SG-PRS-beg-FV AUG-C.(9)

     '[Quoting:] "I'd like a Coke."' [overheard]

(52) Context: Tortoise's child has just told Monkey that Tortoise senior is sad.
     "fi-ki?" "a-fw-ile ɗaaɗa   gw-ake" "n-koolel-e!" a-lınkʋ-sook-a
     8-what 1-die-PFV sister(<SWA) 1-POSS.SG 1-call-IMP   1-NARR-leave-FV
     kajamba, i-kʋ-lıl-a   "hıhıhıhıı, hıhıhıhıı, a-fw-ile, a-fw-ile"
     tortoise(1) 1-PRS-cry-FV of_crying of_crying 1-die-PFV 1-die-PFV

     '[Monkey:] "Why?" [Tortoise's child:] "His sister died" [Monkey:] "Call
     him!" Tortoise came out, he is crying ""hihihihiii, hihihihii, she died, she
     died".'

     po   mwa=n-gambılı   "he?   **baatı**   a-fw-ile ɗaada, ee? po
     then matronym=9-monkey INTERJ hearsay 1-die-PFV sister   yes then
     ndaga"
     thanks

     'Monkey: "So your sister died, yes? My sympathy."' [Monkey and
     Tortoise]

Note that even in the wider discourse context of the preceding examples there
is no referent of noun class 2 which the *ba-* portion could cross-reference. Also
note that *tı* cannot normally be followed by another instance of itself:

(53) * keeta ʋ-t-ile   ʋ-kʋ-tı   n-heesya gw-ıtʋ
      look 2SG-say-PFV AUG-15-say 1-guest   1-POSS.1PL

A homophonous form *baatɪ* is also used as a call for attention (54).[5]

(54) *baatɪ* 'Listen!'

Another use of *tɪ* is that of naming or calling people or entities. Note the object marker in (57), which is otherwise not licensed with this verb.

(55) ijolo   n̩-dw-iho   lw-a   ba-Nyakyʊsa ba-a-lɪ
      old_times 18-11-custom 11-ASSOC 2-Ny.   2-PST-COP
      na=a-ka-jɪɪlo   k-a   n-kiikʊlʊ ʊ-kʊ-n-tiil-a
      COM=AUG-12-custom 12-ASSOC 1-woman AUG-15-1-fear-FV
      ʊ-gwise   gw-a n̩-dʊme, ʊ-jʊ   tʊ-kʊ-tɪ   n-kamwana
      AUG-his_father(1) 1-ASSOC 1-husband AUG-PROX.1 1PL-PRS-say 1-in_law

      'Long ago in the tradition of the Nyakyusa people they had a custom of
      the woman fearing the father of her husband, whom we call Nkamwana.'
      [Should she save a life...]

(56) ky-a-li=po   n=ɪ-kɪ-piki,   tʊ-kʊ-tɪ   ɪ-m-bale
      7-PST-COP=16 COM=AUG-7-stump 1PL-PRS-say AUG-7-type_of_wood

      'There was also a wood. We call it Mbale.' [Clothing long ago]

(57) bi-kʊ-n-tɪ (jo) Mama Tuma
      2-PRS-1-say REF.1 M.   T.

      'They call her Mama Tuma' [ET]

Lastly, *tɪ* features in the conjunction *kookʊtɪ* 'that is to say, that means' (58), in the universal quantifier *kʊkʊtɪ* 'every' (59) and in *ngatɪ* 'as, like' (60).

(58) bo ba-fik-ile   pa-la ba-lɪnkʊ-sy-ag-a   ɪ-n-gambɪlɪ
      as 2-arrive-PFV 16-dist 2-NARR-10-find-FV AUG-10-monkey
      si-tengeene   m-mi-gʊnda gy-abo, si-kʊ-ly-a   ɪ-fi-lombe
      10-live_in_peace.PFV 18-4-field   4-POSS.PL 10-PRS-eat-FV AUG-8-maize
      kangɪ si-kw-ɪmb-a   si-kʊ-tɪ   "ho! ho! ho!" kookʊtɪ   "ee
      again 10-PRS-SING-FV 10-PRS-say INTERJ   that_is_to_say yes
      fi-nunu! ee fi-nunu! ee fi-nunu!"
      8-good   yes 8-good yes 8-good

      'When they arrived there, they found the monkeys looking at home in

---

[5]Note that this parallels Swahili *ati~eti*, which is similarly used as an evidential of report and as an interjection (Madan 1903: 17; Maw 2013: 19). It is unclear if this use of Nyakyusa *baatɪ* is a result of a parallel development or if its usage has been influenced by Swahili..

their fields, eating maize, singing and saying "Ho! Ho! Ho!" That is to say "Yes, it's good! Yes, it's good! Yes, it's good!' (Thieving Monkeys)

(59) ʊ-gwe   ʊ-lɪ   na=a-ma-lʊndɪ lwele, **kʊkʊtɪ** kɪ-lʊndɪ k-oog-a
AUG-2SG 2SG-COP COM=AUG-6-leg eight every 7-leg   2SG.PRS-bath-FV

a-m-ɪɪsi   ɪ-n-dobo   jɪ-mo
AUG-6-water AUG-9-bucket 9-one

'You have eight legs, every leg you bathe in one bucket of water.' [Hare and Spider]

(60) po jʊ-la i-kw-and-a   ʊ-kʊ-bin-a   fiijo
then 1-DIST 1-PRS-begin-FV AUG-15-fall_sick-FV INTENS

n=ʊ-kʊ-ʊbʊk-a   ʊ-ṃ-bɪlɪ   **ngatɪ** lw-ifi
COM=AUG-15-peel_off-FV AUG-3-body like   11-chameleon

'Then that person begins to get very ill and his body peels like a chameleon.' [Killer woman]

10.4 Movement grams

In this section, two auxiliary verbs will be discussed that provide a sense of (figurative) movement:[6] (j)a 'go' and *isa* 'come'. Both verbs are not only related in meaning, but also pattern together in syntactic terms. As their complement, they both take an augmentless infinitive. Further, the simple present of both verbs has undergone further grammaticalization to a futurate, a use in which the infinitive complement can take the imperfective suffix -*aga*.

10.4.1 (j)a 'go'

The movement verb (j)a, which is glossed as 'go' throughout this study is attested only as a movement gram, not as a main verb. Following the infinitive or prefix *kʊ*-, only the vocalic segment is realized, yielding *kwa*. This loss of the consonantal segment is shared with the copula of the same shape (§10.2.1), albeit in a different environment. Use of (j)a construes the state-of-affairs encoded in the lexical verb against a preceding motion event (cf. Wilkins 1991: 251). One possible reading is that of two sequential sub-eventualities, hence 'go (and) verb':

---

[6]The term *movement gram* has been adopted from Nicolle (2002).

(61) po   lınga   a-ba-buʊl-ile a-ba-paapi   ba-ake   pamo
      then if/when 1-2-tell-PFV   AUG-2-parent 2-POSS.SG or

      ʊ-gwise   gw-a   ṇ-dʊmyana jʊ-la, **a-a-j-aga**
      AUG-his_father(1) 1-ASSOC 1-boy   1-DIST 1-PST-go-IPFV

      kʊ-n-sʊʊm-ɪl-a kʊ-gwise   gw-a   n-kiikʊlʊ ʊkʊtɪ
      15-1-beg-APPL-FV 17-his_father(1) 1-ASSOC 1-woman COMP

      "ʊ-mw-anaako,   n-gʊ-lond-a   ʊkʊtɪ eeg-igw-ege
       AUG-1-your_child 1SG-PRS-want-FV COMP 1.marry-PASS-IPFV.SUBJ

      n=ʊ-mw-anangʊ"
      COM=AUG-1-my_child

      'When he had told his parents or his father, he [father] would go to the
      woman's father and ask "Your child, I want her to be married to my
      child."' [Life and marriage long ago]

(62) Context: The researcher is on his way home in the afternoon.
      ʊ-j-ile   **kʊ**-bomb-a?
      2SG-go-PFV 15-work-FV

      'Did you go and work?' [overheard]

In other cases, *(j)a* does not introduce a change of location. This becomes
clearest when it follows a form of the lexical verb *bʊʊka* 'go', as in (63, 64). Instead
of introducing a second motion event, *(j)a* recapitulates the goal-oriented motion
expressed by preceding *bʊʊka*. In (63), this is the explicitly mentioned field, in
(64) the house, which is understood from the context.

(63) bo ka-kınd-ile=po   a-ka-balılo   ka-nandɪ Pakyındɪ **a-lınkʊ-bʊʊk-a**
      as 12-pass-PFV=CMPR AUG-12-time 12-little   P.   1-NARR-go-FV

      kʊ-ṇ-gʊnda. **a-lınkw-a**   kʊ-mmw-ag-a ʊ-n-kasi   n=ʊ-n-nyambala
      17-3-field   1-NARR-go.FV 15-1-find-FV   AUG-1-wife COM=AUG-1-man

      ʊ-jʊ-ngɪ   mu-ṇ-gʊnda mu-la
      AUG-1-other 18-3-field   18-DIST

      'When a short time had passed, Pakyindi went to the field. He (went and)
      found his wife with another man in that field.' [Sokoni and Pakyindi]

(64) Context: Python is hiding in a banana tree outside a house.
      po   j-aa-tɪ   "niine   n-gʊ-bʊʊk-a   bo a-ka-j-a=po
      then 9-SUBSEC-say COM.1SG 1SG-PRS-go-FV as 1-NEG-be(come)-FV=16

      maama   jʊ-la ʊ-n-kiikʊlʊ." po **bo jɪ-bʊʊk-ile** ıı-sota
      mother(<SWA) 1-DIST AUG-1-woman then as 9-go-PFV   AUG-python(9)

j-oope **j-aa-j-ile**   kw-ımb-a
9-also 9-PST-go-PFV 15-sing-FV

'Then it [Python] said "Me too, I'm going when that woman isn't there."
When the python had gone [to the house], it sang.' [Python and woman]

The preceding example illustrates another important point about (*j*)*a*: this construal of a lexical state-of-affairs against the ground of a motion event is often employed in narratives to trace the participants and their actions as they move through space. (65–67) are further examples of this.

(65)   Context: Hare and Skunk are staying together.
po   nsysyı j-oope **a-a-bʋʋk-ile**, **a-a-j-ile**   kʋ-lond-a   a-ma-ani.
then skunk(1) 1-also 1-PST-go-PFV 1-PST-go-PFV 15-search-FV AUG-6-leaf
a-al-iis-ile   na=a-ma-ani   ga-la bo a-gon-ile ʋ-tʋ-lo
1-PST-come-PFV COM=AUG-6-leaf 6-DIST as 1-rest-PFV AUG-13-sleep
kalʋlʋ
hare(1)

'Skunk also went, he (went and) searched for leaves. He came with those leaves, while Hare was asleep.' [Hare and Skunk]

(66)   Context: Hare is trapped in a pit.
a-a-fum-ile   na=a-maka   n-k-iina mu-la. a-a-nyeel-ile
1-PST-come_from-PFV COM=AUG-6-force 18-7-pit 18-DIST 1-PST-jump-PFV
a-a-j-ile   kʋ-tı “tuu!”   p-ii-sıılya
1-PST-go-PFV 15-say of_thunk 16-5-other_side

'He [Hare] came out of that pit with force. He jumped and made "tuu!" on the other side.' [Saliki and Hare]

(67)   Context: A woman has just passed a branch-off.
po   a-lınkʋ-golok-a,   a-lınkʋ-golok-a.   **a-lınkw-a**
then 1-NARR-go_straight-FV 1-NARR-go_straight-FV. 1-NARR-go.FV
kʋ-fik-a   kʋ-jeng-iigwe   kʋ-nunu fiijo.   po   **a-lınkw-a**
15-arrive-FV 17-build-PASS.PFV 17-well   INTENS then 1-NARR-go.FV
kʋ-ba-ag-a ba-lındılıli ba-a   ka-aja   ka-la. ba-lınkʋ-ŋ-daalʋʋsy-a
15-2-find-FV 2-guard   2-ASSOC 12-village 12-DIST 2-NARR-1-ask-FV
ba-lınkʋ-tı “kʋ-lond-a   fi-ki?”
2-NARR-say 2SG.PRS-want-FV 8-what

'She went straight, she went straight. She (went and) arrived at a place well built. She (went and) met the guards of that village. They asked "What do you want?"' [Throw away the child]

The simple present of (*j*)*a* is further grammaticalized as a marker of prospective aspect, which retains a possible spatial or motion reading. This is discussed in §8.5. Note that the movement gram (*j*)*a* cannot express motion with purpose. For this, *bʊʊka* 'go' plus an infinitive marked for locative class 16 or 18 has to be used; see §11.4.1 for a discussion. Lastly, unlike its counterpart *isa* (§10.4.2), the simple present of (*j*)*a* does not have a habitual or generic reading:

(68) * kʊkʊtɪ ky-ɪnja n-gw-a   kʊ-gy-ag-a ɪ-mi-kambɪlɪ   kʊ-mi-gʊnda
      every 7-year 1SG-PRS-go.FV 15-4-find-FV AUG-6-monkey 17-4-field
      gy-ɪtʊ
      4-POSS.1PL

      (intended: 'Every year I go and find damn monkeys in our fields.')

10.4.2 *isa* 'come'

The verb *isa* 'come', when used as an auxiliary, has a figurative meaning of reaching, achieving or being led to a particular condition.

(69) bo a-lɪ   n=ʊ-lw-anda   **iis-aga**   kʊ-pon-a   nalooli
      as 1-COP COM=AUG-11-stomach 1.PST.come-IPFV 15-give_birth-FV really
      ʊ-mw-ana   ʊ-n-kiikʊlʊ
      AUG-1-child AUG-1-woman

      'When she was pregnant, she would eventually give birth to a girl.' [Life and marriage long ago]

(70) mw-ilaamwisye ɪ-n-dagɪlo   sy-angʊ.   ʊ-mw-ana a-ka-bagɪl-a
      2PL-disregard.PFV AUG-10-rule 10-POSS.1SG AUG-1-child 1-NEG-be_able-FV
      ʊ-kw-end-a   kangɪ, **a-ti-kw-is-a**   kʊ-job-a   sikʊ kangɪ
      AUG-15-walk/travel-FV again, 1-NEG-PRS-come-FV 15-speak-FV ever again

      'You have disregarded my rules. The child can't walk, it'll never get to talk.' [Pregnant women]

(71) po   kanunu ʊ-kʊ-j-a   m-bombi gw-abo kʊ-ka-balɪlo
      then well   AUG-15-be(come)-FV 1-worker 1-POSS.PL 17-12-time
      a-ka-a   kʊ-lond-a ʊ-kʊ-kab-a   ɪ-n-dalama   ɪ-sy-a
      AUG-12-ASSOC 15-want-FV AUG-15-get-FV AUG-10-money AUG-10-ASSOC
      k-ʊʊl-ɪl-a   ɪ-fi-bombelo, ɪ-fy-a   **kw-is-a**   kʊ-bomb-el-a
      15-buy-APPL-FV AUG-8-tool   AUG-8-ASSOC 15-come-FV 15-work-APPL-FV

kɪsita   kʊ-lʊmbʊʊs-ɪgw-a
without 15-humiliate-PASS-FV

'And so it is good to be their worker for a time in which you want to get money to buy tools with, for later working with without being disparaged [lit. ...tools of coming to work with ...].' [Types of tools in the home]

(72)   a-ka-pango   a-ka   ki-kʊ-tʊ-many-isy-a   ʊkʊtɪ
      AUG-12-story   AUG-PROX.12   12-PRS-1PL-know-CAUS-FV   COMP

      tʊ-ng-iib-aga,   **tʊ-ng-iis-a**   **kʊ-fw-a**   bo
      1PL-NEG.SUBJ-steal-IPFV   1PL-NEG.SUBJ-come-FV   15-die-FV   as

      lʊʊ~lo   sy-a-fw-ile   ɪ-n-gambɪlɪ   si-la
      REDUPL~REF.11   10-PST-die-PFV   AUG-10-monkey   10-DIST

      'This story teaches us that we should not steal, otherwise we will die [lit. we should not come to die] just like those monkeys died.' [Thieving monkeys]

In the affirmative subjunctive, a variant construction is attested in which the lexical verb is not expressed as an augment-less infinitive, but also figures in the subjunctive paradigm:

(73)   kangɪ   ʊ-swɪl-enge=po   n=ɪ-n-gʊlʊbe   pa-ka-aja   ʊkʊtɪ   bo
      again   2SG-rear-IPFV.SUBJ=16   COM=AUG-10-pig   16-12-homestead   COMP   as

      g-ʊʊl-iisye   ɪ-n-dalama   ɪ-syo   **s-iis-e**
      2SG-buy-CAUS.PFV   AUG-10-money   AUG-REF.10   10-come-SUBJ

      si-kʊ-tʊʊl-ege   ʊ-kʊ-ba-homb-a   a-ba-fundi
      10-2SG-help-IPFV.SUBJ   AUG-15-2-pay-FV   AUG-2-workman(<SWA)

      'And you should be raising pigs at home so that when you have sold them, the money can be helping you to pay the workmen [lit. ...so that the money comes to help you ...].' [How to build modern houses]

Note that the movement gram *isa*, like its counterpart *(j)a* (see §8.5) cannot express motion with purpose. For this, an infinitive marked for locative class 16 or 18 has to be used; see §11.4.1 for a discussion.

As (70) above indicates, the simple present of *isa* has a futurate reading. Another example of this is given in (74). This is also the only use of *isa* discussed by Schumann (1899) and Endemann (1914). As (75) illustrates, the simple present of *isa*, however, also allows for a habitual/generic reading.

(74) lɪlɪno **tʊ-kw-is-a** kʊ-kin-a ʊ-m-pɪla
now/today 1PL-PRS-come-FV 15-play-FV AUG-3-ball

'Today we'll come to play football [ET]'

(75) kʊkʊtɪ ky-ɪnja **n-gw-is-a** kʊ-gy-ag-a ɪ-mi-gambɪlɪ m-mi-gunda
every 7-year 1SG-PRS-come-FV 15-4-find-FV AUG-4-monkey 18-4-farm
gy-ɪtʊ
4-POSS.1PL

'Every year I come to find damn monkeys in our fields.' [ET]

In the futurate use of *isa*, the infinitive complement can take the imperfective suffix -*aga*, which yields a continuous/progressive reading and can add an epistemic flavour (76). Imperfective -*aga* is also used with a habitual/generic reading (77). Lastly, this futurate use of *isa* in the simple present has undergone further grammaticalization, yielding the indefinite future construction (§8.6).

(76) i-kw-is-a kʊ-jeng-aga kʊ-la
1-PRS-come-FV 15-build-IPFV 17-DIST

1. 'He will come to be building there (continuously).'
2. 'He will come to build there (presumably).' [ET]

(77) bi-kw-is-a kʊ-kin-aga ʊ-m-pɪla kʊkʊtɪ ii-sikʊ
2-PRS-come-FV 15-play-IPFV AUG-3-ball every 5-day

'They will come to play football every day.' [ET]

11 Verbal nouns (infinitives)

11.1 Introduction

In this chapter, verbal nouns (infinitives) will be discussed. After a description of their morphological structure and syntactic characteristics (§11.2), the negation of verbal nouns and negative construction containing them will be described (§11.3). This is followed by an discussion of some of their functions (§11.4.1, 11.4.2).

11.2 Structure and characteristics of verbal nouns

Verbal nouns (infinitives) share characteristics of both nouns and verbs. Formally, they are class 15 nouns and can hence be marked for one of the three locative classes or carry the augment (§2.3.2). Like any other noun phrase, infinitives can fulfil the syntactic functions of subjects (1), objects (2), the head of possessives (2), and of the dependent noun of the associative (3).

(1) kɪsita   kʊ-bomb-a   bo ʊ-lo,   kʊ-ka-a-li=ko
     without 15(INF)-do-FV as AUG-REF.11 15(INF)-NEG-PST-COP=17
     ʊ-kʊ-keet-an-a   kʊ-maa-so n=ʊ-kʊ-ponani-a
     AUG-15(INF)-see-RECP-FV 17-6-eye   COM=AUG-15(INF)-greet.RECP-FV
     'Without doing so, there was no looking each other in the eyes or greeting each other.' [Should she save a life...]

(2) n-**kʊ**-meenye   **ʊ-kʊ-pɪɪj-a**   kw-ake
     1SG-15(INF)-know.PFV AUG-15(INF)-cook-FV 15(INF)-POSS.SG
     'I know her cooking.' [ET]

(3) ba-a-tendekesy-aga ngatɪ kɪ-kombe ky-a   **kʊ-nw-el-a**
     2-PST-prepare-IPFV like 7-cup   7-ASSOC 15(INF)-drink-APPL-FV
     a-m-ɪɪsi
     AUG-6-water
     'They prepared them [calabashes] just like a cup for drinking water.' [Lake Kyungululu]

With respect to their verbal characteristics, verbal nouns can be modified by adverbials (4). They can take the complements licensed by the verb stem and accordingly may carry an object marker; see (5, 22) below. Further, infinitives can take post-final clitics; see (24) below.

(4) ʊ-kʊ-jeng-a   panandɪ~panandɪ jɪ-ka-j-a   m-bombo
AUG-15-build-FV REDUPL~a_little   9-NEG-be(come)-FV 9-work
n-gafu
9-difficult
'Building little by little is not difficult work.' [How to build modern houses]

The stem of verbal nouns consists of the base and the default final vowel -*a*. With the movement grams (*j*)*a* and *isa* (§10.4), the infinitive may take the imperfective final suffix -*aga*. The only other token of an infinitive carrying the imperfective suffix is the following example, where -*aga* seems to indicate the generic aspect of the comitative infinitive vis-à-vis its perfective superordinate verb.

(5) a-ba-ndʊ   ba-a-jeng-ile   **n=ʊ-kʊ-tʊʊgasy-aga**   n-ka-aja
AUG-2-person 2-PST-build-PFV COM=AUG-15-settle-IPFV 18-12-homestead
a-ko   looli ba-a-taami-gw-aga   ʊ-kʊ-ga-ag-a   a-m-ɪɪsi
AUG-REF.12 but 2-PST-trouble-PASS-IPFV AUG-15-6-find-FV AUG-6-water
a-g-a   kʊ-nw-a   n-ʊ-kʊ-nw-esy-a   ɪ-mi-tiimo
AUG-6-ASSOC 15-drink-FV COM=AUG-15-drink-CAUS-FV AUG-4-herd
gy-abo
4-POSS.PL
'People (had) built in that village but they had trouble finding water for drinking and watering their cattle.' [Water and toads]

11.3 Verbal nouns and negation

Verbal nouns in Nyakyusa cannot be negated morphologically. To express the negation of an infinitive, periphrastic constructions are used. The most common one is (ʊ)*kʊsita*, (ɪ)*kɪsita* 'without' followed by an augmentless infinitive (6). The former also figures in the negative counterpart to the narrative tense (§7.3).

(6) lɪŋga   a-lɪ   na=ʃʊ   a-bagiile   ʊ-kʊ-bomb-a   ɪ-m-bombo
    if/when 1-COP COM=REF.8 1-be_able.PFV AUG-15-work-FV AUG-9-work

    jo~j-oosa   ɪ-jɪ   i-kʊ-lond-a   ʊ-kʊ-bomb-a   **kɪsita**
    REDUPL~9-all AUG-PROX.9 1-PRS-want-FV AUG-15-work-FV without

    kʊ-taami-gw-a
    15-trouble-PASS-FV

    'If he has them [tools], he can do any kind of work which he wants to do, without being bothered.' [Types of tools in the home]

A construction for constituent negation consists of the substitutive as a pro-clitic to the general negator *mma*, followed by the infinitive carrying the augment.[1]

(7) kʊkʊtɪ ii-sikʊ i-kʊ-kʊ-tʊk-a,   kaŋgɪ i-kʊ-tɪ   "ʊ-ne   **ne=mma**
    every 5-day 1-PRS-2SG-insult-FV   again 1-PRS-say AUG-1SG 1SG=no

    ʊ-kw-eg-igw-a   na Juma, n-ga-ṇ-gan-a"
    AUG-15-marry-PASS-FV COM J.   1SG-NEG-1-love-FV

    'Every day she speaks badly about you and she says "Me, I'm not getting married to Juma, I don't love him."' [Juma, Asia and Sambuka]

This construction, with the class 15 substitutive *ko*, thus *komma*, also serves to form negative commands (8). A free variant *somma* is also found (9, 10).[2] These prohibitives can be adressed to a single person (8, 9) as well as to the second person plural (10).

(8) **komma ʊ-kʊ-nyonyw-a**   ɪ-fi   a-p-eeliigwe
    PROH   AUG-15(INF)-desire-FV AUG-PROX.8 1-give-PASS.PFV

    ʊ-n-nino
    AUG-1-your_companion

    'Do not desire what your neighbour has been given.' [Chief Kapyungu]

(9) **somma ʊ-kʊ-paasy-a!**   lee   po keet-a,
    PROH   AUG-15-worry-FV now/but then watch-FV

    ʊ-ka-a-job-aga   bo ʊ-kaalɪ ʊ-kʊʊ-ny-eeg-a?
    2SG-NEG-PST-speak-IPFV as 2SG-PERS AUG-15-1SG-take-FV?

    'Don't worry! Now look, why didn't you speak before picking me up?' [Crocodile and Monkey]

---

[1]Cf. also Schumann (1899: 69) and Endemann (1914: 84f).
[2]The source of the initial fricative is unclear.

(10) lɪnga   m-b-iigal-iile   **somma ʊ-kʊ-sook-a**   pa-nja
if/when 1SG-2PL-close-APPL.PFV PROH   AUG-15-leave-FV 16-outside
'When I've locked you (pl.) in, don't go outside.' [Python and woman]

11.4 Functions of verbal nouns

11.4.1 Arguments of auxiliaries, modal and motion verbs

Verbal nouns serve as complements of phasal verbs, also called *aspectualizers*, such as *anda* 'begin, start', *mala* 'finish, stop', *leka* 'seize' or *endelela* 'continue'. These take either the infinitive with the augment or the infinitive marked for locative class 16 as their complement. The latter is illustrated in (11). For numerous examples of the first see Chapter 5. It is unclear how far the two differ in meaning and use. Speaker preferences seem to play a role: the younger language assistants used the class 16 form more frequently than the older assistants.

(11) i-kʊ-kwel-a   kangɪ mu-m-piki n=ʊ-kw-**endelel**-a   **pa-kw-ap-a**
1-PRS-climb-FV again 18-3-tree   COM=AUG-15-continue-FV 16-15-pick-FV
a-ma-peasi
AUG-6-pear(<SWA)
'He climbs up the tree again and continues to pick pears.' [Elisha pear story]

    Infinitives, either with the augment or marked for locative class 16, also figure as arguments of modality and manipulation verbs, where they alternate with the subjunctive (§9.3.1.2). The alternation between infinitives and the subjunctive mood is also found following predicative expressions of (dis-)approval or preference, including the invariants *kyajɪpo* '(it is) better' and *paakipo* '(it is) preferable'.

(12) ɲ-dʊ-baatɪko   lw-a   twe ba-Nyakyusa ʊ-n-nyambala
18-11-procedure 11-ASSOC 1PL 2-Ny.   AUG-1-man
ʊ-kʊ-pɪɪj-a,   pamo ʊ-kʊ-suk-a   ɪ-my-enda,   pamo
AUG-15-cook-FV or   AUG-15-wash-FV AUG-4-clothe or
ʊ-kʊ-neg-a   a-m-ɪɪsi   bo ba-li=po a-ba-kiikʊlʊ **mw-iko**
AUG-15-draw_liquid-FV AUG-6-water as 2-COP=16 AUG-2-woman 3-taboo
'In the custom of us, the Nyakyusa people, it is taboo for men to cook or wash clothes or draw water when women are around.' [Division of labour]

Infinitives further function as oblique arguments of modal readings of verbs such as *tola* 'defeat' and its passive *toligwa* 'fail', *kɪnda* 'surpass' or *taamigwa* 'be troubled' (13). See also (5) on p. 324 above and (90b, 90c) on p. 175.

(13) tʊ-tol-iigwe   ʊ-kʊ-lɪ-kol-a   ii-bole
      1PL-defeat-PASS.PFV AUG-15-5-grasp/hold-FV 5-leopard
      'We've failed to catch the leopard.' [Chief Kapyungu]

Infinitives additionally marked for locative classes 16 or 18 also constitute the lexical verb of periphrastic TMA constructions, namely the periphrastic progressive (§6.6.1), the prospective/inceptive (§8.7) and the narrative tense (§7.3). An infinitive with the augment or marked for one of the three locative classes 16–18 may further serve as the complement of the persistive aspect auxiliary (§6.6.2) and augmentless infinitives may serve as the semantic main verb of the movement grams (§10.4).

Lastly, verbs of motion and related verbs such as *ɪma* 'stand, stop' or *tʊma* 'send' often take an infinitive complement additionally marked for one of the three locative classes. Class 16 here indicates that the motion is in relation to a specific place where the eventuality of the verbal noun takes place (14). With class 17, this typically denotes motion with a purpose (15). In a related fashion, a class 17 infinitive can specifically serve as a purpose clause in this context (16). However, a pure motion reading 'to / from' the eventuality is also possible (17). Infinitives marked for class 18 also predominantly give a purposive reading (18), although a locational one is also attested (19).

(14) ɪ-m-bwa   sy-ɪm-aga   **pa-kʊ-ly-a** ɪ-fi-fupa
      AUG-10-dog 10-PST.stand/stop-IPFV 16-15-eat-FV AUG-8-bone
      'The dogs would stop and eat the bones.' [Saliki and Hare]

(15) a-ka-balɪlo ka-mo a-ba-hɪɪji   ba-na ba-a-bʊʊk-ile **kʊ-kʊ-hɪɪj-a**
      AUG-12-time 12-one AUG-2-thief 2-four 2-PST-go-PFV 17-15-steal-FV
      ɪɪ-ng'ombe   pa-kɪ-lo
      AUG-cow(10) 16-7-night
      'One time, four thieves went to steal cows at night.' [Wage of the thieves]

(16) Kalʊlʊ a-lɪnkʊ-bʊʊk-a kʊ-lʊ-bʊbi **kʊ-kʊ-laalʊʊsy-a** lɪnga
      Hare   1-NARR-go-FV   17-11-spider 17-15-ask-FV   if/when
      lʊ-mmw-ag-ile ʊ-n-kiikʊlʊ
      11-1-find-PFV AUG-1-woman
      'Hare went to Spider to ask if it had found a woman.' [Hare and Spider]

(17) bo lʊ-fum-ile   **kʊ-kʊ-hah-a**   ...
      as 11-come_from-PFV 17-15-seduce-FV

      'When it [Spider] returned from seducing ...' [Hare and Spider]

(18) a-ba-ndʊ   ba-a-bʊʊk-ile **n-kʊ-n-keet-a**
      AUG-2-person 2-PST-go-PFV 18-15-watch-FV

      'People went to see her.' [Mfyage turns into a lion]

(19) Saliki a-lɪnkw-is-a   ʊ-kʊ-fum-a   **n-kʊ-jaat-a**
      S.   1-NARR-come-FV AUG-15-come_from-FV 18-15-walk-FV

      'Saliki came from taking a walk.' [Saliki and Hare]

11.4.2 Uses as converbs and related functions

Infinitives can be used in a fashion similar to converbs of simultaneity. The term converb is here understood in Haspelmath's (1995: 3) definition as "a non-finite verb form whose main function is to mark adverbial subordination. Another way of putting it is that converbs are verbal adverbs". Examples (20–22) illustrate this. The use of infinitives in a converb-like manner is especially common with verbs of motion, where each verb provides different components of a single motion event (22).

(20) ba-lɪnkʊ-fimbɪlɪsy-a fiijo   **ʊ-kʊ-n-daalʊʊsy-a** mpaka a-a-job-ile
      2-NARR-persuade-FV INTENS AUG-15-1-ask-FV   until   1-PST-speak-PFV

      a-a-t-ile
      1-PST-say-PFV

      'They interrogated her much until she spoke.' [Killer woman]

(21) **ʊ-kʊ-keet-a**   kʊ-mwanya ki-kʊ-bon-a   ʊ-mu-ndʊ
      AUG-15-watch-FV 17-high   12-PRS-see-FV AUG-1-person

      'Looking up he sees a person.' [Nicholaus Pear Story]

(22) bo i-kw-and-a   itolo ʊ-kʊ-kam-a,   ʊ-n-dʊme   a-lɪnkʊ-sook-a
      as 1-PRS-begin-FV just AUG-15-milk-FV AUG-1-husband 1-NARR-leave-FV

      ʊ-kʊ-fum-a   kʊʊ-sofu   n=ʊ-kʊ-n-kol-a
      AUG-15-come_from-FV 17-room(9) COM=AUG-15-1-grasp/hold-FV

      ʊ-n-kiikʊlʊ   jʊ-la
      AUG-1-woman 1-DIST

      'When she was starting to milk, the husband came out of [lit. left coming from] the bedroom and caught that woman.' [Killer woman]

An infinitive together with a proclitic form of the comitative *na* can be used following another verb to create a tight link between the states-of-affairs of the two, which often occur in sequence. Most commonly the first verb is fully inflected. The relationship between these verbs can be one of cause and consequence (23), preparation and culmination (24), or eventualities based on each other in a more general sense (25). It is also attested with verbs expressing similar or conceptually related meanings (26) and with the last verb in iconic repetitions (27). (28) illustrates coordination with a preceding infinitive complement.

(23) po   jɪ-lɪnkʊ-jɪ-lʊm-a ɪɪ-nine   **n=ʊ-kʊ-jɪ-gog-a**
      then 9-NARR-9-bite-FV AUG-companion.9 COM=AUG-15-9-kill-FV

'It [dog] bit the other one and killed it.' [Dogs laughed about each other]

(24) i-kʊ-pɪmb-a ɪ-kɪ-kapʊ   ky-osa n-ky-eni   mu-n-jɪnga
      1-PRS-lift-FV AUG-7-basket 7-all   18-7-forehead 18-9-bicycle

n=ʊ-kʊ-sook-a=po
COM=AUG-15-leave-FV=16

'He loads a whole basket onto the front of his bicycle and rides away.' [Elisha Pear Story]

(25) ʊ-n-kasi   gw-a   lʊ-bʊbi a-a-b-ambɪliile
      AUG-1-wife 1-ASSOC 11-spider 1-PST-2-receive.PFV

n=ʊ-kʊ-ba-pɪɪj-ɪl-a   ɪ-fi-ndʊ   ɪ-f-ingi   fiijo
COM=AUG-15-2-cook-APPL-FV AUG-8-food AUG-8-many INTENS

'Spider's wife received them and cooked a lot of food for them.' [Hare and Spider]

(26) ŋgoosi a-lɪnkʊ-kʊl-a   **n=ʊ-kʊ-kiikʊlʊp-a**
      N.   1-NARR-grow-FV COM=AUG-15-become_woman-FV

'Ngoosi grew up and became a woman.' [Man and his in-law]

(27) boo=bʊno~bʊ-no   ba-lɪnkw-end-a,   ba-lɪnkw-end-a,
      REF.14=REDUPL~14-DEM 2-NARR-walk/travel-FV 2-NARR-walk/travel-FV

ba-lɪnkw-end-a   **n=ʊ-kw-end-a**
2-NARR-walk/travel-FV COM=AUG-15-walk/travel-FV

'Thus they travelled, travelled, travelled and travelled.' [Pregnant women]

(28) ɪ-n-gwina   j-iis-aga   n-kʊ-j-eeg-a   ɪ-n-gambɪlɪ
      AUG-9-crocodile 9-PST.come-IPFV 18-15-9-take-FV AUG-9-monkey

n=ʊ-kʊ-bʊʊk-a   na=jo   pa-lʊ-sʊngo pa-kw-angal-a
COM=AUG-15-go-FV COM=REF.9 16-11-island 16-15-be_well-FV

'Crocodile used to come to pick up monkey and go with him to an island to spend time together.' [Crocodile and Monkey]

This structure is conventionalized with the verb *enda* 'walk/travel' as the first verb and serves as a marker of sequential events:

(29) ʊ-n-hɪɪj-i ʊ-jʊ   a-a-longwile n-ky-eni
      AUG-1-thief AUG-PROX.1 1-PST-lead.PFV 18-7-forehead

      a-lɪnkw-**end**-a   n=ʊ-kʊ-kol-a   ʊ-lw-igi
      1-NARR-walk/travel-FV COM=AUG-15-grasp/hold-FV AUG-11-door

      'The thief who was going ahead then grabbed the door.' [Wage of the thieves]

Most commonly, only one verb in a sequence is expressed by the comitative infinitive. In a few cases, however, up to three verbs (30) marked in this manner can be found.

(30) a-a-gomok-a   ʊ-mw-anike   jʊ-la **n=ʊ-kʊ-fik-a**
      1-SUBSEC-return-FV AUG-1-young_person 1-DIST COM=AUG-15-arrive-FV

      pa-ka-aja   pa-la **n=ʊ-kʊ-m̩-bʊʊl-a**   **n=ʊ-kʊ-n-nangɪsy-a**
      16-12-homestead 16-DIST COM=AUG-15-1-tell-FV COM=AUG-15-1-show-FV

      ɪ-si   ʊ-n̩-dʊme
      AUG-PROX.10 AUG-1-husband

      'That young woman returned and arrived at home and told and showed her husband these things.' [Man and his in-law]

Other infinitives serve a variety of functions which likely go back to their converb-like use. The infinitive of *tɪ* 'say' amongst other things serves as a complementizer; see §10.3. The reciprocal/associative of *konga* 'follow' is used as an infinitive in a preposition-like manner, together with a comitative phrase expressing reason (31). Similarly the infinitive of *fika* 'arrive', *fuma* 'come from', and *anda* 'start', as well as its applicative *andɪla*, are used in a preposition-like manner. Note that in the case of the first two, the original spatial meaning has been extended to a temporal one. (32, 33) illustrate this use for *fuma* and *andɪla*.

(31) nalooli **ʊ-kʊ-kong-an-a**   n=ʊ-lʊ-gano   ʊ-lʊ   a-a-lɪ
      really AUG-15-follow-RECP-FV COM=AUG-11-love AUG-PROX.11 1-PST-COP

na=lo   ŋgoosi a-lɪnkʊ-jong-a   n=ʊ-n-nyambala jʊ-mo
COM=REF.11 N.   1-NARR-run_away-FV COM=AUG-1-man 1-one

'Because of the love that Ngoosi had, she eloped with a man.' [Man and his in-law]

(32)   ʊ-mu-ndʊ   ʊ-jʊ   a-fumwike   **ʊ-kʊ-fum-a**
       AUG-1-person AUG-PROX.1 1-be(come)_famous.PFV AUG-15-come_from-FV
       pa-tali
       16-long

       'This person has been famous since long ago.' [ET]

(33)   tw-al-iiswisye   ɪ-mi-fuko **ʊ-kw-and-ɪl-a**
       1PL-PST-be(come)_full.CAUS.PFV AUG-4-sack AUG-15-begin-APPL-FV
       n=ʊ-lʊ-bʊnjo   mpaka pa-muu-si
       COM=AUG-11-morning until   16-3-daytime

       'We filled sacks from morning till afternoon.' [ET]

Lastly, the infinitive of *anda* 'begin, start' is further used as the dependent noun in the associative construction as the ordinal number 'first':

(34)   a-lɪnkw-is-a   ʊ-mu-ndʊ   ʊ-gw-a   kw-and-a
       1-NARR-come-FV AUG-1-person AUG-1-ASSOC 15-begin-FV

       'The first person came.' [Chief Kapyungu]

Appendix A: Overview of core TMA constructions

This appendix gives an overview over the core tense, aspect and modality constructions, together with a short summary of their respective functions. Table A.1 lists the present (non-past) and past tense constructions (Chapter 6), Table A.2 summarizes the commonalities and differences of the two narrative markers (Chapter 7), Table A.3 lists the futurate constructions (Chapter 8), and Table A.4 lists mood and modal constructions (Chapter 9).

Table A.1: Major present (non-past) and past tense constructions

Label	Shape	Section	Summary of function(s)
Simple present	SM₂-*kɔ*-VB-*a*	§6.5.1	Non-past progressive, habitual/generic, and futurate
Negative present	SM-*ti-kɔ*-VB-*a*	§6.5.2	Negative counterpart to simple present
Present progressive	SM-*lı pa<-kɔ*-VB-*a*	§6.6.1	Dedicated non-past progressive
Present perfective	SM-VB-ILE	§6.5.3	Non-past, completion of Nucleus (non-inchoatives: completed act; inchoatives: stative or change-of-state)
Persistive	SM-*kaalı* + Verb	§6.6.2	Continuation of a state-of-affairs ('still'); With infinitives: 'not yet'
Neg. present perfective	SM-*ka*-VB-*a*	§6.5.4	Negative counterpart to present perfective
Past perfective	SM-*a(lı)*-VB-ILE	§6.5.5	Past, completion of Nucleus phase (see above)
Neg. past perfective	SM-*ka-a(lı)*-VB-*ile*	§6.5.6	Negative counterpart to past perfective
Past imperfective	SM-*a*-VB-AGA	§6.5.7	Past progressive, habitual, generic; some modal functions
Neg. past imperfective	SM-*ka-a*-VB-*aga*	§6.5.8	Negative counterpart to past imperfective
Past progressive	SM-*a-lı pa<-kɔ*-VB-*a*	§6.6.1	Dedicated past progressive
Past persistive	SM-*a-kaalı* + Verb	§6.6.2	Continuation of a past state-of-affairs ('still'); With infinitives: '(had/was) not yet'

Table A.2: Narrative markers

Label	Shape	Section	Summary of function(s)
Narrative tense	SM-*lmkɔ*-vʙ-*a*	§7.3	The "all-purpose" narrative marker: more frequent than the subsecutive and found in all narratives in the corpus; not subject to sociolinguistic restrictions; unspecified for aspect; does not encode sequential ordering
Subsecutive	SM-*a*-vʙ-*a*	§7.4	Less frequent of the two, not found in all oral narratives; subject to sociolinguistic restrictions: nearly entirely excluded from written texts; specifically perfective semantics; marks advancement of the story; often serves textual function of creating cohesion

Commonalities:

- past time reference (§7.2.3)
- used exlusively with episodic eventualities within the plot proper of narrative discourse (§7.2.3)
- cannot open a text on their own – dependent on an otherwise established specific situation (§7.2.2)
- narrative discourse is structured around the notion of thematic continuity (§6.5.5.3.6)

Table A.3: Futurate constructions

Label	Shape	Section	Summary of function(s)
Future proclitic	*aa*=Verb	§8.2	Shifts to a future reference frame ('D-Domain')
Proclitic (*i*)*sa*	(*i*)*sa*=Verb	§8.3	Function yet unclear; found majoratively at end of paragraphs; limited to lake-shore-plains variety
Proclitic *naa*	*naa*=Verb	§8.4	Portmanteau of COM *na* and *aa*= (?); function vis-à-vis *aa*= yet unclear; limited to southern topolects
Prospective/movement	SM₂-*kw-a kɔ*-VB-*a*(*ga*)	§8.5	Future act with present relevance, typically preceded by motion
Indefinite future	SM-*isakɔ*-VB-*a*(*ga*)	§8.6	Improbable or contingent future state-of-affairs; non-future epistemic reading (presumption) available
Neg. indefinite future	SM-*t-isakɔ*-VB-*a*(*ga*)	§8.6	Negative counterpart to indefinite future
Prospective/inceptive	SM₂-*kɔ-j-a pa-kɔ*-VB-*a*	§8.7	Very near or imminent future state-of-affairs

Table A.4: Major mood and modality constructions

Label	Shape	Section	Summary of function(s)
Imperative	vB-a(ag) vB-e(ge) with OM≠1SG	§9.2	Direct orders to second person singular
Subjunctive	SM-vB-e(ge)	§9.3	Multi-purpose mood, used i.a. in directives to 2PL, jussives (incl. hortatives), volitives, expressions of obligation and not yet realized eventualities; forms part of several complex constructions with tɪ 'say'
Distal/itive subjunctive	SM-ka-vB-e)ge)	§9.3.3	Subjunctive at place other than deictic centre
Negative subjunctive	SM-(lɪ)-ngɑ-vB-a)gɑ)	§9.3.4	Negative counterpart to subjunctive
Desiderative	SM-lɪ-vB-a(gɑ)	§9.4	Bouletic ("boulemaic") modality
Modal future	SM₂-kɔ-vB-agɑ	§9.5	Future state-of-affairs as a settled fact
Negative Modal future	SM-ti-kɔ-vB-agɑ	§9.5	Negative counterpart to modal future
Conditional	ngalɪ + Verb	§9.6	Introduces conditionals (hypotheticals)

Appendix B: Texts

This appendix presents a sample of three texts, all performed orally: two folk narratives and one expository text. For each text, the gender and approximate age of the interlocutor as well as the place and date of recording are provided.

B.1 Narrative: Crocodile and Monkey

This narrative text was told by a male speaker in his 50s in the city of Mbeya in September 2015.

(1) ɪ-n-gwina   n=ɪ-n-gambɪlɪ   ba-a-lɪ   bʊ-manyaani fiijo
AUG-9-crocodile COM=AUG-9-monkey 2-PST-COP 14-friendship INTENS
a-ka-balɪlo a-k-a   ijolo
AUG-12-time AUG-12-ASSOC old_times

'Monkey and Crocodile were good friends long ago.'

(2) ba-a-jaat-an-il-aga   n=ʊ-kw-angal-a   pamopeene
2-PST-walk-RECP-APPL-IPFV COM=AUG-15-be_well-FV together

'They visited and accompanied each other.'

(3) ɪ-n-gwina   j-iis-aga   n-kʊ-j-eega   ɪ-n-gambɪlɪ
AUG-9-crocodile 9.PST-come-IPFV 18-15-9-take-FV AUG-9-monkey
n=ʊ-kʊ-bʊʊk-a   na=jo   pa-lʊ-sʊngo pa-kw-angal-a
COM=AUG-15-go-FV COM=REF.9 16-11-island 16-15-be_well-FV

'Crocodile used to come to pick up Monkey and go with him to an island to spend time together.'

(4) ii-sikʊ lɪ-mo ʊ-n-na   gw-a n-gwina a-a-lɪ   ṃ-bine
5-day 5-one AUG-1-his_mother 1-ASSOC 9-crocodile 1-PST-COP 1-ill

'One day Crocodile's mother was sick.'

(5) po ɪ-n-gwina   j-aa-bʊʊk-ile n-kʊ-jɪ-bʊʊl-a ɪ-n-gambɪlɪ   ʊkʊtɪ
then AUG-9-crocodile 9-PST-go-PFV 18-15-9-tell-FV AUG-9-monkey COMP

"jʊʊba   gw-angʊ ɱ-bine. tʊ-bʊʊk-e   ʊ-ka-n-keet-e"
my_mother(1) 1-POSS.1SG 1-ill   1PL-go-SUBJ 2SG-ITV-1-watch-SUBJ

'So Crocodile went to Monkey to tell him "My mother is sick. Let's go, you should see her."'

(6) ɪ-n-gambɪlɪ   j-aal-iitiike
AUG-9-monkey 9-PST-agree.PFV

'Monkey agreed.'

(7) ba-lɪnkʊ-bʊʊk-a
2-NARR-go-FV

'They went.'

(8) bo j-iitog-ile   pa-mwanya pa-n-gwina   ʊ-kʊ-bʊʊk-a
as 9-mount-PFV 16-high   16-9-crocodile AUG-15-go-FV
kʊ-kʊ-n-keet-a ʊ-n-na   gw-a   n-gwina   bo ba-lɪ
17-15-1-watch-FV AUG-1-his_mmother 1-ASSOC 9-crocodile as 2-COP
pa-katɪ   pa-m-ɪɪsi bi-kw-end-a   ɪ-n-gwina
16-middle 16-6-water 2-PRS-walk/travel-FV AUG-9-crocodile
jɪ-lɪnkw-and-a   ʊ-kʊ-lɪl-a   a-ma-soosi
9-NARR-begin-FV AUG-15-cry-FV AUG-6-tear

'When monkey had mounted Crocodile, going to see Crocodile's mother, when they were travelling in the middle of the water, Crocodile started to cry.'

(9) po ɪ-n-gambɪlɪ   jɪ-lɪnkʊ-tɪ "fi-ki   m-manyaani gw-angʊ
then AUG-9-monkey 9-NARR-say 8-what 1-friend   1-POSS.1SG
kʊ-lɪl-a?"
2SG.PRS-cry-FV

'Monkey said "Why, my friend, are you crying?"'

(10) ɪ-n-gwina   jɪ-lɪnkʊ-tɪ "n-sulumeenie fiijo   paapo ʊlʊ
AUG-9-monkey 9-NARR-say 1SG-afflict.PFV INTENS because now
n-iis-ile   n-kʊ-kw-eg-a   ʊ-ti-kʊ-gomok-a   kangɪ
1SG-come-PFV 18-15-2SG-take-FV 2SG-NEG-PRS-return-FV again

'Crocodile said "I'm very sad, because this time that I've come to pick you up you won't return."'

(11) po ɪ-n-gambɪlɪ   jɪ-lɪnkʊ-tɪ "fi-ki   n-di-kʊ-gomok-a   kangɪ?"
then AUG-9-monkey 9-NARR-say 8-what 1SG-NEG-PRS-return-FV again

'Monkey said "Why won't I return?"'

(12) ɪ-n-gwina   jɪ-lɪnkʊ-tɪ   "tw-a-bʊʊk-ile kʊ-n̩-ganga. ʊ-n̩-ganga
AUG-9-crocodile 9-NARR-say 1PL-PST-go-PFV 17-1-healer. AUG-1-healer

a-a-t-ile   jɪ-kʊ-lond-igw-a   ɪ-n-dumbula j-aa   n-gambɪlɪ. go
1-PST-say-PFV 9-PRS-need-PASS-FV AUG-9-heart 9-ASSOC 9-monkey REF.3

n-kota   gw-a   jʊʊba   gw-angʊ. po i-kʊ-pon-a
3-medicine 3-ASSOC my_mother(1) 1-POSS.1SG then 1-PRS-heal-FV

'Crocodile said: "We went to a witch doctor. The witch doctor said that a monkey's heart is required. That is the medicine for my mother. Then she'll heal."'

(13) ɪ-n-gambɪlɪ   jɪ-lɪnkʊ-tɪ   "somma ʊ-kʊ-paasy-a!   lee   po
AUG-9-crocodile 9-NARR-say PROH   AUG-15-worry-FV now/but then

keet-a,   ʊ-ka-a-job-aga   bo ʊ-kaalɪ ʊ-kʊʊ-ny-eeg-a?"
watch-FV 2SG-NEG-PST-speak-IPFV as 2SG-PERS AUG-15-1SG-take-FV?

Monkey said "Don't worry! Now look, why didn't you speak before picking me up?"'

(14) ɪ-n-gwina   jɪ-lɪnkʊ-tɪ   "n-aa-paasy-aga   ʊkʊtɪ
AUG-9-crocodile 9-NARR-say 1SG-PST-worry-IPFV COMP

aa=kʊ-kaan-a"
FUT=2SG.PRS-refuse-FV

'Crocodile said "I was worrying that you would refuse."'

(15) po ɪ-n-gambɪlɪ   jɪ-lɪnkʊ-tɪ   "ɪno   po ʊ-bomb-ile kabiibi
then AUG-9-monkey 9-NARR-say now/today then 2SG-do-PFV badly

paapo ɪ-n-gambɪlɪ   si-kʊ-j-a   n=ɪ-n-dumbula
because AUG-10-monkey 10-NEG-PRS-be(come)-FV COM=AUG-10-heart

m-mu-nda.   ɪ-n-gambɪlɪ   tʊ-kʊ-si-lek-a   m-mi-piki.
18-3?-inside_of_body AUG-10-monkey 1PL-PRS-10-let-FV 18-4-tree.

pa-la   gʊʊ-ny-aag-ile   mu-m-piki ʊ-ka-fi-bon-a   ɪ-fi
16-DIST 2SG-1SG-find-PFV 18-3-tree   2SG-NEG-8-see-FV AUG-PROX.8

fy-a-syut-aga   fiijo   mu-la?"
8-PST-dangle-IPFV INTENS 18-DIST

'Monkey said "Now you did badly because monkeys don't have their hearts inside the body. Us monkeys we leave them in the trees. There where you met me, in the tree, didn't you see the things that were dangling in there?"'

(16) ɪ-n-gwina   jɪ-lɪnkʊ-tɪ   "ee, m-fi-bwene"
     AUG-9-monkey 9-NARR-say yes, 1SG-8-see.PFV
     'Crocodile said "Yes, I saw them."'

(17) jɪ-lɪnkʊ-tɪ "syo   n-dumbula sy-ɪnʊ   ɪ-si   si-li=po
     9-NARR-say REF.10 10-heart   10-POSS.2PL AUG-PROX.10 10-COP=16
     mu-la? po ʊlʊ tʊ-gomok-e,   tʊ-ka-tʊngʊl-e   jɪ-mo"
     18-DIST then now 1PL-return-SUBJ 1PL-ITV-pick-SUBJ 9-one
     'It said "Are those your hearts in there? Then let's return, let's pick one."'

(18) po ɪ-n-gwina   jɪ-lɪnkʊ-gomok-a mpaka kʊ-m-balɪ kʊ-lw-ɪsi
     then AUG-9-crocodile 9-NARR-return-FV until   17-9-side 17-11-river
     'Crocodile returned to the shore of the river.'

(19) ɪ-n-gambɪlɪ   jɪ-lɪnkʊ-ba-bʊʊl-a a-ba-nine
     AUG-9-monkey 9-NARR-2-tell-FV AUG-2-companion
     'Monkey told the other monkeys.'

(20) jɪ-lɪnkʊ-fyʊk-a mu-m-piki gw-a   baa-mwembe
     9-NARR-climb 18-3-tree 3-ASSOC 2-mango(<SWA)
     'He climbed up a mango tree.'

(21) a-lɪnkʊ-jɪ-koolel-a ɪ-n-gwina   ʊkʊtɪ jɪ-j-e   kɪfuki
     1-NARR-9-call-FV AUG-9-crocodile COMP 9-be(come)-SUBJ near
     paa-si
     16-below
     'He called crocodile so that it would be close below.'

(22) a-lɪnkʊ-si-bʊʊl-a ɪ-n-gambɪlɪ   ɪɪ-nine
     1-NARR-10-tell-FV AUG-10-monkey AUG-companion.10
     'He told the other monkeys.'

(23) si-lɪnkw-and-a   ʊ-kʊ-jɪ-tuuny-a   na=a-baa-mwembe
     10-NARR-begin-FV AUG-15-9-throw-FV COM=AUG-2-mango
     ɪ-n-gwina
     AUG-9-crocodile
     'They started throwing mangoes at Crocodile.'

(24) fyobeene ɪ-n-gwina   ʊ-m-bɪlɪ   gw-ake gʊ-ka-j-a
     therefore AUG-9-crocodile AUG-3-body 3-POSS.SG 3-NEG-be(come)-FV

n-nunu, paapo ba-a-jɪ-tuuny-ile   fiijo
3-good because 2-PST-9-throw-PFV INTENS

'That is why, as for Crocodile, its body is not beautiful, because they threw at it hard.'

(25) j-aaly-and-ile ʊ-kʊ-bop-a   ʊ-kʊ-bop-el-a   m-m-ɪɪsi
9-PST-begin-FV AUG-15-run-FV AUG-15-run-APPL-FV 18-6-water

'It started to run, to run into the water.'

(26) ʊ-bʊ-manyaani bw-a   n-gwina   n=ɪ-n-gambɪlɪ
AUG-14-friendship 14-ASSOC 9-crocodile COM=AUG-9-monkey
bw-a-mal-iike
14-PST-finish-NEUT.PFV

'The friendship between Crocodile and Monkey came to an end.'

(27) a-ka   ko   ka-pango
AUG-PROX.12 REF.12 12-story

'This is the story.'

B.2 Narrative: Hare and Skunk

This narrative was told by a male speaker in his 60s in the village of Lwangwa in December 2014.

(1) po tʊ-kʊ-tɪ   kalʊlʊ na nsyɪsyɪ ba-a-lɪ   ba-manyaani fiijo
then 1PL-PRS-say hare(1) COM skunk(1) 2-PST-COP 2-friend   INTENS

'We say, Hare and Skunk were good friends.'

(2) b-end-aga   b-oosa kʊkʊtɪ kʊ-no   bi-kʊ-bʊʊk-a
2-PST.walk/travel-IPFV 2-all   every 17-PROX 2-PRS-go-FV

'They went together wherever they went.'

(3) po leelo   ii-sikʊ lɪ-mo kalʊlʊ na   nsyɪsyɪ ba-a-bʊʊk-ile
then now/but 5-day 5-one hare(1) COM skunk(1) 2-PST-go-PFV
n-kʊ-fwɪm-a
18-15-hunt-FV

'So one day Hare and Skunk went to hunt.'

(4) po bo bi-kʊ-fwɪm-a ba-a-kol-ile   ii-kanga
then as 2-PRS-hunt-FV 2-PST-grasp/hold-PFV 5-guineafowl

'When they were hunting they caught a guinea fowl.'

(5) po   ba-a-hobwike   fiijo
     then 2-PST-be(come)_happy.PFV INTENS

     'They were very happy.'

(6) po   ba-lɪnkʊ-bʊʊk-a kʊ-ka-aja
     then 2-NARR-go-FV   17-12-homestead

     'They went home.'

(7) bo ba-fik-ile   kʊ-ka-aja   ba-a-peeny-ile
     as 2-arrive-PFV 17-12-homestead 2-PST-remove_feathers-PFV
     ii-kanga   lɪ-la
     5-guineafowl 5-DIST

     'When they arrived home, they removed the feathers from that guinea
     fowl.'

(8) ba-a-peeny-ile,
     2-PST-remove_feathers-PFV

(9) ba-a-peeny-ile
     2-PST-remove_feathers-PFV

     'They removed feathers and removed feathers.'

(10) po   ba-aly-and-ile ʊ-k-ooky-a   m-m-ooto
     then 2-PST-begin-PFV AUG-15-roast-FV 18-3-fire

     'They began to roast it over fire.'

(11) po   bo bi-k-ooky-a   po   nsyɪsyɪ a-lɪnkʊ-m-bʊʊl-a kalʊlʊ
     then as 2-PRS-roast-FV then skunk(1) 1-NARR-1-tell-FV hare(1)
     a-lɪnkʊ-tɪ "ɪɪ-nyama   jɪ-p-iile,   is-aga
     1-NARR-say AUG-meat(9) 9-be(come)_burnt-PFV come-IPFV
     tʊ-ly-ege!"
     1PL-eat-IPFV.SUBJ

     'As they were roasting, Skunk told Hare "The meat is done, come let's
     eat!"'

(12) po   kalʊlʊ a-lɪnkʊ-tɪ "taasi. jɪ-kaalɪ ʊ-kʊ-py-a"
     then hare(1) 1-NARR-say yet   9-PERS AUG-15-be(come)_burnt-FV

     'Hare said "Later. It's not yet done."'

(13) po   nsyɪsyɪ a-lɪnkʊ-tɪ "gwe jɪ-p-iile.   is-aga
     then skunk(1) 1-NARR-say 2SG 9-be(come)_burnt-PFV come-IPFV

tʊ-ly-ege!"
1PL-eat-IPFV.SUBJ

'Then Skunk said "You, it's done. Come, let's eat!"'

(14) kalʊlʊ a-lɪnkʊ-tɪ "jɪ-kaalɪ ʊ-kʊ-py-a"
hare(1) 1-NARR-say 9-PERS AUG-15-be(come)_burnt-FV

'Hare said "It's not yet done."'

(15) ba-lɪnkw-angal-a,
2-NARR-be_well-FV

(16) ba-lɪnkw-angal-a
2-NARR-be_well-FV

'They sat together and sat together.'

(17) kangɪ nsyɪsyɪ a-lɪnkʊ-tɪ "jɪ-p-iile ɪɪ-nyama,
again skunk(1) 1-NARR-say 9-be(come)_burnt-PFV AUG-meat(9)
is-aga tʊ-ly-ege!"
come-IPFV 1PL-eat-IPFV.SUBJ

'Then Skunk again said "The meat is done, come let's eat!"'

(18) Kalʊlʊ a-lɪnkʊ-tɪ "jɪ-kaalɪ ʊ-kʊ-py-a"
hare(1) 1-NARR-say 9-PERS AUG-15-be(come)_burnt-FV

'Hare said "It's not yet done."'

(19) po nsyɪsyɪ a-a-kateele
then skunk(1) 1-PST-be(come)_tired.PFV

'Then Skunk became tired.'

(20) a-aly-and-ile ʊ-kʊ-sipʊk-a
1-PST-begin-PFV AUG-15-doze-FV

'He began to doze.'

(21) po bo i-kʊ-sipʊk-a, bo a-gon-ile ʊ-tʊ-lo po kalʊlʊ
then as 1-PRS-doze-FV as 1-rest-PFV AUG-12-sleep then hare(1)
a-aly-eg-ile ɪɪ-nyama j-oosa
1-PST-take-PFV AUG-meat(9) 9-all

'As he was dozing, as he was asleep, Hare took all the meat.'

(22) a-a-l-iile pyŏ,
1-PST-eat-PFV of_consuming_completely

(23) a-a-l-iile   pyʊ́
      1-PST-eat-PFV o.c.c.
      'He ate it up, he ate it up.'

(24) bo i-kʊ-lembʊk-a   nsyɪsyɪ a-lɪnkw-ag-a   kalʊlʊ a-l-iile   j-oosa
      as 1-PRS-wake_up-FV skunk(1) 1-NARR-find-FV hare(1) 1-eat-PFV 9-all
      ɪɪ-nyama
      AUG-meat(9)
      'When Skunk woke up, he found that Hare had eaten all of the meat.'

(25) po   a-lɪnkʊ-mmw-ani-a kalʊlʊ a-lɪnkʊ-tɪ "ɪɪ-nyama   jɪ-bʊʊk-ile
      then 1-NARR-1-ask-FV   hare(1) 1-NARR-say AUG-meat(9) 9-go-PFV
      kʊʊgʊ?"
      where
      'So he asked Hare "The meat, where has it gone?"'

(26) po   kalʊlʊ a-lɪnkʊ-tɪ "hee.   n-aa-gon-eliile   niine
      then hare(1) 1-NARR-say INTERJ 1SG-PST-rest-INTS.PFV COM.1SG
      ʊ-tʊ-lo.   keet-a,   jɪ-p-iile   j-oosa, jɪ-bwes-ile.
      AUG-13-sleep watch-FV 9-be_burnt-PFV 9-all   9-be_burnt_down-PFV
      jɪ-bwes-ile,   hee"'
      9-be_burnt_down-PFV INTERJ
      'Hare said "Hee, I was also asleep. Look, it all burnt to ashes. It burnt,
      hee."'

(27) po   nsyɪsyɪ a-a-kaleele   fiijo
      then skunk(1) 1-PST-be(come)_angry.PFV INTENS
      'Skunk was very angry.'

(28) a-a-tɪ   "haya!"
      1-SUBSEC-say OK(<SWA)
      'He said "OK!"'

(29) ii-sikʊ ɪ-lɪ-ngɪ   po   ba-lɪnkʊ-bʊʊk-a n-kʊ-lambalal-a
      5-day AUG-5-other then 2-NARR-go-FV   18-15-lie_down-FV
      'Another day they went to sleep.'

(30) po   nsyɪsyɪ j-oope a-a-bʊʊk-ile
      then skunk(1) 1-also 1-PST-go-PFV
      'Skunk also went.'

(31) a-a-j-ile   kʊ-lond-a   a-ma-ani
1-PST-go-PFV 15-search-FV AUG-6-leaf
'He went and searched for leaves.'

(32) a-al-iis-ile   na=a-ma-ani   ga-la bo a-gon-ile ʊ-tʊ-lo
1-PST-come-PFV COM=AUG-6-leaf 6-DIST as 1-rest-PFV AUG-13-sleep
kalʊlʊ
hare(1)
'He came with those leaves, while Hare was asleep.'

(33) a-alɪ-n-kupɪkiile pa-mwanya
1-PST-1-cover.PFV 16-above
'He covered him [with the leaves].'

(34) po   bo a-n-kupɪkiile a-a-lond-ile   ɪ-n-gili,   bo kalʊlʊ a-gon-ile
then as 1-1-cover.PFV 1-PST-search-PFV AUG-9-stick as hare(1) 1-rest-PFV
ʊ-tʊ-lo
AUG-12-sleep
'When he had covered him, he searched for a stick, while Hare was asleep.'

(35) po   nsyɪsyɪ a-a-kom-ile,
then skunk(1) 1-PST-hit-PFV

(36) a-a-kom-ile,
1-PST-hit-PFV

(37) a-a-kom-ile,
1-PST-hit-PFV

(38) a-a-kom-ile
1-PST-hit-PFV
'Then Skunk hit and hit and hit and hit him.'

(39) a-a-kom-ile
1-PST-hit-PFV
'He hit him.'

(40) a-a-bop-ile   pa-nja
1-PST-run-PFV 16-outside
'He ran outside.'

(41) a-a-sook-ile   pa-nja
      1-PST-leave-PFV 16-other
      'He went outside.'

(42) po   kalʊlʊ a-lɪnkʊ-lembʊk-a
      then hare(1) 1-NARR-awake-FV
      'Then Hare woke up.'

(43) i-kʊ-kuut-a "hɪhɪɪ.   ba-n-gom-ile, ba-n-gom-ile, ba-n-gom-ile"
      1-PRS-cry-FV of_crying 2-1SG-hit-PFV 2-1SG-hit-PFV 2-1SG-hit-PFV
      'Then Hare woke up. He cries "Hihii. They've beaten me, they've beaten
      me, they've beaten me."'

(44) po   nsyɪsyɪ "jw-ani a-kʊ-kom-ile?"
      then skunk(1) 1-who 1-2SG-hit-PFV
      'Skunk: "Who's beaten you?"'

(45) "ndɪɪsi,   ndɪɪsi,   ndɪɪsi.   ndɪɪsi,
       I_don't_know I_don't_know I_don't_know I_don't_know
      ndɪɪsi.   ba-n-gom-ile."
      I_don't_know. 2-1SG-hit-PFV
      '[Hare:] "I don't know, I don't know, I don't know. I don't know, I don't
      know. They've beaten me."'

(46) po   "jw-ani a-kʊ-kom-ile, gwe?"
      then 1-who 1-2SG-hit-PFV 2SG
      '[Skunk]: "Who's beaten you?"'

(47) "gwe ndɪɪsi.   ndɪɪsi,   ndɪɪsi."
       2SG I_don't_know I_don't_know I_don't_know
      '[Hare:] "I don't know. I don't know, I don't know."'

(48) ngɪmba mu-n-dumbula i-kʊ-tɪ   "n-gʊ-tosiisye."
      behold 18-9-heart   1-PRS-say 1SG-2SG-pay_back.PFV
      'But in his heart he [Skunk] is thinking "I've paid you back."'

(49) po   leelo   po   ii-sikʊ lɪ-mo ba-a-bʊʊk-ile b-oosa kʊ-kʊ-mog-a
      then now/but then 5-day 5-one 2-PST-go-PFV 2-all   17-15-dance-FV
      ɪ-n-goma
      AUG-9-type_of_drum
      'Then one day they went together to dance to the Ngoma drums.'

(50) po bo ba-fik-ile   pa-la kalʊlʊ a-aly-eg-ile   ɪ-n-goma
      then as 2-arrive-PFV 16-DIST hare(1) 1-PST-take-PFV AUG-9-t.o.drum

      'When they arrived there, Hare took a drum.'

(51) a-aly-and-ile   ʊ-kʊ-kom-a "n-aa-l-iile   j-oosa ɪɪ-nyama
      1-PST-begin-PFV AUG-15-hit-FV 1SG-PST-eat-PFV 9-all   AUG-meat(9)

      m-m-ooto. n-dɪnkʊ-tɪ   jɪ-bwes-ile.   n-dɪnkʊ-tɪ
      18-3-fire 1SG-NARR-say 9-be_burnt_down-PFV 1SG-NARR-say

      jɪ-bwes-ile"
      9-be_burnt_down-PFV"

      'He began to beat it "I ate all the meat on the fire. I said it had burnt. I said
      it had burnt."'

(52) po nsyɪsyɪ a-lɪnkʊ-pɪlɪkɪsy-a
      then skunk(1) 1-NARR-listen-FV

      'Skunk listened.'

(53) po bo a-bɪɪk-ile paa-si   ɪ-n-goma   j-oope nsyɪsyɪ
      then as 1-put-PFV 16-below AUG-9-t.o.drum 1-also skunk(1)

      eeg-a   ɪ-n-goma
      1.SUBSEC.take-FV AUG-9-t.o.drum

      'When he [Hare] had put the drum on the ground, Skunk also took the
      drum.'

(54) a-aly-and-ile   ʊ-kʊ-kom-a   ɪ-n-goma   ʊ-kʊ-tɪ
      1-PST-begin-PFV AUG-15-hit-FV AUG-9-t.o.drum AUG-15-say

      "n-aa-lɪ-kom-ile,   n-aa-lɪ-kom-ile.   n-aa-lɪkomile~lɪ-kom-ile
       1SG-PST-5-hit-PFV 1SG-PST-5-hit-PFV 1SG-PST-REDUPL~5-hit-PFV

      paa-nyuma"
      16-back(9)

      'He started to beat the drum saying "I beat him, I beat him. I beat him on
      the back."'

(55) po kalʊlʊ a-lɪnkʊ-pɪlɪkɪsy-a
      then hare(1) 1-NARR-listen-FV

      'Hare listend.'

(56) po bo i-kʊ-pɪlɪkɪsy-a po   a-a-sumwike   kalʊlʊ
      then as 1-PRS-listen-FV then 1-PST-depart.PFV hare(1)

      'As he was listening, Hare stood up.'

(57) a-lɪnkʊ-m-bʊʊl-a nsyɪsyɪ "ngɪmba jo   ʊ-gwe   gw-alɪ-n-gom-ile?"
    1-NARR-1-tell-FV skunk(1) behold REF.1 AUG-2SG 2SG-PST-1SG-hit-PFV

    'He told Skunk "So it was you who beat me!?"'

(58) j-oope nsyɪsyɪ a-lɪnkʊ-tɪ "ngɪmba jo   ʊ-gwe   gw-a-l-iile
    1-also skunk(1) 1-NARR-say behold REF.1 AUG-2SG 2SG-PST-eat-PFV
    ɪɪ-nyama   j-oosa?
    AUG-meat(9) 9-all

    'Also Skunk said "So you ate all the meat!?"'

(59) "ngɪmba jo   ʊ-gwe   gw-alɪ-n-gom-ile."
    behold REF.1 AUG-2SG 2SG-PST-1SG-hit-PFV

    '[Hare:] "So you beat me!?"'

(60) "n-gʊ-tɪ   "jo   ʊ-gwe   gw-a-l-iile   ɪɪ-nyama   j-oosa.""
    1SG-PRS-say   REF.1 AUG-2SG 2SG-PST-eat-PFV AUG-meat(9) 9-all

    '[Skunk:] "I'm saying "You ate all the meat."""'

(61) "n-gʊ-tɪ   "ngɪmba jo   ʊ-gwe   gw-alɪ-n-gom-ile?"
    1SG-PRS-say   behold 1.REF AUG-2SG 2SG-PST-1SG-hit-PFV
    n-gʊ-kw-ani-a"
    1SG-PRS-2SG-ask-FV

    '[Hare:] "I'm saying "It was you who beat me?" I'm asking you."'

(62) "ngɪmba jo   ʊ-gwe   gw-a-l-iile   ɪɪ-nyama   j-oosa"
    behold REF.1 AUG-2SG 2SG-PST-eat-PFV AUG-meat(9) 9-all

    '[Skunk:] "So you ate all the meat."'

(63) po ba-aly-angɪl-eene   mu-m-bɪlɪ
    then 2-PST-catch-RECP.PFV 18-3-body

    'They grasped each other's bodies.'

(64) kol-aan-a,   kol-aan-a,   kol-aan-a
    grasp/hold-RECP-FV grasp/hold-RECP-FV grasp/hold-RECP-FV
    ba-a-kol-eene
    2-PST-grasp/hold-RECP.PFV

    'Holding each other,[1] holding each other, holding each other, they held
    each other.'

---

[1]This use of *kolaana* is the only attested use of a bare verb stem that does not serve as an imperative.

(65) po   kalʊlʊ a-alɪ-n-kol-ile   nsyɪsyɪ
     then hare(1) 1-PST-1-grasp/hold-PFV skunk(1)

'Hare grasped Skunk.'

(66) a-alɪ-m̩-bind-ile   kʊ-ka-nwa
     1-PST-1-squeeze-PFV 17-12-mouth

'He squeezed around his [Skunk's] snout.'

(67) a-aly-and-ile   ʊ-kʊ-bind-a   kʊ-ka-nwa
     1-PST-begin-PFV AUG-15-squeeze-FV 17-12-mouth

'He began to squeeze around his snout.'

(68) po   j-oope nsyɪsyɪ a-a-kol-ile   ɪ-m-bʊlʊkʊtʊ sy-a   kalʊlʊ
     then 1-also skunk(1) 1-PST-grasp/hold-PFV AUG-10-ear   10-ASSOC hare(1)

'Also Skunk grasped Hare's ears.'

(69) a-aly-and-ile   ʊ-kʊ-luus-a,   ʊ-kʊ-luus-a
     1-PST-begin-FV AUG-15-pull-FV AUG-15-pull-PFV

'He started to pull, to pull.'

(70) ba-lɪnkʊ-lw-a,
     2-NARR-fight-FV

(71) ba-lɪnkʊ-lw-a,
     2-NARR-fight-FV

(72) ba-lɪnkʊ-lw-a
     2-NARR-fight-FV

'They fought and fought and fought.'

(73) po   leelo   j-aal-iis-ile   ɪ-m-bwa
     then now/but 9-PST-come-PFV AUG-9-dog

'Then Dog came.'

(74) j-aa-t-ile   "ʊ-mwe na=mu-lek-e   ʊ-kʊ-lw-a!"
     9-PST-say-PFV   AUG-2PL COM=2PL-let-SUBJ AUG-15-fight-FV

'He said "You (pl.), now stop fighting!"'

(75) po   ba-a-lek-eene
     then 2-PST-let-RECP.PFV

'They released each other.'

(76) po lʊʊ~lʊ   nsyɪsyɪ kʊ-bobonjeele   kʊ-ka-nwa
     then REDUPL~now skunk(1) 17-be(come)_flat.PFV 17-12-mouth

'So now Skunk is flat at the snout.'

(77) kalʊlʊ, ɪ-m-bʊlʊkʊtʊ n-dali
     hare(1) AUG-10-ear   10-long

'As for Hare, his ears are long.'

B.3 Expository: The custom of dancing

This expository text was told by a male speaker in his 40s at Manow mission in October 2015.

(1) a-ka-sumo   ka-a   kʊ-mog-a
    AUG-12-custom 12-ASSOC 15-dance-FV

'The custom of dancing.'

(2) ba-a-li=po a-ba-ndʊ   b-a   ijolo   a-ba-tasi
    2-PST-COP AUG-2-person 2-ASSOC old_times AUG-2-ancestor

'There were the people of old times, the ancestors.'

(3) ba-a-lɪ   n=ii-penenga
    2-PST-COP COM=5-type_of_drum

'They had the Penenga drum.'

(4) ɪ-n-dingala ɪ-jɪ   j-aa-job-igw-aga   ʊkʊtɪ ii-penenga
    AUG-9-drum AUG-PROX.9 9-PST-speak-PASS-IPFV COMP 5-penenga

'This drum was called Penenga.'

(5) po ʊ-lʊ-sumo   lw-ake   ba-a-mog-aga   fiijo
    then AUG-11-custom 11-POSS.SG 2-PST-dance-IPFV INTENS

'As to its custom, they danced much.'

(6) kʊ-kʊ-mog-a kw-ake   ba-a-fwal-aga   kanunu fiijo
    17-15-dance-FV 15-POSS.SG 2-PST-dress/wear-IPFV well   INTENS

'For the dancing they dressed well.'

(7) b-oog-aga   fiijo
    2-PST.bathe-IPFV INTENS

'They bathed well.'

(8) ba-mo ba-a-sanjʊl-aga   n=ɪɪ-nywili
     2-one 2-PST-comb-IPFV COM=AUG-hair(10)
     'Some combed their hair.'

(9) sy-a-fyʊk-aga   fiijo
     10-PST-climb-IPFV INTENS
     'It stood much.'

(10) ba-a-sanjʊl-aga
     2-PST-comb-IPFV
     'They combed it.'

(11) ba-a-t-ɪgɪ   ɪ-fi-bwesi
     2-PST-say-IPFV AUG-8-type_of_hairstyle
     'They called it Fibwesi [hairstyle].'

(12) ba-mo ba-a-sanjʊl-aga
     2-one 2-PST-COMB-IPFV
     'Some combed it.'

(13) ba-a-bɪɪk-aga   n=ɪɪ-syɪti
     2-PST-put-IPFV COM=AUG-parting(9)
     'They parted it.'

(14) ba-a-kol-aga   na=a-ma-koma ng'ombe ga-a
     2-PST-grasp/hold-IPFV COM=AUG-6-hit cow(9)   6-ASSOC
     kʊ-mog-el-a
     15-dance-APPL-FV
     'They also used whips for dancing.'

(15) bo ba-kaalɪ ʊ-kw-and-a   ʊ-kʊ-mog-a   ba-a-fwal-aga
     as 2-PERS AUG-15-begin-FV AUG-15-dance-FV 2-PST-dress/wear-IPFV
     ɪ-my-enda ɪ-my-elu,   pamo a-ma-golole a-m-eelu
     AUG-4-cloth AUG-4-white or   AUG-6-sheet AUG-6-white
     'Before starting to dance, they would put on white clothes, or white
     sheets.'

(16) ga-a-j-aga   a-ma-fume   fiijo
     6-PST-be(come)-IPFV AUG-6-embroidered INTENS
     'They were nicely embroidered.'

(17) ga-a-fwan-aga   mu-ndʊ a-ti-kʊ-kol-a=po
6-PST-resemble-IPFV 1-person 1-NEG-PRS-grasp/hold-FV=PART
'They [were so clean that it] appeared as if a person never held them at all.'

(18) looli leelo   ngɪmba a-ba-ndʊ   bi-kʊ-kol-a   kʊʊ-nongwa
but now/but behold AUG-2-person 2-PRS-grasp/hold-FV 17-issue(9)
j-aa   kʊ-tɪ a-ba-ndʊ   ba-la ba-a-j-aga   b-iifyʊsi
9-ASSOC 15-say AUG-2-person 2-DIST 2-PST-be(come)-IPFV 2-clean
fiijo
INTENS
'But truely, behold, people hold them because those people were very neat.'

(19) po lɪnga   bo ba-lɪ pa-kʊ-mog-a   ba-a-mog-aga
then if/when as 2-COP 16-15-dance-PFV 2-PST-dance-IPFV
'When people were dancing, they danced.'

(20) ba-a-labɪl-aga   ʊ-bʊ-pande   bʊ-mo bw-ene
2-PST-go_in_direction-IPFV AUG-14-side<SWA 14-one 14-self
'They tilted to one side.'

(21) lɪnga   bi-kʊ-sanuk-a kangɪ ba-a-sanuk-ɪl-aga   ʊ-bʊ-pande
if/when 2-PRS-alter-FV again 2-PST-alter-APPL-IPFV AUG-14-side
'When they turned, they turned to the [other] side.'

(22) lʊmo ba-a-bop-el-aga   na n-ky-eni
maybe 2-PST-run-APPL-IPFV COM 18-7-forehead
'Sometimes they would run to the front.'

(23) po a-ba-kiikʊlʊ ba-a-j-anga=po   ba-la ba-a
then AUG-2-woman 2-PST-be(come)-IPFV=16 2-DIST 2-ASSOC
kʊ-luluutɪl-a ʊkʊtɪ "lululululululu"
15-ululuate-FV COMP of_ululating
'As for the women, there were those that ululuated "lululululululu".'

(24) halafu   lɪnga   ba-luluutiile po ba-a-mog-aga   fiijo
afterwards(<SWA) if/when 2-ululate.PFV then 2-PST-dance-IPFV INTENS
'When they [women] had ululuated, they [men] danced much.'

(25) j-oope ɪ-n-dingala ba-a-kʊb-aga   fiijo
      9-also AUG-9-drum 2-PST-beat-IPFV INTENS

      'They also beated the drum hard.'

(26) po lɪnga   ba-kʊb-ile bo ʊ-lʊ,   lɪnga   jɪ-lɪ   kw-Itete kʊ-la,
      then if/when 2-beat-PFV as AUG-PROX.11 if/when 9-COP 17-I.   17-DIST
      j-iis-aga   kʊ-fik-a   mpaka kʊ-no
      9-PST.come-IPFV 15-arrive-FV until   17-PROX

      'When they beated it like this, if it was in Itete over there, it [noise]
      would come to reach this place here.'

(27) po tw-a-many-aga   ʊkʊtɪ kʊ-la ʊ-bw-ite   bʊ-kol-eene
      then 1PL-PST-know-IPFV COMP 17-DIST AUG-14-fight 14-hold-RECP.PFV
      ʊ-bw-a   kʊ-moga
      AUG-14-ASSOC 15-dance-FV

      'Then we would know that a dancing competition was being held.'

(28) a-ka-sumo   ka-tɪ fi,   ka-nog-eliile
      AUG-12-custom 12-say what 12-be_satisfying-INTS.PFV

      'The custom is what?, it is very enjoyable.'

(29) po a-ba-ndʊ   b-iisʊl-aga   pa-la   pa-kʊ-keet-a
      then AUG-2-person 2.PST-be(come)_full-IPFV 16-DIST 16-15-watch-FV

      'People crowded there to look.'

(30) kʊʊ-nongwa j-aa   kʊ-tɪ fi-ki, ba-a-mog-aga   kanunu fiijo
      17-issue(9) 9-ASSOC 15-say 8-what 2-PST-dance-IPFV well   INTENS

      'For what reason, [because] they danced very well.'

(31) lɪnga   ba-lɪ pa-kʊ-sanuk-a kʊʊ-nyuma kʊ-no k-oope
      if/when 2-PST 16-15-alter-FV 17-back(9) 17-PROX 17-also
      ba-a-kyakyatɪl-aga   fiijo bʊno~bʊ-no
      2-PST-move_back_and_forth-IPFV INTENS REDUPL~14-DEM

      'When they were turning back there they would move quickly back and
      forth like this.'

(32) po lɪnga   ba-mog-ile kʊ-lʊ-mogo lw-abo   a-ba-ndʊ
      then if/when 2-dance-PFV 17-11-dance 11-POSS.PL AUG-2-person
      ba-a-hobok-aga   fiijo
      2-PST-be(come)_happy-IPFV INTENS

      'When they danced, people rejoiced much at their dance.'

(33) kʊʊ-nongawa j-aa   kʊ-ti fi-ndʊ fi-ki,   jʊ-la ʊ-gw-a
      17-issue(9)   9-ASSOC 15-say 8-thing 8-what 1-DIST AUG-1-ASSOC
      kʊ-kʊb-a j-oope a-kʊb-ile kanunu, a-ba-a   kʊ-mog-a
      15-beat-FV 1-also 1-beat-PFV well   AUG-2-ASSOC 15-dance-FV
      ba-mog-ile kanunu
      2-dance-PFV well

      'For what reason, [because] the drum player had played well, the dancers
      had danced well.'

(34) po bo ŋdi sisii~si   po lo   lw-iho   lw-ɪtʊ   twe
      then as 18 REDUPL~PROX.10 then REF.11 11-custom 11-POSS.1PL 1PL
      ba-Nyakyusa
      2-Ny.

      'So this is the custom of us, the Nyakyusa people.'

(35) ii-penenga ɪ-lɪ   ba-a-b-oot-aga   n=ʊ-kʊ-b-oot-a
      5-t.o.drum AUG-PROX.5 2-PST-2-invite-IPFV COM=AUG-15-2-invite-FV
      lɪnga   pamo si-li=mo ɪɪ-ʃerehe
      if/when or   10-COP=18 AUG-festivity(9)(<SWA)

      'As for that drum, they invited and invited people when there was a
      celebration.'

(36) po ba-a-bʊʊk-aga kʊ-kʊ-mog-a
      then 2-PST-go-IPFV 17-15-dance-FV

      'So they went to dance.'

(37) po palɪ sisii~si   si-lɪ   m̩-bʊ-pimba, m̩-bʊ-pimba
      then 16 REDUPL~PROX.10 10-COP 18-14-short   18-14-short

      'So this is it in short, in short.'

(38) po si-tumukiile papaa~pa
      then 10-end_at.PFV REDUPL~PROX.16

      'It has finished right here.'

References

Anonymous. 1939. Wörterbuch Deutsch-Kinyakyusa, zum Privatgebrauch der Missionare von Tukuyu, Tanganyika. Unpublished manuscript.

Anonymous. 1969. *Intensive Chichewa.* Lilongwe: Likuni.

Austin, John L. 1962. *How to do things with words.* London: Oxford University Press.

Bain, James Alexander. 1891. *Collections for the Mwamba language, spoken at the north end of the Nyasa.* Livingstonia: Mission Press.

Bar-el, Leora. 2015. Documenting and identifying aspectual classes across languages. In M. Ryan Bochnak & Lisa Matthewson (eds.), *Methodologies in semantic fieldwork*, 75–109. New York: Oxford University Press.

Bastin, Yvonne. 1983. *La finale verbale -ide et l'imbrication en bantou.* Tervuren: Musee Royale de l'Afrique Centrale.

Bastin, Yvonne. 1989a. El prefijo locativo de la clase 18 y la expresión del progresivo presente en bantú (i). *Estudios Africanos. Revista de la Asociación Española de Africanistas (A. E. A.)* 4(6). 35–55.

Bastin, Yvonne. 1989b. El prefijo locativo de la clase 18 y la expresión del progresivo presente en bantú (ii). *Estudios Africanos. Revista de la Asociación Española de Africanistas (A. E. A.)* 4(7). 61–86.

Bastin, Yvonne, André Coupez, Evariste Mumba & Thilo C. Schadeberg. 2002. *Bantu lexical reconstructions 3 / Reconstructions lexicales bantoues 3.* http://www.africamuseum.be/collections/browsecollections/humansciences/blr, accessed 2015-06-23.

Bearth, Thomas. 2003. Syntax. In Derek Nurse & Gerard Philippson (eds.), *The Bantu languages*, 121–142. London: Routledge.

Bennet, William G & Seunghun J. Lee. 2015. A surface constraint in Xitsonga. *li. Africana Linguistica* 21. 3–27.

Berger, Paul. 1933. Konde-Texte. *Zeitschrift für Eingeborenen-Sprachen* 23. 110–154.

Berger, Paul. 1938. Die mit île gebildeten Perfektstämme in den Bantusprachen. *Zeitschrift für Eingeborenensprachen* 28. 81–122, 199–230, 254–286.

References

Bickel, Balthasar. 1997. Aspectual scope and the difference between logical and semantic representation. *Lingua* 102. 115–131.

Bickmore, Lee & Laura Clemens. 2016. *Phonological phrasing in Rutooro.* http://www.lingdomain.org/uploads/2/4/8/4/24841606/acal.pdf, accessed 2017-06-26.

Binnick, Robert I. 1991. *Time and the verb: A guide to tense and aspect.* Oxford: Oxford University Press.

Bochnak, M. Ryan & Lisa Matthewson (eds.). 2015. *Methodologies in semantic fieldwork.* New York: Oxford University Press.

Bohnemeyer, Jürgen. 2002. *The grammar of time reference in Yukatek Maya.* Munich: Lincom Europa.

Bostoen, Koen. 2008. Bantu spirantization. Morphologization, lexicalization and historical classification. *Diachronica* 25(3). 299–356.

Botne, Robert. 1981. *On the nature of tense and aspect: Studies in the semantics of temporal reference in English and Kinyarwanda.* Evanston: Northwestern University dissertation.

Botne, Robert. 1983. On the notion 'inchoative verb' in Kinyarwanda. In Francis Jouannet (ed.), *Le kinyarwanda, langue bantu de rwanda,* 149–180. Paris: SELAF.

Botne, Robert. 1986. The temporal role of eastern Bantu -ba and -li. *Studies in African Linguistics* 17. 303–317.

Botne, Robert. 1998. The evolution of future tenses from serial 'say' constructions in central eastern Bantu. *Diachronica* 15(2). 207–230.

Botne, Robert. 1999. Future and distal -ka-'s: Proto-Bantu or nascent form(s)? In Larry M. Hyman & Jean-Marie Hombert (eds.), *Bantu historical linguistics: Theoretical and empirical perspectives,* 473–515. Stanford: CSLI.

Botne, Robert. 2003a. Dissociation in tense, realis, and location in Chindali verbs. *Anthropological Linguistics* 45(4). 390–412.

Botne, Robert. 2003b. To die across languages: Towards a typology of achievement verbs. *Linguistic Typology* 7. 233–278.

Botne, Robert. 2005. Cognitive schemas and motion verbs: Coming and going in Chindali (eastern Bantu). *Cognitive Linguistics* 16(1). 43–80.

Botne, Robert. 2006. Motion, time and tense: On the grammaticization of come and go to future markers in Bantu. *Studies in African Linguistics* 35(2). 127–188.

Botne, Robert. 2008. *A grammatical sketch of Chindali (Malawian variety).* Philadelphia: American Philosophical Society.

Botne, Robert. 2010. Perfectives and perfects and pasts, oh my!: On the semantics of -ile in Bantu. *Africana Linguistica* 16. 31–63.

Botne, Robert & Tiffany L. Kershner. 2000. Time, tense and the perfect in Zulu. *Afrika und Übersee* 83. 161–180.

Botne, Robert & Tiffany L. Kershner. 2008. Tense and cognitive space: On the organization of tense/aspect systems in Bantu languages and beyond. *Cognitive Linguistics* 19(2). 145–218.

Botne, Robert, Hannington Ochwada & Michael R. Marlo. 2006. *A grammatical sketch of the Lusaamia verb*. Cologne: Köppe.

Bresnan, Joan & Lioba Moshi. 1990. Object asymmetries in comparative Bantu syntax. *Linguistic Inquiry* 21(2). 147–185.

Breu, Walter. 1984. Zur Rolle der Lexik in der Aspektologie. *Die Welt der Slaven* 29(8). 123–148.

Brinton, Laurel J. 1988. *The development of English aspectual systems: Aspectualizers and post-verbal particles*. Cambridge: Cambridge University Press.

Budd, Peter. 2014. Partitives in Oceanic languages. In Silvia Luraghi & Thomas Huumo (eds.), *Partitive cases and related categories*, 523–561. de Gruyter.

Buffin, Jules Marc. 1925. *Remarques sur les moyens d'expression de la durée et du temps en français*. Paris: Impr.-édition les Presses universitaires de France.

Busse, Joseph. 1940. Lautlehre des Inamwanga. *Zeitschrift für Eingeborenen-Sprachen* 30. 250–272.

Busse, Joseph. 1942. Konde-Texte. *Zeitschrift für Eingeborenen-Sprachen* 32. 201–224.

Busse, Joseph. 1949. Aus dem Leben von Asyukile Malongo (Nyakyusa-Texte). *Zeitschrift für Eingeborenen-Sprachen* 35. 191–227.

Busse, Joseph. 1957. Nyakyusa-Rätsel. *Zeitschrift für Phonetik und allgemeine Sprachwissenschaft* 10(2). 108–119.

Busse, Joseph. 1960. *Die Sprache der Nyiha in Ostafrika*. Berlin: Akademie Verlag.

Busse, Joseph. n.d. Nyakyusa dictionary. Unpublished manuscript.

Bybee, Joan L., William Pagliuca & Revere D. Perkins. 1991. Back to the future. In Elizabeth Closs Traugott & Bernd Heine (eds.), *Approaches to grammaticalization*. Vol. 2: *Types of grammatical markers*, 17–58. Amsterdam: Benjamins.

Bybee, Joan L., Revere Dale Perkins & William Pagliuca. 1994. *The evolution of grammar: Tense, aspect and modality in the languages of the world*. Chicago: University of Chicago Press.

Carlson, Gregory N. 2009. Generics, habituals and iteratives. In Keith Allen (ed.), *Concise encyclopedia of semantics*, 375–378. Amsterdam: Elsevier.

Carlson, Robert. 1992. Narrative, subjunctive, and finiteness. *Journal of African Languages and Linguistics* 1(13). 59–86.

Carlson, Robert. 1994. *A grammar of Supyire*. Berlin: de Gruyter.

Chafe, Wallace (ed.). 1980. *The pear stories: Cognitive, cultural, and linguistic aspects of narrative production.* Norwood: Ablex.

Christensen, Lisa. 1997. *Framtidsuttrycken i svenskans temporala system.* Lund: Lund University dissertation.

Cleve. 1904. Über die Frauensprache. *Zeitschrift für Ethnologie* 3. 460–463.

Cole, Desmond T. 1955. *An introduction to Tswana grammar.* London: Longmans, Green & Co.

Comrie, Bernard. 1976. *Aspect.* Cambridge: Cambridge University Press.

Comrie, Bernard. 1985. *Tense.* Cambridge: Cambridge University Press.

Contini Morava, Ellen. 1987. Text cohesion and the sign: Connectedness between events in Swahili narrative. In David Odden (ed.), *Current approaches to African linguistics 4*, 107–122. Dordrecht: Foris.

Contini Morava, Ellen. 1989. *Discourse pragmatics and semantic categorization: The case of negation and tense-aspect with special reference to Swahili.* Berlin: de Gruyter.

Cook, John. 2004. The semantics of verbal pragmatics: Clarifying the roles of wayyiqtol and weqatal in Biblical Hebrew prose. *Journal of Semitic Studies* 49(2). 247–273.

Cover, Rebecca Tamar. 2010. *Aspect, modality, and tense in Badiaranke.* Berkeley: University of California dissertation.

Cover, Rebecca Tamar. 2015. Semantic fieldwork on TAM. In Lisa Matthewson & M. Ryan Bochnak (eds.), *Methodologies in semantic fieldwork*, 233–268. Oxford: Oxford University Press.

Cover, Rebecca Tamar & Judith Tonhauser. 2015. Theories of meaning in the field: Temporal and aspectual reference. In M. Ryan Bochnak & Lisa Matthewson (eds.), *Methodologies in semantic fieldwork*, 306–349. New York: Oxford University Press.

Crane, Thera Maria. 2011. *Beyond time: Temporal and extra-temporal functions of tense and aspect marking in Totela, a Bantu language of Zambia.* Berkeley: University of California dissertation.

Croft, William. 2012. *Verbs. Aspect and causal structure.* Oxford: Oxford University Press.

Crowley, Terry. 2007. *Field linguistics: A beginner's guide.* Oxford: Oxford University Press.

Dahl, Östen. 1985. *Tense and aspect systems.* Oxford: Basil Blackwell.

Dahl, Östen (ed.). 2000a. *Tense and aspect in the languages of Europe.* Berlin: de Gruyter.

Dahl, Östen. 2000b. The grammar of future time reference in European languages. In Östen Dahl (ed.), *Tense and aspect in the languages of Europe*, 309–328. Berlin: de Gruyter.

Devos, Maud & Daniël van Olmen. 2013. Describing and explaining the variation of Bantu imperatives and prohibitives. *Studies in Language* 37(1). 1–57.

Diercks, Michael. 2011. Incorporating location in argument structure: The Lubukusu locative clitic. In Eyamba G. Bokamba, Ryan K. Shosted & Bezza Tesfaw Ayalew (eds.), *Selected proceedings of the 40th annual conference on African linguistics*, 65–79. Sommerville: Cascadilla Proceedings Project.

Dimmendaal, Gerrit J. 2011. *Historical linguistics and the comparative study of African languages*. Amsterdam: Benjamins.

Doke, Clemens. 1935. *Bantu linguistic terminology*. London/New York: Longmans, Green.

Dom, Sebastian & Koen Bostoen. 2015. Examining variation in the expression of tense/aspect to classify the Kikongo language cluster. *Africana Linguistica* 21. 163–211.

Dooley, Robert A. & Stephen H. Levinsohn. 2000. *Analyzing discourse: A manual of basic concepts*. Dallas: SIL International.

Downing, Laura J. 2001. Ungeneralizable minimaliy in Ndbele. *Studies in African Linguistics* 30(1). 33–58.

Dowty, David R. 1979. *Word meaning and Montague Grammar. The semantics of verbs and times in generative semantics and in Montague's PTQ*. Dordrecht: D. Reidel.

Duranti, Alessandro. 1977. Notes on Nyakyusa syntax. Unpublished manuscript.

Eaton, Helen. 2013. *A comparison of narrative verb forms in Bena, Nyakyusa, Malila and Nyiha*. http://bantu5.sciencesconf.org/conference/bantu5/GS_EATON_Bantu5_HO.pdf, accessed 2016-05-05.

Eaton, Helen. 2015. *Narrative discourse in Malila*. http://www.sil.org/resources/publications/entry/61298, accessed 2015-07-09.

Eaton, Helen. n.d. Vwanji. In Koen Bostoen & Mark van de Velde (eds.), *The Bantu languages*, 2nd edn., (in print). London: Routledge.

Ebneter, Theodor. 1973. *Das bündnerromanische Futur. Syntax der mit vegnir und habere gebildeten Futurtypen in Gegenwart und Vergangenheit*. Bern: Franck.

Ehret, Christopher. 1973. Patterns of Bantu and Central Sudanic settlement in central and southern Africa (ca. 1000 B.C. – 500 A.D.) *Transafrican Journal of History* 3. 1–71.

Ehret, Christopher. 2001. *An African classical age. Eastern and southern Africa in world history. 1000 b.c. to a.d. 400*. Charlottesville: University Press of Virginia.

Endemann, Karl. 1900. Zur Erklärung einer eigenthümlichen Verbalform in Konde. *Mittheilungen des Seminars für orientalische Sprachen* 3(3). 93–95.

Endemann, Karl. 1914. Erste Übungen in Nyakyusa. *Mitteilungen veröffentlicht vom Seminar für Kolonialsprachen in Hamburg* 31(Beiheft 10). 1–92.

von Essen, Otto & Emmi Kähler-Meyer. 1969. Prosodische Wortmerkmale im Nyaykusa. In Hans-Jürgen Greschat & Hermann Jungraithmayr (eds.), *Wort und Religion: Kalima na Dini. Studien zur Afrikanistik, Missionswissenschaft, Religionswissenschaft. Ernst Dammann zum 65. Geburtstag*, 34–56. Stuttgart: Evangelischer Missionsverlag.

Evans, Vyvyan & Melanie Green. 2006. *Cognitive linguistics. An introduction.* Edinburgh: Edinburgh University Press.

Fauconnier, Gilles. 1994. *Mental spaces: Aspects of meaning construction in natural language.* New York: Cambridge University Press.

Felberg, Knut. 1996. *Nyakyusa-English-Swahili & English-Nyakyusa dictionary.* Daressalaam: Mkuki na Nyota.

Felberg, Knut. 2010. *The Nyakyusa homepage.* www.nyakyusa.com, accessed 2016-05-05.

Filip, Hana. 2011. Aspectual classes and aktionsart. In Klaus von Heusinger, Claudia Maienborn & Paul Portner (eds.), *Semantics. An international handbook of natural language meaning*, vol. 2, 1186–1216. Berlin: de Gruyter.

von Fintel, Kai. 2006. Modality and language. In Donald M. Borchert (ed.), *Encyclopedia of philosophy*, 2nd edn., 20–27. Detroid: MacMillan.

Fleisch, Axel. 2000. *Lucazi grammar. A morphosemantic analysis.* Cologne: Köppe.

Fleischman, Suzanne. 1982. *The future in thought and language. Diachronic evidence from Romance.* Cambridge: Cambridge University Press.

Fleischman, Suzanne. 1985. Discourse functions of tense-aspect oppositions in narrative: Toward a theory of grounding. *Linguistics* 23(6). 851–882.

Fleischman, Suzanne. 1990. *Tense and narrativity.* London: Routledge.

Fourshey, Catherine Cymone. 2002. *Agriculture, ecology, kinship and gender. A social and economic history of Tanzania's corridor 500 bc to 1900 ad.* Los Angeles: University of California dissertation.

Freed, Alice. 1979. *The semantics of English aspectual complementation.* Dordrecht: D. Reidel.

Fülleborn, Friedrich. 1906. *Das Deutsche Njassa- u. Ruwuma-Gebiet, Land und Leute, nebst Bemerkungen über die Schire-Länder.* Berlin: Reimer.

Givón, Talmy. 1984. *Syntax: A functional-typological introduction.* Amsterdam: Benjamins.

Givón, Talmy. 1994. Irrealis and the subjunctive. *Studies in Language* 18(2). 265–337.

Givón, Talmy. 2001. *Syntax. An introduction*. Amsterdam: Benjamins.

Good, Jeffrey Craig. 2007. Slouching towards deponency: A family of mismatches in the Bantu verb stem. In Matthew Baerman, Greville G. Corbett, Dunstan Brown & Andrew Hippisley (eds.), *Deponency and morphological mismatches*, 203–230. Oxford: Oxford University Press.

Gray, Hazel. 2013. *Locatives in Ikizu*. Universiteit Leiden MA thesis.

Gray, Hazel. n.d. *Kisi language description*. Unpublished manuscript.

Greenway, P.J. 1947. A veterinary glossary of some tribal languages of Tanganyika territory. *East African agricultural journal of Kenya, Tanganyika, Uganda and Zanzibar* 13. 237–244.

Güldemann, Tom. 1996. *Verbalmorphologie und Nebenprädikation im Bantu. Eine Studie zur funktional motivierten Genese eines konjugationalen Subsystem.* Bochum: Brockmeyer.

Güldemann, Tom. 1999. The genesis of verbal negation in Bantu and its dependency on functional features of clause types. In Larry M. Hyman & Jean-Marie Hombert (eds.), *Bantu historical linguistics: Theoretical and empirical perspectives*, 545–587. Stanford: CSLI.

Güldemann, Tom. 2000. When 'say' is not say: The function versatility of the Bantu quotative marker ti with special reference to Shona. In Tom Güldemann & Manfred von Roncador (eds.), *Reported discourse. A meeting ground for different linguistic domains*, 253–287. Amsterdam: Benjamins.

Güldemann, Tom. 2003. Grammaticalization. In Derek Nurse & Gerard Philippson (eds.), *The Bantu languages*, 182–194. London: Routledge.

Guthrie, Malcolm. 1967. *Comparative Bantu: An introduction to the comparative linguistics and prehistory of the Bantu languages*. Farnborough: Gregg.

Haspelmath, Martin. 1995. The converb as a cross-linguistically valid category. In Martin Haspelmath & Ekkehard König (eds.), *Converbs in cross-linguistic perspective. Structure and meaning of adverbial verb forms - adverbial participles, gerunds*, 1–55. Berlin: de Gruyter.

Haspelmath, Martin. 1998. The semantic development of old presents. New futures and subjunctives without grammaticalization. *Diachronica* 15(1). 29–62.

Haspelmath, Martin. 2006. Against markedness (and what to replace it with). *Journal of Linguistics* 42(1). 25–70.

Haspelmath, Martin. 2013. Argument indexing: A conceptual framework for the syntactic status of bound person forms. In Dik Bakker & Martin Haspelmath (eds.), *Languages across boundaries: Studies in memory of Anna Siewierska*, 192–226. Berlin: de Gryuter.

Hawkinson, A.K. 1976. *A semantic characterisation of verbal agreement and word order in several Bantu languages.* Dar es Salaam: University of Dar es Salaam MA thesis.

Heine, Bernd. 1972. Zur genetischen Gliederung der Bantu-Sprachen. *Afrika und Übersee* 56(61). 164–185.

Heine, Bernd, Ulrike Claudi & Friederike Hünnemeyer. 1991. *Grammaticalization. A conceptual framework.* Chicago: University of Chicago Press.

Hodson, T.C. 1934. Name giving among the Wasokile. *Man: A monthly record of anthropological science* 21.

Hopper, Paul J. 1979. Aspect and foregrounding in discourse. In Talmy Givón (ed.), *Discourse and syntax*, 213–241. New York: Academic Press.

Hopper, Paul J. 1982. Aspect between discourse and grammar: An introductory essay for the volume. In Paul J. Hopper (ed.), *Tense-aspect: Between semantics and pragmatics*, 3–18. Amsterdam: Benjamins.

Hyman, Larry M. 1999. The historical interpretation of vowel harmony in Bantu. In Larry M. Hyman & Jean-Marie Hombert (eds.), *Bantu historical linguistics: Theoretical and empirical perspectives*, 235–295. Stanford: CSLI.

Hyman, Larry M. 2002. Suffix ordering in Bantu: A morphocentric approach. In Geert M. Booji (ed.), *Yearbook of morphology 2002*, 423–458. Dordrecht: Kluwer.

Hyman, Larry M. 2003. Sound change, misanalysis, and analogy in the Bantu causative. *Journal of African Languages and Linguistics* 24(1). 55–90.

Hyman, Larry M. 2007. Niger-Congo verb extensions: Overview and discussion. In Doris L. Payne & Jaime Peña (eds.), *Selected proceedings of the 37th annual conference on African linguistics*, 149–163. Sommerville: Cascadilla Proceedings Project.

Hyman, Larry M. 2013. Penultimate lengthening in Bantu. In Balthasar Bickel, Lenore A. Grenoble, David A. Peterson & Alan Timberlake (eds.), *Language typology and historical contingency: In honor of Johanna Nichols*, 309–330. Amsterdam: Benjamins.

Hyman, Larry M. & Francis X. Katamba. 1991. The augment in Luganda tonology. *Journal of African Languages and Linguistics* 12(1). 1–45.

Hyman, Larry M. & Francis X. Katamba. 1993. The augment in Luganda: Syntax or pragmatics? In Sam A. Mchombo (ed.), *Theoretical aspects of Bantu grammer*, 209–256. Stanford: CSLI.

Jakobson, Roman. 1957. *Shifters, verbal categories and the Russian verb.* Cambridge: Harvard University Press.

Johanson, Lars. 1996. Terminality operators and their hierarchical status. In Betty Devrient, Louis Goossens & Johan van der Auwera (eds.), *Complex structures: A functionalist perspective*, 229–258. Berlin: de Gruyter.

Johanson, Lars. 2000. Viewpoint operators in European languages. In Östen Dahl (ed.), *Tense and aspect in the languages of Europe*, 27–187. Berlin: de Gruyter.

Johnston, Henry Hamilton. 1897. *British Central Africa.* New York: Edward Arnold.

Johnston, Henry Hamilton. 1977. *A comparative study of the Bantu and Semi-Bantu languages.* Oxford: Clarendon Press.

Jones, Larry B. & Linda K. Jones. 1979. Multiple levels of information in discourse. In Linda K. Jones (ed.), *Discourse studies in Mesoamerican languages.* Vol. 1: *Discussion*, 3–27. Dallas: Summer Institute of Linguistics.

Kamp, Hans & Uwe Reyle. 1993. *From dicourse to logic. Introduction to modeltheoretic semantics of natural language, formal logic and discourse representation theory.* Dordrecht: Springer.

Karels, Jacob. 2014. *Relative Constructions in Nyiha: An Investigation of the syntax, semantics and activation status of information in relative constructions in Nyiha, a Bantu language of Southwestern Tanzania (M23).* http://www.sil.org/resources/publications/entry/59430, accessed 2015-12-01.

Katamba, Francis X. 2003. Bantu nominal morphology. In Derek Nurse & Gerard Philippson (eds.), *The Bantu languages*, 103–120. London: Routledge.

Kemmer, Suzanne. 1993. *The middle voice.* Amsterdam: Benjamins.

Kenny, Anthony. 1969. *Action, emotion and will.* London: Routledge/Kegan Paul.

Kershner, Tiffany L. 2002. *The verb in Chisukwa: Aspect, tense and time.* Bloomington: Indiana University dissertation.

de Kind, Jasper, Sebastian Dom, Gilles-Maurice de Schryver & Koen Bostoen. 2015. Event-centrality and the pragmatics-semantics interface in Kikongo: From predication focus to progressive aspect and vice versa. *Folia Linguistica Historica* 36(1). 113–163.

Kishindo, Pascal J. 1999. Ikyangonde: A preliminary analysis. *Journal of Humanities* 13. 59–86.

Kisseberth, Charles. 2003. Makhuwa (P30). In Derek Nurse & Gerard Philipson (eds.), *The Bantu languages*, 546–565. London: Routledge.

Kisseberth, Charles & David Odden. 2003. Tone. In Derek Nurse & Gerard Philippson (eds.), *The Bantu languages*, 59–70. London: Routledge.

Kittilä, Seppo. 2009. Causative morphemes as non-valency increasing devices. *Folia Linguistica* 43(1). 67–94.

Klein, Wolfang. 1994. *Time in language.* London: Routledge.

Kolbusa, Stefanie. 2000. *Schwiegermeidung bei den Nyakyusa.* Bayreuth: Universität Bayreuth dissertation.

Konter-Katani, Maggy. 1988. A Nyakyusa-English wordlist. Unpublished manuscript.

Konter-Katani, Maggy. 1989. *Sound correspondences of Nyakyusa (M30) and Ndali: Reflexes of Proto-Bantu voiceless stops.* Leiden: Rijksuniversiteit Leiden MA thesis.

Krifka, Manfred, Francis J. Pelletier, Gregory N. Carlson, Gennaro Chierchia, Godehard Link & Alice ter Meulen. 1995. Introduction to genericity. In Gregory N. Carlson & Francis J. Pelletier (eds.), *The generic book*, 1–124. Chicago: University of Chicago Press.

Kröger, Rüdiger. 2011. Dokumentation afrikanischer Sprachen durch Herrnhuther Missionare in Deutsch-Ostafrika. In Thomas Stolz, Christina Vossmann & Barbara Dewein (eds.), *Kolonialzeitliche Sprachforschung: Die Beschreibung afrikanischer und ozeanischer Sprachen zur Zeit der deutschen Kolonialherrschaft.* 161–186. Berlin: Akademie Verlag.

Kutsch Lojenga, Constance. 2007. Minimality and morae in Malila (M.24). In Doris L. Payne & Jaime Peña (eds.), *Selected proceedings of the 37th annual conference on African linguistics*, 77–87. Sommerville: Cascadilla Proceedings Project.

Labov, William. 1997. Some further steps in narrative analysis. *Journal of narrative and life history* 7. 395–415.

Labov, William & Joshua Waletzky. 1967. Narrative analysis: Oral versions of personal experience. In June Helm (ed.), *Essays on the verbal and visual arts*, 12–44. Seattle: University of Washington Press.

Labroussi, Catherine. 1998. *Le couloir de lacs: Contributions linguistique à l'histoire des populations du sud-ouest de la tanzanie.* Paris: INALCO dissertation.

Labroussi, Catherine. 1999. Vowel system and spirantisation in southwest Tanzania. In Jean-Marie Hombert & Larry M. Hyman (eds.), *Bantu historical linguistics: Theoretical and empirical perspectives*, 335–377. Stanford: CSLI.

Lehmann, Christian. 2012. *Speech act participants in modality.* http://www.christianlehmann.eu/publ/lehmann_modality.pdf, accessed 2015-06-11.

Levinsohn, Stephen H. 2007. *Self-instruction materials on narrative discourse analysis.* http://www-01.sil.org/~levinsohns/narr.pdf, accessed 2015-01-16.

Levinson, Steven C. 1983. *Pragmatics.* Cambridge: Cambridge University Press.

Lewis, M. Paul (ed.). 2009. *Ethnologue: Languages of the world*. Dallas: SIL.

Lindfors, Anna-Lena, Mark Woodward, Louise Nagler & Susanne Krüger. 2009. *A sociolinguistic survey of the Nyiha and Nyika language communities in Tanzania, Zambia and Malawi*. http://www.sil.org/resources/publications/entry/9168, accessed 2017-09-20.

Lindsted, Jouko. 2000. The perfect – aspectual, temporal and evidential. In Östen Dahl (ed.), *Tense and aspect in the languages of Europe*, 365–384. Berlin: de Gruyter.

Longacre, Robert E. 1990. Storyline concerns and word order typology in east and west Africa. *Studies in African Linguistics* supplement 10. 1–181.

Longacre, Robert E. 1996. *The grammar of discourse*. 2nd edn. New York: Plenum.

Lusekelo, Amani. 2007. *Tense and aspect systems in Kinyakyusa*. Dar es Salaam: University of Dar es Salaam MA thesis.

Lusekelo, Amani. 2008a. A descriptive account of the Bantu verbal extensions in Kinyakyusa. *Journal of Research in African Languages and Linguistics* 8. 83–116.

Lusekelo, Amani. 2008b. Lexicalization of motion events in Kiswahili and Kinyakyusa. *KISWAHILI: Journal of the Institute of Kiswahili Research* 71. 11–23.

Lusekelo, Amani. 2009a. *A description of Kinyakyusa reduplication*. http://www.skase.sk/Volumes/JTL14/pdf_doc/02.pdf, accessed 2016-05-05.

Lusekelo, Amani. 2009b. The structure of the Nyakyusa noun phrase. *Nordic Journal of African Studies* 18(4). 305–331.

Lusekelo, Amani. 2010. Adverbs as a word category in Kinyakyusa. *Journal of the National Council of Less Comonly Taught Languages* 8. 59–88.

Lusekelo, Amani. 2012. *Inflectional and derivational morphology in Optimality Theory. multiple object-nouns and co-occurrence of verbal extensions in Kinyakyusa*. Gabarone: University of Botswana dissertation.

Lusekelo, Amani. 2013. *Tense-aspect, modality and negation in Kinyakyusa. A Bantu language of Tanzania and Malawi*. Saarbrücken: LAP Lambert Academic Publishing.

Lusekelo, Amani. 2016. The nature of conditional sentences in Nyakyusa. *Journal of Education, Humanitites & Sciences* 5(1).

Madan, Arthur Cornwallis. 1903. *Swahili-English dictionary*. Oxford: Clarendon Pres.

Maho, Jouni Filip. 1999. *A comparative study of Bantu noun classes*. Gothenburg: Acta Universitatis Gothoburgensis.

Maho, Jouni Filip. 2003. A classification of the Bantu languages: An update of Guthrie's referential system. In Derek Nurse & Gerard Philippson (eds.), *The Bantu languages*, 639–652. London: Routledge.

Maho, Jouni Filip. 2009. *NUGL Online: The online version of the new updated Guthrie list, a referential classification of the Bantu languages*. http://goto.glocalnet.net/mahopapers/nuglonline.pdf, accessed 2017-09-20.

Marlo, Michael R. 2014. Exceptional patterns of object marking in Bantu. *Studies in African Linguistics* 43. 85–123.

Mathangwane, Joyce T. 2001. Suffix ordering in the Ikalanga verb stem: A case against the repeated morph constraint. *South African Journal of African Languages* 21(3–4). 396–409.

Maw, Joan. 2013. *Narrative in Swahili*. London: Routledge.

McCawley, James D. 1971. Tense and time reference in English. In Charles Filmore & D. Terence Langendoen (eds.), *Studies in linguistic semantics*, 97–113. New York: Holt Rinehart.

Meeussen, A. E. 1967. Bantu lexical reconstructions. *Africana Linguistica* 3. 80–122.

Meinhof, Carl. 1966. *Grundrisse eine Lautlehre der Bantusprachen*. Neldeln: Kraus.

Merensky, Alexander. 1894. *Deutsche Arbeit am Njaßa, Deutsch-Ostafrika*. Berlin: Buchhandlung der evangelischen Misisonsgesellschaft.

Method, Samuel. 2008. *Aspects of kiNyakyusa phonology – The Case of kiMwamba dialect*. Dar es Salaam: University of Dar es Salaam MA thesis.

Meyer, Theodor. 1919. Regeln für die Schreibung im Kinyakyusa. Unpublished manuscript.

Meyer, Theodor. 1989. *Die Konde – Ethnographische Aufzeichnungen (1891–1916) des Missinssuperintendanten Theodor Meyer bei den Nyakyusa (Tanzania)*. Sylvia Träbing (ed.). Hohenschäftlarn: Renner. published posthumously by Träbing.

Michaelis, Laura A. 2004. Type shifting in Construction Grammar: An integrated approach to aspectual coercion. *Cognitive Linguistics* 15. 1–67.

Miestamo, Matti. 2005. *Standard negation. The negation of declarative verbal main clauses in a typological perspective*. Berlin: de Gruyter.

Miestamo, Matti. 2007. Negation – an overview of typological research. *Language and Linguistics Compass* 1(5). 552–570.

Moens, Marc. 1987. *Tense, aspect and temporal reference*. Edinburgh: University of Edinburgh dissertation.

Moens, Marc & Mark Steedman. 1988. Temporal ontology and temporal reference. *Computational linguistics* 14(2). 15–28.

Möhlig, Wilhelm J. G. 1981. Die Bantusprachen im engeren Sinne. In Bernd Heine, Thilo C. Schadeberg & Ekkehard Wolff (eds.), *Die Sprachen Afrikas: Mit zahlreichen Karten und Tabellen*, 78–116. Hamburg: Buske.

Morrison, Michelle Elizabeth. 2011. *A reference grammar of Bena*. Houston: Rice University dissertation.

Mous, Maarten. 2007. *Language documentation as a challenge to description.* http://home.planet.nl/~gongg010/veldwerk/Language%20documentation%20as%20a%20challenge_article.pdf, accessed 2015-06-11.

Mreta, Abel Yamwaka. 1998. *An analysis of tense and aspect in Chasu: Their form and meaning in the affirmative constructions.* Hamburg: LIT.

Mulinda, M.F. 1997. *An evaluation of the degree of simliarity between five Bantu languages: Kihaya, Kihehe, Kinyakyusa, Kishambala and Kisukuma.* Unpublished manuscript.

Muzale, Henry R.T. & Josephat M. Rugemalira. 2008. Researching and documenting the languages of Tanzania. *Language Documentation & Conservation* 2(1). 68–108.

Mwakasaka, Christon S. 1975. Trends and development in the oral poetry of the Banyakyusa in this century. *UMMA* 5(1). 35–47.

Mwakasaka, Christon S. 1978. *The oral literature of the Banyakyusa.* Nairobi: Kenya Literature Bureau.

Mwalilino, Walusako A. 1995. *A bibliography on the Nyakusa-Ngonde people of Tanzania and Malawi.* Silver Spring: Institute of Nyakyusa-Ngonde Studies.

Mwangoka, Ngapona & Jan Voorhoeve. 1960a. *Cursus kiNyakyusa.* Vol. 2: *Cursus praktische Taalbeheersing.* Leiden: Rijksuniversiteit.

Mwangoka, Ngapona & Jan Voorhoeve. 1960b. *Cursus kiNyakyusa.* Vol. 4: *Nyakyusa word list.* Leiden: Rijksuniversiteit.

Mwangoka, Ngapona & Jan Voorhoeve. 1960c. *Cursus kiNyakyusa.* Vol. 3: *Outline of Nyakyusa grammar.* Leiden: Rijksuniversiteit.

Mwangoka, Ngapona & Jan Voorhoeve. 1960d. *Cursus kiNyakyusa.* Vol. 1: *Text.* Leiden: Rijksuniversiteit.

Nedjalkov, Vladimir P. & Sergej Je. Jaxontov. 1988. The typology of resultative constructions. In Vladimir Petrovich Nedjalkov (ed.), *Typology of resultative constructions*, 3–61. Amsterdam: Benjamins.

Nicolle, Steve. 2002. The grammaticalisation of movement verbs in Digo and English. *Revue de Sémantique et Pragmatique* 11. 47–67.

Nicolle, Steve. 2013. *A grammar of Digo: A Bantu language of Kenya and Tanzania.* Dallas: SIL International.

References

Nurse, Derek. 1979. Description of sample Bantu languages of Tanzania. *African Languages* 5. 1–150.

Nurse, Derek. 1988. The diachronic background to the language communities of southwestern Tanzania. *Afrika und Übersee* 9. 15–115.

Nurse, Derek. 1999. Towards a historical classification of east African Bantu languages. In Jean-Marie Hombert & Larry M. Hyman (eds.), *Bantu historical linguistics: Theoretical and empirical perspectives*, 21–41. Stanford: CSLI.

Nurse, Derek. 2008. *Tense and aspect in Bantu*. Oxford: Oxford University Press.

Nurse, Derek & George Park. 1988. Regional anthropology and historical linguistics. *Sprache und Geschichte in Afrika* 9. 7–14.

Nurse, Derek & Gerard Philippson. 2003a. Introduction. In Derek Nurse & Gerard Philippson (eds.), *The Bantu languages*, 1–13. London: Routledge.

Nurse, Derek & Gerard Philippson (eds.). 2003b. *The Bantu languages*. London: Routledge.

Nurse, Derek & Gerard Philippson. 2003c. Towards a historical classification of Bantu languages. In Derek Nurse & Gerard Philippson (eds.), *The Bantu languages*, 164–181. London: Routledge.

Nuyts, Jan. 2005. Modality: Overview and linguistic issues. In William Frawley (ed.), *The expression of modality*, 1–26. Berlin: de Gruyter.

Ogden, Charley Kay & Ivor Armstrong Richards. 1923. *The meaning of meaning. A study of the influence of language upon thought and of the science of symbolism*. London: Kegan Paul, Trench, Trübner.

Palmer, Frank R. 2007. *Mood and modality*. 2nd edn. Cambridge: Cambridge University Press.

Payne, Doris L. 1992. Narrative discontinuity versus continuity in Yagua. *Discourse Processes* 15(3). 375–394.

Payne, Doris L. & Shahir Shirtz. 2015. Discourse structuring and typology: How strong is the link with aspect? In Doris L. Payne & Shahar Shirtz (eds.), *Beyond aspect. The expression of discourse functions in African languages*, 1–22. Amsterdam: Benjamins.

Persohn, Bastian. 2016. When the present is in the past and what is normal is to come: Old and new present tenses in Nyakyusa (Bantu). *Afrikanistik und Ägyptologie Online* vol. 2016. https://www.afrikanistik-aegyptologie-online. de/archiv/2016/4523.

Persohn, Bastian. 2017a. Aspectuality in Bantu: On the limits of Vendler's categories. *Linguistic Discovery* 15. (accepted).

Persohn, Bastian. 2017b. Postfinals in Nyakyusa. *Africana Linguistica* 23. (in print).

Persohn, Bastian & Rasmus Bernander. 2016. *A note on the present tenses in some southern Tanzanian Bantu languages.* Unpublished manuscript.

Persohn, Bastian & Maud Devos. 2017. Postfinal locatives in Bantu: Axes of variation and non-locative functions. *Africana Linguistica* 23. (in print).

Portner, Paul. 2003. The (temporal) semantics and (modal) pragmatics of the perfect. *Linguistics and Philosophy* 26. 459–510.

Prein, Phillipp. 1995. *Differenz und Identität in Rungwe (Tansania) während der deutschen Kolonialzeit (1890-1914).* Hamburg: Universität Hamburg MA thesis.

Prince, Ellen F. 1981. Toward a taxonomy of given-new information. In Peter Cole (ed.), *Radical pragmatics*, 281–297. New York: Academic Press.

Prince, Ellen F. 1992. The ZPG letter: Subjects, definiteness, and information-status. In William C. Mann & Sandra A. Thompson (eds.), *Discourse description: Diverse linguistic analyses of a fund-raising text*, 295–326. Amsterdam: Benjamins.

Reichenbach, Hans. 1947. *Elements of symbolic logic.* New York: MacMillan.

Ritz, Marie-Eve. 2012. Perfect tense and aspect. In Robert I. Binnick (ed.), *The oxford handbook to tense and aspect*, 881–907. Oxford: Oxford University Press.

Robar, Elisabeth. 2014. *The verb and the paragraph in Biblical Hebrew. A cognitive-linguistic approach.* Leiden: Brill.

Rose, Sandra R., Christa Beaudoin-Lietz & Derek Nurse (eds.). 2002. *A glossary of terms for Bantu verbal categories, with special emphasis on tense-aspect.* Munich: Lincom Europa.

van Sambeek, Jan Cornelius. 1955. *A Bemba grammar.* London: Longmans.

Sasse, Hans-Jürgen. 1991. Aspekttheorie. In Hans-Jürgen Sasse (ed.), *Aspektsysteme*, 1–35. Cologne: Institut für Sprachwissenschaft.

Sasse, Hans-Jürgen. 2002. Recent activity in the theory of aspect. *Linguistic Typology* 6(2). 199–271.

Schadeberg, Thilo C. 2003a. Derivation. In Derek Nurse & Gerard Philippson (eds.), *The Bantu languages*, 71–89. London: Routledge.

Schadeberg, Thilo C. 2003b. Historical linguistics. In Derek Nurse & Gerard Philippson (eds.), *The Bantu languages*, 143–163. London: Routledge.

Schadeberg, Thilo C. & Clement Maganga. 1992. *Kinyamwezi: Grammar, texts, vocabulary.* Cologne: Köppe.

Schumann, K. 1899. Grundriss einer Grammatik der Kondesprache. *Mittheilungen des Seminars für orientalische Sprachen* 2(3). 1–86.

Seidel, Frank. 2008. *A grammar of Yeyi: A Bantu language of Southern Africa.* Cologne: Köppe.

Seidel, Frank. 2015. Rethinking narrative tenses based on data from Nalu (Atlantic) and Yeyi (Bantu). In Doris L. Payne & Shahar Shirtz (eds.), *Beyond aspect. The expression of discourse functions in African languages*, 177–218. Amsterdam: Benjamins.

Simons, Gary F. & Charles D. Fenning (eds.). 2017. *Ethnologue: Languages of the world.* Dallas: SIL International.

Smith, Carlota S. 1997. *The parameter of aspect.* 2nd edn. Dordrecht: Kluwer.

Smith, Carlota S. 2003. *Modes of discourse. the local structure of texts.* Cambridge: Cambridge University Press.

Stassen, Leon. 2005. Zero copula for predicate nominals. In Martin Haspelmath, Matthew S. Dryer, David Gil & Bernard Comrie (eds.), *The world atlas of language structures*, 486–489. Oxford: Oxford University Press.

Stassen, Leon. 2013. Comparative constructions. In Martin Haspelmath & Matthew S. Dryer (eds.), *The world atlas of language structures online.* Leipzig: Max Planck Institute for Evolutionary Anthropology. http://wals.info/chapter/121, accessed 2017-07-01.

Stolz, Adolf. 1934. Die Namen einiger afrikanischer Nutzpflanzen in der Konde-Sprache. *Zeitschrift für Eingeborenen-Sprachen* 24(2). 81–99.

Swilla, Imani N. 1998. Tenses in Chindali. *Afrikanistische Arbeitspapiere* 54. 95–125.

Talmy, Leonard. 1985. Lexicalization patterns: Semantic structure in lexical forms. In Timothy Shopen (ed.), *Language typology and syntactic description.* Vol. 3: *Grammatical categories and the lexicon*, 57–149. Cambridge: Cambridge University Press.

Tatevosov, Sergej. 2002. The parameter of actionality. *Linguistic Typology* 6(3). 317–401.

Timberlake, Alan. 2007. Aspect, tense, mood. In Timothy Shopen (ed.), *Language typology and syntactic description.* Vol. 3: *Grammatical categories and the lexicon*, 280–333. Cambridge: Cambridge University Press.

Toews, Carmela. 2015. *Topics in Siamou tense and aspect.* Vancouver: University of British Columbia dissertation.

Tomlin, Russel S. 1985. Foreground-background information and the syntax of subordination. *Text* 5. 85–122.

Traugott, Elizabeth Closs. 1978. On the expression of spatio-temporal relations in language. In Joseph H. Greenberg, Charles A. Ferguson & Edith A. Moravcsik (eds.), *Universals of human language.* Vol. 3: *Word structure*, 367–400. Stanford: Stanford University Press.

Vendler, Zeno. 1957. Verbs and times. *The Philosophical Review* 66. 143–160.

Verkuyl, Henk J. 1972. *On the compositional nature of aspect.* Dordrecht: D. Reidel.

Voorhoeve, Jan. n.d. A grammar of Safwa: Preliminary draft based on previous research by J. van Sambeek, checked by C. K. Mwachusa. Leiden. Unpublished manuscript.

van der Wal, Jenneke & Saudah Namyalo. 2016. The interaction of two focus marking strategies in Luganda. In Doris L. Payne, Sara Pacchiarotti & Mokaya Bosire (eds.), *Diversity in african languages*, 355–377. de Gruyter.

Walsh, Martin T. 1982. Nyakyusa greetings. *Cambridge anthropology* 7(3). 31–44.

Walsh, Martin T. & Imani N. Swilla. 2002. *Linguistics in the Corridor: A review of the research on the Bantu languages of South-West Tanzania, North-East Zambia, and North Malawi.* Unpublished manuscript.

Watters, David E. 2002. *A grammar of Kham.* Cambridge: Cambridge University Press.

Weber, Paul. 1998. *Ritual und Identität: Vorkoloniale Geschichte in Unyakyusa von ca. 1600 bis 1897.* Hamburg: LIT.

Weinreich, Harald. 1964. *Tempus. Besprochene und erzählte Welt.* Stuttgart: Kohlhammer.

Welmers, William Everett. 1974. *African language structures.* Berkeley: University of California Press.

Werner, Alice. 1919. *Introductory sketch of the Bantu languages.* London: Kegan Paul.

Wilkins, David P. 1991. The semantics, pragmatics and diachronic development of 'associated motion' in Mparntwe Arrernte. *Buffalo Papers in Linguistics* 1. 207–257.

Wilson, Godfrey. 1936. An African morality. *Africa: Journal of the International African Institute* 9(1). 75–99.

Wilson, Godfrey. 1937. Introduction to Nyakyusa law. *Africa: Journal of the International African Institute* 10(1). 16–36.

Wilson, Monica. 1958. *The peoples of the Nyasa-Tanganyika corridor.* Cape Town: University of Cape Town.

Wilson, Monica. 1963. *Good company. A study of Nyakyusa age-villages.* Boston: Beacon Press.

Wolff, R. 1905. *Grammatik der Kinga-Sprache (Deutsch-Ostafrika, Nyassagebiet). Nebst Texten und Wörterverzeichnis.* Berlin: Kommissionsverlag von Georg Reimer.

Ziegeler, Debra. 2006. *Interfaces with English aspect. Diachronic and empirical studies.* Amsterdam: Benjamins.

References

Ziervogel, Dirk, Jacobus Abraham Louw & Petrus C. Taltjaardt. 1981. *A handbook of the Zulu language*. 3rd edn. Pretoria: van Schaik.

Name index

Language index

Subject index

length, 30–32, 37, 38, 52^1, 57, 60, 61, 85, 86, 89, 94, 108, 146, 146^5, 150, 150^8, 151, 155, 167, 260, 261, 268, 304, 311
vowel height harmony, 29, 80–82

www.ingramcontent.com/pod-product-compliance
Lightning Source LLC
Chambersburg PA
CBHW080917100426
42812CB00007B/2308